VOLUNTEER USA

VOLUNTEER USA

**Andrew Carroll
with Christopher Miller**

Fawcett Columbine • New York

A Fawcett Columbine Book
Published by Ballantine Books

Copyright © 1991 by Andrew Carroll

All rights reserved under International and Pan-American Copyright Conventions. Published in the United States by Ballantine Books, a division of Random House, Inc, New York, and simultaneously in Canada by Random House of Canada Limited, Toronto.

Library of Congress Catalog Card Number: 90-82342

ISBN: 0-449-90577-2

Text design by Michaelis/Carpelis Design Associates
Cover design by Sheryl Kagan

Manufactured in the United States of America

First Edition: April 1991

10 9 8 7 6 5 4 3 2 1

This book is dedicated to America's volunteers. They are a community of individuals unlike any in the world.

CONTENTS

Foreword xiii
Doing Good in America
   Why Help Is Needed 1
   What You Can Do 3
   Community Resources and Organizations 6
   National Organizations 9
Doing Good Full-Time and for the Long Term (Internships, Summer Programs, and Professional Opportunities)
   What You Can Do 22
   National Organizations 25
Money Matters: Socially Responsible Consumerism and Investing
   What You Can Do 26
   National Organizations that Monitor Corporations and Socially Responsible Investments 29
   National Socially Responsible Networks, Investments, and Services 32
AIDS (Acquired Immune Deficiency Syndrome)
   Why Help Is Needed 40
   What You Can Do 41
   National Organizations 47
Alcohol and Drugs
   Why Help Is Needed 55
   What You Can Do 57
   National Organizations 62
   National Organizations Against Drinking and Driving 72
   National Alcohol and/or Drug Self-Help Organizations 74
Animals
   Why Help Is Needed 78
   What You Can Do 79
   National Organizations 86
   Companion Animals (Particularly Cats and Dogs)
   What You Can Do 97

National Organizations 98
Marine Life
What You Can Do 100
National Organizations 101
Wildlife and Endangered Species
What You Can Do 104
National Organizations 105

Blood and Organ/Tissue Donations
Blood Donations
Why Help Is Needed 111
What You Can Do 111
Questions and Answers About Donating Blood 112
Organ/Tissue Donations
Why Help Is Needed 113
What You Can Do 114
Questions and Answers About
Becoming an Organ/Tissue Donor 115
National Organizations 116

Children and Young Adults
Why Help Is Needed 119
What You Can Do 121
National Organizations 126
National Child Sponsorship Organizations 140
Adoption (of Special-Needs Children and Youth)
What You Can Do 142
National Organizations 143
Child Abuse and Neglect
What You Can Do 145
National Organizations 147
Foster Care
What You Can Do 150
National Organizations 151
Missing Children
What You Can Do 152
National Organizations 153

Crime and Victim Assistance
Why Help Is Needed 157
What You Can Do 158
National Organizations 168

Disabilities
Why Help Is Needed 176
What You Can Do 177

National Organizations 185
National Organizations for the Employment
of Individuals with Disabilities..194
National Sports and Recreational Organizations
for Individuals with Disabilities..195
Blindness and Visual Impairments
What You Can Do 198
National Organizations 201
Deafness and Hearing Loss
What You Can Do 203
National Organizations 206
Mental Illnesses
What You Can Do 208
National Organizations 209
Mental Retardation
What You Can Do 211
National Organizations 212

Education and Illiteracy
Why Help Is Needed 215
What You Can Do 217
National Education Organizations 221
National Literacy Organizations 228

Elderly Persons
Why Help Is Needed 233
What You Can Do 234
National Organizations 237

The Environment
Why Help Is Needed 245
What You Can Do 251
National Organizations 259
Air Pollution, Deforestation, and Global Warming
What You Can Do 278
National Organizations 283
Chemicals and Hazardous Wastes
What You Can Do 289
National Organizations 296
Energy Conservation
What You Can Do 300
National Organizations 306
Recycling
What You Can Do 309
National Organizations 317

Water Conservation and Preservation of Natural Resources (Particularly Lakes, Oceans, and Rivers)
    What You Can Do 319
    National Organizations 322

Homelessness and Housing
    Why Help Is Needed 327
    What You Can Do 328
    National Organizations 333

Hunger
    Why Help Is Needed 340
    What You Can Do 341
    National Organizations 345

Suicide
    Why Help Is Needed 352
    What You Can Do 353
    National Organizations 353

Veterans
    Why Help Is Needed 356
    What You Can Do 357
    National Organizations 359

Voicing Your Opinion
    How to Contact Government Representatives 363

Wise Giving
    Tips on Making Charitable Donations 366

General Index 371
Geographical Index 379

Acknowledgments

Until now, I had never realized how essential the acknowledgments section of a book is. If it were not for the following people, this book simply could not have been written. First of all, I want to extend a hearty thank-you to Carole Jackson and Megan Bartsch for their support and for helping me find Ballantine Books, the greatest publisher a writer could have. At Ballantine I am indebted to Jöelle Delbourgo, Mary Sagripanti, and Emily Pearl for their confidence and assistance. I'm still amazed that they gave me the opportunity to work with them; it was truly an honor.

I am grateful for the constant support of my friends and family which carried me through this project. I would especially like to thank my father, who provided me with everything I needed both to meet my deadlines and maintain my general well-being while writing this book. His love and encouragement were invaluable. I want to thank my mom for her infinite support and understanding, which she has always given but which I especially appreciated during this project.

I also want to thank all of the organizations and institutions who sent me materials, helped me with information, and gave me advice. I only hope this book will provide them with additional volunteers and support.

In particular, I want to say thank-you to Christopher Miller, my right-hand assistant and good friend. Not only did he write and help edit a significant portion of the book, he helped me keep my sanity when the pressure was on. His assistance and humor were indispensable, and I am extremely grateful for everything he did.

On a somewhat different note, I want to thank Professor Robert Herman at Pomona College for helping me better appreciate volunteerism and the value of community spirit and service. His advice, along with one of his recommended readings—*Habits of the Heart*, by Robert N. Bellah—truly inspired me. And, along the lines of inspiration, I want to thank the person who has influenced me the most concerning volunteer work—Marian Wright Edelman. Through her guidance, she has helped me begin to see that "service is the rent we pay for living." Although this book is dedicated to America's volunteers, I would like to make a special dedication to Mrs. Edelman. I wish I could better express my gratitude for all that she has done for me, but I hope that this is, at least, a start.

FOREWORD

If you're interested in volunteering your time and energy, this book will help you get started. You will find hundreds of ideas on volunteer opportunities, reasons to consider working for certain causes, and organizations that work with or refer volunteers. This book, however, is just a starting point. It is not a list of every organization involved in volunteer work in America, nor does it present every idea on how you can become involved with an issue. Your interests, as well as the needs and resources of your community, will determine what you end up doing. What this book hopefully will show you is that no matter what your skills or interests, and no matter what the needs of your community, you can help.

The information in this book is presented in as orderly a fashion as possible. Aside from the obvious—the organizations and chapters are listed in alphabetical order—the What You Can Do ideas and suggestions are listed in increasing order relative to the amount of sacrifice or time they require. What constitutes a "sacrifice" will no doubt vary from reader to reader, but in a general sense, the easiest tips come first, the harder ones, later.

It won't take you long to notice that some of the organizations in this book are not strictly "volunteer" organizations. There are mail-order companies that sell environmentally safe products, publishing companies that sell books on social issues, and organizations that serve as information clearinghouses; I selected the organizations in this book because I believed they were important components in addressing the issues with which they are associated. Some of the organizations may be too aggressive for some people, some may be too passive. Some may be too liberal, others too conservative. It was not possible to make judgments about the organizations in the selection process or to look into their full histories, financial practices, and activities. Unless stated otherwise, the fact that an organization, service, or product is listed in this book *does not* mean that it is being endorsed. Before you volunteer or donate money, read the organization's literature thoroughly, look into its past activities and/or programs, talk with friends or family who may have heard of it, and address any concerns or questions you may have to the organization's staff. If you find an organization to be disagreeable, simply find another one—there are plenty to choose from.

Here are a few other suggestions to help you get the most out of this book:

1. Although volunteer ideas are listed in the What You Can Do section of every chapter, the descriptions of the national organizations may provide more ideas. These organizations often have their own projects that may not have been mentioned in the What You Can Do section. Also, issues may sometimes overlap, so check similar chapters for additional information. For example, those interested in animals may find helpful information in The Environment chapter as well as in the chapter titled Animals. A few suggestions, such as "read up on the issue," or "volunteer to work at a nonprofit organization addressing the issue," are given in more than one section. That way, if a person wants to focus on a single issue/chapter, he or she won't miss those ideas.

2. Don't be surprised if some organizations are difficult to reach or don't respond to your inquiry right away. Almost all the organizations in this book are nonprofit, and they are often short on staff and supplies. If you deal with government programs (for example, adopting a baby through your local social services department), you may confront a good deal of red tape. Be patient, but be persistent.

3. Information on every organization listed in this book was verified by phone or by mail. (If there is no telephone number—or in some cases, fax number—given, this was requested by the organization.) Consequently, the addresses, phone numbers (including TTY and TDD numbers—for individuals who are deaf or hard of hearing), publications (if any), and descriptions should be correct. It is possible, however, for an organization to move, change its membership, shift its goals, or change its phone number before this book comes out. Also, volunteer opportunities may change. There is no guarantee that listed opportunities will still be available at the time of publication (or even if they are, that everyone can participate).

4. If you are interested in a particular issue but do not see a specific program or organization addressing that issue, check Doing Good in America, specifically the sections on Community Resources and Organizations (page 6) and National Organizations (page 9). This chapter covers resources and organizations that address a variety of issues.

It is inevitable that important ideas and organizations have been overlooked. Every effort was made, however, through talking with the organizations listed and looking through other directories, to include all the major national organizations focusing on the issues presented. To those organizations left out, please accept my apologies. I will make every effort to include relevent organizations that were missed in later editions of the book.

I am donating one-third of the royalties which I receive for this book (after the advance) to those nonprofit organizations listed in the book that I think are deserving.

VOLUNTEER USA

DOING GOOD IN AMERICA

Why Help Is Needed

The United States is suffering from millions of individual tragedies—tragedies so knotted together and so severe that, in many ways, the situation seems hopeless. Alcohol and drugs are wasting away thousands of lives every day; millions of children are living in poverty, many of them homeless; AIDS is racing through the country, taking lives and spreading prejudice, ignorance, and fear; countless people are suffering from severe hunger; tens of thousands of people are killing themselves every year; and thousands of violent crimes are being committed every day. The list goes on and on. Even more discouraging is the extent to which these problems feed upon each other. Wherever substance abuse exists, crime is often not far away. Wherever there is illiteracy or poor schooling, unemployment and lack of self-esteem are also usually close by. As these problems become more intertwined, the overall magnitude becomes so tremendous that the individual faces and stories are lost. It is difficult to believe that there could be any hope stirring within such a mess of despair.

There is. It is, quite simply, the presence of determined and selfless individuals working to provide the help that is needed, wherever it is needed. Their sacrifices are not necessarily sweeping acts of courage or heroism—often they are simple acts of compassion. Nevertheless, they remind those who have met hard times that they are still worthy of support. And although the vicious cycles of this nation's problems may be powerful, goodwill can be just as strong. An ordinary act of kindness can result in an extraordinary chain of positive effects. Teaching a person to read not only produces another reader, it creates the potential for one more productive employee (or employer) in the work force, one more volunteer to help another person learn to read, or one more parent who can read to his or her children. Providing homeless parents with the counseling and necessary resources to find a job helps not only those parents but their children, who will not have to be raised on the streets or in a shelter. Even something as simple as cleaning up a littered park or playground may inspire others to do the same. Doing good rarely stops with one person or one cause.

The need to confront America's problems is critical for the welfare of every citizen, but it is especially urgent for the sake of our nation's young people. As this country searches for desperately needed doctors, nurses, scientists, teachers, and countless other professionals, energetic and creative minds are slipping away every day. These lost minds belong to the young people suffocated by cities swarming with drugs and violence, the young people given no encouragement to succeed, no foundation to build on, and few role models to emulate. The energy of America's youth needs to be channeled more effectively. Provided with the proper direction, this energy can help illuminate solutions to the nation's problems and offer the power needed to solve them.

No one individual is going to solve the hunger problem, stop the AIDS epidemic, or save the environment. One individual can, however, feed one hungry person, offer support for one person with AIDS, or plant one tree. Even those who may need assistance in one area may be able to help in another. A frail elderly person, for example, may need help with household chores, but that same elderly person could teach another adult how to read. An individual who uses a wheelchair may need help with transportation but could be a Big Brother or Big Sister to a disadvantaged teenager. There is, quite clearly, no "us" and "them" when it comes to doing good. We are all an essential part of the American community, we can all do good, and we are all needed.

Getting involved, however, is seldom a glamorous or effortless task. Volunteers may be met with mistrust, the work can be draining, and the progress can seem painfully slow. But when results do come, they are often as rewarding for the volunteer as for the person receiving assistance. The look of a homeless child who has been given a Christmas toy, the excitement of an adult who has just read a book, cover to cover, for the first time, or simply the embrace or smile from someone in need can make all the sacrifices and time worthwhile. The feeling of this shared success cannot be fully expressed in any book or manual on volunteerism. It can only be experienced.

While the problems confronting America are, without a doubt, enormous in size and scope, the millions of individual tragedies have been and will continue to be met successfully by millions of volunteers and selfless individuals. It is these individuals in every community of this nation who are building, one person at a time, one day at a time, a better America. Together, their acts of kindness are not a small hope for America's survival; they are one of the nation's most promising hopes.

What You Can Do

☞ **Educate yourself and others on the need to do good in America.** Read articles and books on volunteers and volunteerism. Becoming informed about volunteerism in general and about specific causes will help you know what to expect as a volunteer, understand the need for volunteers in this country, and learn about additional ideas for getting involved. Whatever you do, encourage others—family members, friends, classmates, co-workers—to join you. Volunteering as a group or with a friend not only provides more helping hands, it makes the activity more enjoyable. Also, consider writing to your local newspaper to encourage it to focus on volunteers working to improve the community.

☞ **Whatever you do as a volunteer, know your abilities, be persistent, but don't set your expectations too high.** Some people end up trying to do too much and become frustrated when problems are not solved as quickly as they would like, especially with volunteer work that requires serious commitment, such as helping someone learn to read, becoming a mentor, or building low-income housing. Recognize that change takes time and that one-shot efforts rarely have lasting results. Volunteers are desperately needed for one-on-one services, and these are often the most rewarding volunteer experiences. However, if you do volunteer to help people on a one-on-one basis, especially in a crisis situation (such as working on a suicide hotline or in a shelter for the homeless or for battered women), be sure you are emotionally prepared. No matter how much training you receive, it can be very difficult to see people suffering on a constant basis. Also, make sure you have an idea of how much time and effort your volunteer work may require. Talk with others who have done the same thing, read any literature the organization may have, and ask a lot of questions before you get started.

☞ **Don't throw away old books, toys, clothes, sports equipment, or other items you no longer need.** Local Goodwill agencies (see Disabilities, page 188), hospitals, shelters for the homeless, schools, nonprofit organizations, youth centers, and religious congregations will put virtually all of these items to good use. (If you have only a few items to donate, see if your friends or neighbors have anything that can be donated, too. Take turns collecting and bringing in donations—this will save everybody time and energy in the long run.) If you want more ideas on items (and services) such organizations often need, the **Junior League of Washington** distributes *The Community Wish Book* free of cost. This book lists hundreds of items and services local (i.e., Washington, D.C.) organizations "wish" for to make their work easier. Even if you don't live in the Washington, D.C., area, the book can give you ideas on how to help organizations near you. Write to the Junior League for more information: *3039 M St., N.W., Washington, DC 20007*; (202) 337-2001.

☞ **For Christmas, Chanukah, or birthdays, consider gift ideas that help promote doing good in some way.** Here are a few to keep in mind:

- **A donation or membership to a nonprofit organization the recipient supports.** (Sometimes it's best to let the recipient choose.)
- **A poster, book, or handmade gift sold by one of the organizations in this book.** (If an organization does sell such items, it is noted in the description.) Consider a handmade craft from the **Save the Children Craft Shop** (see Money Matters, page 28), or a wildlife poster from **Defenders of Wildlife** (see Animals, page 105).
- **A tree or houseplant.**
- **Cosmetics, perfume, or cologne from a company that does not test its products on animals** (see Animals, page 81).
- **Stationery or other paper products made from recycled paper** (see The Environment, page 312).
- **Stock in a socially responsible company** (see Money Matters, page 32).

☞ **Offer administrative assistance to a nonprofit organization near you.** This can include stuffing envelopes, answering phones, typing, editing a newsletter, or helping with fundraising. Administrative work is generally not as exciting as one-on-one volunteer work, such as becoming a Big Brother or Big Sister, but it is essential to the organization and enables it to serve the community better.

☞ **Look for ways you can help the greater community and use your imagination and resources to respond accordingly.** This book is just a starting point for ideas; specific problems and situations require specific responses. Don't assume that if no one is doing something about a particular problem, nothing can be done. Often, it is a lack of initiative, not need, that hinders involvement. Any individual or institution can help make a difference. For example:

- **If you are a student,** work with your classmates to address community issues that you feel are being neglected. This may include making sandwiches for a soup kitchen, cleaning up a littered playground, or bringing elderly persons to school events like plays and concerts.
- **If you are a member of a religious congregation,** work with other members and use the congregation's facilities to provide the community with needed services, such as a day-care facility, a shelter for the homeless, or a "safe house" for latchkey kids whose parents don't come home from work until dinnertime.
- **Use your business or professional skills or supplies to contribute to needy causes.** If you own a hardware store, volunteer to donate supplies to a local housing project. If you are an athletic coach, help with recreational activities at a local youth club. If you work at a restaurant or bakery, see if excess food could go to feed the hungry. If you are in advertising, volunteer to help a nonprofit company spread its message. If you have financial expertise, offer to help a nonprofit organization manage its budget. Even if you don't think your business can offer anything to a needy cause, you can still organize a blood drive with your co-workers or clean up a neighborhood park together.

Here are a few resources that show how others are addressing some national problems:

- ***Business Ethics*** (see Money Matters, page 26) is an excellent publication for those interested in learning how other businesses and professionals have used their resources and business sense in a socially responsible manner.
- **The Giraffe Project** is a national nonprofit organization working to find and recognize people who have "stuck their necks out," acting above and beyond the call of duty. People who are recognized include students, homemakers, businesspeople, teachers, doctors, retired citizens, and hundreds of others who have made significant sacrifices for the common good. If you know someone you feel should be recognized by the program, contact TGP at *P.O. Box 759, Langley, WA 98260*;

1-800-344-TALL (8255). TGP also sells T-shirts, bumper stickers, coffee mugs, and sweatshirts, and publishes *The Giraffe Gazette*, a quarterly journal with profiles of Giraffes, ideas on sticking your neck out, editorials, book reviews, and other informative and inspiring features and news items. One copy costs $3 (plus $1 for postage and handling) but comes free with TGP membership ($25).

Community Resources and Organizations

☞ **Check the phone book for a section called "Community Services Numbers" (usually in the front of the book), which lists local services that help the greater community.** If you find an organization you'd like to help, see if volunteer opportunities are available. Also, check under "Human Services Organizations" or "Social Services Organizations." While these are not listed by issue and the names may not always tell you what the organizations do, something may catch your eye.

☞ **Your city or town government should have a volunteer office that can help you find opportunities specific to the needs of the community.** Sometimes these offices are part of the human services or social services department. Check the government pages of the phone book.

☞ **Consult the phone book for the Volunteer Clearinghouse near you.** A clearinghouse may be listed under "Voluntary Action Center," "Volunteer Bureau," "Volunteer Office," or "Volunteer Information and Referral." Or write or call **VOLUNTEER—The National Center** (see page 20) for the address of the affiliate near you. These clearinghouses have information on numerous organizations in your community that need help in a variety of areas, including tutoring, providing assistance to individuals with disabilities, helping the homeless, reading or delivering meals to elderly persons, being a mentor for at-risk youths, fundraising for nonprofit organizations, working on crisis hotlines, and providing health services (opportunities will vary depending on the affiliate). Clearinghouses often have newsletters with information on community programs, legislation concerning volunteerism, and volunteer opportunities. Clearinghouses themselves may need volunteers to help with administrative work, editing newsletters, and recruiting and placing other volunteers. These organizations are indispensable resources for volunteers.

☞ **Contact the United Way of America** for information about health- and human-care issues and services that assist families and individuals in need. There are more than 2,300 community-based United Way organizations throughout America. Each one is separately incorporated and governed by a local volunteer board of directors working to assess and address critical community needs. More than 37,000 human-service agencies and programs receive United Way support to help the homeless, the hungry, individuals with disabilities, disadvantaged youth, children, elderly persons, and countless other people needing assistance. Ask the United Way in your area for an *Agency Directory*, a free booklet that lists the agencies United Way supports in the community. The directory is an essential resource for anyone interested in volunteer opportunities with community-based nonprofit organizations. If you cannot find the United Way in your community, write or call United Way of America at *701 N. Fairfax St., Alexandria, VA 22314*; (703) 836-7100.

☞ **Contact the United Black Fund** for a comprehensive listing of nonprofit organizations working to "meet the unmet needs" in your community. These organizations are involved with child care, illiteracy, crime prevention, drug and alcohol prevention, and support and companionship programs for youths, elderly persons, and individuals with disabilities. Most of them need volunteers. If you cannot find the UBF in your community, write or call the national headquarters at *1012 14th St., N.W., Suite 300, Washington, DC 20005*; (202) 783-9300, TDD: (202) 783-9304.

☞ **Look up the Community Action Agency in your area.** CAAs focus attention on specific problems affecting the community, then mobilize resources and create solutions to help the people in need and attack the root of the problem. Most CAAs track local low-income housing, economic development, and employment and training programs, and offer information on Head Start and programs for the elderly. If you cannot find the CAA in your area, contact the **National Association of Community Action Agencies** at *1775 T St., N.W., 1st Floor, Washington, DC 20009*; (202) 265-7546, FAX: (202) 265-8850.

Many communities also have a **Jewish Community Center** that addresses a variety of community needs. JCC volunteer opportunities include working with disadvantaged children and at-risk youth; offering assistance to elderly persons; visiting individuals in hospitals; feeding the hungry; cleaning and rehabilitating shelters, transitional homes, and youth and community centers; assisting the homeless;

improving intercultural relations; and working with individuals with disabilities. If you cannot find the JCC in your community, contact the **Jewish Community Centers Association of North America** at *15 E. 26th St., New York, NY 10010-1579*; (212) 532-4949.

☞ **See if there's a Neighborhood Center near you.** These centers, which are affiliated with the **United Neighborhood Centers of America, Inc.** (a national, nonprofit voluntary organization), provide a variety of needed services to their communities. Centers nationwide are addressing such issues as teen pregnancy, chronic youth unemployment, homelessness and malnutrition, neglect and abuse of elderly residents and children, teenage gangs, drug and alcohol dependencies, and illiteracy. Local centers work to foster neighborhood pride, local decision-making and control, and concern for one's neighbors. Volunteers can help with practically all of these issues in a variety of ways from providing person-to-person assistance to helping with administrative work. To find out if there's a UNCA affiliate near you, contact UNCA at *4801 Massachusetts Ave., N.W., Suite 400, Washington, DC 20016*; (202) 895-1667.

☞ **If you belong to a synagogue, church, or other religious congregation, find out what volunteer opportunities are available.** Many religious congregations sponsor food drives, provide services for elderly persons, take care of homeless individuals, and sponsor recreational activities for young people. If there is an issue that interests you but that is not addressed by your congregation, consider starting your own group or committee with other members. Volunteers may also be needed to help the congregation itself in a variety of ways: maintaining the facilities (for example, making small repairs, planting trees, painting), assisting the clergy, helping with fundraising, and teaching religion classes for children. If you do not belong to a religious congregation or organization but would be interested in working with one, check under "Religious Organizations" in the telephone book.

☞ **If you are an employee, find out if your company sponsors any volunteer activities.** Many major corporations, in particular, have established programs for employees who want to become volunteers. (Employees sometimes even receive paid time off to volunteer.)

☞ **Check with the following places in your community to see if there are any volunteer opportunities available:**

- **Fire departments.** Many fire departments need volunteer-firefighters, as well as volunteer paramedics and ambulance workers. You will have to go through some training, and not everyone is eligible; call your local station for more information.
- **Hospitals.** Contact your local hospital and ask for the volunteer coordinator (or similar title). Volunteers can staff mobile libraries, offer clerical assistance, provide support and care for patients, and comfort young children or "boarder babies," who have been abandoned and are often victims of drug abuse and/or who have AIDS. Donations of books, games, magazines, and other items are almost always needed, especially around the holiday seasons. If you have a four-wheel-drive automobile, the local hospital may need your help during a snowstorm (primarily to help get doctors and nurses to the hospital).
- **Libraries.** Library volunteers assist people looking for particular books or materials, help with organizing of books, and provide a variety of other services.
- **Nursing homes.** (See Elderly Persons, page 234, for volunteer opportunities.)
- **Police station or sheriff's office.** (See Crime, page 160, for volunteer opportunities.)
- **Schools.** (See Education and Illiteracy, page 218, for volunteer opportunities.)

National Organizations

ACTION, The National Volunteer Agency
Washington, DC 20525
(202) 634-9108

ACTION is the federal domestic volunteer agency dedicated to promoting the spirit and practice of volunteerism. ACTION helps volunteers of every age and socioeconomic background become involved with nearly every needed service, including teaching individuals who are illiterate, preventing crime, feeding the hungry, offering companionship for elderly persons, and sharing professional expertise to help solve specific community needs. ACTION also helps countless other neighborhood volunteer activities and community projects by providing grants, technical assistance, and a vast knowledge of volunteer resources, activities, and programs. ACTION has five main programs for volunteers:

Foster Grandparent Program

FGP matches older Americans with special- or exceptional-needs children. Although the program initially worked with low-income seniors (who received a modest hourly stipend for their services), it now encourages all older Americans to become involved. All Foster Grandparents attend to the physical, mental, and emotional needs of disadvantaged children. The volunteers work in various environments, including schools for children who are mentally retarded, Head Start programs, juvenile detention centers, boarding schools, foster-care homes, and, in special cases, a child's own home.

Retired Senior Volunteer Program

RSVP, ACTION's largest program, works with thousands of retired Americans who are volunteering their time, energy, and wisdom. RSVP volunteers give almost sixty-five million hours of their time each year to programs related to preventing crime, tutoring, operating shelters for runaways, counseling troubled youths, working on crisis hotlines, providing various services at food banks, and using their skills to help young people in similar professions. If you are retired, semi-retired, or sixty years or older, contact RSVP for more information on how you can help.

Senior Companion Program

SCP matches older Americans with frail elderly persons. Most Senior Companions help the homebound elderly gain the confidence and positive mental attitude needed for successful independent living, assisting with shopping, doctor's visits, and managing finances. Companions also help those who have been hospitalized readjust to normal life, assist people facing terminal illness, and offer support to individuals with mental illnesses. (Although most Senior Companions are low-income volunteers who receive a modest stipend, individuals who do not meet those income requirements are needed for the program, too.)

Student Community Service Program

SCSP encourages students to enroll in volunteer activities in their communities and to serve the needs of low-income individuals. Volunteers are assigned on a part-time basis to projects that meet a variety of community needs, such as companionship for individuals with disabilities, tutoring, health and nutrition education for the elderly, crime prevention, and neighborhood improvements. The benefits of the program are mutual—while helping people in need, student volunteers gain valuable work experience and a sense of commitment to their communities. Student volunteers do not receive a stipend and must be enrolled in high school, college, or junior college.

Volunteers In Service To America

VISTA is the oldest program in ACTION, established to alleviate poverty in America by using volunteers (eighteen years or older) to work (full-time, for at least a year) with low-income individuals to improve the conditions of their lives. Volunteers, about one-third of whom are low income themselves, live and work in urban locations, rural areas, or on Native American reservations. VISTA volunteers address such issues as illiteracy, unemployment, drug and alcohol abuse, child abuse, hunger, and neighborhood revitalization. ACTION provides a basic subsistence allowance for volunteers' housing, food, and incidentals.

For more information on ACTION programs and requirements or to sign up for a program, contact your regional office:

Region I
10 Causeway St., Room 473
Boston, MA 02222-1039
(617) 565-7000
Connecticut, Maine, Massachusetts, New Hampshire, Vermont, and Rhode Island

Region II
6 World Trade Center, Room 758
New York, NY 10048
(212) 466-3481
New Jersey, New York, Puerto Rico, and the Virgin Islands

Region III
U.S. Customs House, Room 108
2nd & Chestnut Sts.
Philadelphia, PA 19106-2912
(215) 597-9972
Kentucky, Maryland, Delaware, Ohio, Pennsylvania, Virginia, West Virginia, and Washington, DC

Region IV
101 Marietta St., N.W., Suite 1003
Atlanta, GA 30323-2301
(404) 331-2860
Alabama, Florida, Georgia, Mississippi, North Carolina, South Carolina, and Tennessee

Region V
175 W. Jackson Boulevard, Suite 1207
Chicago, IL 60604-2702
(312) 353-5107
Illinois, Indiana, Iowa, Michigan, Minnesota, and Wisconsin

Region VI
1100 Commerce St., Room 6B11
Dallas, TX 75242-0696
(214) 767-9494
Arkansas, Kansas, Louisiana, Missouri, New Mexico, Oklahoma, and Texas

Region VIII*
Executive Tower Building, Suite 2930
1405 Curtis St.
Denver, CO 80202-2349
Colorado, Wyoming, Montana, Nebraska, North Dakota, South Dakota, and Utah

Region IX
211 Main St., Room 530
San Francisco, CA 94105-1914
(415) 744-3013
Arizona, California, Hawaii, Nevada, Guam, and America Samoa

Includes states that were formerly part of Region VII.

Region X
Federal Office Building, Suite 3039
909 First Ave.
Seattle, WA 98174-1103
(206) 442-1558
Alaska, Idaho, Oregon, and Washington

American Red Cross
17th and D Sts., N.W., Washington, DC 20006
(202) 737-8300

The **Red Cross** is the nation's foremost volunteer emergency services organization. Red Cross and its volunteers work tirelessly to improve the quality of human life, including helping people avoid, prepare for, and cope with emergencies. The Red Cross has more than 2,700 chapters located throughout the U.S. and its territories, and is assisted by 1.1 million volunteers who are working with homeless people, offering programs for latchkey children of working parents, working in blood donation centers, visiting and caring for elderly persons, providing transportation for individuals with disabilities, repairing or rebuilding homes damaged by fire or other natural disasters, creating food pantries and programs for the hungry, educating the community on AIDS, and providing numerous other needed services. Young people are also involved, counseling other young people with drug and alcohol abuse problems, sponsoring blood drives, visiting nursing homes, and delivering meals to the homebound. Whatever your age (even young children can help through some affiliates) or interests, and regardless of how much time you can devote, you can help out your local Red Cross chapter. Also, if you are interested in learning first aid, swimming, CPR, and other lifesaving skills, the Red Cross can provide you with the proper training. Ask for *The Red Cross Course Catalog* for more information. (See also Blood and Organ/Tissue Donations, page 111.)

Association of Jewish Family & Children's Agencies
P.O. Box 248, Kendall Park, NJ 08824-0248
(201) 821-0909 or 1-800-634-7346

The association is the national service organization for the 139 **Jewish Family & Children's Agencies** in North America. The agencies provide a variety of needed services for their communities, including offering adoption/foster-care services; providing family counseling; offering job assistance; visiting with and providing companionship to frail elderly persons and individuals with disabilities; collecting, sorting, and delivering food; driving elderly persons and individuals with disabilities to plays, concerts, and other cultural events; interpreting for people who are not fluent in English; providing tutorial aid to children with learning disabilities and to newly arrived immigrants; and helping out with administrative duties in agency offices (for example, answering phones, sorting mail, fundraising). If you cannot find the agency near you (it may be listed as "Jewish Family Service" in the telephone book), contact the national headquarters.

The Box Project
P.O. Box 435, Plainville, CT 06062
(203) 747-8182

TBP is a nonprofit organization dedicated to helping low-income families, elderly persons, and college students living in poverty areas nationwide. TBP focuses on helping families help other families through its "sister-family" program. Through this program, a family exchanges letters with another family about once a month and sends a box of clothing, food, and other needed items (as well as their friendship) on a consistent basis. TBP also sponsors an Education/Scholarship program for promising young students, supports community centers with material donations, and sponsors a Holiday Santa project, in which "Santas" send a package to a family at Christmastime. Write to or call TBP for information on becoming a sister-family to a family in need, a Santa, or a sponsor for the scholarship program. The yearly membership fee for TBP is $25.

Campus Outreach Opportunity League
University of Minnesota, 386 McNeal Hall,
St. Paul, MN 55108-1011
(612) 624-3018

COOL is a national nonprofit organization that promotes and supports student involvement in community service. Created and directed by recent college graduates, COOL has developed a network of 600 colleges and universities. Its goal is to help students address such issues as hunger, homelessness, illiteracy, and cultural diversity. If you are interested in starting or strengthening a community service program on your campus, COOL staff members will make campus visits to help you develop a strategy. The organization can also help you plan activities that are consistent with the needs of your community and student body. COOL publishes a bimonthly newsletter (during the school year), *Campus Outreach*, and numerous other publications, including *Hunger/Homelessness Action: A Resource Book for Colleges and Universities; On Your Mark, GO! Get Set: From Campus Ideals to Community Involvement;* and *Break Away: A Guide to Organizing an Alternative Spring Break.*

Catholic Charities U.S.A.
1319 F St., N.W., Washington, DC 20004
(202) 639-8400

Catholic Charities U.S.A. is a nonprofit organization dedicated to supporting high-quality services to those in need, advocating for social justice, and calling all people of goodwill to do the same. Catholic Charities U.S.A. and its more than 630 member agencies have advocated for the needy in the social services, juvenile justice, and welfare systems. Local Catholic Charities member agencies have maintained and defended residential care for those with special needs; offered a long history of high-quality adoption services, family and child counseling, pregnancy services, employment programs, and community self-help programs; and provided a variety of other services for the homeless, elderly persons, individuals with disabilities, and children. The Catholic Charities U.S.A. national social policy staff has collaborated with other social justice networks and worked with congressional leaders on behalf of programs for the unemployed, national housing legislation, encouragement of health insurance programs for wage earners, federal funding for specialized care of children with severe disabilities, improvement of welfare legislation, and provision of medical care to low-income pregnant women. Individual memberships ($25) include a subscription to *Charities USA*, a bimonthly news magazine that covers agency service programs, current issues of concern, and pertinent legislation. Contact Catholic Charities U.S.A. for more information on its national services and activities, publications, and membership and volunteer opportunities, or for the location of a local affiliate.

Family Service America
Communications
11700 W. Lake Park Drive, Park Place, Milwaukee, WI 53224
FAX: (414) 359-1074

FSA is a nonprofit organization of 290 member agencies in the U.S. and Canada and approximately 10,000 volunteers working to strengthen family life in North America. FSA agencies assist individuals and families with problems relating to marital difficulties, parent-child tensions, drug and alcohol dependency, teenage pregnancy, aging, child abuse, family violence, and other complex issues. Volunteers are needed at the local agencies for a variety of services, including fundraising, delivering meals to or visiting elderly persons, working on crisis hotlines, becoming mentors for at-risk youths, and working in day-care centers. FSA also has a publications catalog listing books (such as *Effective Stepparenting*, *Parenting Children of Divorce*, and *Parent-Child Communication*) and other materials. Contact the FSA agency in your area or send a self-addressed, stamped envelope to the national headquarters for referral information.

Four-One-One
7304 Beverly St., Annandale, VA 22003
(703) 354-6270, FAX: (703) 941-4360

A national clearinghouse on volunteerism, **Four-One-One** covers community volunteer programs, national organizations, and agencies concerned with human services/community needs; elementary and secondary schools; and colleges, universities, and libraries. If you're having trouble finding a particular activity or program to volunteer for, this is the organization to contact. Four-One-One provides comprehensive references for information needed to plan, design, and manage successful volunteer programs. It also maintains a library of 3,000 volumes related to volunteers on the local level and sponsors charitable programs, including **Super Volunteers**, which encourages young people to become involved with community service and recognizes those who have made significant contributions. Four-One-One sells Super Volunteers materials (including T-shirts, club kits, a newsletter, and a program idea list), a volunteer board game, and a coloring book. If you're looking for a *very* comprehensive directory on volunteerism, contact Four-One-One and ask about *Volunteerism: The Directory of Organizations, Training, Programs, and Publications* ($95), which lists more than 5,000 local and national volunteer organizations. This is an indispensable resource for people and institutions who want up-to-date information on volunteer organizations in the U.S. and other aspects of volunteerism.

INDEPENDENT SECTOR
1828 L St., N.W., Washington, DC 20036
(202) 223-8100

IS is a nonprofit coalition of 700 corporations, foundations, and voluntary organizations with an interest in and impact on philanthropy and voluntary action nationwide. The organization's mission is to create a national forum capable of encouraging the giving, volunteering, and not-for-profit initiatives that serve people, communities, and causes. Since 1980 IS has fought legislative battles, published research data, and worked for better management in the nonprofit world. In addition, in 1986 IS launched a major national campaign, **Give Five**, to encourage all Americans to volunteer five hours of their time a week and to give five percent of their annual income to causes they care about. IS also distributes publications, including *Volunteers in Action; Youth Service: A Guidebook for Developing and Operating Effective Programs;* and *Giving and Volunteering in the United States—Findings from a National Survey*. (The latter is the largest study on volunteerism ever undertaken, providing the fullest assessment to date about patterns, motivations, and satisfactions of giving and volunteering.) Although voting members are organizations, associate membership ($50) is available for interested individuals. Associate membership includes a subscription to *UPDATE*, a monthly newsletter that provides the latest information on research and legislative activity, and other news about giving and volunteering; complimentary copies of *Government Relations Information and Action*, which addresses a variety of issues involving the relationship between government and the independent sector; and thirty percent discounts on IS publications.

National Association of Community Action Agencies
(see Community Resources and Organizations, page 7)

National Association of Service & Conservation Corps
1001 Connecticut Ave., N.W., Suite 827
Washington, DC 20036
(202) 331-9647

A nonprofit membership organization, **NASCC** serves as the focal point for youth corps, promoting them at the federal, state, regional, county, and municipal levels. NASCC also works to broaden the national consensus for youth service, and provides information and technical assistance to existing and nascent conservation and service corps programs. Youth corps participants are economically disadvantaged people, ages fourteen to twenty-five, who provide a variety of services to better the communities in which they work. Nationwide, youth corps participants are building trails, planting trees, fighting fires, assisting the homebound elderly, renovating low-income housing, providing support services for teachers of individuals with mental disabilities, and delivering food to the hungry. If you would like to become involved with a youth corps program or know of someone who would, contact the national headquarters for information on available programs. Anyone can support youth corps by becoming a member of NASCC. Membership includes the NASCC newsletter, job announcements, and other publications. Individual memberships cost $25 (contact NASCC for other membership opportunities). Many NASCC member corps also draw on the talents of volunteers who help out as mentors, teachers, and supervisors. A nationwide listing of programs and other publications on corps program development and operation (for potential volunteers and participants alike) is available from the national headquarters.

National Urban League, Inc.
The Equal Opportunity Building
500 E. 62nd St., New York, NY 10021
(212) 310-9000

The **National Urban League** is one of the most influential and effective social service and civil rights organizations in America. A nonprofit, nonpartisan community-based agency, the league has 113 affiliates and more than 30,000 volunteers throughout the U.S. working to secure equal opportunities for African-Americans and other minorities. Aside from providing a powerful voice for minorities and maintaining a renowned research department, the organization offers assistance in employment, housing, education, social welfare, teen pregnancy, AIDS education, and crime prevention. Services include the **Comprehensive Youth Development Program**, which teaches remedial skills, provides employment counseling, and offers guidance in social and personal areas to at-risk young people; the **AIDS Initiative**, which educates the African-American community on the dangers of AIDS; and the **Stop The Violence Campaign**, a partnership between the National Urban League and some of today's best rap artists working to end the homicide of African-American males by other African-American males. There are many other effective campaigns, services, and programs initiated by NUL, all of which need support. If you are interested in helping, contact the affiliate near you.

The Salvation Army
799 Bloomfield Ave., Verona, NJ 07044
(201) 239-0606

The Salvation Army is a nonprofit, Christian-based organization motivated by a love of God and a practical concern for the needs of humanity. TSA works to preach the Gospel, supply basic human necessities, provide personal counseling, and undertake the spiritual and moral regeneration and physical rehabilitation of all persons in need. (Salvation Army officers, however, must believe in Christ and the doctrines of the organization, which relate to Christianity.) There are more than 10,000 Salvation Army centers nationwide, which provide emergency shelters, day-care centers, youth programs, summer camps for low-income children, victim assistance, assistance for the homeless and hungry, emergency disaster services, and missing persons services. Members visit hospitals, convalescent and nursing homes, correctional institutions, and children's homes to provide care and support and bring writing materials, magazines, Bibles, and various other gifts. At Christmastime, the Salvation Army collects and distributes food for the homeless, toys and clothing for homeless children and children of prisoners, and special gifts to persons in hospitals and nursing homes. Most important to members is their commitment to bring spiritual light and love to people in need at Christmas. If you are interested in working with the Salvation Army, contact the affiliate in your area.

20/20 Vision
(see The Environment, page 274)

United Black Fund
(see Community Resources and Organizations, page 7)

USO
World Headquarters
601 Indiana Ave., N.W., Washington, DC 20004
(202) 783-8121, FAX: (202) 638-4716 or (202) 638-0901

The **United Services Organization** is a civilian, voluntary nonprofit organization supported solely by private contributions. It is not part of the U.S. government and receives no direct federal funding. The USO serves the needs of military personnel and their families, helping them adjust to the unique hardships of a transient life while promoting strong and lasting relationships between military and host civilian communities around the world. At more than 155 locations in the states and worldwide the USO assists the U.S. Armed Forces community through **Airport Centers** (which provide infant nurseries, temporary rest/sleeping areas, and assistance with flight delays/cancellations, missing luggage, and meeting family members), **Fleet**

Centers (which offer assistance with transportation, currency exchange, and other travel services), **Family and Community Centers** (which help with finding day care, budgeting, housing, job placement, and crisis intervention), **Orientation and Intercultural Programs** (which foster friendship and understanding between the visiting military and permanent host communities), and **Celebrity Entertainment**. Volunteers are needed for many of these activities. Also, if you are interested in sending Christmas or other holiday gifts or letters to servicemen and -women overseas, contact your local USO office or the national headquarters for the necessary addresses (ask for the Programs and Community Relations Office).

United Way of America
(see Community Resources and Organizations, page 7)

VOLUNTEER—The National Center
1111 N. 19th St., Suite 500, Arlington, VA 22209
(703) 276-0542

VOLUNTEER is a nonprofit organization working to strengthen the volunteer sector in the U.S. The organization seeks to increase involvement in volunteering, develop and sustain strong local structures to promote volunteerism, increase public awareness of the importance of volunteering, and demonstrate innovative ways of applying volunteer energies to specific needs. In addition to disseminating information, VOLUNTEER has developed a network of nearly 400 local **Volunteer Clearinghouses** throughout the U.S. (These centers are sometimes listed in the telephone book under "Voluntary Action Center," "Volunteer Bureau," or "Volunteer Information and Referral.") Volunteer clearinghouses match volunteers with organizations that need help (see page 6 for more information). VOLUNTEER has a comprehensive catalog of books and materials (primarily for nonprofit administrators), including *101 Ideas for Volunteer Programs; Volunteers: How to Find Them, How to Keep Them;* and *Volunteering: A National Profile.* The organization also offers posters, T-shirts, tote bags, buttons, and other items with messages encouraging people to become volunteers. If you cannot find the Volunteer Center in your community, call the national headquarters. (If there is no center in your community, VOLUNTEER can help you develop one.)

Volunteers of America
3813 N. Causeway Boulevard, Metairie, LA 70002
(504) 837-2652

VOA is a nonprofit, Christian-based human services organization offering over 400 programs in more than 200 communities across the U.S. Here is just a partial list of what VOA provides: meals to elderly persons and homebound individuals; food, clothing, and household items to the needy; day care for children and adults with disabilities; support services for people with AIDS; personal and family counseling; crisis and suicide prevention; halfway houses for individuals with mental illnesses; job training; transitional living for ex-prisoners; emergency shelter for the homeless; nursing-home care; apartments for elderly persons; and help with reading skills. Check your phone book or contact the VOA headquarters for an affiliate near you.

**Young Men's Christian Association
of the United States of America**
101 N. Wacker Drive, Chicago, IL 60606
(312) 977-0031

The **YMCA** is a nonprofit, Christian-based organization dedicated to helping men and women of all ages, incomes, abilities, races, and religions grow in body, mind, and spirit. Each local YMCA functions independently and has an all-volunteer board responding to the specific needs of its community. The major U.S. programs include health and recreation programs (for example, first aid and CPR training, infant/parent aquatic classes, youth basketball), day camps, and child care. YMCAs may also provide housing, job training, literacy programs, substance-abuse programs, and a variety of services for senior citizens, as well as classes and services for people with disabilities. Volunteers of all ages, religions, races, and economic backgrounds are welcome at the more than 2,000 YMCAs nationwide. Contact your local YMCA for more information.

**Young Women's Christian Association
of the United States of America**
726 Broadway, New York, NY 10003
(212) 614-2700, FAX: (212) 677-9716

The **YWCA** is a nonprofit organization rooted in the Christian faith and dedicated to empowering women and fighting racism. With over 4,000 locations nationwide, the YWCA is a coalition of four million women, girls, and their families, reflecting diversity in age (twelve and up), ethnicity, religion, race, lifestyle, and interests. Most YWCA activities stress education and personal development for women and girls, focusing on such areas as peer counseling, teen pregnancy prevention, domestic abuse, career counseling, and child and health care. Local centers may offer classes and services for seniors, refugees, and individuals with disabilities. The YWCA also sponsors **ENCORE**, an exercise and education program for those who have had breast cancer surgery, and the **Mothers' Center** program for young mothers. Write or call the national headquarters if you cannot find the affiliate in your area.

> **Youth Service America**
> 1319 F St., N.W., Suite 900, Washington, DC 20004
> (202) 783-8855, FAX: (202) 347-2603

YSA is a nonprofit organization that promotes service by young people of all racial, class, and cultural backgrounds. Volunteers work with programs that are improving urban living conditions, protecting natural resources, cleaning up neighborhoods, caring for older Americans, tutoring at-risk youngsters, helping with day care, working in shelters for the homeless, and much more. YSA is also an aggressive advocate for the thousands of youth service programs across the U.S., providing coherence to the movement and emphasizing to both policymakers and the private sector the needs and benefits of youth service. If you are interested in joining or supporting YSA, contact the national headquarters. YSA also distributes several publications that discuss youth service and national service in general. These include *Community Service Programs in Independent Schools* and *National Service: What Would It Mean*. Programs and organizations can become professional affiliates for an annual fee of $200.

Doing Good Full-Time and for the Long Term
(Internships, Summer Programs, and Professional Opportunities)

What You Can Do

☞ **Many of the organizations listed in this book have internships and other positions available, so if you find an organization that appeals to you, see if it has full-time or long-term opportunities.** The geographical index will help you find nonprofit organizations near you (not all such organizations have volunteer opportunities, however).

☞ **If you are interested in becoming involved with long-term volunteer opportunities, including internships, summer programs, or working at camps, Native American reservations, or rural areas nationwide, here are some resources to help you get started:**

• ***Community Jobs*** is a monthly newsletter listing jobs and internships available with nonprofit organizations that address such issues as the environment, consumer advocacy, housing, education, and homelessness. Jobs are listed by region, with a special section on opportunities in Washington, D.C. One issue costs $3.50, and a one-year subscription costs $15 for individuals, $18 for nonprofit organizations, and $30 for institutions. For more information, contact **Community Careers Resource Center** at *1601 Connecticut Ave., Suite 600, N.W., Washington, DC 20009*; (202) 667-0661.

• ***Connections*** is a free directory of Catholic volunteer opportunities, published by the **St. Vincent Pallotti Center for Apostolic Development**. The directory lists several hundred opportunities for people interested in helping elderly persons, disadvantaged young people, individuals with disabilities, refugees, prisoners, and others who may be in need of assistance. Volunteer opportunities relating to education, homelessness, low-income housing, hunger, social justice, poverty, and peace are also listed. Write to or call the St. Vincent Pallotti Center at *715 Monroe St., N.E., Washington, DC 20017-1755*; (202) 529-3330.

• ***Good Works: A Guide to Careers in Social Change*** by Joan Anzalone is a valuable resource for people who are really serious about "doing good" and promoting social change. The book lists more than 600 companies and organizations involved with such issues as the environment, civil rights, hunger, homelessness, and poverty. If you can't find a copy in bookstores, contact the publisher, **Dembner Books** at *80 8th Ave., New York, NY 10011*; (212) 924-2525.

• ***New Careers: A Directory of Jobs and Internships in Technology and Society*** is a 255-page guide to nonprofit organizations working in such areas as energy and the environment, peace, health, and general science. Approximately 150 organizations, located in more than thirty major cities nationwide, are listed. The directory costs $20, $12 for students (these prices include $2 for shipping and handling), and is published by **Student Pugwash U.S.A.** (see The Environment, page 273). Write or call SP USA at *1638 R St., N.W., #32, Washington DC 20009*; (202) 328-6555.

● *Opportunity to Serve!* is a comprehensive listing of volunteer opportunities in the U.S. and abroad distributed free by the **Mennonite Board of Missions**. The booklet lists approximately a hundred long-term and short-term volunteer opportunities in such areas as education, health care, homelessness and low-income housing, and a variety of services relating to poverty and social justice. Write or call the Mennonite Board of Missions at *Box 370, Elkhart, IN 46515-0370*; (219) 294-7523 (Voice or TTY).

● *The Response* is a free, comprehensive listing of more than 140 Christian-based volunteer opportunities in the U.S. and around the world. Opportunities include working with individuals with disabilities, teaching, assisting individuals who are homeless, offering companionship and support to disadvantaged young people, providing health services, and feeding the hungry. *The Response* also lists opportunities for married/single parents, people over fifty-five, people under eighteen, and married couples. There is no age requirement, and the programs vary in terms of time commitment required (some call for a commitment of less than three weeks). Write or call the **International Liaison of Lay Volunteers in Mission** at *4121 Harewood Road, N.E., Washington, DC 20017*; 1-800-543-5046 or (202) 529-1100.

● *Volunteer! The Comprehensive Guide to Voluntary Service in the U.S. and Abroad* is a fantastic resource for people who are interested in volunteering for short or extended periods of time. It includes organizations and programs in the U.S. and abroad working in such areas as homelessness, low-income housing, hunger, peace, social justice, and poverty-related issues. The book is 155 pages long and costs $8.30 (which includes $1.35 for postage and handling)—quite a bargain for an extremely useful book on volunteerism. Write the **Commission on Voluntary Service and Action** at *Box 347, Newton, KS 67114-0347*. (CVSA is a nonprofit council of private North American organizations that sponsor and/or support voluntary service projects worldwide.)

● *Volunteer Program Guide* ($2), put out by **Service Civil International/USA**, lists hundreds of volunteer opportunities around the U.S. and abroad, including opportunities to improve the environment, work with adults with mental disabilities, rehabilitate houses on Native American reservations, and address such issues as peace, women's rights, and low-income housing. Contact SCI/USA for more information at *Innisfree Village, Route 2, Box 506, Crozet, VA 22932*; (804) 823-1826 (office hours are Mon., Wed., and Thurs. 9 a.m.–noon, EST).

See also The Environment (page 256), and Hunger (page 345), for other long-term volunteer opportunities.

National Organizations

Fourth World Movement
7600 Willow Hill Drive, Landover, MD 20785
(301) 336-9489

FWM is a nonprofit organization of dedicated volunteers fighting for the human rights of the poorest individuals in the U.S. and eighteen other countries. It sponsors more than 300 volunteer-run projects in abandoned and isolated towns, villages, urban ghettos, and shantytowns. Involvement in the U.S. includes providing street libraries (which bring learning activities, books, and arts and crafts to children), advocacy, support, and literacy programs for low- and no-income persons. FWM also distributes *The Human Face of Poverty* (1990), by Vincent Fanelli, which looks back on two decades of involvement of FWM volunteers in some of New York's poorest neighborhoods. Write to or call FWM for more information on the book, internships, or volunteer opportunities.

Lutheran Volunteer Corps
1226 Vermont Ave., N.W., Washington, DC 20005
(202) 387-3222

LVC is a nonprofit organization that encourages people of all Christian faiths to commit themselves to a year of full-time service, explore a simplified lifestyle, and live in an intentional Christian community. All placements are domestic, start at the end of August, and are in urban social-justice organizations. People of all racial, ethnic, and cultural backgrounds are encouraged to participate, but they must be twenty-one when their term of service begins (there is no upper age limit). Depending on your skills and interests, you may teach in an inner-city preschool, write a newsletter for a food pantry, staff a shelter for homeless individuals, or work with lawyers on low-income housing issues. Program information is available upon request.

Volunteers for Peace
43 Tiffany Road, Belmont, VT 05730
(802) 259-2759, FAX: (802) 259-2922

VFP is a nonprofit organization that coordinates the **International Workcamps** program for people interested in participating in workcamps in the U.S. and abroad. Workcamp activities include building houses and community centers, cleaning up the environment, working with individuals with disabilities, and feeding the hungry. Participants donate a nominal fee (usually around $80 to $90 for two to three weeks) for the unique experience of working with people from different countries. Ninety percent of the workcamps take place from June through September, so if you're looking for a productive summer activity, write to or call VFP for more information. VFP can provide you with its *International Workcamper Newsletter* and the *International Workcamp Directory*, which costs $10 and lists over 800 programs overseas and in the U.S.

Money Matters
Socially Responsible Consumerism and Investing

What You Can Do

☞ **Keep up on socially responsible companies, products, and investments and tell others about them.** There are countless companies in America that are as concerned with making the world a better place as they are with making a profit. Here are a few publications that will help you inform yourself and others about companies that are making a difference and those that are not:

- ***Business Ethics*** is a highly informative and very enjoyable magazine. For $49 (the one-year subscription rate), you get a high-quality, bimonthly magazine that presents stories on professionals and businesses having a positive effect on the world. *Business Ethics* provides its readers with ideas that they can put to use in their businesses, directories of socially responsible businesses, book reviews and notices, and a variety of in-depth articles and features. You can even receive a free copy to check it out. For more information, write to or call *1107 Hazeltine Boulevard, Suite 530, Chaska, MN 55318*; (612) 448-8864.
- ***The Corporate Examiner*** is a newsletter put out by the **In-**

terfaith Center on Corporate Responsibility** that examines the policies of major U.S. corporations on nine issues: apartheid, Star Wars, nuclear weapons, minorities, women, alternative investments, energy, the environment, and international marketing. A one-year, ten-issue subscription costs $35. Contact ICCR at *475 Riverside Drive, Room 566, New York, NY 10115*; (212) 870-2936. (See page 31 for more information on ICCR.)

• ***The Clean Yield*** ($85 for a one-year subscription) is an informative stock-market newsletter for investors who would like to make timely and profitable investments in publicly traded companies that pass certain social-responsibility tests. Companies are screened for South African involvement, weapons production, environmental practices, labor and community relations, affirmative action, tobacco production and gambling, nuclear power generation, and corporate frankness. Those companies that successfully mix financial prosperity and social responsibility and whose stocks show above-average promise are profiled and actively followed. (In fact, for more than four years, *TCY*'s "clean" companies have outperformed the market.) Write to or call Clean Yield Publications at *Box 1880, Greensboro Bend, VT 05842*; (802) 533-7178.

• ***Shopping for a Better World*** is a pocket-size guide that rates the makers of more than 1,300 brand-name products on eleven social issues, including giving to charity, women's advancement, minority advancement, military contracts, animal testing, disclosure of information, community outreach, nuclear power, South Africa, the environment, and family benefits. The book costs $5.95 (which includes $1 for shipping and handling). If your local bookstore doesn't have it, the **Council on Economic Priorities** (see page 30) distributes the book.

☞ **The next time you need to get personal checks, contact the Message!Check Corporation.** M!C can provide you with beautiful, eye-catching personal checks featuring the name of a nonprofit organization you'd like to support (from a list of about fifteen participating nonprofit organizations, including **Mothers Against Drunk Driving, Greenpeace U.S.A., National Audubon Society**, and **Vietnam Veterans of America**). M!C checks provide visibility for nonprofit organizations, and with every order you make, M!C donates $1 to the organization noted on your check (single-style orders—200 checks—cost $14). M!C checks can be used with checking accounts at any U.S. financial institution. Write to M!C for an information packet at *P.O. Box 3206-V, Seattle, WA 98114*.

28 VOLUNTEER USA

☞ **Be a socially responsible consumer.** You can buy virtually everything you need (especially gifts) from companies that practice good ethics and help people and/or causes in need. Here are a few important resources and organizations:

- **Co-op America** has one of the most outstanding mail-order catalogs available. Here are just a few items you can purchase through its "Alternative Catalog":

    - cloth diapers
    - cloth grocery bags
    - fluorescent bulbs
    - high-quality handmade crafts and clothes
    - nontoxic cleaners
    - organic foods
    - recycled paper products
    - T-shirts, posters, children's toys and games, books, calendars, and other items that promote women's rights, peace, love, the environment, and related issues

    Write or call Co-op America at *2100 M St., N.W., Suite 403, Washington, DC 20063*; (202) 872-5307, 1-800-424-2667, TTY: (202) 872-5399. (See page 33 for more information on Co-op America.)

- **Save the Children**, a child sponsorship organization (see Children and Young Adults, page 142, for more information), runs an excellent mail-order company featuring folk art and crafts, many handmade by poor people in the U.S. and around the world. Here is a sampling of the items you can purchase:

    - bead necklaces and bracelets
    - brass candlesticks
    - ceramic masks
    - colorful tin ornaments
    - copper plates
    - Guatemalan doll ornaments
    - handcrafted wood bookends
    - handwoven pillow covers
    - handwoven and silk scarves
    - multi-striped handwoven napkins
    - multi-striped vests
    - painted tiles

    Write or call for a free catalog: **Save the Children Craft Shop**, *P.O. Box 166, Peru, IN 46970; 1-800-833-3154 (8 a.m. to 9 p.m.).* If you're in the area, you can visit an STC retail shop at *54 Wilton Road, Westport, CT 06880*; (203) 226-7271.

- Write to or call **SELFHELP Crafts** for information on purchasing crafts in its retail stores nationwide. The crafts are made by poor people all over the world, including the U.S., providing employment and a fair amount of income for more than 30,000 needy families. The items are handmade, very inexpensive, and strikingly detailed. You can purchase, among many other items:

- bamboo planters and trays
- baskets
- bracelets
- brass bowls
- ceramic boxes and vases
- stuffed animals
- tablecloths
- wall hangings
- wooden animals
- wooden backgammon sets
- wooden tables and shelves
- wool sweaters

Contact SELFHELP Crafts at *704 Main St., P.O. Box 500, Akron, PA 17501-0500*; (717) 859-4971. Wholesalers interested in selling products from SELFHELP Crafts can also call for more information. Volunteers are needed at the shops, so if there's a store near you, see how you can help out.

● **Trade Wind** is a nonprofit mail-order company that sells beautiful, high-quality crafts and clothes handmade by small families and poor people in Central America and in the U.S. Here is a partial list of the items available:

- brass earrings
- children's clothes
- dresses
- kimonos
- men's and women's shirts
- patchwork bags
- purses and wallets
- shawls
- shorts
- tablecloths and napkins
- ties
- wall art

Write to or call Trade Wind for a free catalog at *P.O. Box 380, Summertown, TN 38483*; (615) 964-2334 or 1-800-445-1991.

See also The Environment (page 245) and Animals (page 78) for companies that sell environmentally safe and cruelty-free products.

National Organizations that Monitor Corporations and Socially Responsible Investments

Catalyst
P.O. Box 1308, Montpelier, VT 05601
(802) 223-7943

Catalyst is a nonprofit activist organization working to promote a greater awareness of the interconnections between economics, ecology, and human rights. Its focus is on research, education, outreach, and action from an Earth-centered perspective. Catalyst sponsors many projects and petition drives and has a wealth of information on socially responsible investments and corporate practices. The organization publishes a quarterly newsletter, *Catalyst*, packed with in-depth articles, information on upcoming projects, business investment news, recommended publications, and ideas on how you can respond to particular irresponsible corporations. The newsletter is free to members (membership is $50 and up—call for more information) or $25 for nonmembers. Catalyst offers several other publications (such as *Economics As If the Earth Really Mattered*), as well as posters and T-shirts.

Council on Economic Priorities
30 Irving Place, New York, NY 10003
(212) 420-1133 or 1-800-822-6435

CEP is a nonprofit, public-interest research organization concerned with corporate policies that affect citizens around the world. The council publishes more than 1,000 books, reports, and newsletters on subjects as diverse as air pollution, toxic waste, child care, arms control, and the politics of defense contracting. CEP is an indispensable organization for those who want to find out how companies really act behind their sleek advertising campaigns. The cost of a regular membership is $25 ($15 for people with limited incomes), and includes a one-year subscription to CEP's monthly newsletter, *Research Report*, and *Shopping for a Better World*, a pocket guide rating brand-name products on eleven issues, including the environment, promotion of women, animal testing, and South Africa ($5.95, which includes $1 for shipping and handling, for nonmembers). Contact CEP for information on other membership possibilities and volunteer opportunities.

GOOD MONEY Publications
Box 363, Worcester, VT 05682
1-800-535-3551, In Vermont: (802) 223-3911

A nonprofit organization, **GM** is an excellent resource for ethically and socially concerned investors. GM publishes two newsletters, *Good Money*, a twelve-page bimonthly, and *Netback*, a four-page quarterly. Both newsletters present socially responsible and irresponsible businesses and business practices, commentary on a variety of business issues, and related features and articles. GM also publishes *Issue Papers* ($20 each)—detailed papers on important social issues such as animal rights, the environment, minorities, and the military; social funds guides; and other informative publications. Contact GM for a full price sheet.

Interfaith Center on Corporate Responsibility
475 Riverside Drive, Room 566, New York, NY 10115
(212) 870-2936

ICCR is a nationwide coalition of investors who utilize church investments and other resources to change unjust or harmful corporate policies and practices. The center sponsors shareholder resolutions; meets with management; divests from companies that are not socially responsible; conducts public hearings and investigations; publishes special reports; testifies at the United Nations, the Securities and Exchange Commission, and Congress; and sponsors actions such as prayer vigils, consumer boycotts, and letter-writing campaigns. An ICCR membership is open to any religious group or denominational agency. The minimum annual dues are $1,750. Individuals can still benefit from and help ICCR by subscribing to *The Corporate Examiner* (see description on page 26). ICCR also has a comprehensive list of publications on important social issues (for example, *Chemical Weapons; Cutting Ties to Apartheid: What the Churches Say on Divestment*) available to anyone.

Investor Responsibility Research Center
1755 Massachusetts Ave., N.W., Suite 600
Washington, DC 20036
(202) 234-7500

A not-for-profit corporation, **IRRC** researches and publishes impartial reports on contemporary business and public policy issues affecting corporations and investors. The center follows such issues as corporate governance, South Africa, energy and the environment, military contracting, and Northern Ireland. IRRC also offers research, consulting, and database searches specifically tailored to the needs of the client, on a contract basis. Publications include *The Impact of Sanctions on South Africa; Stones in a Glass House: CFCs and the Ozone Depletion Controversy;* and *Animal Testing and Consumer Products*. IRRC also publishes *News for Investors*, a monthly newsletter that keeps readers up-to-date on developments affecting corporate social responsibility in such areas as investment in South Africa, animal testing, the Valdez principles for the environment, and related areas (cost: $200 per year); the *Corporate Governance Bulletin*, a bimonthly publication that features reports and analyses of current corporate governance issues and policy developments in Congress, regulatory agencies, the courts, and other government bodies (cost: $225 per year); and *South Africa Reporter*, a quarterly newsletter covering the events and trends that will shape the future of South Africa (cost: $100 per year). Contact IRRC for more information on its publications and services.

National Socially Responsible Networks, Investments, and Services

Affirmative Investments
129 South St., 6th Floor, Boston, MA 02111-0250
(617) 350-0250 or 1-800-633-2747

AI works with individuals, institutions, and organizations to help them channel their funds into investments that, while being solid in financial terms, also create positive social change. AI investments address such national and global issues as homelessness and housing, education, health, and the environment. The organization locates, evaluates, negotiates, recommends, and monitors direct investments, specializing in raising equity capital for the development of low- and moderate-income housing. AI makes a very strong distinction between investing, which should produce a good return, and "gifting." In mutual funds, it demands affirmative screening, rather than benign investments. AI can help you with portfolio management, lending, tax planning, housing development, real estate finance, and securities. (The company does not, however, manage stock or bond portfolios or provide general financial planning services.)

Calvert Group
Calvert Social Investment Fund
4550 Montgomery Ave., Suite 1000N, Bethesda, MD 20814
(301) 951-4814 or 1-800-368-2750

Serving more than 180,000 investors, the **Calvert Group** offers the nation's first and largest family of socially screened funds. Since its beginning in 1976, Calvert's assets have grown to more than $3 billion. Six of its twenty investment options, representing more than $650 million, are socially and environmentally responsible mutual funds, representing the broadest range of such funds in the industry. **Calvert Social Investment Fund (CSIF)**, with its money market, bond, equity, and managed growth (balanced) portfolios, is generally recognized as applying the industry's most stringent social and environmental criteria to its investment decisions. Not only do the investments have high promise on total return relative to risk, but the companies involved must also negotiate fairly with their workers; deliver safe products and services in ways that sustain the natural environment; provide an environment supportive of their employees' wellness; provide equal opportunities for women, individuals with disabilities, and others; and foster awareness of commitment to human goals, such as creativity, productivity, and responsibility to others. CSIF will not invest in enterprises that produce nuclear energy or that manufacture equipment to produce such energy; operate in South Africa or lend to the government, state-owned corporations, or privately owned corporations in that country; manufacture alcoholic beverages or tobacco products, or operate gambling casinos; or have significant involvement in the manufacture of weapons systems. The newest addition to Calvert's family of funds, introduced in January 1990—**Calvert-Ariel Appreciation Funds**—incorporates similar criteria on the issues of South Africa, weapons systems, and nuclear weapons, as well as employing a strong environmental screen. Contact Calvert for more information on its standards and investment opportunities.

Co-op America
2100 M St., N.W., Suite 403, Washington, DC 20063
(202) 872-5307, 1-800-424-2667, TTY: (202) 872-5399

Co-op America is a nonprofit, member-controlled, worker-managed association linking socially responsible businesses and consumers in a national network. The group enables consumers to align their buying habits with companies and products concerned about protecting the environment and promoting peace and justice. Co-op America also helps businesses, co-ops, and nonprofit organizations expand the market for their goods and services. The organization's catalogs offer hundreds of useful, hard-to-find products (natural-fiber clothing, books, music, magazine subscriptions, furniture, nonsexist toys and games, posters, and Third World products) as well as valuable information. Membership includes a subscription to *Building Economic Alternatives*, a quarterly magazine filled with insightful articles on strategies for changing the systematic injustice of world economy systems. Members also have access to a network of socially responsible companies, banks, and credit unions; are offered health and life insurance from socially responsible companies; and can take advantage of the Co-op America travel service, offering the most comprehensive range of socially responsible travel options with all of the guarantees of other travel agencies (lowest advertised airfares, hotel, car rental, tour bookings, and a toll-free **Travel-Links** number). A basic membership starts at $20 ($15 for people with a limited income).

Cooperative Development Foundation
National Cooperative Business Association
1401 New York Ave., N.W., Suite 1100
Washington, DC 20005
(202) 638-6222, FAX: (202) 638-1374

CDF finances cooperative ventures that help needy individuals build better lives for themselves. In the U.S., for example, CDF provides grants to assist with constructing housing, providing health care, stimulating adult education, and creating and marketing crafts for low-income families. If you make a contribution to the CDF fund, you will receive a certificate of appreciation and CDF's quarterly newsletter, which covers cooperative developments in the U.S. and abroad. Contact CDF for more information.

Ethical Investments
430 First Ave., North, Suite 204, Minneapolis, MN 55401
(612) 339-3939

EI offers a broad range of investment services, from consultation and advice to complete portfolio management. Counselors work with clients to find fiscally sound investments that meet positive social criteria on issues such as sensitivity to the environment; high-quality employee relationships, including female and minority participation at all levels of management; product safety, quality, and usefulness; and participation in community interests. EI does not recommend investments with any involvement with South Africa; weapons production, both nuclear and conventional; nuclear power; or liquor, tobacco, and gambling. The company can develop a comprehensive plan for you that considers your financial needs and specific attitudes on business ethics, religion, family obligations, and philanthropy. Initial consultants are available without fee or obligation.

Franklin Research and Development Corporation
711 Atlantic Ave., Boston, MA 02111
(617) 423-6655 or 1-800-548-5684

FRDC is an employee-owned registered investment adviser company that helps individuals and institutions who want socially responsible criteria applied to the management of their funds. Currently, FRDC maintains extensive social-service assessments on more than 750 companies and follows selected social issues on another 1,000. Company evaluations focus on the following areas: environment, employee relations, responsible citizenship in local and world communities, South Africa, efficient and safe use and/or production of energy, weapons production, and product/service quality and social usefulness. FRDC researches corporations by reviewing their literature, interviewing corporate managers, and seeking verification from third-party nonprofit research groups, government agencies, and stakeholder groups. FRDC also publishes a monthly newsletter, *Insight*, which addresses socially responsible investing ($19.95 for a one-year subscription).

The Institute for Community Economics
57 School St., Springfield, MA 01105
(413) 746-8660

ICE is a nonprofit corporation that provides organizational development assistance nationwide to community groups working to regain control over their land, housing, and capital resources, including community land trusts, limited-equity housing co-ops, mobile home park co-ops, community loan funds, and other grass-roots organizations. The institute places a priority on assisting groups that meet the urgent needs of the poor within a broader community empowerment strategy which creates and preserves lasting community resources such as permanently affordable housing and land. It also provides low-cost financing to such groups through its **Revolving Loan Fund**, which accepts and manages loans from socially concerned individual and institutional investors. ICE works closely with the members of these organizations on an equal basis, seeing them not as "clients" but as co-workers in a common struggle. The institute's guiding principles include recognizing that the social and economic changes underpinning successful community development efforts require both personal and institutional changes, as well as an increased public willingness to deal with the root causes of economic justice, such as property speculation and absentee ownership. ICE publishes a quarterly newsletter, *Community Economics*, which provides information about community land trusts (CLTs), community loan funds (CLFs), and other innovative community development activities. It also distributes a variety of publications on CLTs, CLFs, socially responsible investments, and the widening gap between rich and poor. Contact ICE for free information on its programs and how you can become involved through community investing, a one-year internship, a newsletter subscription, community land trust development, and more.

New Alternatives Fund
295 Northern Boulevard, Great Neck, NY 11021
(516) 466-0808

NAF is a diversified open-end investment company that seeks long-term capital gains through equity investment, concentrating its investments in companies with an interest in solar and alternative energy development. Investments may include solar cells, natural gas, fuel cells, biomass, resource recovery, passive and active architectural products, forest products, conservation systems, and energy-efficient apparatus and controls. Contact NAF for more information on environmentally responsible investments, a look at NAF's track record so far, and a prospectus summary.

The Parnassus Fund
244 California St., San Francisco, CA 94111
(415) 362-3505 or 1-800-999-3505

The Parnassus Fund follows both a socially responsible investment policy and a "contrarian" policy, investing in stocks that are out of favor with the financial community and, therefore, undervalued. The fund looks for companies that provide high-quality products or services, show sensitivity to the communities where they operate, treat their employees well, and are not involved with weapons, nuclear power, South Africa, alcohol, tobacco, or gambling. Contact the organization if you are interested in more information on "contrarian" principles or have general questions about the fund.

Pax World Fund
224 State St., Portsmouth, NH 03801
(603) 431-8022 or 1-800-767-1729

PWF is a no-load, open-end, balanced mutual fund that applies both economic and social criteria to investments. The fund supports companies that produce life-supportive goods and services, non-war-related industries, firms with fair-employment practices; and companies with sound environmental practices. PWF also invests in such areas as health care, education, and pollution control, and avoids investing in liquor, tobacco, and gambling industries. Contact the organization for more information on services, accounts, and management and auditing practices.

Progressive Asset Management
1814 Franklin St., Suite 710, Oakland, CA 94612
(415) 834-3722 or 1-800-527-8627

A full-service financial counseling group, **PAM** provides sound investment advice with a conscience. Its consultants help investors avoid companies that contribute to or support South Africa and other repressive regimes, nuclear weapons production (or significant involvement in war-related production), environmental pollution, use of nuclear power, or the generation of toxic waste. PAM does, however, support companies that promote fair hiring, employment, and union policies, as well as affirmative action for minorities and women; production of safe, healthful products; energy conservation; and the practice of good corporate citizenship, community investment, and involvement. The company publishes a bimonthly newsletter, *Progressive Investor*, which provides economic analysis, investment advice, and information about other responsible investment organizations. The annual subscription fee is $15; a complimentary copy is available upon request.

Progressive Securities Financial Services
5200 S.W. Macadam, Suite 350, Portland, OR 97201
(503) 224-7828
Toll-free: 1-800-PROGRES (776-4737)
or
767 Willamette, Suite 301, Eugene, OR 97401
(503) 345-5669

Progressive Securities assists individuals and institutions with socially responsible investments, taking into consideration such issues as South Africa, the environment, equal opportunity, weapons production, employee relations, and product quality and safety. The company offers a full range of services, including stock and bond portfolio management, financial planning, community development, insurance, money markets, and mutual funds. The investments provide competitive returns while supporting companies making a positive impact with their products, services, and business ethics.

Social Investment Forum
430 1st Ave., N., Minneapolis, MN 55401
(612) 333-8338

SIF is a nonprofit association of companies and individuals interested in socially responsible investing. Its purpose is to promote financially sound investing consistent with a commitment to peace, a healthy environment, social justice, and related social concerns. The group networks with similar organizations, sharing socially responsible investing trends with them, the public, and the media. The SIF newsletter, *The Forum*, is a quarterly publication with in-depth profiles and articles on SIF member organizations and individuals. Most notably, SIF publishes *Social Investment Services Guide to Forum Members* ($10), a 100-page guide with more than 200 listings of organizations in one of four categories: advisers and investment funds, community-targeted programs, information providers, and venture capital funds.

Working Assets Funding Service
230 California St., San Francisco, CA 94111
(415) 788-0777 or 1-800-522-7759

Working Assets Funding Service is a socially responsible consumer services company offering credit cards, long-distance phone service, and travel services to socially concerned individuals. Every time a **Working Assets VISA** or **MasterCard** is used to make a purchase, five cents goes to a fund that helps selected nonprofit action groups working for the environment, human rights, peace, and economic justice. (Contact the organization for a list of these groups.) Every time a new card is issued, $2 automatically goes to the fund. Whenever a **Working Assets Long Distance** user makes a long-distance call, one percent of the charge is donated to the fund; with **Working Assets Travel Service**, two percent of a member's charge is also donated to the fund. Working Assets Travel Service provides all of the services of a regular travel agency, including free bookings, guaranteed lowest fares available, and a twenty-four-hour emergency hotline.

Working Assets Money Fund
230 California St., Suite 500, San Francisco, CA 94111
1-800-533-3863, FAX: (415) 989-5920

Working Assets Money Fund is the largest socially responsible money fund in the country, and the fund's social screening process is one of the strictest in the social investing industry. Working Assets avoids investing in companies that operate or maintain business ties in South Africa; have substantial military contracts; build or operate nuclear power plants or equipment; show a consistent record of environmental violations; and have records of employment discrimination, and poor labor relations and worker safety standards. The fund seeks out companies with positive records on the environment, affirmative action, labor relations, and charitable giving. A minimum investment of $1,000 is required to open a money fund account, and the shareholder's money is always accessible either through the check-writing privilege (free of charge for checks over $250) or through the transferral of funds by phone, using the toll-free number. Working Assets also provides unlimited check writing, automatic deposits, retirement plans, and a quarterly newsletter, *Money Matters*. All investments are either commercial paper or CDs with the highest financial rating by Moody's or Standard & Poor's; or government-backed agency securities. Write or call for a free prospectus.

The resources and ideas listed in this chapter should give you a good start to making a positive difference in America. The remainder of the book is organized by specific causes, so if you're interested in a particular issue, read on.

AIDS
(Acquired Immune Deficiency Syndrome)

Why Help Is Needed

The Centers for Disease Control (CDC) estimate that since June 1981, 100,777 Americans have died as a result of AIDS.[1] Thousands continue to die every month. CDC also estimates that one to one and a half million people in the U.S. are infected with the HIV virus. By 1991, it is believed that AIDS will be the leading cause of death for Americans between twenty-five and forty-four years of age.[2] AIDS is killing people of all ages, races, and religions; it is not a disease that discriminates.

People, however, sometimes do. The prejudices, judgments, and attacks that have accompanied AIDS can be as destructive emotionally as the disease is physically. People with AIDS have been run out of offices, schools, religious congregations, apartment complexes, even their own homes. This is why friends, family members, and volunteers are so essential—they offer the support and care that any individual with a life-threatening illness would welcome. Having someone over to play a game of cards, to celebrate a birthday or holiday, or just to talk can be extremely gratifying. Even a simple handshake or a hug can inspire a smile and positive feelings. These friends and volunteers demonstrate an understanding not only of the human need for acceptance and companionship, but of AIDS itself. They recognize, above all, that casual contact does not spread AIDS and that their assistance is too valuable to be lost as a result of myths and rumors.

Education, prevention, and understanding will fight AIDS and the hysteria that has accompanied it, not blame, indifference, or hostil-

[1] Centers for Disease Control report, Oct. 31, 1990.
[2] "AIDS: An Expanding Emergency" (editorial), *Washington Post*, May 5, 1990, A20.

ity. Until a cure is found, it will be up to caring people to provide the support and compassion needed. It is the most inexpensive and effective medicine available, and anyone can offer it.

What You Can Do

☞ **Know the facts.** One of the most disturbing aspects of the AIDS crisis is that ignorance has fostered prejudice and insensitivity toward adults and children with AIDS. Almost all of the national organizations listed in this chapter can provide you with informative literature. You can also contact the local chapter of the Red Cross as well as local bookstores and libraries for materials on AIDS and related topics.

☞ **Keep up on AIDS-related legislation and voice your concern or approval.** Many of the organizations listed in this chapter have legislative updates and newsletters, and the **AIDS Action Council** (page 47) is an especially good source of information. (See also Voicing Your Opinion, page 363)

☞ **Work to educate others about AIDS and related issues.** Myths about AIDS not only encourage discrimination and fear, they obscure the real causes for the spread of the virus. For information and materials, check out the **San Francisco AIDS Foundation** (page 53) and the **Health Education Resource Organization** (page 51). Here are some additional ideas:

- **Talk with your children about AIDS.** Although most of the organizations listed in this chapter will have the information you'll need, *How to Talk to Your Child About AIDS* is a valuable resource for parents who wish to discuss AIDS and related issues openly and honestly with their children. The sixteen-page booklet (published in English and Spanish) is free. Send a self-addressed, stamped envelope to **Sex Information and Education Council of the U.S.**, 130 W. 42nd St., Suite 2500, New York, NY 10036; (212) 819-9770.
- **If you are a high school or college student,** see if you can put up posters, show videos or films, or distribute informative publications on AIDS. Since this usually requires a good deal of effort and money, work with an established school organization to get started.
- **If you are a teacher or coach,** see if you can implement

curricula on AIDS and related issues. School is an excellent place to educate kids about AIDS because it is often the only formal setting kids have to discuss such a serious issue. Once students know the facts, they can better educate their peers and family members.

• **Educate your co-workers or employees about AIDS and the (non)threat of AIDS in the workplace.** The office is an excellent place to provide AIDS information for adults, for it may be the only formal setting available for them to learn about and openly discuss the issue. It may also directly benefit the business, preventing antagonism and mistrust among employees unnecessarily afraid of becoming infected with the AIDS virus.

• **Buy a SHIRTS BY ZACK T-shirt or sweatshirt from the Pediatric AIDS Foundation** (page 52). These shirts have a picture of a cat, bear, or train on them, printed from drawings by a little boy named Zachary Fried who contracted AIDS and died when he was five and a half years old. The back of the shirts read, "HOPE FOR CHILDREN WITH AIDS." Not only will you help a worthy cause by buying a shirt, but every time you wear it you will remind people that children develop AIDS and need help, too.

☞ **Volunteer to work with a community-based AIDS organization.** The organization may need people to provide one-on-one care and support for people with AIDS or simply to help with sending out envelopes, answering phones, fundraising, and similar activities. To find such an organization in your community, look under the community-service numbers in the phone book or try the local government's human services or social services department, specifically a health-services office or division. Also, you can call the **National AIDS Hotline** (page 49) for information on organizations in your area.

☞ **Volunteer to work on an AIDS hotline.** You will need some training for this, but it is an educational opportunity and a much-needed service. To find out about local hotlines, look under the community-service numbers in your phone book. AIDS hotlines may also be listed under a subcategory such as "Survival Numbers," "Hotlines," or "Crisis Assistance." You can also call the **National AIDS Hotline** (page 49) for information on hotlines in your area.

☞ **Check with local hospitals to see if you can volunteer to work with "boarder babies."** These are babies who actually live in hospitals because their parents either have abandoned them or

AIDS (Acquired Immune Deficiency Syndrome) 43

have died (often from AIDS or drug overdoses). The hospital nursing staff may not have the time to devote individual attention to the babies, so volunteers fill in to provide the extra bit of TLC. Hospitals are listed in the phone book (usually the Yellow Pages) individually, under "Hospitals" or "Children's Hospitals," and sometimes under community-service numbers. If your local hospital has no such volunteer program, ask if another hospital in the area might.

☞ **Volunteer to work with an organization that delivers food to people with AIDS.** These organizations are located in most major cities across the country. Volunteer opportunities may include cooking or preparing food, delivering meals to peoples' homes, answering office phones, writing letters, and helping with fundraising. People can also donate food and the use of cars or vans.

The following organizations can provide you with the necessary information on food-delivery programs and volunteer opportunities:

Community Servings
c/o American Jewish Congress, Suite 310
1 Lincoln Plaza
Boston, MA 02111
(617) 330-9630
Serving the Boston area

Cure AIDS Now
2240 S. Dixie Highway
Miami, FL 33133
(305) 856-8378
Serving the Miami area

Food & Friends
P.O. Box 70601
(or 400 Eye St., S.W.)
Washington, DC 20024
(202) 488-8278
Serving the Washington metropolitan area

God's Love We Deliver
P.O. Box 1776
Old Chelsea Station
New York, NY 10113
(212) 874-1193
Serving New York City and Jersey City, NJ

Moveable Feast
P.O. Box 38445
Baltimore, MD 21231
(301) 243-4604
Serving the Baltimore area

Project Angel Food
1550 N. Hayworth Ave., Suite 1
Los Angeles, CA 90046
(213) 874-1677
Serving the Los Angeles area

Project Open Hand
2720 17th St.
San Francisco, CA 94110
(415) 558-0600
Serving the San Francisco area

Project Open Hand Atlanta, Inc.
1080 R Euclid Ave., N.E.
Atlanta, GA 30307
(404) 525-4620
Serving the Atlanta area

If you cannot find an organization in your community, call the **National AIDS Hotline** (page 49). If there is no food-delivery organization in your community, consider starting one up. This will require a group of very dedicated individuals who can sacrifice a lot of time, energy, and probably money. Contact a few of the organizations listed above for more information.

☞ **If you do volunteer to work on a one-on-one basis with a person with AIDS, or if you know of someone with AIDS whom you'd like to help,** here are a few things you may want to consider (adapted, with permission, from *When a Friend Has AIDS*, by Dixie Beckham, Diego López, Luis Palacios-Jimínez, Vincent Patti, and Michael Shernoff, © 1990, Chelsea Psychotherapy Associates, New York, NY):

- **Call before you visit.** The person may not feel up to a visit that day. If that is the case, however, don't hesitate to phone again and visit on another occasion. Tell the person what you'd like to do to help. If he or she agrees, make sure to keep any promises you make.

- **Don't be afraid to shake hands, hug, or touch the person as you would anyone else.** Human contact is a wonderful form of comfort and support, and AIDS cannot be passed on by touching or casual contact.
- **If the person is a friend of yours, it's okay to ask about the illness, but be sensitive to whether your friend wants to discuss it or not.** Simply ask, "Do you feel like talking about it?" The person may be tired of talking about symptoms, doctors, and treatments and may be more interested in current events, mutual friends, and other common interests. Take your cues from the person with AIDS.
- **Like everyone else, a person with AIDS can have both good and bad days.** On good days, treat the person as you would any other friend, and on bad days, treat him or her with extra care and compassion.
- **If the person expresses concern about his or her looks, be gentle, but acknowledge these feelings.** Just your listening may be all that is needed. Try pointing out some positive physical traits. It may make the person feel better.
- **Offer to go out for a walk or outing to get some fresh air, but ask about and know the person's limitations.** If he or she really doesn't seem to want to go out, don't push it.
- **Offer to take the person somewhere if he or she is in need of transportation,** such as to the store, the bank, the doctor, a movie, church or synagogue, or the park.
- **If you and the person with AIDS are religious, ask if you could pray or attend services together.** Don't hesitate to share your faith with the person (but only if he or she wants to). Spirituality can be very important at this time.
- **Appointments with Social Security or Medicaid can often be frustrating and exhausting.** Offer to accompany the person and to help fill out the forms. Be sure to stay with him or her until the business is finished.
- **Be creative when you come over.** Bring books, periodicals, taped music, a poster, home-baked cookies, or anything else that shows that you were thinking of the person. Before you cook a special meal or snack, make sure that it is something the person is able to eat. Bring the food in disposable containers so the person won't have to worry about washing dishes (unless you can also help with this).
- **Help celebrate holidays and other special occasions by offering to decorate the person's home or hospital room.** Bring flowers or other special gifts. Include the person in holiday

plans, even if he or she has to celebrate the holiday on a different date.

- **Offer to help out with household chores,** such as watering plants, washing dishes, taking out the laundry, or walking and feeding pets. The person may also need help answering phone calls or writing letters. However, don't do things he or she can do or wants to do. Ask before helping.
- **Don't feel as if you always have to talk when you come over.** Even if you just read, listen, or watch a movie, the fact that you're there to provide support and companionship is enough.
- **Check in with others who are taking care of the person with AIDS.** They, too, may be suffering and may need a break from the illness from time to time. Offer to stay with the person with AIDS in order to give the loved ones some free time. Invite them out or offer to accompany them. Remember, they may need someone to talk with as well.
- **If the person with AIDS is a parent, ask about and offer to help care for any children.** If the children are not living with the person, offer to bring them for a visit. If there are young children living with the person, offer to take them to or pick them up from school or day care. Ask if you could make them lunch or supper or take them to the dentist, doctor, etc.
- **Be prepared for the person to get angry with you for no obvious reason, although you have been there and done everything you could.** Permit this, but try not to take it personally. Remember, when a person is very ill, he or she often takes out anger and frustration on the people most loved and needed because it's safe and will be understood.
- **Be sure to include the person in decision-making whenever possible.** Illness can bring about a loss of control over many aspects of life. Don't deny the person with AIDS the opportunity to make decisions, no matter how simple or trivial they may seem to you.
- **Don't lecture or become angry with the person if he or she seems to be handling the illness in a way that you think is inappropriate.** The person may not be where you expect or need him or her to be, but different people deal with life-threatening illnesses in different ways.
- **Don't confuse the person's acceptance of the illness with defeat.** In fact, acceptance can be a very positive step, for it may free the person, providing him or her with a sense of power.

- **Talk with the person about the future: tomorrow, next week, next year.** It is helpful to look toward the future without denying the reality of today. Hope is especially important at this time.
- **Don't take on more than you can handle, but don't underestimate what you can offer**—many volunteers and friends help out just by being there, and that is enough.

National Organizations

AIDS Action Council
2033 M St., Suite 802, Washington, DC 20036
(202) 293-2886, FAX: (202) 296-1292

AAC is the only national nonprofit organization focused solely on the public policy issues created by the AIDS crisis. AAC seeks to bring the concerns and experiences of those on the front line of the crisis into the public policy debate. The organization strives to assure adequate support for the community-based groups that provide prevention education activities and primary care and support for people with AIDS. AAC promotes nationwide, targeted public education, prevention, and risk-reduction programs; champions antidiscrimination protection for people infected with the human immunodeficiency virus (HIV); and provides many other services. The council also works with members of Congress and their staffs on AIDS-related legislation and serves as an information clearinghouse for the general public.

AIDS Coalition To Unleash Power
496A Hudson St., Suite G4, New York, NY 10014
(212) 989-1114, FAX: (212) 989-1797

ACT UP is a nonprofit organization that focuses attention on critical AIDS issues and provides direct action to end the AIDS crisis. ACT UP organizes vocal demonstrations and other forms of protest, meets with government and public health officials, and researches and distributes the latest medical information on AIDS and related issues. Active volunteer opportunities are available in its chapters all across the U.S. ACT UP also has posters, buttons, stickers, caps, T-shirts, sweatshirts, and postcards bearing the "Silence=Death" logo and encouraging people to "ACT UP." Write or call the national headquarters if you cannot find the affiliate in your community.

AIDS Project Los Angeles
6721 Romaine St., Los Angeles, CA 90038
(213) 962-1600
Toll-free information hotline: 1-800-922-AIDS (2437)
TDD: 1-800-533-AIDS (2437)
Asian and Middle-Eastern languages: 1-800-922-2438

APLA is a nonprofit, community-based organization committed to improving the quality of life of people affected by AIDS. The organization provides vital human services and risk-reduction education programs, and actively advocates for fair and effective public policies. APLA operates more than twenty programs, serving almost seventy percent of the people with AIDS in Los Angeles County. Some of APLA's services include the **Case Management Program** (works to ensure that people affected by AIDS are connected to appropriate services and benefits); the **Necessities of Life Program** (provides free groceries, vitamins, new clothing, and other necessities for people affected with AIDS); the **Buddies Program** (recruits and connects volunteers—who offer support and assistance—with people affected by AIDS); and the **Hospital Visitation Volunteers Program** (recruits and trains volunteers who provide emotional support for the lovers, spouses, and other primary caretakers of people with AIDS). Although the organization primarily works with volunteers in the L.A. area, anyone can call its toll-free hotline, which can provide callers with information on AIDS, counseling, and referrals (for example, community-based AIDS organizations). APLA publishes two free newsletters—*The Optimist* (quarterly) and *Update* (approximately every other month)—which report on APLA activities, fundraising and advocacy efforts, drug trials, national issues, and other information for people affected by AIDS. APLA also disseminates brochures and other educational materials on AIDS.

American Foundation for AIDS Research
5900 Wilshire Blvd., 2nd Floor, E. Satellite, Los Angeles, CA 90036-5032
(213) 857-5900
or
1515 Broadway, Suite 3601, New York, NY 10036-8901
(212) 719-0033

AmFAR is the nation's leading private-sector funding organization dedicated to AIDS research, education, and public policy. The foundation works to identify major gaps in AIDS biomedical, clinical, and social science research and education, and provides funding to support innovative projects designed to fill those gaps. Approximately eighty percent of the grants underwrite scientific research for a vaccine and effective treatments for AIDS, with the other twenty percent going to education, prevention, and public policy. AmFAR sponsors several major publications, including the *AIDS/HIV Treatment Directory* and *Learning AIDS*. The organization also has volunteer opportunities nationwide. Individuals can assist with AmFar's **ART AGAINST AIDS** fundraising event or with the **Community-Based Clinical Trial Network**, with over forty community-based research centers nationwide. Local CBCTs conduct clinical trials that produce data acceptable to the FDA, while at the same time accelerating the pace of AIDS research and providing increased access for people with AIDS/HIV to promising experimental AIDS therapies. Volunteers are needed to help with administrative work and other duties. Contact AmFAR for more information on services and volunteer opportunities and internships (particularly in the Los Angeles and New York offices).

American Social Health Association
National AIDS Hotline
P.O. Box 13827, Research Triangle Park, NC 27709
Hotline: 1-800-342-AIDS (2437)
Spanish hotline: 1-800-344-SIDA (7432)
TTY: 1-800-AIDS-TTY (243-7889)

A nonprofit organization, **ASHA** provides information, education, and leadership in the fight against sexually transmitted diseases. The association runs the National AIDS Hotline, which operates twenty-four hours a day, seven days a week. The hotline provides callers with confidential information on AIDS and related issues, and referrals to public health clinics, hospitals, alternative HIV test sites, food-delivery organizations, local hotlines, counseling and support groups, and legal services (many of which need people with legal expertise to help people with AIDS). ASHA can also arrange for a mailing of free printed materials on AIDS. The hotline is an outstanding resource for people with AIDS, those interested in information about AIDS, and volunteers looking for local organizations and services to which they can offer their assistance.

COSSMHO
The National Coalition of Hispanic Health and Human Services Organizations
1030 15th St., N.W., Suite 1053, Washington, DC 20005
(202) 371-2100

COSSMHO is a nonprofit organization dedicated to improving the health and psychosocial well-being of the nation's Hispanic population. The coalition conducts demonstration programs, coordinates research, and serves as a source of information, technical assistance, and policy analysis for issues such as AIDS and substance abuse, teen pregnancy, and child abuse/neglect prevention. COSSMHO distributes numerous publications, including *AIDS: A Guide for Hispanic Leadership; AIDS Service Directory for Hispanics;* and *The COSSMHO AIDS Update*, a quarterly newsletter covering a variety of issues concerning AIDS and the Hispanic community ($40 for nonmembers, $30 for members). Membership to COSSMHO costs $40 for individuals and $10 for students and senior citizens. Members and nonmembers alike can call COSSMHO to find out if any of its programs or activities in their area need volunteers.

Gay Men's Health Crisis
129 W. 20th St., New York, NY 10011
(212) 807-6664
Hotline: (212) 807-6655, TDD: (212) 645-7470

GMHC is a nonprofit organization that educates the public about AIDS, advocates for fair and effective AIDS public policy, and provides a variety of direct services to individuals who have AIDS. GMHC also develops and distributes materials that address various aspects of AIDS (for example, general information, risk reduction, medical and psychological issues, testing, health insurance, and legal concerns). Publications include *I'm HIV Positive—What Next?; Ten Minutes That Can Change Your Life; Legal Answers* and *Medical Answers About AIDS;* and *Loving, Caring, Sharing*. The organization conducts public forums, seminars for health-care professionals, and workshops for people at risk. It also provides support services for people with AIDS, including crisis intervention counseling, a "buddy" program (for example, helping with daily living tasks, such as meals and shopping), recreational programs, a pediatrics program, support and therapy groups (for people with AIDS and their care partners), and legal, financial, and health-care advocacy. GMHC publishes a newsletter, *Treatment Issues* ($20), ten times a year which contains information on experimental AIDS therapies. If you would like more information on volunteer opportunities, call *(212) 337-3593.*

Health Education Resource Organization
101 W. Reed St., Suite 825, Baltimore, MD 21201
(301) 685-1180

One of the most valuable educational resource organizations on AIDS in the country, **HERO** is a nonprofit community group formed to provide accurate, up-to-date information and assistance to people concerned about AIDS and the HIV virus. HERO can supply you with informative brochures (for example, *You Don't Have to Be White or Gay to Get AIDS*), reference cards (such as *Women, Infants, and AIDS*), booklets (for example, *Questions and Answers About the HIV Antibody Test*), matchbook condom packets, posters (including *AIDS in the Black Community*), and videos (for example, *Personal Perspectives on AIDS*). All of the materials are high quality, informative, and relatively inexpensive, and many of them are available in English and Spanish.

The Names Project Foundation
2362 Market St., San Francisco, CA 94114
(415) 863-5511

The Names Project Foundation brought some much-needed attention to the AIDS epidemic when, in 1987, it organized the **AIDS Memorial Quilt**, an enormous project dedicated to those who have died of AIDS. The quilt has more than 12,000 individual memorial panels and covers fourteen acres overall (it is growing every year). The organization takes portions of the quilt across the country to illustrate the impact of the AIDS epidemic by showing the humanity behind the statistics, to provide a positive and creative means of expression for those whose lives have been touched by the epidemic, to raise funds, to encourage support for people with AIDS and their loved ones, and to encourage people to take action to stop the epidemic. Although the quilt's home is in San Francisco, the foundation has chapters nationwide that, among other things, serve as "host" locations for the quilt. Volunteers are needed at the local chapters for a variety of services, including assisting with quilting bees, sewing panels, fundraising, organizing small quilt displays, and offering emotional support. Contact The Names Project Foundation for more information on the memorial quilt (especially if you want to contribute a panel) or for information on volunteer opportunities.

National AIDS Hotline
(see American Social Health Association, page 49)

The National Gay & Lesbian Task Force
(see Crime and Victim Assistance, page 172)

National Minority AIDS Council
300 I St., N.E., Suite 400, Washington, DC 20002
(202) 544-1076, FAX: (202) 544-0378

NMAC is a nonprofit organization created to examine and respond to the impact of AIDS in minority communities, to increase the participation of nonwhite AIDS volunteers, to increase public awareness about AIDS, and to decrease its spread. The council provides technical assistance to both existing and developing organizations responding to HIV/AIDS-related needs in minority communities, works to educate people of color and influence those who shape public opinion through **Project HEAL** (Health Education and AIDS Leadership), seeks to place AIDS high on the legislative agenda of people of color at the national and local level, and provides many informative resources. The organization's bimonthly newsletter, *NMAC Update*, contains information on the growth and direction of NMAC and HIV/AIDS-related issues in general. NMAC also publishes the *NMAC HEALer*, a quarterly publication focusing on the effects and responses to HIV/AIDS in people-of-color communities and related information. NMAC can also provide you with the *Volunteer Program Development Manual*, which addresses the history of volunteerism among ethnic minorities and the need for nonwhites as volunteers, and describes how NMAC volunteers are screened, trained, and directed to communities in need.

Pediatric AIDS Foundation
2407 Wilshire Boulevard, Suite 613, Santa Monica, CA 90403
(213) 395-9051 or 1-800-552-0444

PAF, a nonprofit organization dedicated to confronting problems unique to children with AIDS, seeks to identify and fund critically needed pediatric AIDS research. The foundation also supports a model program in Los Angeles for dealing with pediatric AIDS in the community; provides emergency assistance to hospitals around the country that serve children with AIDS; and raises public awareness about pediatric AIDS issues, stressing knowledge, compassion, and action. PAF also sells **SHIRTS BY ZACK** T-shirts ($15) and sweatshirts ($25) that have designs on them drawn by Zachary Fried, a little boy who contracted AIDS from a transfusion and died when he was five and a half years old. The clothing has the logo "HOPE FOR CHILDREN WITH AIDS" along with Zack's drawings of trains, cats, and bears.

People with AIDS Coalition
31 W. 26th St., New York, NY 10010
(212) 532-0290, NYC hotline: (212) 532-0568
National hotline: 1-800-828-3280

The **PWA Coalition** is a nonprofit organization created by and for people with AIDS, people with AIDS-related complex, and concerned friends. The organization fosters "self-empowerment" and promotes a sense of personal responsibility for one's own health and well-being. It also disseminates information about all facets of living with AIDS and related complexes and provides pertinent services. The *PWA Coalition Newsline* is a highly informative and often moving monthly publication filled with stories, news items, poems, and a comprehensive AIDS resource directory (for people in the New York area). The subscription price is $35 a year for people who do not have AIDS, but for those persons with AIDS or ARC, the publication is free.

Ryan White National Fund
(see Athletes & Entertainers for Kids, page 126)

San Francisco AIDS Foundation
P.O. Box 6182, San Francisco, CA 94102-6182
(415) 864-4376
Toll-free hotline (in Northern California: 1-800-FOR-AIDS (367-2437); in San Francisco: (415) 863-AIDS (2437)
TDD hotline: (415) 864-6606
All numbers are trilingual (English/Spanish/Tagalog) and open 9 A.M. to 9 P.M. Mon.–Fri., 11 A.M. to 5 P.M. Sat. and Sun.

Since 1982, **SFAF**, a nonprofit organization, has been at the forefront of the battle against AIDS, working to combat ignorance, prejudice, and fear, with education, compassion, and understanding. In association with **Project Open Hand** (see page 44), the foundation provides tens of thousands of bags of groceries for people with AIDS through the **AIDS Food Bank Program**, finds shelter for dozens of clients each month through the **Emergency Housing Program**, distributes millions of educational pieces on AIDS, answers tens of thousands of calls on its trilingual English/Spanish/Tagalog hotline, and sponsors hundreds of educational events. SFAF is an especially good resource for teachers and employers looking for informative kits and materials to use at school or in the office. It offers (in both English and Spanish) posters, books, brochures, videos, and other materials that address prevention, drugs, pregnancy, and general information for young adults, children, the general public, ethnic communities, women, and health-care providers. Brochures include *When a Friend Has AIDS; Fact vs. Fiction; Your Child and AIDS; Women and AIDS;* and *Straight Talk About Sex and AIDS.* SFAF is one of the best sources for information on AIDS and related issues.

ALCOHOL AND DRUGS

Why Help Is Needed

Every minute and a half, another cocaine addict is born in America. Literally. According to a recent congressional report, an estimated 375,000 babies who have been exposed to cocaine during pregnancy are born in this country each year.[1] These babies do not experience any sort of "high" from the cocaine they have received. Instead, they cry, some suffer from "the shakes," and some will have heart attacks and die. This is just one horrible aspect of America's drug problem; the rest isn't much better.

Drugs are destroying careers, wrecking families, and laying waste to communities. Drug-related crimes are flooding the nation's courts and prisons, and drug-related injuries are overwhelming emergency facilities and staffs in hospitals nationwide. The Media-Advertising Partnership for a Drug-Free America estimates that businesses lose $100 billion a year because of drug-related problems. Drug abusers are four times as likely to be involved in an accident on the job as nonabusers, and their absentee rate is four times higher than normal.[2] Drugs are also spreading the AIDS virus through intravenous drug use, representing the single largest source of new HIV/AIDS virus infections.[3] Drug gangs are disrupting communities, and innocent people are being killed in the crossfire of rival dealers.

Drug abuse is not confined to a specific area or group of people. It is everywhere. One out of three Americans has used illicit drugs, and one in ten uses them regularly.[4] There are approximately sixteen million regular users of marijuana, six million cocaine users, half a million heroin users, and another half a million users of other drugs.[5] "Crack" cocaine is being used in rural areas, by employees of major

---

[1] Senate Finance Committee, June 28, 1990.
[2] National Crime Prevention Council, "Crime Prevention Is . . . A Community Affair," 1989, 10.
[3] "*National Drug Control Strategy*," September 1989, 1.
[4] According to the Phoenix House Foundation, the nation's largest private, nonprofit drug-abuse service agency, *164 W. 74th St., New York, NY 10023*, (212) 595-5810.
[5] Morton M. Kondracke, "Don't Legalize Drugs," *The New Republic*, June 27, 1988, 16.

businesses, and by upper- and middle-class individuals.[6] Drugs are by no means just an adult problem, however. More than half of all high school seniors use drugs, and more than a quarter use them regularly.[7] The Media-Advertising Partnership for a Drug-Free America also reports that one out of six American children ages nine to twelve has been offered drugs, and the median age for first use of illegal drugs in this country is under twelve.

These statistics should not overshadow the severity of the nation's problems with alcohol—approximately seventeen million Americans are alcoholics, according to the Will Rogers Institute.[8] Alcoholism does much of the same damage as drug abuse: it kills both abusers and innocent people, destroys families, and ruins careers. Alcohol abuse, claims the National Council on Alcoholism and Drug Dependence (NCADD), costs businesses nearly seventy-one billion dollars annually in lost employment and reduced productivity. The National Crime Prevention Council (NCPC) estimates that fifty-five percent of all arrests, sixty-five percent of all homicides, and almost seventy percent of all assaults involve alcohol. NCPC also estimates that in families with at least one alcoholic spouse, the rate of separation and divorce is seven times that of the general population. Children of alcoholics suffer, too, experiencing a wide range of psychological problems, and they are at much greater risk of becoming alcoholics themselves. According to NCADD, approximately half of all children of alcoholic parents become alcoholics.

Drunk driving has, in itself, become a national crisis. NCADD reports that about 24,000 Americans are killed in alcohol-related highway crashes each year, while another 534,000 people are injured—an average of one person injured each minute. The National Highway Traffic Safety Administration claims that alcohol-related fatalities constitute about half of all traffic deaths, and they are the number one killer of fifteen-to-twenty-four-year-olds. The administration also estimates that two out of every five people in the U.S. will be involved in an alcohol-related crash in their lifetime.

Alcohol and drugs clearly represent severe and immediate problems. Although they may not be direct, immediate problems for every individual or every family, they do, ultimately, affect the lives of every American. The increase in crime, the enormous costs of drug-

---

[6]Philip Elmer-De Witt, "A Plague Without Boundaries," *Time*, November 6, 1989, 95.
[7]According to the Phoenix House Foundation.
[8]According to The Will Rogers Institute, a nonprofit organization dedicated to providing information to the public on a variety of health issues; *785 Mamaroneck Ave., White Plains, NY 10605*, (914) 761-5550.

and alcohol-abuse treatment and prevention, the loss of neighborhoods to dealers and users, and the hundreds of thousands of cocaine babies born every year are distressing examples of how abusers are not the only victims of abuse.

What You Can Do

☞ **Educate yourself and others about alcohol and drug abuse in America.** There is a great deal of information, but the more you stay on top of current issues, the better you will know how you can help. Understanding the facts will help you discuss the issues intelligently with friends and family members as well as help you better express your opinions to your government representatives on pending legislation related to drugs and alcohol. (See also Voicing Your Opinion, page 363.)

☞ **Learn the effects of using drugs and alcohol.** Knowing the hazards will help you educate others and discourage drug and alcohol use. Knowing the signs of alcohol and drug abuse will help you be able to recognize them in friends and family members. Almost all of the national organizations listed in this chapter can provide you with extensive information on abuse. Pharmacies and hospitals often have information, too.

☞ **If you have children, make sure you talk with them about drug and alcohol use.** Many kids say that their parents have never talked to them about these issues. The national organizations in this chapter can provide you with information on alcohol and drugs and suggestions on how to talk to your children about substance abuse.

☞ **If you, a friend, or a family member is having a problem with alcohol or drugs, get help as soon as possible.** Coming to grips with an alcohol or drug problem or talking with someone who may have a problem is not easy. Treatment centers and support groups are very effective in helping individuals break a drug or alcohol habit. Even if you're not certain that you or someone you know has a problem, going to a self-help group at least once isn't a big sacrifice. Here are some resources for finding self-help and treatment centers in your community:

- **Under community-service numbers** in the phone book, check "Alcohol and Drug Abuse," or look for separate entries

under "Alcoholism" or "Drug Abuse." Hospitals also usually have information on resources for drug and alcohol abusers.
- **Check the National Self-Help Organizations** listed on page 74. If you cannot find a chapter near you, contact the national headquarters for a referral.
- **Call any of these toll-free numbers for a referral** (although they may seem specific, any one of them can help substance abusers or the people who live with them):

1-800-662-HELP (4357)
National Institute on Drug Abuse
Information and Referral Line
Mon.–Fri.: 9 A.M. to 3 A.M.,
Sat./Sun.: noon to 3 A.M.

1-800-622-2255
National Council on Alcoholism and Drug
Dependence Hotline
7 days a week, 24 hours a day

1-800-COCAINE (262-2463)
Cocaine Helpline
7 days a week, 24 hours a day

☞ **Work to fight drug and alcohol abuse in your school, office, or religious congregation.** On the simplest level, this may involve putting up posters or distributing informative pamphlets and brochures in common areas. Educating your friends or co-workers about substance abuse may help them recognize the seriousness of the problem and motivate them to get involved. Your local police department or sheriff's office should have drug-prevention information, and many of the national organizations listed in this chapter can provide you with information. Here are two others, in particular, to check out:

- **Employers can call the National Institute on Drug Abuse's Drug-Free Workplace Helpline** *(1-800-843-4971)* for information, referrals, publications, and other materials on drug-related issues in the workplace, including drug testing, policy issues, and employee assistance programs. The hotline is available Monday through Friday, 9 A.M. to 8 P.M.
- The **U.S. Department of Education** has an informative booklet, *Schools Without Drugs*, which provides information

about the nature and extent of the drug problem, and what parents, schools, students, teachers, and communities can do. For a free copy, contact Schools Without Drugs: The Challenge at *1717 K St., N.W., Suite 601, Washington, DC 20036*; 1-800-624-0100, (in D.C. 732-3627).

☞ **Never, under any circumstances, drive while drunk (or high), and don't let anyone you know do so, either.** If you go out drinking with your friends or co-workers, make sure there is at least one person who won't drink at all. If someone is drunk and insists on driving, take the keys from him or her and call a cab or drive the person home. Remember, according to NCADD, well over 23,000 people die each year in alcohol-related accidents (534,000 more are injured).

☞ **Participate in or set up organizations in your school, office, or community that work to stop drinking and driving.** This can be simple, such as putting up posters in public areas and encouraging films or slide shows to be presented, or more involved, such as organizing a free ride service with a local cab company. These services are always needed, but are especially important around holidays, school events (graduation, homecoming, etc.), and large social gatherings. See National Organizations Against Drinking and Driving, page 72 for more information.

☞ **Volunteer to work with babies who have been exposed to drugs.** Call your local hospital and ask if they have volunteer opportunities for people who want to work with "boarder babies," infants left in hospitals by their mothers who are often drug addicts or AIDS victims. Although inner-city hospitals are the most likely to have such opportunities, many other hospitals do care for these babies, or can refer you to a nearby hospital that does. Often these babies just need to be held and played with, because the hospital staff, overloaded with other responsibilities, may not have time for this.

☞ **Volunteer to work on a substance-abuse crisis hotline or at an organization in your community working to stop alcohol and drug abuse (and/or helping people who abuse alcohol or drugs).** Although self-help groups use only their members as volunteers, other organizations need help with administrative work, fundraising, and various other tasks. (Note: People who want to work on hotlines will probably need training.) Check the phone book for "Alcohol and Drug Abuse" under community-service listings. Hotline numbers are also listed in the front of the phone book, usually under "Hotlines," "Survival Numbers," or "Crisis Assistance and/or Information." In addition, contact any of the national organizations listed here to see if local chapters are in need of volunteers.

☞ **If you have had any experiences with drug or alcohol abuse, volunteer to talk with students or community groups.** Experiences may include actually having had a substance-abuse problem, living in a family in which one or more members had such a problem, having been injured by a drunk driver, losing a friend or family member to a drunk driver, or having injured someone else as a drunk driver. Discussing such personal experiences, especially with strangers, can be difficult, but it will probably have a much greater impact on an audience than any list of statistics.

☞ **If you are an employer, make an effort to hire individuals who are recovering from alcohol or drug abuse.** Call your local employment office, usually listed as "Employment/Unemployment" under the community service numbers in the phone book. If it's not listed there, check the government pages of the phone book under "Employment Services, Department of." The employment office can direct you to a job bank or referral program in your community.

☞ **If there is a drug problem in your community, work to stop it. If there isn't a problem, work to prevent one from occurring.** Concerned individuals have proven to be powerful forces in the war on drugs. Antidrug groups have literally run drug dealers out of their neighborhoods and shut down crack houses. Here are some suggestions for people who want to keep their communities drug-free (adapted, with permission, from materials provided by the **Citizens Committee for New York City**):

- **Report any drug activity that you see in your neighborhood.** Contact the local police department or sheriff's office for training on how to report information safely and effectively. Don't assume that someone else is going to do it or that the police already know about it. Try to take down descriptions of the dealers and buyers, the location of transactions, any license plate numbers, and other related information. Even an anonymous call to the police is better than no call at all.
- **Become part of an anticrime group, or start a group if there isn't one.** Contact the local police or sheriff's office for

information on existing programs or assistance in establishing one. Before you take action:
- Analyze the community's drug problem so that you can accurately design strategies. Work with a group of neighbors you can trust; don't, however, have one individual be seen as the group leader or driving force. Anonymity is critical to safety.
- Recognize that time, follow-up work, and possibly even money will be necessary in order to achieve results. One-shot or short-term actions rarely have lasting effects.
- Try to get all members of the community together, including teens, elderly persons, businesspersons, and civic and religious leaders. See if area businesses will help pay for flyers, newsletters, and other materials to attract attention and publicize the group's activities.
- Be sure to invite new neighbors into the group so that they feel welcome and know that they are joining a neighborhood concerned about safety.
- Be sure your goals, plans, and activities are well thought out and articulated so that there is no confusion over direction or responsibilities. It's important that the group works together to achieve its aims, so it is critical that goals are understood by everyone.
- Exchange home and work telephone numbers with group members, and share information about daily routines, vacation plans, etc. A phone "tree," or network, will help you get information out quickly and effectively.
- Push the local Department of Public Works for better lighting and other improvements, if they are needed.
- Patrol the streets or apartment buildings at night in small groups. Bring noisemakers (whistles, air horns) to scare away offenders, as well as two-way radios to communicate with patrols on other blocks. If you or your friends have car phones or CB radios, consider organizing a civilian motor patrol in cooperation with the police. **REMEMBER: Do not put yourself or neighbors in jeopardy by confronting armed or dangerous offenders. Let the law-enforcement officers handle the confrontational work.**

If you do start up a Community Watch, here are some organizations that can provide you with valuable information and ideas:

- **Citizens Committee for New York City.** Although CCNYC focuses on helping New Yorkers, it can provide excellent guidelines and tip sheets on creating safer communities anywhere.

Publications include *Tools and Tactics for Building Neighborhood Organizations; Lend a Hand to Improve Your Schools; Strategies for Drug-Free Communities;* and *Improving Intergroup Relations.* If you live in New York, CCNYC is an indispensable resource for making the city a better place, providing information on crime, drugs, the environment, education, and a variety of other social issues. Write to or call CCNYC at *3 West 29th Street, New York, NY 10001;* (212) 684-6767.

• **National Crime Prevention Council** (see Crime and Victim Assistance, page 171) can provide you with or direct you to a variety of informative pamphlets, booklets, and books, and Community Watch posters, signs, and stickers.

See also Crime and Victim Assistance, page 158, for more information on general crime prevention tips and crime prevention organizations.

National Organizations

The American Council for Drug Education
204 Monroe St., Suite 110, Rockville, MD 20850
(301) 294-0600

ACDE is a nonprofit organization that works to prevent drug abuse through public education. The council produces educational materials, reviews scientific findings, and develops educational media campaigns. ACDE also assists educators, parents, employers, and industry leaders in their efforts to address drug use, and hosts conferences and workshops for concerned parents and professionals. The organization has more than fifty informative pamphlets and monographs (such as *Marijuana and Driving; Cocaine: The Bottom Line;* and *Marijuana and Alcohol*), books (*Getting Tough on Gateway Drugs: A Guide for the Family; Thinking About Drugs and Society: Responding to an Epidemic*), films, and other materials explaining the health hazards associated with alcohol or drugs, especially for adolescents, young working adults, women of childbearing age, and elderly persons. ACDE can also supply schools and businesses with appropriate kits, films, posters, and other educational materials to help prevent drug and alcohol abuse. A basic membership ($25, $5 for those under 18) includes a subscription to ACDE's quarterly newsletter, *The Drug Educator.*

BACCHUS of the U.S., Inc.
National Headquarters
P.O. Box 10430, Denver, CO 80210
(303) 871-3068

BACCHUS (Boost Alcohol Consciousness Concerning the Health of University Students) is a nonprofit organization devoted to promoting education, prevention, research, networking, and national initiatives to eliminate substance-abuse problems on college and university campuses. There are presently over 400 chapters nationwide, each motivated by the philosophy that young adults play an important role—unmatched by professional educators—in encouraging their peers to reflect on, talk honestly about, and develop responsible habits and attitudes toward alcohol consumption. BACCHUS offers numerous pamphlets, videos, books, posters, stickers, and designated driver materials. If you are interested in starting a group in your area, contact the national headquarters.

CAMPUSES WITHOUT DRUGS, Inc.
2530 Holly Drive, Pittsburgh, PA 15235
(412) 731-8019

A nonprofit organization dedicated to drug prevention through education, **CAMPUSES** seeks to achieve long-term social change in attitudes and behavior toward alcohol and other drugs. Community-wide drug prevention is addressed by meeting the drug education needs of teachers, administrators, and businesses, as well as those of students, youth programs, and parent groups. Special emphasis is placed on educating and mobilizing young adults in high schools, colleges, vocational schools, workplaces, and communities to actively contribute their energies to drug-prevention efforts. CAMPUSES offers seminars, conferences, technical and consulting services, drug information materials, T-shirts, posters, and informative books, brochures, fact sheets, and other publications. Membership ranges from individual ($20, $10 for students) to business/institution (call for information) and includes a one-year subscription to CAMPUSES' quarterly newsletter, a highly informative publication about current drug issues that includes editorials, international drug and alcohol updates and reports, and other news. If you are planning on setting up a substance-abuse prevention program in your school, business, or anywhere else, CAMPUSES has a great deal of information on other prevention programs. If you have concerns or questions about particular programs, especially those that work with young people, give CAMPUSES a call.

The Chemical People Institute
1615 Penn Ave., Pittsburgh, PA 15222
(412) 391-0900

CPI is a nonprofit organization of parents, schools, media, civic leaders, and professionals committed to increasing community awareness and action concerning alcohol and other drug problems. The institute promotes community outreach, education, and research programs, primarily through community task forces. Task forces are coalitions of people working in a community, providing support and encouragement for friends and neighbors dealing with a substance-abuse problem. Task forces also establish hotlines that teens or parents in trouble can turn to for help and information, publish community newsletters, provide alternative activities for youth, and sponsor seminars and workshops on the problem of school-age drug and alcohol abuse. Contact CPI if you are interested in starting a task force in your community.

Committees of Correspondence, Inc.
Drug Awareness Information
57 Conant St., Room 113, Danvers, MA 01923
(508) 774-2641

A nonprofit drug-education resource organization, **COC** disseminates up-to-date information on drugs and related issues. Materials include books (such as *How to Save Your Child from Drugs; Keep Off the Grass*), pamphlets (*What Parents Must Learn About Marijuana; Marijuana: More Harmful Than You Think*), booklets (for example, *How to Identify and Prevent Drug Abuse by Youth*), posters, audio-cassettes, and teachers' guides. Of special note is the *Drug Prevention Resource Book*, a valuable resource for people who are concerned about substance abuse and are looking for the necessary information to get involved. The directory costs $21 spiral-bound, $25 in a three-ring binder.

CompCare Publishers
2415 Annapolis Lane, Minneapolis, MN 55441
(612) 559-4800 or 1-800-328-3330

CompCare has a large selection of books, audiocassettes, and videos on alcohol, drugs, and related issues and problems. Here is a partial list of titles: *The All American Cocaine Story; Drug Data; Young Alcoholics; Suicide: The Hidden Epidemic; Kids and Drinking;*

ALCOHOL AND DRUGS

Women and Drugs: Getting Hooked, Getting Clean; Coming Home: Adult Children of Alcoholics Stories; A Day at a Time. Write or call CompCare for a free catalog.

**COSSMHO
The National Coalition of Hispanic Health and Human Services Organizations**
(see AIDS, page 50)

Hazeldon Educational Materials
15251 Pleasant Valley Road, P.O. Box 176,
Center City, MN 55012-0176
*1-800-328-9000; in Minnesota: 1-800-257-0070;
in Alaska: (612) 257-4010*

Hazeldon is a mail-order company that offers a large selection of publications, audiovisuals, and other materials on alcohol and drug abuse and recovery from addiction for people of all ages. Titles include *Raising Drug-Free Kids in a Drug-Filled World; Staying Clean: Living Without Drugs; Children of Alcoholics; A Parent's Survival Guide: How to Cope When Your Kid Is Using Drugs;* and *I'll Quit Tomorrow.* Catalogs are available upon request.

Institute on Black Chemical Abuse
2616 Nicollet Ave., S., Minneapolis, MN 55408
(612) 871-7878
or
1041 Selby Ave., St. Paul, MN 55102
(612) 227-0299

A nonprofit organization established in response to concern about substance abuse in the Black community, **IBCA** provides substance-abuse prevention and intervention services, drug and alcohol information, family counseling, and other essential services. The institute strives to increase awareness of the incidence, severity, and causes of alcohol and drug abuse in the Black community; to reduce alcohol- and drug-related family problems; and to encourage Blacks to enter the field of substance-abuse prevention. IBCA also distributes many informative publications (for example, *Marketing Booze to Blacks; Black, Beautiful and Recovering; Alcohol and Drug Abuse in Black America: A Guide for Community Action*). People interested in volunteer opportunities or internships should contact the national headquarters.

"Just Say No" International
1777 N. California Boulevard, Suite 210
Walnut Creek, CA 94596
(415) 939-6666 or 1-800-258-2766

"Just Say No" International is a nonprofit organization that provides support and direction to "Just Say No" clubs. These clubs are made up of young people, ages seven to fourteen, committed to leading drug-free lives and helping their peers do the same. The groups develop educational, social/recreational, community service, and outreach activities for after school, weekends, and vacations. For more information about the clubs, contact "Just Say No" International. The program manual, *The "Just Say No" Club Book*, is available for $10 postpaid.

Narcotics Education, Inc.
12501 Old Columbia Pike, Silver Spring, MD 20904
(301) 680-6740 or 1-800-548-8700

NEI has a large selection of information for teachers, parents, and anyone interested in drug- and alcohol-related issues. Here is a partial list of NEI materials: posters, magazines, audiovisuals (for example, *Drunk and Deadly; Marijuana: Myths and Misconceptions*), teaching aids (such as, *Consequences of Alcohol; Consequences of Drug Use*), coloring books, informative pamphlets and brochures (including *Alcohol: The Inside Story; Is Marijuana Really All That Bad?*), computer software, books and booklets (for example, *Cocaine in the Workplace; Kids and Drugs*), materials for skits, T-shirts, and drug identification kits. Write or call NEI for a free catalog.

National Asian Pacific American Families Against Substance Abuse
6303 Friendship Court, Bethesda, MD 20817
(301) 530-0945

NAPAFASA is a nonprofit organization committed to eliminating alcohol and drug abuse among Asian Pacific American families. The association supports those societal and cultural values that reinforce a drug-free society by promoting leadership from the Asian Pacific American community, enhancing public awareness, and participating in the formulation of public policy. NAPAFASA distributes information on the nature and extent of substance abuse among Asian Pacific American communities, supports the development of model community programs, and helps develop substance-abuse literature, videos, films, and other materials. Contact the national headquarters for more information or your local affiliate for volunteer opportunities. An individual membership costs $15 ($5 for students and senior citizens).

National Association for Children of Alcoholics
31582 Coast Highway, Suite B, South Laguna, CA 92677
(714) 499-3889, FAX: (714) 499-0044

NACoA is the only national nonprofit organization that serves as an advocate for children (of all ages) of alcoholics. The organization works to increase public awareness of alcoholism and its effects on children; supports schools, businesses, communities, and individuals who are working for the benefit of children of alcoholics; facilitates the exchange of resources and ideas through a national network; directs volunteers to state chapters; and publishes materials for CoA education (for example, *It's Elementary: Meeting the Needs of High-Risk Youth in the School Setting*). Membership costs $35 a year.

National Association on Drug Abuse Problems
355 Lexington Ave., New York, NY 10017
(212) 986-1170

A nonprofit organization, **NADAP** is dedicated to fighting drug and alcohol abuse in the family, the community, and the workplace. Among other things, the association provides a forum for the exchange of information on drug- and alcohol-abuse issues, establishes family and community-based prevention programs, helps recovering abusers find and maintain employment, helps companies in the development of programs that aid employees with drug- and alcohol-abuse problems, and sponsors research on issues of drug and alcohol abuse. Contact NADAP for publications on alcohol and drug abuse; referrals to programs that help drug and alcohol abusers and their families; vocational rehabilitation, education, and placement services for recovering persons; information on maintaining a drug-free office; and various other activities and programs. NADAP also publishes *NEWS/REPORT*, a forum for discussion on current drug- and alcohol-abuse issues. Volunteers nationwide are needed to work with NADAP.

National Black Alcoholism Council
1629 K St., Suite 802, Washington, DC 20006
(212) 296-2696

NBAC is a nonprofit organization of Black individuals concerned with alcoholism and drug abuse among Black people. The council is committed to advocating increased services for alcoholics and their families; ensuring that Blacks have accessible and affordable treatment and prevention services; educating the public by collecting and disseminating information about alcohol abuse among Blacks; providing community education on drinking and driving through its **BADD (Blacks Against Drunk Driving)** campaign; encouraging the creation of a Black coalition concerned with alcoholism, drug abuse, and mental health; and sponsoring an intensive **Black Alcoholism Institute**. The basic membership fee is $45 ($15 for the unemployed, students, and senior citizens).

National Clearinghouse for Alcohol and Drug Information
P.O. Box 2345, Rockville, MD 20852
(301) 468-2600 or 1-800-SAY-NO-TO (729-6686)

For information and materials on substance abuse and its prevention, **NCADI** is nationally unsurpassed. Its catalog lists hundreds of publications, including pamphlets and fact sheets (for example, *Facts About Alcohol; Alcohol and Youth: Fact Sheet; Cocaine/Crack: The Big Lie*), books (such as *Drug-Free Communities: Turning Awareness Into Action; What Works: Workplaces Without Drugs*), posters (*Live the Dream, Say No to Alcohol and Drug Abuse*—featuring Dr. Martin Luther King, Jr.), newsletters, and audiovisual materials (which are lent free of charge). There are publications aimed at families, women, scientists and researchers, health-care providers, employers, minorities, educators, children, and elderly persons. Anyone looking for general and prevention information on drugs, alcohol, and related issues can find it here. NCADI's catalog and a copy of the president's *National Drug Control Strategy* are free.

National Collegiate Athletic Association Committee on Competitive Safeguards and Medical Aspects of Sports
6201 College Boulevard, Overland Park, KS 66211-2422
(913) 339-1906

This committee of the **NCAA** works to provide drug-education materials and establish substance-abuse prevention programs for grade school, high school, and collegiate student-athletes. Its services include a speakers' bureau, a grants program, public-service announcements, workshops, and two youth programs, the **National Youth Sports Program (NYSP)** and the **Youth Education through Sports (YES)** program, both of which provide grade schoolers with information about preventing drug use. Publications and educational materials include *Drugs and the Athlete . . . a Losing Combination*, a nine-page, full-color booklet with information about frequently abused drugs; posters, videotapes (*The NCAA Drug-Testing Program* and *Drugs and the Collegiate Athlete*); drug-education research reports; and a quarterly newsletter that covers innovative programs, new educational materials, and related issues. Contact the NCAA if you are interested in starting a youth drug-education program or if you want to purchase individual materials.

National Council on Alcoholism and Drug Dependence
12 W. 21st St., New York, NY 10010
(212) 206-6770 or 1-800-NCA-CALL (622-2255)

NCADD is a nonprofit organization established to inform the public about alcoholism and other forms of drug dependence and to prevent illegal drug use through education and public advocacy. The council distributes educational, scientific, and medical information and materials (such as *What Can You do About Someone Else's Drinking; Alcohol and Youth; What Are the Signs of Alcoholism?—The NCA Self-Test*); offers assistance and prevention programs for schools, organizations, and communities; and answers questions from the public, legislative bodies, and the media. Through its 200 state and local affiliates, NCADD provides information and referral services to families and individuals seeking help with drinking- and drug-related problems. (Volunteers are needed at these affiliates; contact the national headquarters for locations.) NCADD also sponsors **National Alcohol Awareness Month** (April) and the **National Alcohol-Related Birth Defects Awareness Week** (beginning on Mother's Day each year).

National Families in Action
2296 Henderson Mill Road, Suite 204, Atlanta, GA 30345
(404) 934-6364

A nonprofit organization, **NFIA** works to educate the public about the dangers of substance abuse by providing the most accurate, up-to-date information available about drugs and alcohol. For this purpose, it maintains a public collection of 500,000 documents from medical journals, newspapers, and various other publications. The organization publishes a quarterly, *Drug Abuse Update* ($7 per issue, $25 for a one-year subscription), and answers telephone and mail inquiries. (NFIA can direct volunteers to various opportunities in their area.) It also publishes the *FIA Manual*, a 164-page guide to forming a parent support group. The manual, which costs $10, has helped create thousands of community-based prevention groups nationwide.

National Federation of Parents for Drug-Free Youth
1423 N. Jefferson, Springfield, MO 65802
(417) 836-3709

NFP is a nonprofit organization which believes that America's children should be able to grow up drug-free and that the best way to achieve this is through education. The federation unites individual group efforts nationwide to form a recognizable force in the fight against drug use. NFP works with Congress, the media, and numerous action groups to spread its message. It sponsors **REACH** (Responsible Educated Adolescents Can Help), a youth leadership training program, to help high school students educate younger children about the dangers of drugs; the **National Red Ribbon Campaign**, an awareness program designed to mobilize communities and reduce the demand for drugs; and **Lifers**, a program for seventh- and eighth-grade adolescents that provides positive motivation to discourage the use of drugs through education and peer support. NFP also distributes media and educational kits and informative pamphlets and brochures on substance abuse for parents, teachers, and other concerned individuals. Coordinators in every state can provide interested individuals with a variety of volunteer opportunities (for example, fundraising, establishing community groups, sending out notices, speaking at schools). Community chapter membership costs $100.

National Federation of State High School Associations
TARGET
P.O. Box 20626, 11724 Plaza Circle, Kansas City, MO 64195
(816) 464-5400 or 1-800-366-6667

NFSHA is a nonprofit organization that sponsors **TARGET**, a program that focuses on fighting alcohol and drug abuse among America's youth. TARGET's services include training volunteers to help develop programs and workshops in their communities, and providing a national resource center for parents, teachers, coaches, and concerned individuals with free or low-cost publications (*Prevention Is Everybody's Business; What, When, and How to Talk to Students About Alcohol and Other Drugs—A Guide*; and *Crack—The Facts*), and videos and films (such as *Crackdown; No Matter How You Say It—Say No; Children of Denial*). NFSHA also makes referrals to important national and state organizations addressing alcohol and other drug concerns. Contact NFSHA for its extensive catalog of publications and materials or for information on starting a program in your school.

Parents' Resource Institute for Drug Education (PRIDE)
50 Hurt Plaza, Suite 210, Atlanta, GA 30303
(404) 577-4500 or 1-900-988-PRIDE (7743)

PRIDE is a nonprofit organization established to fight the epidemic of drug abuse, especially among adolescents and young adults, through education and information networks. The institute administers a questionnaire that has become a leading national source of adolescent drug-use information; publishes numerous resources, including books, pamphlets, films, and surveys; and sponsors the **America's PRIDE Program**, an intensive nationwide program which educates students about drugs and encourages discussions on peer pressure, parent-child communication, and helping friends with a substance-abuse problem. Each spring, PRIDE hosts the world's largest symposium and trade show on drug-abuse prevention. Hundreds of leading authorities on all aspects of drug abuse join parents and youth from every state and dozens of nations at the PRIDE World Drug Conference. PRIDE also has drug-prevention and fact kits for both schools and the media, as well as a toll-free drug message system for anyone who has access to a touch-tone phone. (Callers punch in numbers for information on such topics as "Alcohol," "Marijuana," "Legal Issues," and "Parental Concerns." Messages are in both Spanish and English. Calls cost $1 per minute.) The membership fee is $25, which includes the *PRIDE Quarterly* newsletter and other benefits.

Youth to Youth
700 Bryden Road, Suite 321, Columbus, OH 43215
(614) 224-4506

YtY is a nonprofit community drug-prevention program for middle school and high school students. The program was founded in Columbus, Ohio, and has since served as a model for hundreds of schools and communities across the U.S. It is designed to promote a drug-free lifestyle through youth involvement in the planning and implementation of the program, the use of current community resources in a comprehensive prevention effort, and the backing of schools, civic organizations, and parent groups. YtY provides an extensive selection of educational publications and materials (such as *Youth to Youth—A Classroom Curriculum*, and *Positive Peer Prevention: Putting the Pieces Together*), buttons, T-shirts, sweatshirts, and posters. Write or call for information on starting a program in your school.

National Organizations Against Drinking and Driving

Business Against Drunk Drivers, Inc.
1101 N. Market St., Milwaukee, WI 53202
(414) 273-BADD (2233)

A nonprofit organization, BADD utilizes the resources of business and industry in the growing effort to combat drunk driving. It provides its members (who include individuals, corporations, and government agencies) with suggested policy guidelines and corporate statements concerning drinking and driving, information on implementing designated-driver programs, legal and insurance information, information on speakers available for employee groups, and a comprehensive selection of literature and materials on drinking and driving (including audiocassettes, T-shirts, videocassettes, brochures, buttons, posters, bumper stickers, national and local reports, and a quarterly newsletter). Materials are available to nonmembers. Annual dues are $250, but less expensive associate memberships are available.

Mothers Against Drunk Driving
511 E. John Carpenter Freeway, Suite 700, Irving, TX 75062
(214) 744-6233
Victim crisis line: 1-800-GET-MADD (438-6233)

The largest nonprofit victim assistance organization in the world, **MADD** was formed to stop drunk driving and to support victims of drunk drivers. The group sponsors extensive public awareness programs such as the **National Red Ribbon Campaign** during the holidays, **Project Prom/Graduation, Keep It a Safe Summer (KISS)**, and **Drive for Life** over Labor Day Weekend. MADD provides forty-hour training programs for victim advocates and offers numerous brochures in English and Spanish, two books, and a magazine, **MADDvocate**, for victims of drunk driving. The organization responds to more than 350 calls per month on its victim crisis line. It also offers a compendium listing MADD's legislative goals and strategies, a free quarterly newsletter (*MADD In Action*), and numerous publications for adolescents and young adults.

National Commission Against Drunk Driving
1140 Connecticut Ave., N.W., Suite 804
Washington, DC 20036
(202) 452-0130

NCADD is a private, nonprofit organization working to reduce the incidence of drunk driving and resulting accidents. The successor body to the Presidential Commission on Drunk Driving, NCADD monitors the implementation of the commission's recommendations. It has published several informative reports, including *Zeroing in on Repeat Offenders*, and *Youthful Driving Without Impairment* (which addresses the problems of underage drinking and driving), and the *Checklist of State Countermeasures*, an annual survey that monitors the status of drunk-driving legislation in all fifty states. NCADD also holds public hearings on pertinent issues and provides testimony before state legislators to encourage laws to reduce drinking and driving. In conjunction with the National Highway Traffic Safety Administration and corporate members, NCADD sponsors the **Network of Employers for Traffic Safety (NETS)**, which encourages businesses to become involved with drunk-driving-prevention programs. The commission issues two quarterly publications, *Network Newsnotes* and *NETS Notes*, which describe model programs and report on developments in the field.

Remove Intoxicated Drivers
P.O. Box 520, Schenectady, NY 12301
Victim's hotline: (518) 372-0034 or (518) 372-9624
FAX: (518) 370-4917

RID is the oldest nonprofit grass-roots organization working to rid the nation's streets and highways of drunk drivers. It is also the only anti-drunk-driving citizen's action organization that has never accepted money from brewers or national broadcasters. There are more than 150 autonomous chapters in forty states. Ninety percent of the money raised by each chapter is kept in the community to fight drunk driving, help victims obtain justice, monitor the courts, raise public awareness, and push for better and tougher laws. At the national level, RID advocates a **Sane National Alcohol Policy**, in accord with the Surgeon General's guidelines, which suggests raising taxes on alcohol and curbing advertisements and promotions aimed at youth. The organization also publishes a quarterly newsletter containing legislative updates, information on upcoming conferences and events, and general news on drunk driving and related issues. A one-year subscription costs $10. Send a self-addressed, stamped envelope to RID for general information or if you cannot locate a RID affiliate in your community.

> **Students Against Driving Drunk**
> P.O. Box 800, Marlboro, MA 01752
> (508) 481-3568

SADD is a nonprofit organization working to prevent deaths and injuries from alcohol- and drug-related car accidents. The organization encourages students to use positive peer pressure to prevent other young people from using alcohol and drugs, and conducts parent and community-awareness programs that promote the care-giving triangle of home, school, and community. SADD sponsors college, middle school, and high school programs, a **Student Athletes Detest Drugs** project, and various other innovative efforts. If you are interested in starting a SADD chapter, or need information and materials, SADD can provide you with numerous publications, T-shirts, decals, bumper stickers, and other items. There are SADD chapters in all fifty states and offices throughout Europe.

National Alcohol and/or Drug Self-Help Organizations

> **Adult Children of Alcoholics Interim World Service Organization**
> P.O. Box 3216, 2522 W. Sepulveda Boulevard, Suite 200
> Torrance, CA 90505
> (213) 534-1815

ACA is a twelve-step support group of men and women who were traumatized in childhood by physical and or emotional abuse usually resulting from the effects of alcoholism (although some other form of family dysfunction may initially be more identifiable). Members work toward recovery by expressing their feelings and sharing their experiences, strengths, and hopes with other members. Send a self-addressed, stamped envelope to the national headquarters if you cannot find a meeting near you, or if you would like to start a chapter.

Al-Anon/Alateen Family Group Headquarters
862 Midtown Station, New York, NY 10018-0862
(212) 302-7240, Public information number: 1-800-356-9996

A nonprofit organization with thousands of groups nationwide, **Al-Anon** serves one very important purpose: helping friends and relatives of alcoholics. Members share their common experiences in order to solve their common problems. If you are interested in starting a chapter in your community, Al-Anon can send you all of the necessary information. Al-Anon also has a comprehensive catalog of books, pamphlets, leaflets, audiovisual materials, and posters.

Alcoholics Anonymous World Services
P.O. Box 459, Grand Central Station, New York, NY 10163
(212) 686-1100

AA is a fellowship of men and women acting as a support network to help one another recover from alcoholism. The program, consisting of twelve steps (it was the model for all the twelve-step programs listed in this chapter), helps alcoholics develop a satisfying life without alcohol. AA sponsors several different types of meetings, including open speaker meetings (open to the general public), at which recovering alcoholics explain how they became involved with AA and how AA has helped them; open discussion meetings (also open to the public), at which one member recalls his or her drinking experience, then begins a discussion on AA recovery or a drinking-related problem anyone brings up; and closed discussion meetings, conducted in the same manner as open discussion meetings but open only to AA members and prospective members. AA has many informative pamphlets and publications (such as *Young People and AA; Time to Start Living; 44 Questions*).

Cocaine Anonymous World Services
3740 Overland Ave., Suite G, Los Angeles, CA 90034
(213) 559-5833; Toll-free meeting referral line: 1-800-347-8998

CA is a nonprofit organization of men and women who desire to help themselves and others recover from addiction. The only requirement for membership is a desire to stop using cocaine and all other mind-altering substances. CA has several informative brochures (for example, *The First Thirty Days; A Power Greater Than Ourselves*), key chains, books, stickers, and a kit for individuals interested in starting a meeting in their community.

Families Anonymous
P.O. Box 528, Van Nuys, CA 91408
(818) 989-7841

FA is a nonprofit organization established to help family members and friends of drug abusers. Through public meetings and free membership, families are introduced to the twelve-step program for family recovery. The organization offers books, pamphlets, posters, cards, bookmarks, cassettes, and other materials. If there is no family support in your area, FA will provide you with everything you'll need to start one. FA also has a bimonthly newsletter, the *Twelve Step Rag*, for relatives and friends concerned about another's use of drugs or related behavioral problems. A one-year subscription costs $4.50.

Nar-Anon Family Group Headquarters, Inc.
P.O. Box 2562, Palos Verdes Peninsula, CA 90274
(213) 547-5800

A support group to **Narcotics Anonymous**, Nar-Anon follows the same twelve-step program for family recovery. Services are aimed at families and relatives of drug users. Nar-Anon works to offer a constructive program whereby its members learn to achieve peace of mind and gain hope for the future, accept addiction as a disease, reduce family tension, and encourage the drug user to seek help for his or her own problem. Contact the national headquarters if you cannot find a meeting near you.

Narcotics Anonymous
P.O. Box 9999, Van Nuys, CA 91409
(818) 780-3951

NA is a nonprofit organization of men and women with drug-abuse problems who meet regularly to help one another stay drug-free. The organization encourages complete abstinence, unity, and strong support for each and every member. NA also has informative books, and pamphlets, including *Am I an Addict?* and *Narcotics Anonymous: Who, What, How, and Why*. Contact the national headquarters to find a chapter near you.

Animals

Why Help Is Needed

The number of animals that suffer and are killed in this country has reached astounding proportions. According to the World Society for the Protection of Animals, more than one hundred million animals are killed every year for their fur alone. Of the approximately fifty million animals caught each year in "instant-kill" devices (which really have only about a forty-percent "instant" success rate), twenty-five million are considered "trash" and thrown away. Nor do the traps discriminate; cats, dogs, and endangered species are also inadvertently caught and die.[1] The International Society for Animal Rights estimates that more than fifteen million animals suffer and die each year in tests to determine the safety of cosmetics and household products. According to Friends of Animals, animal shelters nationwide euthanize as many as eighteen million dogs and cats each year, many of whom were neglected or abandoned by their owners. In many states, pound animals are even used for laboratory experiments.

Other statistics are just as discouraging. As a result of poaching, industrial expansion, and other threats by humans, entire species of animals in the sea, on land, and in the air are nearing extinction. People for the Ethical Treatment of Animals reports that every year an estimated 100,000 seals, whales, and porpoises and a million birds become entangled in drift nets (which can extend from one to thirty miles) and die. Another one million seabirds, 100,000 marine mammals, and 50,000 fur seals are killed each year because of plastics dumped in the ocean.[2] The National Audubon Society estimates that 11,000 endangered sea turtles drown in shrimp fishing nets annually. The U.S. Fish and Wildlife Service reports that blue whales, timber wolves, tigers, leopards, and California condors are all endangered. Even America's national symbol, the bald eagle, was on the brink of

---

[1] Barbara Sleeper, "Living with Animals," *Animals*, March/April 1990, 23.
[2] John Elkington, Julia Hailes, and Joel Makower, *The Green Consumer*. (New York: Penguin Books, 1988), 9.

extinction just a few years ago. After legislative actions and grass-roots efforts, however, it has made a comeback and today is considered merely "threatened."

With numbers as high as these and with the threatened extinction of animal species, it is not surprising that animal welfare has become an intensely debated issue in this country. On one side is the belief that animals deserve equal protection under the law—cruelty to them is no different from cruelty to people. On the other side is the belief that animals are part of the renewable resources of nature and that people are entitled to use them for their own purposes. Most people find themselves somewhere between these beliefs, a position that can prove to be full of tricky moral dilemmas. For example, is using animals in medical research acceptable under any circumstances, only in certain cases, or not at all? Is buying a fur coat the same as buying leather shoes? If a person refuses to eat meat, should milk and eggs be avoided as well? Is fishing the same as hunting wildlife? For many people, these can become complex issues. It's unfortunate, however, that many well-intentioned individuals are overwhelmed by the arguments and moral questions and end up doing nothing. This need not happen. Even simple actions can help prevent a great deal of animal suffering, and considering the suffering involved, the need to help could hardly be greater.

What You Can Do

☞ **Keep up on animal welfare issues.** Although most of the national organizations listed in this chapter have newsletters and publications, here are a few periodicals in particular that provide in-depth coverage:

- *Animals,* a bimonthly, full-color magazine, is filled with comprehensive articles, stunning photography, and a variety of other features and departments. It is published by the **Massachusetts Society for the Prevention of Cruelty to Animals**. Contact MSPCA at *350 S. Huntington Ave., Boston, MA 02130*; (617) 522-7400. A one-year subscription costs $15.
- *The Animals' Agenda* is a comprehensive, full-color periodical filled with profiles, news, reviews, national events, employment opportunities, and a variety of features all related to animals. The magazine also offers sources for nonleather and cruelty-free merchandise (T-shirts, posters, notecards, etc.). A one-year subscription (ten issues) costs $22, $39 for two years.

Contact *The Animals' Agenda, Subscription Dept.*, P.O. Box 6809, Syracuse, NY 13217-9953; 1-800-825-0061.

• **The Animals' Voice Magazine** is a bimonthly, full-color publication filled with investigative reports, national and world news, legislative information, and comprehensive articles and features on a variety of animal issues. A one-year subscription costs $20. Write or call *The Animals' Voice Magazine* at P.O. Box 16955, North Hollywood, CA 91615-9931; (for credit card subscription orders): 1-800-82-VOICE (828-6423), (general information): (213) 204-2323.

☞ **Keep up on legislation affecting animal welfare and endangered species and express your concern or approval.** (See Wildlife and Endangered Species, page 104, for information on finding out about endangered species and related legislation.) Most of the organizations listed in this chapter track legislation. The **National Alliance for Animal Legislation**, page 93, and **The Write Cause**, page 96, are especially good sources of information. (See also Voicing Your Opinion, page 363.)

☞ **Work to educate others about animal welfare.** You can help by putting up posters, stickers, and other materials in public places, wearing T-shirts, or showing films, videos, or slides to your school, community club, or any other group. Most of the national organizations listed in this chapter have educational materials and publications. Some groups even give out or loan items free of charge.

☞ **If you are a parent, encourage your children to learn about and appreciate animals and the environment.** Encourage them to watch educational TV programs on the animal world and provide them with books or magazines about animals, such as *Ranger Rick* (see **National Wildlife Federation**, page 107) and *WORLD* (see **National Geographic Society**, page 267). Many of the national organizations listed in this chapter, especially those in the wildlife and marine life sections, have stunning books and videos for children and adults. Another resource is **Animal Town**, a mail-order company offering a large collection of items that encourage young people to learn about and appreciate animals and the environment. Animal Town sells games (for example, *Dam Builders; Predator and Pollution*), books (such as *The Man Who Planted Trees; Legends of the Sun and Moon*), toys, tapes (such as *Beautiful Bird Songs; Sounds of the Jungle Tape*), and much more. Its items encourage cooperation, family unity, and old-time fun—that is, fun without television or video games. Animal Town is an excellent resource for parents looking for wholesome activities, books, and games for their children. Write or call Animal Town at *P.O. Box 485, Healdsburg, CA 95448*; 1-800-445-8642 (8 A.M. to 5 P.M., Pacific Time).

☞ **Become a "cruelty-free" shopper and encourage your friends, family members, and others to do the same.** Cruelty-free products contain no animal ingredients and are made without killing animals or causing them to suffer. (There is no law in the U.S. that requires cosmetics or household products to be tested on animals.) Cruelty-free products do not differ in quality from "regular" products; you may even be using some of them—such as Nexxus, Paul Mitchell, or Tom's of Maine—without even knowing it. Most magazines on animal issues, especially those mentioned on page 79 and the national organizations listed in this chapter (such as **Animal Protection Institute of America**, page 88, **Beauty Without Cruelty**, page 89, **National Anti-Vivisection Society**, page 94, and **People for the Ethical Treatment of Animals**, page 94) are excellent sources of information on cruelty-free products. Here are a few companies that sell cruelty-free products:

- **The Body Shop** offers a wide variety of items, including cosmetics, soaps, perfumes, and lotions. All of the products are 100% cruelty-free and environmentally friendly. Check the phone book to see if there's a store near you, or contact the mail-order center at *Hanover Technical Center, 45 Horsehill Rd., Cedar Knolls, NJ 07927*; 1-800-541-2535; in New Jersey: (201) 984-9200.
- **The Compassionate Consumer, Inc.** is one of the best sources for cruelty-free products. Here are just a few items this mail-order company sells:

  - air fresheners
  - baby products
  - bath oils
  - cards, T-shirts, buttons, and books (including, *Animal Liberation, Country Life Natural Foods Cookbook*, and *Cookbook for People Who Love Animals*)
  - companion animal products (collars, food, shampoos, flea repellents)
  - conditioners
  - cosmetics
  - deodorants
  - fabric softeners
  - facial cleaners
  - fragrances
  - household cleaners
  - laundry detergents

- moisturizers
- nonleather wallets, purses, keyholders, change purses, and belts
- nonleather shoes for men and women (athletic sneakers, boat deck shoes, dress shoes, sandals, and flat-heel and mid-heel pumps)
- shampoos
- soaps
- toothpaste

Five percent of every order goes to the animal rights, animal shelter, or environmental protection group of your choice. Write to or call The Compassionate Consumer, Inc. at *P.O. Box 27, Jericho, NY 11753*; (718) 445-4134. (Catalogs cost $1.)

● **Eco-Choice** sells beautiful baskets of cruelty-free personal products. The baskets make great gifts and are an excellent way to introduce someone to cruelty-free and environmentally friendly products. You can also buy a wide array of individual items, including:

- all-purpose cleaners
- baby care products
- bubble bath
- carpet shampoos
- cloth diapers
- cosmetics
- deodorants
- dishwashing liquid
- fabric softeners
- facial soaps
- hair dyes
- insect repellents
- laundry detergents
- pain-relieving creams
- pest controls
- polish waxes
- recycled paper products
- shampoos and conditioners
- skin care lotions
- sun-care lotions
- toothpaste

Contact Eco-Choice at *P.O. Box 281, Dept. 5020, Montvale, NJ 07645-0281*; 1-800-535-6304.

● **EveryBody Ltd.** is a store and mail-order company that sells a wide variety of cruelty-free products, including:

- air fresheners
- bath and shower products
- body and skin care
- child and baby products (such as bubble bath, powders, and shampoos)
- cosmetics
- deodorants
- foot-care products
- shaving cream
- soaps
- sun protection lotions

Write or call EveryBody Ltd. at *1738 Pearl St., Boulder, CO 80302*; (303) 440-0188; for catalogs only: 1-800-748-5675.

• **Heartland Products, Ltd.** sells a large assortment of non-leather shoes, including boots, aerobic hightops, Oxfords, and slingback pumps. Send $1 (credited toward purchase) for a price list to *Box 218, Dakota City, IA 50529*; (515) 332-3087.

• **Home Service Products Co.** sells a variety of household-cleaning products that have not been tested on animals, contain no animal ingredients, and are safe for the environment. HSP products include:

- all-purpose spray cleaners
- bleaches
- dishwasher detergents
- fabric softeners
- laundry detergents

Contact HSP at *P.O. Box 269, Bound Brook, NJ 08805*; (201) 356-8175.

• **lion & lamb, inc.** sells several hundred all-natural cruelty-free products, including:

- baby products
- bath and shower products
- bleaches
- deodorants
- laundry detergents
- lotions
- makeup
- nail polishes
- shampoos
- soaps
- sun-care products

Write or call lion & lamb, inc. at *29-28 41st Ave., Suite 813, Long Island City, NY 11101*; (718) 361-5757. (Free samples of makeup are available.)

• **Rainbow Concepts** is a mail-order company that sells a wide array of cruelty-free and environmentally safe products, including:

- bath oils
- body oils
- cosmetics
- dishwashing liquids
- eye creams
- fabric softeners
- lip-care products
- moisturizers
- mouthwash
- night creams
- sculpting gels and mousses
- shampoos and conditioners
- shaving cream
- tanning oils
- toothpaste

Contact Rainbow Concepts at *Route 5, Box 569-H, Pheasant Mountain Road, Taccoa, GA 30577*; (404) 886-6320. (Catalogs cost $1, which can be credited toward purchase.)

- **Spare the Animals, Inc.** sells a variety of cruelty-free and environmentally friendly products including:

  - all-purpose cleaners
  - baby powder
  - cosmetics
  - deodorants
  - dishwashing liquids
  - laundry detergents
  - shampoos
  - soaps
  - toothpaste

Write or call Spare the Animals, Inc. at *P.O. Box 233, Dept. V, Tiverton, RI 02878*; (401) 625-5963.

- **Sunrise Lane** sells a wide array of cruelty-free and environmentally safe products, including:

  - air sprays
  - baby powders
  - bleaches
  - conditioners
  - cosmetics
  - creams and moisturizers
  - dishwasher detergents
  - facial products
  - floor soaps
  - hair colors
  - laundry detergents
  - liquid soaps
  - lotions
  - perfumes
  - shampoos
  - suntan lotions

Contact Sunrise Lane at *780 Greenwich St., New York, NY 10014*, (212) 242-7014.

See also The Environment, page 252, for information on environmentally safe products and mail-order companies, most of which also sell cruelty-free products.

☞ **Write to magazines, advertisers, newspapers, department stores, and mail-order companies that you feel glamorize, sell, or advertise products or clothing that are not cruelty-free.** Consumers can have a tremendous impact on companies' marketing practices and/or products. Case in point: Due to the efforts of concerned individuals, the largest canned tuna companies announced in the spring of 1990 that the fishing practices used to catch tuna (which at the same time killed hundreds of thousands of dolphins) would be changed.

☞ **If you are a student opposed to dissecting animals in science class, learn about your right to refuse.** The **Student Action Corps for Animals** (page 95) counsels students, case by case, on a variety of issues related to dissecting animals in schools.

☞ **Volunteer to work for an animal welfare group or participate in animal welfare activities in your community.** Many of the national organizations listed in this chapter have local and regional offices and/or activities across the U.S. in need of volunteers. Volunteers can help out by answering phones, sending out legislative alerts, raising funds, writing articles for newsletters, and much more.

☞ **Consider adopting a more vegetarian diet.** There is an unfortunate misconception that vegetarian meals consist of little more than lettuce and bean sprouts. In reality, there are countless recipes for people interested in eating healthy, appetizing, and filling vegetarian meals. Go to your local bookstore or health food store for books with recipe ideas. Here are a few publications and organizations in particular to look out for:

- The **American Vegan Society** is a nonprofit educational organization that promotes the benefits of vegetarianism. AVS has a large selection of publications and recipes for vegetarians. Membership ($15) includes the quarterly newsletter *Ahimsa*, which covers a variety of issues concerning animal rights and a total vegetarian lifestyle. Contact AVS at *501 Old Harding Highway, Malaga, NJ 08328*; (609) 694-2887. (Sample issue of magazines are available.)
- **EarthSave** (see The Environment, page 263).
- The **North American Vegetarian Society** is a nonprofit educational organization dedicated to promoting the vegetarian way of life. NAVS provides information to its members, the public, local groups, interested organizations, and the media; sponsors regional and national conferences; and distributes books and other educational materials (such as *Vegetarian Cooking for a Better World* and *Diet for a New America*). NAVS also publishes *Vegetarian Voice*, a quarterly newsmagazine with recipes, book reviews, vegetarian group and contact listings, reports on health findings, and practical ideas and resources for healthy and compassionate living. Both regular (no meat, fish, or fowl) and associate (not yet a vegetarian) memberships cost $15 and include discounts on NAVS literature and a one-year subscription to the *Voice*. Contact NAVS for more information at *P.O. Box 72, Dolgeville, NY 13329*; (518) 568-7970.
- **Vegetarian Awareness Network (VEGENET)** is a national clearinghouse for vegetarian information, with a large database of restaurants, cookbooks, products, services, speakers, health

professionals, and much more. For more information about **VEGENET** or vegetarianism in general, write or call *P.O. Box 50515, Washington, DC 20004*; 1-800-USA-VEGE (872-8343). Volunteer opportunities are also available for people in the Washington, D.C., area to staff the phone line.

● ***Vegetarian Times*** is a monthly magazine filled with vegetarian recipes, dietary information, updates on animal rights issues, and a variety of related features and news items. A one-year subscription costs $24.95 (a six-month subscription is available for $12.47). Contact VT at *P.O. Box 446, Mt. Morris, IL 61054*; 1-800-435-0715, in Illinois: 1-800-892-0753.

Most of the national organizations listed in this chapter have information on vegetarianism, especially the **Farm Animal Reform Movement** (page 90) and **The Humane Farming Association** (page 91).

☞ **If you are a lawyer, law student, or paralegal, volunteer your legal skills to help animal groups and causes. The Animal Legal Defense Fund** (page 87) will help you find organizations, humane societies, and activists near you in need of legal assistance.

See also The Environment chapter for more information on things to do to help the earth and its inhabitants.

National Organizations

American Anti-Vivisection Society
Noble Plaza, Suite 204, 801 Old York Road
Jenkintown, PA 19046
(215) 887-0816

AAVS is a nonprofit educational organization dedicated to the abolition of vivisection and other forms of animal experimentation. If you need information on animal experimentation, AAVS is an excellent resource. The society offers a variety of brochures (for example, *Animal Experiments and the Welfare of Man; The Call to Compassion; What Can I Do to Help?;* and *Pet Owners Beware*), books and booklets (such as, *The Cruel Deception—The Use of Live Animals in Research and Testing* and *In Pity and in Anger—A Study of the Use of Animals in Science*), and audiovisual aids. Membership ($10) includes a subscription to the monthly journal *The AV Magazine*, which contains in-depth reports and commentary, book reviews, facts and figures, educational materials available from AAVS, and other informative items.

The American Society for the Prevention of Cruelty to Animals
441 E. 92nd St., New York, NY 10128
(212) 876-7700

The **ASPCA** was the first humane society in America and is now one of the largest in the world. Through its shelters in New York, the ASPCA cares for more animals each year than any other humane society in America. It is also a powerful legislative force, helping to pass laws protecting America's wild animals and working to ensure that the laws passed are obeyed. The society's staff of professionals, including specialists in ethology and biology, work to educate the public on animal protection and humane ethics issues. The **Pet Adoption Vans** program finds homes for orphaned pets, and its ambulance service rescues more than 25,000 sick and injured animals each year in New York City. Contributors of $20 or more receive a membership card, a one-year subscription to the *ASPCA Report* (a full-color magazine that contains a variety of news items, in-depth articles, and information on legislation and on numerous ASPCA materials, including posters, ties, buttons, and T-shirts), and other benefits. Volunteers are needed at the ASPCA shelters in New York. (The local SPCAs, located all across America, are independent from the ASPCA. Volunteers are often needed at SPCAs. For more information, see page 98.)

The Animal Legal Defense Fund
1363 Lincoln Ave., San Rafael, CA 94901
(415) 459-0885

ALDF is a nonprofit, nationwide network of hundreds of attorneys who use their skills to protect and promote animal rights. Whenever and wherever animals require legal defense against abuse and exploitation, the ALDF works to provide assistance. ALDF's quarterly newsletter, *The Animals' Advocate* (free when you become a supporter—$15 and up), is an excellent resource for those interested in what's going on with legislation and other important issues concerning the welfare of animals. If you are an attorney interested in joining ALDF, contact the national headquarters for more information.

Animal Protection Institute of America
P.O. Box 22505, Sacramento, CA 95822
(916) 731-5521

API is a nonprofit organization of more than 150,000 members dedicated to advancing the well-being of all animals. The institute monitors activities affecting animals in America and throughout the world, conducts research (particularly on endangered species), and can provide you with audiovisual materials, brochures (such as *Endangered Species* and *How to Become Actively Involved for Animals in Your Community*), books (for example, *Animal Activists' Handbook*), posters (such as *Wildlife Under Attack* and *Petwatch*), bumper stickers, informational packets, protest packages, and various other publications and materials (including the *Shopper's Guide to Cruelty-Free Products*, which lists 300 cruelty-free products and a dozen or so distributors). If you become a member ($20 or more), you will receive API's quarterly publication, *Mainstream*, as well as campaign and project mailings.

Animal Rights Mobilization!
P.O. Box 1553, Williamsport, PA 17703
(717) 322-3252

ARM! (formerly **Trans-Species Unlimited**) is a national grass-roots networking organization dedicated to eliminating animal abuse and exploitation. A unifying force for the grass-roots animal-rights movements, ARM! has affiliated groups in cities and towns across the country. Through its highly visible, dramatic events and high-powered educational and outreach activities, ARM! is helping to make animal rights a mainstream political issue. Contact ARM! to find out how you can link up with the movement and join an affiliate in your area. Contributors of $15 or more receive all mailings and *Movement Mag*, the organization's periodic publication.

Animal Welfare Institute
P.O. Box 3650, Washington, DC 20007
(202) 337-2332

Established almost forty years ago, **AWI** is a nonprofit organization dedicated to reducing animal suffering caused by humans. AWI's goals include enforcing humane treatment of lab animals, finding nonanimal alternatives for research, reforming cruel methods of trapping wild animals, banning the importation and sale of exotic birds caught in the wild, preserving species threatened by extinction, reforming cruel treatment of farm animals, and much more. AWI has an extensive list of publications (including *Facts About Furs; The Endangered Species Handbook;* and *Beyond the Laboratory Door*), audiovisuals (such as *The Great Whales* and *Save the Dolphins*), and other materials. The regular membership ($15, $5 for students and senior citizens), entitles you to a subscription to *The AWI Quarterly*, opportunities to receive free copies of selected AWI books, special mailings on pressing issues, and AWI's annual progress report.

Beauty Without Cruelty U.S.A.
175 W. 12th St., New York, NY 10011
(212) 989-8073

A nonprofit organization, **BWC** informs the public about animal suffering in the fashion and cosmetics industries, and provides information about substitute fashions and cosmetics that do not involve the death, confinement, or suffering of any animal. BWC can keep you up-to-date on companies that are using animals and those that are not. It also has publications and fact sheets on alternatives to dissection and using animals in cancer research and other issues.

The Delta Society
P.O. Box 1080, Renton, WA 98057-1080
(206) 266-7357
Hearing Dog Resource Center: 1-800-869-6898 (voice/TDD)

Delta is a nonprofit organization established in response to a new interdisciplinary field of study—the interactions between people, animals, and the environment. Delta is now the world's leading professional association in this field. The organization has chapters across the country, each of which offers a variety of services and projects, including providing information to the community and local media about the human-animal bond; encouraging animal-assisted therapy in places such as nursing homes; providing assistance to HIV/AIDS patients so that they can keep their animals; placing and maintaining aquariums in children's wards of local hospitals; providing vaccinations for animals owned by low-income elderly persons and street people; advocating for individuals with disabilities who are denied access to public places with their assistance animals; and training volunteers and their companion animals to provide animal visitation to local institutions. Delta has a large selection of books, videos, and other items on human-animal bonds. It publishes a quarterly magazine (free with membership) that profiles human-animal relationships, chapter activities, and related news; a quarterly journal *Anthrozoos* ($35 a year), which presents scientific data relating to the benefits of human-animal relationships; and *Alert*, a free quarterly newsletter on hearing dogs and hearing-dog programs. The basic membership fee is $35 ($25 for students, seniors, and individuals with disabilities). Contact the national headquarters for more information on membership, the location of a chapter near you (or materials for starting one), volunteer opportunities, information on assistance and hearing-dog programs nationwide that work with volunteers, and society publications and audiovisuals.

Farm Animal Reform Movement
P.O. Box 30654, Bethesda, MD 20824
(301) 530-1737

Formed by animal, consumer, and environmental-protection advocates, **FARM** is a nonprofit public information organization working to expose and stop animal abuse, particularly factory farming. FARM sponsors three national annual campaigns in cooperation with hundreds of local groups: **The Great American Meatout**, **World Farm Animals Day**, and the **Veal Ban Campaign**. FARM can send you a variety of informative publications on the abuses and dangers (for animals and humans) of factory farming, as well as T-shirts, tote bags, aprons, buttons, and bumper stickers. Basic membership ($20) includes an introductory information packet and a quarterly newsletter. Those who contribute $30 receive a copy of *Animal Factories*, an illustrated exposé of factory farming, or a T-shirt with the slogan "Fight Factory Farming."

Friends of Animals
Box 1244, Norwalk, CT 06856
(203) 866-5223

FoA is a nonprofit organization working to reduce and eliminate animal suffering and to achieve humane treatment of all animals. The group identifies, investigates, and exposes inhumane practices, implementing programs to bring them to an end, pushes for animal welfare legislation, and works to ensure that current animal-protection laws and regulations are properly administered and enforced. FoA also works to stop dog and cat overpopulation, protect farm animals, wildlife, and marine mammals, and stop the cruel use of animals for experimental purposes. *Act'ionLine* magazine features in-depth articles, investigative reports, and legislative updates (often listing the name and a brief description of legislation being considered). FoA also sells calendars, bumper stickers, posters, T-shirts, sweatshirts, buttons, decals, sports duffels, and other items. Annual membership costs $20 ($10 for students and senior citizens) and includes a subscription to *Act'ionLine*.

The Fund for Animals, Inc.
200 W. 57th St., New York, NY 10019
(212) 246-2096, FAX: (212) 246-2633

A nonprofit organization dedicated to improving the welfare of all animals, **TFA** works to stop such activities as laboratory abuses, the clubbing of baby seals, bullfighting, the use of animals for furs, and sport hunting. TFA's newsletter is an excellent source of information, not only on the organization's activities but also on various issues pertaining to animal welfare. The newsletter also identifies pressing needs in certain regions of the country and tells what people living in those areas can do to help. The basic membership fee ($20, $10 for students) includes a subscription to the newsletter.

The Humane Farming Association
1550 California St., Suite 6, San Francisco, CA 94109
(415) 485-1495

HFA is a nonprofit organization of public health specialists, veterinarians, consumer advocates, family farmers, and other concerned individuals united to protect consumers from the misuse of chemicals in food production and to eliminate severe abuses inflicted on farm animals. HFA has many informative brochures, consumer information materials, books (including, *Animal Factories; Modern Meat;* and *Diet for a New America*), posters, bumper stickers, and T-shirts. The basic $10 membership fee includes an education packet and a subscription to *Watchdog*, which contains legislative information, interviews, and a listing of HFA activities.

Humane Society of the United States
2100 L St., N.W., Washington, DC 20037
(202) 452-1100

The **Humane Society** is a nonprofit organization working to stop the exploitation and cruel treatment of animals nationwide. HSUS has begun an aggressive anti-fur campaign ("You Should Be Ashamed to Wear Fur"), placing ads in major magazines and gaining the support of several celebrities, including Candice Bergen, Margaux Hemingway, and Betty White. The society also promotes programs to help stray dogs and cats, and projects to stop sport hunting and animal testing. Its catalog of publications, a valuable resource for anyone interested in animal issues, includes video documentaries, bumper stickers, legislative alerts, buttons, posters (for example, *Animals . . . It's Their World Too* and *Remember the Elephants . . . Forget Ivory!*), books (such as *Animal Rights and Human Morality*), periodicals, pamphlets, and materials for educators. The basic membership ($10) includes a subscription to *HSUS NEWS*, a quarterly magazine covering the organization's involvement with a variety of animal issues, and periodic *Close-Up Reports*.

In Defense of Animals
816 W. Francisco Blvd., San Rafael, CA 94901
(415) 453-9984

IDA is a national nonprofit organization committed to defending the rights, welfare, and habitats of nonhuman species. It has been instrumental in orchestrating anti-fur demonstrations, lawsuits against illegal use of animals in research, campaigns promoting a cruelty-free environment, and many other direct action campaigns. Some of IDA's accomplishments include freeing nineteen greyhounds from the Army's proposed bone-breaking experiments, helping coordinate **World Laboratory Animal Liberation Week** in more than forty-one cities nationwide, and maintaining a twenty-four-hour hotline—*(415) 453-9994*—to give people within the research community the opportunity to report and describe abuses as they occur (their anonymity is protected). Membership ($20) includes a subscription to IDA's quarterly newsletter, information on IDA-coordinated demonstrations in members' areas, and updates on pertinent issues, along with suggestions on who to call or write. For a donation of $25, contributors also receive a free copy of *Animals, Nature, and Albert Schweitzer*.

International Society for Animal Rights, Inc.
421 S. State St., Clarks Summit, PA 18411
(717) 586-2200, FAX: (717) 586-9580

A nonprofit organization that believes animals have rights that are being denied every day, **ISAR** works to expose and end animal suffering and exploitation. The organization is aggressively working to stop the use of animals for cosmetics analyses and other experiments and to develop policies that will eliminate the use of animals in such testing. ISAR publishes a wide variety of books (including *Animal Rights—A Symposium* and *The Case for Animal Rights*), brochures (such as *Human Rights and Animal Rights* and *10 Easy Ways To Be Kind*), and other materials on vivisection, vegetarianism, and wildlife. ISAR also sells posters, pins, T-shirts, and bumper stickers. Membership ($15) includes a subscription to *ISAR Report*, which comes out six times a year and provides up-to-date information on a variety of animal-rights issues.

The Latham Foundation
Latham Plaza Building, Clement and Schiller
Alameda, CA 94501
(415) 521-0920

TLF is a nonprofit organization established to promote respect for the environment and all forms of life through education. In particular, the foundation emphasizes how much animals help people by providing companionship and by supporting individuals with disabilities. TLF distributes many publications, films, and videos. Its quarterly newsletter, *The Latham Letter*, addresses issues affecting the welfare of animals, children, and the environment. A one-year subscription costs $10.

National Alliance for Animal Legislation
P.O. Box 75116, Washington, DC 20013-5116
(703) 684-0654

ALLIANCE is a nonprofit animal protection league working to monitor and promote animal-welfare legislation. The organization also coordinates lobbying efforts among grass-roots groups across the country, helps its members become effective lobbyists, and updates them on legislative issues. Membership ($25, $15 for students and senior citizens) includes *The Capitol Hill Report*, a newsletter with items on legislative activity concerning animals. Members also receive the *ALLIANCE Alert* (when urgent action is needed for specific legislative matters) and the *Congressional Report Card*, which lists cosponsors of animal welfare–related bills.

National Anti-Vivisection Society
53 W. Jackson Boulevard, Suite 1552, Chicago, IL 60604-3795
(312) 427-6065

The **National Anti-Vivisection Society** was established to oppose animal experimentation and educate government officials, scientists, and the public at large. The organization provides funding for alternative research, works to repeal laws enabling laboratories to use animals from pounds, and stops a variety of cruel animal-testing practices. NAVS also distributes *Personal Care with Principle: A Guide to Choosing Cruelty-Free Cosmetics and Products from Major Manufacturers*, which is extremely useful for anyone interested in purchasing cruelty-free products. The booklet presents hundreds of firms, listing whether they do or do not currently practice animal testing. One copy of the booklet is free, but each additional copy is $1. The basic membership fee is $10 ($5 for students and senior citizens).

People for the Ethical Treatment of Animals
P.O. Box 42516, Washington, DC 20015
(301) 770-7444

A nonprofit organization, **PETA** is dedicated to promoting the rights and improving the lives of all animals by educating the public and policymakers, encouraging people to change their lifestyles, and exposing cruelty to animals. PETA brings members of the scientific, judicial, and legislative communities together to halt abusive practices. Its investigative work, congressional involvement, and international media coverage have resulted in widespread short- and long-term changes that have improved the lives of thousands of animals. PETA's informative literature (for example, *Tofu Cookery; Diet for a New America; The Farm Vegetarian Cookbook; The PETA Guide to Compassionate Living;* and *The PETA Cruelty-Free Shopping Guide*) will help you to eat, dress, and live cruelty-free. PETA also distributes notecards, sweatshirts, posters, children's books, mugs, T-shirts, fact sheets, and cruelty-free cleaners, detergents, fabric softeners, and beauty products. Annual membership ($15) includes a subscription to the bimonthly magazine *PETA NEWS*, which covers PETA activities, legislative information, national animal-welfare news, and related issues.

Physicians Committee for Responsible Medicine
P.O. Box 6322, Washington, DC 20015
(202) 686-2210

PCRM is a nonprofit national network of physicians and others concerned with ethical and practical issues (primarily the issue of animal research) in modern medicine. Many of the doctors in PCRM have provided professional testimony to public agencies concerned with animal experimentation and to local and national animal protection groups. The committee's publications offer alternatives to animal experimentation; *Alternatives in Medical Education: Non-Animal Methods*, for example, promotes computer models, videotapes, and other products in medical education. PCRM also distributes free publications providing nutrition information and recipes, and publishes the *Guide to Healthy Eating*, a bimonthly newsletter containing nutrition information and tips on healthy eating (the annual subscription rate is $12.95). Basic membership ($20 for physicians and nonphysicians alike, $10 for medical students) includes a subscription to *PCRM Update*, which is filled with articles on modern medicine and research and alternatives to animal experiments.

Scientists Center for Animal Welfare
4805 St. Elmo Ave., Bethesda, MD 20814
(301) 654-6390, FAX: (301) 907-3993

SCAW is an educational, nonprofit organization of scientists and other concerned individuals promoting responsible and humane treatment of laboratory, farm, and wild animals involved in research. SCAW believes that the humane treatment of animals is complementary to good science and good ethics. It opposes redundant research involving animals and encourages alternatives to animal use. As an information and resource center, SCAW publishes a quarterly newsletter, proceedings of conferences, and other educational materials; organizes seminars; and offers a speakers' bureau. An individual membership ($35, $15 for students) includes a one-year subscription to the newsletter and other information about current issues and events (institutional membership is also available).

Student Action Corps for Animals
P.O. Box 15588, Washington, DC 20003-0588
(202) 543-8983

A nonprofit advocacy, education, and information organization,

SACA specializes in empowering junior high, high school, and college students to work for animal rights. The group offers comprehensive and individualized assistance to students nationwide who refuse to dissect animals and who need information about their rights. SACA can provide individuals with informative literature (such as *Say No to Dissection* and *Suggestions for Student Animal Rights Groups*), posters (for example, *Their Eyes Don't Lie*), buttons, T-shirts, stickers, and a newsletter, *SACA NEWS*, which features articles about student rights and students organizing for animal rights. Membership costs $7 for students ($15 for nonstudents) and includes a subscription to the newsletter.

United Action for Animals, Inc.
205 E. 42nd St., Room 1923, New York, NY 10017
(212) 983-5315

UAA is a nonprofit organization established to end the abuse and death of billions of animals used in duplicative, inconclusive, and wasteful experiments. The association works to expose myths regarding animal research, to find alternatives to the use of live animals in experiments, and to stop redundant testing. UAA has many free publications (such as *Animal Agony in Addiction Research: Science or Savagery;* and *Science Gone Insane*). The basic membership fee is $15 and includes a subscription to UAA's newsletter, *UAA Reports*, which addresses legislative issues and a variety of news items related to animal welfare.

The Write Cause
P.O. Box 751328, Petaluma, CA 94975
(707) 769-0116

TWC is an organization working to get concerned individuals involved with legislation related to animal welfare and the environment. For an annual membership fee of $37 ($64 per couple), members receive TWC's monthly newsletter listing summaries of pertinent issues. Members simply choose the two issues they would like to target and then send the list back to TWC in the stamped, addressed envelope provided. Within two weeks, members receive two personalized letters (both are preaddressed and stamped) addressed to individuals who can influence the welfare of animals. Members just sign the letters and send them out. It's a simple and effective way to express your views to government representatives, corporations, foreign governments, and animal-research facilities.

Companion Animals
(Particularly Cats and Dogs)

What You Can Do

☞ **If you plan to get a companion animal, here are a few things to keep in mind:**

- **Above all, be sure that you will have the money, time, commitment, and energy to care properly for a companion animal.** According to **People for the Ethical Treatment of Animals (PETA)**, millions of dogs and cats are abandoned every year, many of whom starve to death or become sick and die. When you consider the cost of a companion animal, figure in money for food, medical bills, flea and tick supplies, and various other expenses. More importantly, make sure you will have the time to train, feed, groom, walk, and provide love and companionship for the animal.
- **Consider adopting an animal from your local animal shelter instead of buying one from a pet store or a breeder.** Look in the yellow pages under "Animal Shelters" or "Humane Societies." These shelters are filled with puppies, kittens, and older animals who will make excellent companion animals. Some humane societies will even spay or neuter your animal, as well as provide follow-up veterinary services, free of charge. (Local humane societies are independent organizations—they are not affiliates of any national organization, such as the **Associated Humane Societies** or the **Humane Society of the United States**.)

☞ **If you have a companion animal, remember the following:**

- **Consider having the animal spayed or neutered.** The **National Dog Registry** reports that there are almost 100 million cats and dogs in 50 million homes in America. Because too many of these animals are not spayed or neutered, more than 60,000 puppies and kittens are born every day, according to PETA. Many of them are abandoned, used for animal experimentation, or become lost and die. For spaying and neutering services, look under "Veterinarian" in the yellow pages. Also check with local humane societies to see if free or low-cost spaying and neutering services are offered.
- **Make sure your companion animal wears a tag with your**

name, address, and telephone number, so that he or she can be returned if lost. Also, consider having your companion animal tattooed with an identification number, so that if the name tag falls off (or is ripped off) the animal can still be identified. The tattoo process is completely painless and could save the animal's life. The **National Dog Registry** (page 99) can provide you with the necessary information.

• **Do not leave animals in cars on hot days.** On an average summer day, the inside of a car can quickly become hot enough to kill your animal. An animal left for even a short period of time can suffer brain damage. You may want to reconsider leaving companion animals in cars altogether, because of the prevalence of animal thieves who sell animals to research laboratories.

☞ **If your friends or neighbors get a new cat or dog, encourage them to have the animal spayed or neutered, and educate others on the importance of this.** Some of the national organizations listed in this chapter can provide you with posters, stickers, and other materials to put up in public places. (The **International Society for Animal Rights**, page 92, also sells dog- and cat-overpopulation materials.)

☞ **If you know of poor or inhumane conditions at an animal store, dog-breeding operation, or similar business, contact the local humane society.**

☞ **Volunteer to work at an animal shelter in your community.** These shelters may need volunteers for administrative work, fundraising, and help with the animals (for example, walking the animals, petting and playing with them, etc.). Also, if you have extra animal food, bowls, leashes, or similar items, see if your local shelter needs them. To find a shelter near you, check the phone book under "Humane Society" or "Society for the Prevention of Cruelty to Animals."

National Organizations

American Humane Association
Animal Protection Division
63 Inverness Drive East, Englewood, CO 80112
(303) 792-9900

AHA was the first national nonprofit organization to protect animals from neglect, abuse, and exploitation. Training programs for animal care and control professionals, innovative humane education materials for children and adults, and emergency relief for injured animals and animal victims of natural disasters are just some of the services AHA provides. The association has sponsored such programs as **Adopt a Pet from Your Local Animal Shelter, Be Kind to Animals Week**, and **Adopt-a-Cat** month. The Los Angeles office protects performing animals in motion pictures, television programs, and commercials, and the Washington, D.C., office aggressively advocates animal protection legislation. Contributors of $15 or more receive *The Advocate,* AHA's quarterly magazine on animal protection issues. Volunteers are needed at the local chapters.

The American Society for the Prevention of Cruelty to Animals
(see page 87)

Associated Humane Societies
124 Evergreen Ave., Newark, NJ 07114
(201) 824-7080

AHS is a nonprofit organization dedicated to promoting the well-being of animals, particularly cats and dogs. AHS provides such services as cruelty investigations, an adoption program, education projects, low-cost spaying and neutering clinics, tatooing, grooming, a lost-pet service, and wildlife rescue and release operations. In the **Share-a-Pet** program, sponsors donate $10 a month to be designated for the care of a particular homeless cat or dog. (Almost all of the animals in this program are unadoptable and must stay with the AHS because of age, disabilities, medical problems, etc.) Sponsors receive a photo of the animal every four months and are welcome to visit, walk, feed, and take photos of him or her. Membership ($10) includes a subscription to *Humane News,* a monthly newsletter that features a variety of articles and AHS activities, and lists supplies for companion animals, donations the organization needs to help animals (such as can openers, birdseed, leashes), and various posters and gift items.

Humane Society of the United States
(see page 91)

National Dog Registry
Box 116, Woodstock, NY 12498
(914) 679-2355

NDR works aggressively to stop animal theft, particularly theft of cats and dogs. The registry provides its members with numerous services to increase the likelihood that their companion animal will be returned if lost. (Recovery rate for NDR's member animals is over ninety-five percent.) For a one-time fee of $35, members receive information on finding a tattooer near them, a tattoo number for the animal (the tattoo is painless), a complete owner's kit, missing-animal posters, and access to a twenty-four-hour, 365-days-a-year hotline *(1-800-NDR-DOGS [3647])* for reporting a lost or found animal. NDR has been featured in many publications and articles; the list of these articles can serve as an excellent bibliography for people with companion animals (for example, *Dog Owner's Bible; Protecting Your Pets at Home and Away; Your Pet's Health from A to Z*). NDR also publishes a full-color, bimonthly newsmagazine, *RESCUE*, filled with statistics and general information on pets, NDR activities, and success stories. Although NDR is not a nonprofit organization, it sponsors the nonprofit **National Dog Registry's Rescue Fund, Inc.** The fund provides needed monies for people nationwide who cannot afford catastrophic veterinary costs for their animals (particularly elderly persons and individuals with disabilities).

Marine Life

What You Can Do

☞ **Educate yourself and others on marine life and the problems confronting marine animals.** All of the national organizations in this chapter have information on marine life, and most of them can provide you with T-shirts, fact sheets, posters, videos, and other materials to help you educate others.

☞ **Keep up on legislation that affects marine life and write to your government representatives to express your concern or approval.** The national organizations in this chapter can provide you with the necessary information. (See also Voicing Your Opinion, page 363.)

☞ **Adopt a whale.** The **International Wildlife Coalition** (page 102) and **Ocean Alliance** (see The Environment, page 326) sponsor whale-adoption projects. Contributors select a whale from a list of many and receive a picture and information on the whale, reports on its progress, and other notices and updates. This is also a unique gift idea.

☞ **If you go boating or fishing, remember to dump any garbage you have in a trash receptacle on land and encourage**

others to do the same. Plastic six-pack holders, for example, can strangle seabirds and suffocate various sea animals.

☞ **Participate in a beach cleanup.** Not only good for the environment, a beach cleanup keeps garbage from washing into the ocean and killing marine life. Try to get classmates, co-workers, neighbors, or members of your religious congregation to participate. Here are a few resources to help you get involved:

- The **Oregon Department of Fish and Wildlife** has a free publication, *Get the Drift and Bag It: A Nuts and Bolts Guide to Organizing a Beach Cleanup Campaign the Easy Way.* Write to or call the ODFW at *P.O. Box 59, Portland, OR 97207*; (503) 229-5400 (ext. 432—Public Affairs).
- *COASTWEEKS* is both a three-week project of nationwide beach cleanups and a public-education campaign to increase awareness of our nation's saltwater and freshwater shores. COASTWEEKS also sponsors boat cruises, coastal walks, seminars, conferences, art shows, photography contests, library and museum exhibits, and more. For information on the next COASTWEEKS and a calendar of events, contact the **Coastal States Organization** at *Hall of the States, 444 N. Capitol St., N.W., Suite 312, Washington, DC 20001*; (202) 628-9636.

National Organizations

American Cetacean Society
P.O. Box 2639, San Pedro, CA 90731
(213) 548-6279

ACS is a nonprofit organization dedicated to protecting whales and dolphins through research, conservation, and education. Activities have included studying and preventing the killing of dolphins by tuna fishermen, fighting to stop whaling, and studying ocean pollution and gill net and drift net problems. ACS distributes pamphlets discussing the threats marine mammals face and what you can do to help protect them, books (for example, *The Book of Whales; Coloring Book of Sea Mammals;* and *The Bottlenose Dolphin in the Wild*), T-shirts, pins, stickers, videos, posters, audiocassettes, teaching kits, fact packs on whales and dolphins, and other merchandise. ACS also sponsors whale watches and other marine expeditions. Membership ($25) includes a subscription to the quarterly *Whalewatcher* magazine, which covers research and conservation information, and the *WhaleNews* newsletter, which addresses a variety of issues related to whales and other marine animals.

Center for Marine Conservation
1725 DeSales St., N.W., Washington, DC 20036
(202) 429-5609, FAX: (202) 872-0619

CMC is a nonprofit organization dedicated to protecting marine wildlife and habitats and to conserving coastal and ocean resources. CMC also works with other conservation groups, governments, private industries, and concerned citizens to protect all wildlife species threatened by international trade. The center conducts policy-oriented research, promotes public awareness through education, and involves citizens in public policy decisions. The organization has four major program areas: protecting and conserving marine habitats, protecting and conserving marine species and biodiversity, fighting marine pollution, and protecting and conserving marine fisheries. CMC also has a *Whale Gifts* catalog, filled with posters, videos, mugs, T-shirts, glasses, stuffed animals, ties, audiotapes, books, and a variety of other high-quality items. Membership ($20) includes a subscription to *Marine Conservation News*, a quarterly newsletter featuring legislative updates, and articles on CMC's programs and marine mammals and their habitats.

The Cousteau Society
(see The Environment, page 261)

Greenpeace U.S.A.
(see The Environment, page 265)

International Wildlife Coalition
634 N. Falmouth Highway, Box 388
North Falmouth, MA 02556
(508) 564-9980

A nonprofit organization, IWC, through its **Whale Adoption Project**, gives you a chance to "adopt" a whale of your choice from a list IWC maintains. For $15, you will receive an Official Whale Adoption Certificate in your name and the name of your adoptee; a Whale Calendar and Whale Migration Map to keep track of the movements of IWC whales; *Whalewatch*, an illustrated quarterly newsletter (published in both adult and child versions) containing the latest news on IWC whales; and an Honorary First Mate Card, which provides discounts on whale-watching trips off Cape Cod. IWC also has beautiful T-shirts, wind socks, wind chimes, tote bags, and duffels.

National Coalition for Marine Conservation
P.O. Box 23298, Savannah, GA 31403
(912) 234-8062

NCMC is a national nonprofit organization dedicated exclusively to conserving ocean fish and protecting the marine environment for all of its inhabitants. The coalition believes that conservation means preventing overexploitation of the ocean and habitat destruction before it occurs, not repairing the damage afterward, and that sound resource management must be based on scientific principle, not political or economic expedience. NCMC's programs focus on fishery management and habitat preservation. NCMC also monitors and works to influence public policy and legislation at all levels of government. Membership ($30) includes a subscription to the bimonthly newsletter *Marine Bulletin*, which contains legislative updates, articles, and features on threats to ocean life and what is being done to counter them.

Sea Shepherd Conservation Society
P.O. Box 7000-S, Redondo Beach, CA 90277
(213) 373-6979

A nonprofit organization, **SSCS** works to protect marine animals and marine habitats by serving as an international enforcement body, and by policing nations and individuals engaged in illegal slaughtering activities. SSCS is made up entirely of volunteers who actively work to prevent dolphin killings by the tuna industry, protect pilot whales, and rescue whales and marine animals in distress. SSCS also works to educate the public about the illegal slaughter of hundreds of thousands of marine animals every year and what needs to be done to stop it. Contributors of $25 or more receive a subscription to the quarterly newsletter *Sea Shepherd Log*, containing SSCS activities, successes, anticipated actions, and a variety of features and articles on marine life. Volunteers *with sea experience and marine skills* are welcome to participate in SSCS activities.

See also Water Conservation and Preservation of Natural Resources, page 322 for other national organizations concerned with the ocean and its inhabitants.

Wildlife and Endangered Species

What You Can Do

☞ **Keep up on wildlife and endangered species issues so you can educate your friends, family members, and others.** Almost all of the national organizations in this chapter can provide information on both general and specific issues, including materials (such as posters, videos, literature) you can use to educate others. Your local library should also have information on endangered species and the laws created to protect them. If you want a free list of endangered or threatened animal and plant species, contact the **U.S. Fish and Wildlife Services—Division of Endangered Species** at *1849 C St., N.W., Room 130, ARLSQ, Washington, DC 20240*; (703) 358-2171.

☞ **Write to your government representative expressing your opinion on legislation affecting endangered species and wildlife.** Congress votes on many important pieces of wildlife legislation each year. Expressing your views can be one of the most effective ways to help save wildlife and endangered species. (See also Voicing Your Opinion, page 363.)

☞ **Circulate petitions that encourage the protection of wildlife and endangered species.** The **Elsa Wild Animal Appeal** (see page 105) usually has petitions that need signatures. Check with other organizations you're interested in to see if they have any petitions in need of support.

☞ **Don't buy exotic animals.** Keep these animals in their native habitat and instead look for domestic animals such as cats and dogs, plenty of whom need to be adopted by a loving family. (See Companion Animals, page 97, for more information.)

☞ **Volunteer to clean up trails, wooded areas, and other locations where there may be wildlife.** Encourage your friends and family members to help (especially if you are on vacation in the outdoors). See The Environment, page 256, for short- and long-term opportunities to work to keep the environment clean for the sake of wildlife.

☞ **Go on wildlife tours or participate in an ecology workshop or camp.** These programs are fantastic ways to learn about animals in their natural habitats. Many of the national organizations in this chapter, particularly the **National Audubon Society** (page 106) and the **Wildlife Preservation Trust International** (page 109) have excellent opportunities for interested individuals.

National Organizations

Defenders of Wildlife
1244 19th St., N.W., Washington, DC 20036
(202) 659-9510

Defenders is a nonprofit organization working to preserve, enhance, and protect wildlife and the habitats critical for its survival. It is the only natural membership organization group that dedicates all of its resources to advocating for the protection and restoration of all species of wild animals and plants in their natural communities. Defenders uses public education, litigation, scientific studies and conferences, expert testimony, and grass-roots action to effect change. The organization has led a successful four-year campaign to strengthen the Endangered Species Act and has pressed for government action to protect grizzlies, bald eagles, and mountain lions. Defenders has also fought to save seals, whales, and other marine wildlife. The organization distributes high-quality publications, clothing, duffel bags, coffee mugs, and other gifts. (Defenders posters are absolutely stunning.) You can even get a Defenders VISA or MasterCard (a portion of the annual fee goes to the organization). Membership ($20 and up) includes a one-year subscription to the bimonthly *Defenders* magazine, one of the most informative natural periodicals available, featuring the work of some of the world's finest wildlife writers, photographers, and artists; invitations to special events and presentations; and offers of limited-edition wildlife prints and photos.

Elsa Wild Animal Appeal
Elsa Clubs of America
P.O. Box 4572, North Hollywood, CA 91617-0572
(818) 761-8387

A nonprofit organization, **EWAA** is dedicated to the conservation of the environment and wildlife, especially endangered species, through education and legislative activities. EWAA develops and distributes education materials designed for children and adolescents. Membership ($15 for adults, $7.50 for children) includes a subscription to the triannual *Born Free News* and a wildlife kit that can be used at home, in classrooms, or with community groups such as the Boy Scouts or 4-H. Examples of available kits include *North American Predators* and *Marine Mammals of the World*. The kits include booklets, posters, projects, games, and ideas on various activities. Youth members also receive *Action Alerts* throughout the year (for example, *Elephant Ivory Bans; Save the Whales*) with information on specific problems and suggestions on what kids can do to help. The kits are $7 for nonmembers.

International Council for Bird Preservation
c/o WWF US, 1250 24th St., N.W., Washington, DC 20037
(202) 778-9563

ICBP is a nonprofit organization dedicated to conserving birds and their habitats and preventing the extinction of any species or subspecies. The council works to protect endangered birds all over the world and promote public awareness of their ecological importance. Through its network of scientists and conservationists, ICBP gathers and disseminates information, identifies and carries out high-priority projects, and advocates and implements conservation measures where they are most needed. Activities have included monitoring the status of susceptible bird populations, fostering international cooperation in bird preservation efforts, and addressing environmental issues that affect the welfare of birds, including acid rain, oil spills, chemical pollutants, forest clearing, wetland drainage, and pesticide use. ICBP also distributes numerous books, study reports, and publications, including two newsletters (the *Bulletin*, which highlights ICBP's conservation achievements in Latin America, and a quarterly newsletter, *World Birdwatch*, which keeps members up-to-date on a variety of bird issues). Membership ($35 and up) includes a subscription to *World Birdwatch*.

National Audubon Society
950 Third Ave., New York, NY 10022
(212) 832-3200

NAS is one of America's best-known grass-roots conservation organizations. Although the society was established to protest the cruel and thoughtless slaughter of birds, its goals have expanded to helping and protecting all wildlife, natural habitats, and the environment. NAS patrols eighty wildlife and natural areas around the country (ranging in size from 12 to 26,000 acres). The organization also monitors and works to influence legislation that affects wildlife and the environment. NAS conducts comprehensive scientific studies and works to educate its members and the general public through a variety of workshops, camps, trips, seminars, informative publications, videos, and other materials. With the regular $20 membership, you will receive a subscription to *Audubon* magazine, a bimonthly periodical filled with outstanding photos, commentaries, conservation news, and in-depth reports about various environmental issues. Contact NAS for more information on its programs, activities, and literature, and for the location of a chapter near you.

National Institute for Urban Wildlife
10921 Trotting Ridge Way, Columbia, MD 21044
(301) 596-3311

NIUW is a nonprofit educational and scientific organization dedicated to the conservation of wildlife in urban, suburban, and urbanizing areas. It is the only private national organization whose programs deal almost exclusively with fish and wildlife in the metropolitan environment. NIUW conducts extensive research on the relationship between humans and wildlife under urban conditions and distributes information on maintaining, enhancing, and controlling certain wildlife species in urban areas. As a result of NIUW's efforts, people in urban areas can enjoy and appreciate what animals and the environment have to offer. The institute distributes many publications, including *A Guide to Urban Wildlife Management; Feeding Birds in Winter; Butterflies in Your Garden; A Simple Backyard Pond;* and *Keeping the Wild in Wildlife*. With the regular membership fee of $25, you will receive a subscription to *Urban Wildlife News*, a ten percent discount on NIUW publications, invitations to NIUW activities and programs, and the hotline number for free advice and counsel from the staff of urban wildlife biologists.

National Wildlife Federation
1400 16th St., N.W., Washington, DC 20036
(202) 797-6800; Legislative hotline (24-hour recorded message): (202)-797-6655; Merchandise and membership information: 1-800-432-6564

A nonprofit organization, **NWF** works to preserve and better the environment and its inhabitants. NWF's organizational, educational, editorial, scientific, legal, legislative, and artistic skills have made it one of the world's largest and most influential conservation organizations. The federation has 5.8 million members and supporters and a network of fifty-one state and territorial affiliate organizations (all of whom need volunteers), enabling it to monitor local activities and act quickly and effectively when needed. The organization has an excellent catalog featuring bird feeders, books (such as *Kingdom of the Cats; Wonders of the Jungle; Endangered Animals*), posters, mugs, T-shirts, and periodicals, including the *Ranger Rick* magazine for kids. Contact NWF about internships, conservation summits, and its wildlife camps. The regular membership ($15) includes a subscription to NWF's award-winning *National Wildlife* magazine, a bimonthly publication full of outstanding wilderness photography and articles about animals, the environment, and natural sciences.

The Nature Conservancy
(see The Environment, page 268).

North American Wildlife Foundation
102 Wilmont Road, Suite 410, Deerfield, IL 60015
(708) 940-7776, FAX: (708) 970-3739

NAWF is a nonprofit organization dedicated to soil and water conservation, wetlands research, and waterfowl protection. The foundation works especially to correct the misconception that wetlands are wastelands. NAWF's research, particularly through its several research stations, highlights the importance of wetlands to the environment as one of the earth's most productive ecosystems, playing a critical role in the life cycle of waterfowl and a huge variety of plants and animals. Contact NAWF for more information.

Wildlife Information Center, Inc.
629 Green St., Allentown, PA 18102
(215) 434-1637

WIC is a nonprofit organization that disseminates information at the local, state, national, and international levels on wildlife conservation, research, and recreation (for example, information on whale watching, bird-watching, ecotourism, and photographing wildlife). The center sponsors wildlife conferences; presents expert testimony at public hearings; conducts public wildlife walks; and advocates nondestructive uses of wildlife, such as photographing, observing, and drawing and painting animals. Projects include securing a ban on the importation and sale of live wild birds as pets, and addressing issues such as acid rain, destruction of tropical forests and their wildlife, pesticide use, endangered species, and the impact of development on wildlife habitats. WIC distributes books, action alerts, bibliography sheets, and fact sheets in a variety of wildlife emergencies and issues (including *Lawn Care Chemicals; Tropical Forests; Balloon Releases;* and *Marine Wildlife*). Membership ($25 or more) includes a subscription to *Wildlife Activist* and other selected reports and newsletters.

Wildlife Preservation Trust International
34th St. and Girard Ave., Philadelphia, PA 19104
(215) 222-3636, FAX: (215) 222-2191

A nonprofit organization dedicated to the preservation of endangered species, **WPTI** rescues animals endangered in the wild and allows them to breed in the safety of captivity while studying their behavior, biology, and ecology. The organization also teaches young professionals in the animal field techniques of conservation and captive breeding, works to reintroduce animals to the wild where they belong, and endeavors to make the public aware of the urgent need to preserve wildlife and natural land. WPTI is especially concerned with the "rarest of the rare," those species so close to extinction that they may vanish in a few years or decades. Membership ($25, $15 for students and senior citizens) includes a subscription to the newsletter *On The Edge*, which comes out three times a year, and a variety of other benefits.

World Wildlife Fund and The Conservation Foundation
1250 24th St., N.W., Washington, DC 20037
(202) 293-4800, FAX: (202) 293-9211

The **WWT and TCF** is the largest nonprofit international conservation organization. The organization works to preserve the diversity and abundance of life on earth and the health of ecological systems by protecting natural areas and wild populations of plants and animals, including endangered species; by promoting sustainable approaches to the use of renewable natural resources; and by advocating for more efficient use of resources and energy and the maximum reduction of pollution. Over the past thirty years, WWF and TCF has sponsored more than 1,400 conservation projects in 100 countries and has been a leading force in rescuing endangered animals from extinction, establishing and protecting national parks and reserves, and sponsoring scientific investigations that spark protective actions. Regular membership ($15) includes the bimonthly newsletter *Focus*, which includes information on group activities and a variety of environmental and wildlife-related news, announcements of WWF and TCF events and presentations nationwide, and invitations to participate in the members' international travel program. The organization also produces a wide array of books, fact sheets, films, videos, reports, and educational kits. Of particular interest is the *WWF and TCF Letter*, which comes out six times a year and focuses on topics of current interest (the *Letter* costs $1.50 a copy). A catalog of publications and audiovisuals is available on request.

Xerxes Society
10 Southwest Ash St., Portland, OR 97204
(503) 222-2788

A nonprofit organization, the **Xerxes Society** promotes the global protection of invertebrates (especially butterflies) and their habitats, and works to increase general understanding of invertebrates' critical role in all biosystems. The society maintains a regularly updated networking and referral system; sponsors conservation projects; and distributes several full-color publications for scientists and the general public, including *Wings: Essays on Invertebrate Conservation*, a triannual magazine filled with spectacular photographs and articles on insects, butterflies, and other invertebrates, and *Butterfly Gardening: Creating Summer Magic in Your Garden*, a colorful book about insect-plant interactions and conservation aimed particularly at gardeners. The organization also sells butterfly greeting cards, sweatshirts, coloring books, T-shirts, and stickers. Membership ($25 for individuals, $15 for students and retired citizens) includes a subscription to *Wings*.

BLOOD AND ORGAN/ TISSUE DONATIONS

Blood Donations
Why Help Is Needed

In 1989 alone, the American Red Cross received more than 6.2 million pints of blood from volunteers. This blood went to thousands of hospitals and other facilities nationwide, saving the lives of patients who simply could not have survived without it. Unfortunately, 6.2 million pints is not enough. Blood is *always* needed. The American Red Cross reports that each minute, more than 36 pints of blood or blood products are used by patients all over the country, adding up to nearly 52,000 pints of blood a day.

Blood donations are absolutely essential because there is simply no artificial substitute for human blood. According to the American Red Cross, a single donation, after being separated into components, can help several patients. Whole blood helps patients suffering from massive bleeding; the protein in plasma helps hemophiliacs; platelets help individuals with leukemia and other forms of cancer; white blood cells are given to help patients, including newborns, fight severe infections; and red blood cells help treat anemia.

If you've never donated blood, or if you haven't done so in a while, consider taking a small amount of your time to make a donation. It's easy, it's safe, and it's a way to make a direct difference in someone's life.

What You Can Do

☞ **Set up an appointment at your local community blood center and make a donation.** To find the blood center near you, look up the *American Red Cross* (see page 13) in the phone book, or under "Community Blood Center" (it may be listed as simply "Blood Center") in the Yellow Pages.

☞ **Ask friends and family members to go with you when you donate.** This will encourage more donations, and going as a group can make the experience more enjoyable.

☞ **Encourage your school, religious congregation, or co-workers to sponsor a blood-donation drive.** The local Red Cross chapter can provide you with all of the posters and materials you'll need free of charge.

☞ **Volunteer at your local blood center.** Volunteers can help by answering phones, registering volunteer donors, driving donors who don't have transportation to the center, working at the canteen, and providing a variety of other services. (Opportunities may vary from center to center.)

Questions and Answers About Donating Blood

1. What are the requirements for becoming a donor?
According to the American Red Cross:

- You should be in good health.
- You must weigh more than 110 pounds.
- You must be seventeen years of age or older.
- You should not drink alcohol before you donate. This includes the night before the donation.
- You should eat a substantial breakfast or lunch before donating.

If you have any specific medical questions, ask the staff at the local community blood center before you make your appointment.

2. How long does it take to give blood?
The actual donating process takes only about ten minutes. The entire process—answering questions about your health, donating, and resting—generally takes about forty-five minutes (this may be longer if there's a wait).

3. Does it hurt?
Only for a second. Once the donating process starts, you won't really feel anything. Afterward your arm should feel fine, as long as you

don't bump the area from which the blood was drawn. A small number of people do get an upset stomach or experience faintness or dizziness, but these experiences are not common.

4. How long after I donate can I play sports or exercise?
It's best if you don't exert yourself too much for the rest of the day. So do your exercising before you donate or wait a day.

5. Is there any chance that I'll get AIDS by donating?
You cannot contract AIDS by donating blood. The equipment used in the donating process is sterile and is discarded after the blood is taken.

Organ/Tissue Donations

Why Help Is Needed

According to the United Network for Organ Sharing (UNOS)*, which maintains the only national patient waiting list in the U.S., the need for organ/tissue donors in America is greater than ever. Medical advancements have created a greater need for such donors as doctors, with increasing success, are giving life and sight to people who would have had little hope in the not-so-distant past. As of July 1990, approximately 20,000 people were on the UNOS waiting list for solid organ transplants. This number is increasing daily. The need for donors is great in other areas, too. According to the American Red Cross National Tissue Services, half a million people could have the quality of their lives improved with tissue transplants. As with blood donations, one person can, depending on the situation, provide organ and/or tissue donations for several individuals.

Volunteering to become a potential organ/tissue donor takes only a few seconds; you simply have to sign an organ/tissue donor card indicating your willingness to donate and carry the card with you. There is probably no other volunteer opportunity listed in this book that is so simple and yet can do so much good.

---

*For more information on organ donation, or for a free organ-donor card, write or call UNOS at *Dept. V, 1100 Boulders Parkway, Suite 500, P.O. Box 13770, Richmond, VA 23225*; 1-800-24-DONOR (243-6667).

What You Can Do

☞ **Talk with family members about becoming an organ donor, then sign a donor card and carry the card with you.** Almost all of the national organizations listed in this chapter can provide you with a donor card; you also can have "organ donor" indicated on your driver's license. It is very important that you discuss this arrangement with your family, because without the consent of the next of kin, you cannot donate.

☞ **Encourage others to become donors.** Most people don't acquire donor cards simply because they've never thought about it, or they have some misconceptions about it. Most of the national organizations listed in this chapter can provide you with materials to show your friends, family members, co-workers, or classmates. Let them know how easy and valuable it is (but don't push—some people just don't like the idea of becoming an organ or tissue donor, and that should be respected, too).

☞ **If you are deaf or hard of hearing, contact the National Temporal Bone Banks Program** (page 118) about becoming a temporal bone donor. Temporal bone donations are used for medical research dealing with hearing disabilities.

☞ **Consider becoming a bone marrow donor.** This is different from becoming an organ/tissue donor as the donation is made while you are alive. Becoming a bone marrow donor is a truly generous act, for although the actual procedure lasts only about forty-five minutes, donors are usually advised to stay in the hospital overnight (which is paid by the recipient or the recipient's insurance company). According to the **National Marrow Donor Program**, some donors experience discomfort for a day or two. Most donors, however, are back to their usual routine after a few days. For the estimated 16,000 children and adults stricken with fatal blood diseases each year, a bone marrow transplant may be their only hope. If you are interested in becoming a donor, contact the National Marrow Donor Program (page 117) for more information.

Questions and Answers About Becoming an Organ/Tissue Donor*

1. If I were to become a donor, would my family be billed for any costs or receive any payment related to the donation?
No. Donor families are never billed for expenses related to a donation, nor do they receive any payment.

2. Should my age or health condition influence my decision to sign a donor card?
No. While the age and health of the donor may affect the use of some organs and tissues, it often does not prevent the use of others.

3. If I am less than eighteen years old, can I sign a donor card?
Yes, but only with the consent of your parent or guardian.

4. If I become a donor, will I have a normal funeral?
Yes. Donation does not affect funeral arrangements whatsoever, nor does it affect the appearance of the donor.

5. Do organ, tissue, or eye donations conflict with religious beliefs?
No. Organ, tissue, and eye donations are consistent with beliefs and attitudes of major religions. If you have doubts, talk with a member of the clergy.

6. If I sign a donor card today, can I change my mind later?
Yes. Simply destroy your donor card and notify your next of kin that you have changed your mind.

7. Will the recipients be told who donated the organ(s), and will the families of donors be told who the recipient was?
No. All donations are made anonymously. Donor families and recipients can be given some general information about each other, if desired.

8. If I sign a donor card, does that mean that any organs or tissues may be donated?
The choice is up to you. You can indicate on a donor card if you'd

---

*Reprinted, with permission of the **National Kidney Foundation, Inc.** from the booklet "Organ Donor Program."

like to donate only specific organs or tissues or if you want to donate whatever is most needed. Assuming that they are in good shape, any organs or tissues may be used *if you so desire*.

National Organizations

American Red Cross National Tissue Services
4050 Lindell Boulevard, St. Louis, MO 63108
(314) 289-1155 or 1-800-2-TISSUE (284-7783)
FAX: (314) 531-FAXS (3297)

Although the **Red Cross** is best known for its blood donation program, the organization also runs an excellent tissue donation program. More than forty Red Cross tissue centers nationwide give tissues to thousands of recipients each year, enabling them to see, hear, walk, or live. The Red Cross can provide you with several pamphlets discussing the donating process and explaining the need for donors, and can also supply you with organ/tissue donor cards.

Eye Bank Association of America
1725 Eye St., N.W., Suite 308, Washington, DC 20006
(202) 775-4999

Since 1961, the nonprofit **Eye Bank Association** has helped more than 300,000 men, women, and children receive the gift of sight. If you are interested in becoming a potential donor, EBAA will send you information along with a donor card.

LifeBanc
1909 E. 101st St., Cleveland, OH 44106
(216) 791-LIFE (5433) or 1-800-558-LIFE (5433)

LifeBanc is a nonprofit donor organization that can provide you with several informative pamphlets (in English and Spanish) on becoming a potential tissue and/or organ donor. LifeBanc can also supply you with a donor card and a "Key to Life" key ring you can carry with you to indicate that you are a potential donor. The organization runs a toll-free hotline for anyone with questions about organ/tissue donations.

The Living Bank
P.O. Box 6725, Houston, TX 77625
(713) 528-2971 or 1-800-528-2971

A nonprofit organization, **TLB** maintains the largest computerized multi-organ and tissue donor registry in the world, serving all fifty states and sixty-three foreign countries. TLB provides donor forms with detailed information on becoming an organ and tissue donor, the donation process, and the need for additional donors. It also maintains a toll-free telephone line, staffed by personnel trained to answer questions on organ donation. For a small charge, TLB can provide you with medallions, key chains, decals, and other items that will identify you as a potential organ donor (donor cards are free).

The National Kidney Foundation, Inc.
30 East 33rd St., New York, NY 10016
(212) 889-2210 or 1-800-622-9010

NKF, a nonprofit organization, is the major national voluntary health agency dedicated to the prevention, treatment, and cure of kidney and urinary tract diseases. The foundation works to help millions of Americans who suffer from kidney diseases by providing donor and patient services, research, advocacy, professional education, and public information. If you are interested in becoming a potential kidney donor, NKF can provide you with a donor card, detailed information, and question-and-answer pamphlets on all aspects of becoming a donor.

National Marrow Donor Program
3433 Broadway St., N.E., Minneapolis, MN 55413
(612) 378-2044

NMDP is a nonprofit organization that maintains an international computerized data bank to match potential donors with patients desperately in need of bone marrow transplants. If you are interested in becoming a marrow donor, NMDP is the organization to contact. The organization can send you a list of donor centers around the nation and some comprehensive pamphlets on becoming a donor. NMDP also operates a toll-free hotline for people who have questions about marrow donations.

**National Temporal Bone Banks Program
of the Deafness Research Foundation**
Massachusetts Eye and Ear Infirmary
243 Charles St., Boston, MA 02114
(617) 573-3711

If you are hearing impaired and are interested in donating temporal bone for use in research, contact the **National Temporal Bone Banks Program**. This program, administered by the nonprofit **Deafness Research Foundation**, can provide you with information on becoming a potential temporal bone donor (and on the need for donors in the U.S.), including comprehensive pamphlets, a list of regional centers, and a medical form your doctor will need to fill out.

CHILDREN AND YOUNG ADULTS

Why Help Is Needed

There are only two lasting bequests we can hope to give our children. One of those is roots; the other, wings.

Hodding Carter*

Even a brief look at the state of America's young people reveals that too many of them are not only without wings, but their roots are embedded in abuse and poverty. Unfortunately, this is not an overstatement. A statistical snapshot of an average day in the United States demonstrates the severity of the problem.[1]

- Every 26 seconds, a child runs away from home.
- Every 47 seconds, a child is abused or neglected.
- Every 67 seconds, a baby is born to a teenage mother.
- Every 90 seconds, a baby is born suffering from exposure to cocaine.[2]
- Every 53 minutes, a child dies because of poverty.
- Every day, 3 children die from child abuse.
- Every day, 105 babies die before their first birthday.
- Every day, 130 young people attempt to kill themselves. Thirteen succeed.[3]
- Every day, 2,989 children see their parents divorce.
- Every day, at least 100,000 children are homeless.

One teenage suicide, one homeless child, one abused child is a tragedy. When these numbers reach the thousands, hundreds of thousands, even millions, it is a national crisis. The problem is as broad as it is deep. Young people of all races, socioeconomic backgrounds,

---

*State Department Press Secretary during the Carter Administration.
[1] Children's Defense Fund, "S.O.S. America! A Children's Defense Budget," 1990, 5–6.
[2] Senate Finance Committee, June 28, 1990.
[3] According to the American Association of Suicidology.

and religions are suffering. Rich kids run away from home just as poor kids do. Both white and minority children are abducted. Children are being abused in inner-city apartments as well as in suburban split-levels.

Many of these problems are getting worse. According to the Child Welfare League of America, the incidence of child abuse is up 80 percent and that of child sexual abuse, 277 percent since 1981. CWLA also estimates that fatalities from abuse are up 36 percent (from 1985 to 1988 alone). The Children's Defense Fund reports that the fastest-growing segment of the homeless population is families with children. CDF finds that children, who are by far the poorest Americans (they are almost twice as likely to be poor as adults), have grown even poorer in recent years. Today, one in five children (twelve million in all) lives in poverty, and if recent trends continue, by the end of this century, these rates will have risen to one in four.[4]

Nor are children the only victims; all of America suffers. Children who are illiterate are more likely to grow up to be illiterate. Children who are homeless are more likely to grow up to be homeless. Children who are abused are more likely to grow up and be abusers. So it goes with substance abuse, teenage pregnancy, crime, and an array of other problems. What is so terribly frustrating is that these same young people could have become the nation's scientists, writers, teachers, doctors, political leaders, and, of course, volunteers. The impact of these losses is doubly severe; the source of energy and talent needed to build a better future is instead contributing to the decay of today's foundations.

This vicious cycle, however, need not continue. The first major step in breaking the cycle is for people to realize that these problems are community problems and require community responses. Concerned individuals can fight for policies that support young people and help them excel, provide hospital "boarder babies" with a warm hug and someone to play with, offer counseling for at-risk youths, or assist young runaways on the street and in shelters. Foster parents are also desperately needed nationwide. According to the U.S. House Select Committee on Children, Youth, and Families, more than 300,000 young people are in out-of-home placement, and many of them are in need of good foster homes. Caring adults are also needed to adopt the tens of thousands of special-needs youngsters waiting to become part of a family.[5] Whether by reading stories to homeless

---

[4] Children's Defense Fund, 2, 4.
[5] Mary Cronin, Elizabeth Taylor, and James Wilwerth. "The Baby Chase," *Time*, October 9, 1989, page 86.

children in day-care centers or providing a home for a child with a disability, every person can make a contribution to better the welfare of the nation's young people.

It was once said, "Babies are such a nice way to start people." Just about anyone who has held a smiling infant knows how true this is. Babies, like all young people, embody the hope that their world will be, although not perfect, at least better than the one their parents knew. With the incredible abundance and opportunity this nation has to offer, this hope is still possible today for every young person. The future of our youth, however, will depend on the encouragement and support they are offered now. Given the confidence to risk, the courage to fail, and the resources to succeed, they will soar.

What You Can Do

☞ **Keep up on current issues concerning the welfare of children and young adults in the U.S., especially legislation that affects young people.** The more you know about the plight of millions of America's young people, especially those in the inner cities and in rural areas, the more you will know how to get involved and where help is needed most. Write to your government representative to express your concern or approval of pending legislation. (This is especially important because children cannot vote for the laws that will affect them.) The **Children's Defense Fund** (page 129) and the **Child Welfare League of America** (page 129) can provide you with the necessary information. These national organizations, along with others listed in this chapter, can also provide you with materials (such as posters, videos, and literature) to educate others on the need to help America's young people. (See also Voicing Your Opinion, page 363.)

☞ **Volunteer to help with "boarder babies" at a hospital near you.** These babies who actually live in hospitals because their parents have either died or abandoned them, are often victims of substance abuse or AIDS. Volunteers can help simply by holding and playing with the infants; often the babies do not receive much attention or personal care because the nursing staff is busy with countless other duties. Look under "Hospitals" in the Yellow Pages to find a children's hospital near you, and ask for the volunteer coordinator.

☞ **Sponsor a child through one of the groups listed in National Child Sponsorship Organizations,** page 140. Or consider having your office, school, religious congregation, or family sponsor a child. It's an excellent way to make a direct impact on a child's life, and through correspondence and notices, you'll be able to follow the child's progress.

☞ **Participate in programs and projects that work to bring comfort and cheer to children who are sick or homeless, or who have disabilities.** Some programs need volunteers to visit the children; others simply appreciate contributions of toys, books, and similar items. Here are a few organizations and activities to check out:

- **Good Bears of the World** is a nonprofit organization that delivers teddy bears to children of all ages as well as to elderly persons in hospitals, institutions, and other places nationwide. Although GBW does accept donations of new bears, the organization prefers that you purchase one of GBW's official teddy bears (prices start at $8.50). Write GBW for general information or for the GBW chapter near you (or for information on starting your own chapter), *2352 Valeway, Toledo, OH 43613*.
- **The Holiday Project** is a nonprofit organization of thousands of volunteers in more than 400 communities nationwide who visit people confined to hospitals, nursing homes, and other institutions during the Christmas and Chanukah seasons, and on other holidays throughout the year. Even if you aren't able to visit, you can still help by making or wrapping gifts and by donating goods and services (such as providing wrapping paper or driving volunteers). You can also help just by spreading the word; students can encourage their classmates to get involved and members can organize religious congregations. Write to or call The Holiday Project for general information, the location of a chapter near you, or information on starting a chapter, at *P.O. Box 6829, FDR Station, New York, NY 10150-1921*; (212) 532-0353.
- **Mail for Tots** is a nonprofit organization that keeps a mailing list of thousands of shut-in or seriously ill children who would like to receive letters or cards. For further information, send a self-addressed, stamped envelope to *25 New Chardon St., P.O. Box 8699, Boston, MA 02114*.
- **Donate a new, unwrapped toy** to the **TOYS FOR TOTS** program sponsored by the **United States Marine Corps Reserve.** The program collects toys for needy children at Christmas. (The toys are donated unwrapped so that they may be

categorized by age and gender for appropriate distribution.) Right after Thanksgiving, the USMCR will begin accepting donations, so watch for a drop-off point near you, or call the local office of the Marine Corps Reserve (see the U.S. government listings in the phone book).

• **Variety Clubs International** (page 138) has a wide array of volunteer opportunities for individuals interested in helping sick children and children with disabilities.

☞ **Volunteer at a nonprofit organization that helps children.** These organizations often need help with fundraising, editing newsletters, writing letters to government representatives, sending out notices to members, and similar activities. See if one of the national organizations listed here has a chapter in your community.

☞ **Help out at your local youth center or Boys & Girls Club** (page 128). These centers often need volunteers to counsel or act as mentors to young people, coach or help out with sporting and recreational events, work on crafts projects, decorate or help renovate facilities, provide administrative assistance, and offer a variety of other services. (Anyone, regardless of particular skills or time constraints, can volunteer.) Donations of games, toys, sports equipment, and other items are almost always needed, too. If you cannot find a Boys & Girls Club in your community, check the telephone book under "Youth Organizations & Centers" or a similar listing. Also see Community Resources and Organizations (page 6) and National Organizations (starting on page 13). Many of the organizations listed there sponsor youth centers or can direct you to one.

☞ **Volunteer to become a tutor, a mentor, or a Big Brother or Big Sister.** Many schools sponsor mentor programs (see Education and Illiteracy, page 218) for interested adults and other students. The **National Black Child Development Institute** (page 134) also has information on tutorial programs. Thousands of kids around the country need **Big Brothers** and **Big Sisters** (see page 127) with whom they can play sports, go to movies and museums, or simply talk. The time commitment to be a Big Brother or Big Sister is usually only a couple of hours a week, and it is an extremely rewarding way to get directly involved with a young person and make a significant difference in his or her life.

☞ **Volunteer to work at a day-care or child-care center in your community, particularly one that helps low-income children.**

Religious congregations, shelters for the homeless, **Head Start** programs (page 137), and **Family Service America** (page 15) all need volunteers for a variety of services. You can read stories to young children, help provide supervision, play games and make crafts, decorate or renovate centers, or simply help out with administrative work or financial support. You may find information on centers listed under "Child-Care Information" under "Community Service Numbers" in the phone book or under "Social Services" or "Human Services" (check the government pages).

☞ **Volunteer to work at a shelter for runaways.** Shelters usually need volunteers to help with food distribution, counseling, mentoring, and administrative and fundraising activities. Contributions of food, clothing, blankets, furniture, towels, hygiene supplies, books, games, and other items are also often needed. See **Covenant House** (page 130), **The National Network of Runaway and Youth Services** (page 136), the **National Runaway Switchboard** (page 136), and **Youth Development, Inc.** (page 139) for a wide array of volunteer opportunities. Also, check the "Community Service Numbers" in the phone book under "Emergency Assistance, Food, Clothing, and Shelter."

☞ **Volunteer at a Children's Home or residential center in your community.** These homes provide a variety of services and activities for children who are emotionally disturbed and/or who have been abused. Although services may vary from home to home, volunteers are usually needed to work with the children (for example, storytelling, arts and crafts activities, tutoring, recreational activities) or to help the home (for example, administrative assistance, fundraising, and recruitment of other volunteers). Check the phone book to see if there's a Children's Home near you. Also, you can contact the **American Association of Children's Residential Centers**, a national organization representing many of the residential centers in America, to see if there's a center near you. Contact AACRC at *440 First St., N.W., Suite 310, Washington, DC 20001*; (202) 638-1604.

☞ **Volunteer to work on a crisis hotline for children or young people in distress** (runaways or suicidal teens, for example). Look in the phone book under "Community Service Numbers," specifically under the headings "Survival" and "Crisis." (See also Suicide, page 353, and the runaway organizations mentioned above.)

☞ **Join a scouting organization or a similar group working**

CHILDREN AND YOUNG ADULTS 125

with young people. Organizations such as the **Boy Scouts** (page 127), **Girl Scouts** (page 132), **Camp Fire Boys and Girls** (page 128), and **National 4-H** (page 135) need volunteers to help with a variety of services, including outings, sports and recreational activities, fundraising, and administrative work.

☞ **If you are fifty-five or older, consider volunteering for The Family Friends Program run by The National Council on the Aging.** (See Disabilities, page 187 for more information.) This program matches older volunteers with children twelve or younger who are chronically ill or who have disabilities. Write or call NCOA for referrals to a program near you at *600 Maryland Ave., S.W., West Wing 100* (After June 1, 1991: *409 3rd St., S.W., 2nd floor*); *Washington, DC 20024*; (202) 479-1200.

☞ **If you are a doctor or have any medical experience, consider using your skills to help poor children and families in poverty-stricken areas.** The **International Child Health Foundation** (page 132), and **Project Concern International** (page 137) are two organizations that can help interested doctors, nurses, medical students, and other individuals work with those in need.

☞ **If you have any legal expertise, volunteer to work for a child advocacy organization.** The **National Court Appointed Special Advocate Association** (page 150) needs lawyers to help train CASA volunteers and provide other services. **The National Center for Youth Law** (page 135) and the **Youth Law Center** (page 140) also work with volunteers with legal expertise.

☞ **If you are an employer, make an effort to hire young people from low-income families.** Check the phone book (usually in the government pages) for the nearest "Employment/Unemployment" office. Also check the phone book under "Social Services" or "Human Services" for the "Youth Services Administration" or the "Juvenile Justice Department." You may want to contact a **Private Industry Council** (PIC) near you. Under the Job Training Partnership Act, PICs were established to provide training to economically disadvantaged youths and adults. Local PICs can help employers find workers who have skills in such areas as word processing, carpentry/rehabilitation, telephone installation, and accounting. If you cannot find a PIC in your community (check the white pages of the phone book), write or call the **National Association of Private Industry**

Councils at *1201 New York Ave., N.W., Suite 800, Washington, DC 20005*; (202) 289-2950.

National Organizations

The ASPIRA Association, Inc.
1112 16th St., N.W., Suite 340, Washington, DC 20036
(202) 835-3600

ASPIRA is the only national nonprofit organization devoted solely to serving Puerto Rican, Latino, and other disadvantaged youths through leadership development and education. ASPIRA takes its name from the Spanish verb *aspirar*, which means "to aspire to something greater." Motivated by the philosophy that at-risk youths can and should succeed, ASPIRA has focused on the positive for thirty years by developing the capacities of Latino youths to be leaders. The association's twelve offices are located in Florida, Illinois, New Jersey, New York, Pennsylvania, Puerto Rico, and the District of Columbia. Those offices network with over 2,000 community-based organizations, local and national policymakers, and corporate representatives. With a combined staff of 220 and over 900 volunteers, ASPIRA yearly serves more than 13,000 Aspirantes—those youths who seek a brighter future—through internship programs, career guidance programs, and high school clubs. Students and adults are encouraged to participate in ASPIRA's volunteer programs, which include mentoring, hospital work, food and clothing drives, blood drives, campaigns to help the homeless, and peer counseling.

Athletes and Entertainers for Kids
P.O. Box 191, Building B, Gardena, CA 90248
1-800-933-KIDS (5437)

AEFK is a nonprofit organization working to brighten the lives of children and teens through educational and community service programs, targeting the most urgent needs of today's youths. In less than three years, AEFK has worked with more than 100,000 young people, serving in schools, community groups, hospitals, social service agencies, and rehabilitation centers and homes. Activities include **The Ryan White National Program**, which works to educate the public about AIDS, especially about how it has affected children; and **Kareem's Kids**, which works to provide positive role models for at-risk youths, to provide basic needs for young children beginning school (school supplies, lunch tickets, and clothing), and to introduce youngsters to positive alternatives to gangs and other destructive activities. Other programs include **Back to School and Stay in School**, substance- and alcohol-abuse education and counseling, and remedial reading tutoring. (The athletes and entertainers often help with direct services, but they mostly work to bring much-needed publicity to the issues, as Elton John did with Ryan White and his program.) Call AEFK for information about volunteer opportunities (most, though not all, of which are in California).

Big Brothers/Big Sisters of America
230 N. 13th St., Philadelphia, PA 19107
(215) 567-7000

BB/BSA is a nonprofit organization with over 480 affiliated agencies nationwide providing one-on-one friendships between caring adults and children in need of stability and companionship. Big Brothers and Big Sisters serve as mentors and role models to at-risk school-aged children, most of whom live with a single parent. Each volunteer makes a commitment of four to six hours a week for a minimum of one year. Being a Big Brother or Big Sister isn't hard work; it involves taking trips to the zoo, tossing a football, going fishing, or just sitting on a park bench listening to what's going on in a child's life and giving advice when asked. Tremendous care goes into the recruitment, screening, and matching process so that the relationship is beneficial for both individuals, and trained staff members are always available to help and give support. Some 40,000 children are on the organization's waiting list, and minority volunteers are especially needed. Even if you would prefer not to become a Big Brother or Big Sister, you can still help out in many ways, so contact your local chapter of BB/BSA to see how you can get involved.

Boy Scouts of America
1325 Walnut Hill Lane, P.O. Box 152079, Irving, TX 75015
(214) 580-2000

A nonprofit organization, **BSA** provides educational programs for boys, ages seven to twenty, to build character, provide training in the responsibilities of citizenship, and develop physical fitness. The group works to instill in its members a high degree of self-reliance and resourcefulness and the desire to help others. BSA, in fact, represents one of our nation's greatest sources of energy, commitment, and altruism; among many other activities, Boy Scouts work to fight hunger, save the environment, provide clothes for those in need, and encourage blood and organ donations. Approximately 1.2 million men and women serve as adult BSA volunteers, making BSA one of the largest volunteer organizations in the U.S. These men and women serve as unit leaders, chairpersons of troop committees, and scouting coordinators. Regardless of your skills, interests, or time constraints, your help is needed, so contact the BSA in your area for more information.

Boys & Girls Clubs of America
771 First Ave., New York, NY 10017
(212) 351-5900

BGCA is a nonprofit organization of 600 local clubs providing more than 1.4 million young people, ages six to eighteen with support services, new opportunities for personal growth and achievement. Essentially, BGCA works to make a positive impact on young lives by building self-esteem and encouraging the development of values and skills during critical periods of childhood. It is the only major national youth agency whose primary mission is to provide services to boys and girls from disadvantaged circumstances. BGCA is truly an oasis in many metropolitan areas. All local clubs are professionally staffed and offer daily programs in youth employment promotion, citizenship and leadership development, alcohol- and drug-abuse prevention, outdoor and social recreation, and health care. Volunteers are needed to help with these and many other programs. No matter what your skills or time constraints may be, your local club needs your help.

Camp Fire Boys and Girls
4601 Madison Ave., Kansas City, MO 64112
(816) 756-1950

Through a program of informal education, **Camp Fire** provides opportunities for young people to realize their potential and to become responsible, caring, self-directed individuals. Camp Fire also works to improve those conditions in society that adversely affect youth. Each year the nonprofit organization serves more than 500,000 young people across the U.S.; members include boys and girls from infancy to age twenty-one. Camp Fire reaches young people through its clubs, camping programs, self-reliance courses, and child-care activities. The members of Camp Fire do not, however, simply receive various services. They are active in running food programs; working to prevent crime, teen suicide, drug abuse, and teen pregnancy; and providing support to peers and younger children. Camp Fire needs volunteers to help keep these activities and services going. Just a few hours a month, working from your home or out in the community, would help Camp Fire a great deal, so contact your local chapter for more information. Camp Fire also has an extensive catalog of books, clothing, and other products.

Child Welfare League of America
440 First St., N.W., Suite 310, Washington, DC 20001
(202) 638-2952, FAX: (202) 638-4004

The oldest and largest voluntary membership organization in North America, **CWLA** is devoted entirely to protecting and promoting the well-being of troubled children. CWLA develops internationally recognized child-welfare standards and legislative initiatives that guide policies on issues such as adoption, child care, child abuse and neglect, foster care, and child protective services. CWLA has a catalog of first-rate posters and publications (for example, *Lost and Found— The Adoption Experience; Children and AIDS: The Challenge for Child Welfare; Foster Parenting Young Children; Homeless Children and Their Families: A Preliminary Study;* and *Child Abuse*). The **Center for Program Excellence** provides management consulting to public and private organizations that work with children and families in the U.S. and Canada. CWLA also sponsors a child advocacy network—the **Children's Campaign**—concerned with changing laws to benefit children. Contact CWLA for information on membership fees and its newsletters (*Children's Voice; Children's Campaign News; Children's Monitor; Washington Social Legislation Bulletin;* and *Child Welfare Journal*).

Children's Defense Fund
122 C St., (After July 1: 25 E St.) N.W., Washington, DC 20001
(202) 628-8787

CDF is a nonprofit organization dedicated to providing a strong and effective voice for America's youth, with particular emphasis on the needs of poor and minority children and children with disabilities. Its goal is to educate the nation about the needs of children and to encourage preventive measures before children get sick, drop out of school, get into trouble, or suffer a family breakdown. If you want information on the plight of children (as well as on other social problems in America), CDF is a valuable resource. The organization addresses such issues as health and child care, child welfare and family supports, adolescent pregnancy prevention, youth employment, and homelessness. CDF confronts these issues through public education, research and policy analysis, training and technical assistance, coalition building, and legislative efforts. CDF has an extensive catalog of informative materials, including clearinghouse reports (for example, *Preventing Children Having Children; Teens and AIDS: Opportunities for Prevention;* and *Tackling the Youth Unemployment Problem*), books (such as *Vanishing Dreams: The Growing Economic Plight of America's Young Families* and *Families in Peril: An Agenda for Social Change*), posters (for example, *Dear Lord Be Good to Me, The Sea Is So Wide and My Boat Is So Small;* and *Education Costs Less Than Ignorance*), and videos (such as *When I Dream*, a thirteen-minute tape that examines the nation's teen pregnancy problem), as well as calendars and T-shirts. CDF also publishes *CDF Reports* ($29.95 for a one-year subscription), a monthly newsletter presenting a wide array of news items, in-depth features, legislative information, and more.

Children's Rights of America, Inc.
12551 Indian Rocks Road, Suite 9, Largo, FL 34644
(813) 593-0090

A nonprofit child-advocacy and youth-services organization, **CRA** works to collect and disseminate accurate statistics on missing and abused or exploited children. It also advocates for better care of runaways and teens in crisis, educates the public concerning the prevention of kidnapping and physical and sexual abuse of children, and pushes for stiffer penalties for those who abuse children. CRA offers a multitude of services for incidents involving missing children, including case-by-case location assistance, support counseling, and a twenty-four-hour emergency hotline *(1-800-874-1111)* for parents and law-enforcement (and other) agencies working with missing or abused children. The organization also offers youth outreach services, helping runaways, child prostitutes, and homeless or abandoned youths. It sponsors a twenty-four-hour **National Youth Crisis Hotline** *(1-800-442-HOPE [4673])* for troubled youths who are suicidal, drug- or alcohol-dependent, depressed, abused, or abandoned. Contact CRA for more information on its services and on how to become a volunteer.

Covenant House
460 W. 41st St., New York, NY, 10036
1-800-999-9999

CHILDREN AND YOUNG ADULTS   131

Covenant House and its corps of dedicated volunteers provide food, clothing, shelter, medical attention, vocational training, counseling, and compassion to tens of thousands of kids every year who have no place to go for help. Every young person seeking help receives it quickly and with no questions asked. Covenant House also provides long-term care. Through its **Rights of Passage** program, the group helps young people get jobs, offers educational services to help them graduate from high school or college; provides mentors who act as role models, advisers, and confidants; provides child care for young women who are trying to get jobs; and offers a host of other services. One of its main services is **Nineline**, a toll-free, twenty-four-hour hotline that anyone can call, including runaways, parents of runaways, and children and teens complaining of child abuse or neglect at home. Nineline has received millions of calls since it first began in the fall of 1987. There are Covenant House facilities nationwide, all of which need volunteers for a variety of services (opportunities may vary from facility to facility), including working on the Nineline, working as a mentor or tutorial assistant, employing a runaway, or working in the child-care department. Covenant House also has a long-term volunteer program (**Faith Community**) for people who are willing to spend thirteen months working in shelters and other facilities. Contact the national headquarters for more information.

Family Friends Program
The National Council on the Aging, Inc.
(see Disabilities, page 187)

The Fresh Air Fund
1040 Avenue of the Americas
New York, NY 10018
(212) 221-0900
(To host children): 1-800-367-0003

A nonprofit organization, **The Fresh Air Fund** has provided free summer vacations to more than 1.6 million disadvantaged New York City children since 1877. Each year, more than 10,000 children ages six to sixteen attend Fresh Air Fund camps and visit host families who live in rural and suburban communities in thirteen northeastern states and Canada. Children stay with their host families for two weeks; for their first vacation. Youngsters invited back may spend the entire summer in the country. There are no financial requirements for hosting a child—most volunteers simply want to share their homes with someone less fortunate. The Fund also has a program for placing children with special physical or emotional needs. Call for more information if you're interested in getting involved. To see if there's a similar program near you, contact the local office of the **United Way** (page 7) or the local **Volunteer Clearinghouse** (page 6). These programs do not exist in every state, but there are others in the U.S.)

Girl Scouts of the United States of America
830 Third Ave. and 51st St., New York, NY 10022
(212) 940-7500

GSUSA is a not-for-profit organization providing girls ages five through seventeen with opportunities to develop their potential, make friends, and become a vital part of their community. With more than 3.1 million members, the Girl Scouts program is the largest voluntary organization for girls in the world. Its 750,000 adult members work as troop leaders, consultants, and board members—going camping, providing after-school care, assisting with fundraising, and organizing the annual cookie sales campaign. No matter what your skills or interests may be or how much time you have to offer, the local Girl Scouts council needs your help.

International Child Health Foundation
P.O. Box 1205, Columbia, MD 21044
(301) 596-4514

ICHF is a nonprofit organization dedicated to saving the lives of desperately poor children all over the world. Through its corps of volunteers the foundation provides oral rehydration therapy (ORT), an inexpensive mixture of grain cereal, salt, and water which keeps babies and toddlers from becoming dehydrated and dying. In addition to educating families on administering ORT, ICHF offers emergency relief and services, conducts clinical research, and sponsors training programs for inner-city mothers, focusing on disease prevention and management. Volunteer opportunities (periodic, regular, and long-term) are always available. A one-year subscription to *The International Child Health Foundation Newsletter*, which covers ICHF activities and related information, costs $20.

Joint Action in Community Services, Inc.
5225 Wisconsin Ave., N.W., Suite 404, Washington, DC 20015
(202) 537-0996

JACS is a nonprofit volunteer organization whose major responsibilities are to the Department of Labor's Job Corps program. Job Corps was created in 1965 as one of the first major government efforts directed to address the problem of hard-core, unemployable youth. Job Corps enrollees are generally ninth-grade dropouts whose reading and math skills are at a sixth-grade level. Instead of allowing these disadvantaged young people to slip into poverty and hopelessness, Job Corps takes them from their communities and puts them in residential training centers around the country to receive intensive and individualized vocational, educational, and social-skills training to prepare them for permanent employment. Annually, JACS works to organize personalized community support nationwide (including Alaska, Hawaii, and Puerto Rico) for 40,000 young people, ages sixteen to twenty-one, returning from Job Corps. JACS volunteers do this by helping former Job Corps students find a place to live, giving advice on money problems, helping with transportation during job hunting, finding community agencies to help with personal and family problems, and offering a variety of other services depending on the needs of the student. JACS also provides on-center counseling for students enrolled in training. If you are interested in helping out a former Job Corps student in your community, contact JACS for more information.

Making the Grade
National Assembly of National Voluntary Health and Social Welfare Associations
1319 F. St., N.W., Suite 601, Washington, DC 20004
(202) 347-2080, FAX: (202) 393-4517

The **National Assembly** (a coalition of major national social-service organizations, most of which are listed in this book) sponsors the **Making the Grade** project, which is designed to raise public awareness of the problems facing America's youth and stimulate collaboration to address these issues. If you are a parent, educator, policymaker, clergy member, or other concerned individual, Making the Grade can help you assess the current local network of youth services, identify unmet needs, establish local priorities, and develop a collaborative action plan for addressing and solving these problems. The project provides technical assistance, training, written materials (including *Issue and Option* papers, which focus on six problem areas—functional illiteracy, juvenile crime, school dropout rate, substance abuse, teenage pregnancy, and youth unemployment) for local communities to use in town meetings, and follow-up activities to publicize and support the implementation of community action plans. Contact the National Assembly for more information.

March of Dimes Birth Defects Foundation
(see Disabilities, page 188)

National Association for the Advancement of Colored People
Youth and College Division
4805 Mt. Hope Drive, Baltimore, MD 21215
(301) 358-8900

The **Youth and College Division** of the **NAACP**, the nation's oldest, largest, and most powerful civil-rights organization, is a coalition of 600 local units and 50,000 members working to promote and provide assistance to Black and other minority youth. Although local units have different agendas and programs, many of them provide remedial academic programs to high school students, conduct Scholastic Aptitude Test (SAT) counseling sessions, hold food drives to help out needy families, and run a **Resumé Retrieval Project**, which seeks to identify talented minority youths and transmit their names directly to a growing list of participating businesses. Through its education programs, the NAACP works to nurture and reward academic achievement among high school students, particularly through the **Academic, Cultural, Technological and Scientific Olympics (ACT-SO)**. The NAACP also has a **Back to School/Stay in School** program, which monitors and rewards regular attendance and fosters academic improvement through an after-school program of remediation and counseling. Volunteers of all ages and races are welcome to help out with most of the NAACP programs. Membership costs $10 ($5 for people twenty-one or younger) and includes a one-year subscription to *Crisis* magazine, which comes out ten times a year and addresses a variety of civil-rights issues and NAACP activities.

National Black Child Development Institute
1463 Rhode Island Ave., N.W., Washington, DC 20005
(202) 387-1281
For volunteer opportunities: (202) 673-7700

A nonprofit organization, **NBCDI** is dedicated to improving the quality of life for Black youth on the national and local levels. The institute focuses on issues and services that fall within four major areas: health, child welfare, education, and child care. NBCDI has an affiliate network that provides direct services to Black children and youth, such as tutorial programs, help for homeless children looking for adoptive families, and cultural heritage programs. It also monitors public policy issues that affect Black children and works to educate the public by sponsoring annual conferences and other forums. The organization publishes periodic reports and two quarterly newsletters, *Black Child Advocate*, which offers legislative and policy updates, and *Child Health Talk*, which addresses a variety of issues related to children's health. Membership ($20 for individuals, $10 for students) includes discounts on these publications. NBCDI is a valuable resource for anyone who is concerned about the welfare of Black children and young adults in America, and who would like to do something to help out.

The National Center for Youth Law
114 Sansome St., Suite 900, San Francisco, CA 94104-3820
(415) 543-3307, FAX: (415) 956-9024

A nonprofit organization devoted to improving the lives of underprivileged youth in the United States, the **National Center for Youth Law** provides specialized assistance to attorneys and others who work on behalf of poor children. NCYL helps through consultations, training programs, and dissemination of publications, including *Youth Law News*, a journal published six times a year that addresses problems affecting poor children and possible legal solutions. Attorneys, paralegals, and others with legal or secretarial skills can help by volunteering for NCYL projects nationwide. Write to or call NCYL to see if there's a project near you.

National Court Appointed Special Advocate Association
(see page 150)

National 4-H Council
7100 Connecticut Ave., Chevy Chase, MD 20815
(301) 961-2800, FAX: (301) 961-2895

The **National 4-H Council** is a not-for-profit organization that uses private resources to enhance and expand the 4-H program. 4-H is the development program of the Extension Service of the U.S. Department of Agriculture and the state land grant university system. More than five million boys and girls ages nine to nineteen and nearly 650,000 volunteer leaders participate in the program. These 4-H'ers are active in a host of self-esteem-building programs in such areas as community service, science and technology, and natural resources. 4-H sponsors environmental conservation, drug-abuse prevention, youth safety, and peer support programs. The organization helps young people acquire knowledge, develop life skills, and form attitudes that will enable them to become self-directed, productive, and contributing members of society. For information on how you can become involved, contact the county Cooperative Extension office listed in the government pages of the phone book. (If you cannot find it, call the National 4-H Council.)

The National Network of Runaway and Youth Services
1400 I St., N.W., Suite 330, Washington, DC 20005
(202) 682-4114, FAX: (202) 289-1933

The National Network of Runaway and Youth Services is a nonprofit organization whose members provide support for at-risk youths and their families to help them lead safe, healthy, and productive lives. The network represents more than 900 community-based organizations offering such programs as **Safe Choices**, a comprehensive AIDS/HIV prevention-education project providing materials, training, and technical assistance to youth-serving agencies; **Youth-to-Youth**, a substance-abuse peer-counseling program; and a resource clearinghouse of information on the latest issues and legislation concerning youths and families. The National Network also publishes *Network News*, a quarterly newsletter that highlights National Network activities, services, and member accomplishments, and the *Policy Reporter*, a quarterly newsletter containing legislative information and a variety of news items pertaining to youth services. Individual membership ($50) includes a one-year subscription to the two newsletters, program updates, and other benefits. (Organization membership is also available; contact the national office for more information.)

National Runaway Switchboard
3080 N. Lincoln Ave., Chicago, IL 60657
(318) 880-9860
Hotline: 1-800-621-4000

Although based in Chicago, **NRS** provides confidential, nonjudgmental, crisis-intervention services for at-risk, runaway, and homeless youths calling from anywhere in the nation. The toll-free hotline is open twenty-four-hours a day, seven days a week. NRS can also refer callers to agencies across the country which deliver a wide array of services. (NRS's computerized database contains more than 7,000 agency resources nationwide.) Chicago residents can volunteer to work on the hotline.

Project Concern International
3550 Afton Road, San Diego, CA 92138
(619) 279-9690
Mailing address: P.O. Box 85323, San Diego, CA 92138

PCI is a nonprofit organization dedicated to improving the health of individuals, particularly children, worldwide. The international association trains volunteer health workers, provides disease-prevention assistance (including immunization and information, on proper nutrition, sanitation, and hygiene), and sponsors various other treatments and services for poor families and children. (PCI not only assists poor people with basic health care and related education, it encourages them to participate in the process of their own development.) Through its **OPTIONS/SERVICE** and **CHAP** programs, the organization recruits medical professionals to work in communities where services are desperately needed. PCI distributes a quarterly publication, *Options Newsletter*, which lists positions available for medical and development personnel around the world ($10 for a one-year subscription). Each year, PCI sponsors the **WALK FOR MANKIND** walkathon in which tens of thousands of volunteers of all ages participate to raise money to help underprivileged persons worldwide.

Project Head Start
U.S. Department of Health and Human Services
Administration for Children, Youth and Families
330 C St., S.W., Washington, DC 20201
(202) 245-0560

Head Start is a federally funded comprehensive child-development program that helps children ages three to five from low-income families gain self-confidence and provides the necessary nutritional and educational tools to help them perform at their best when they enter school. At least ten percent of enrollment nationwide is set aside for children with disabilities. There are four major components to the program: (1) education—providing children with a variety of learning experiences and encouraging them to express their feelings and learn to work with others; (2) health—helping children meet daily nutritional needs and providing basic physical and mental health examinations; (3) parent involvement—encouraging parents to participate in classes and workshops on child development (many parents also work as volunteers in the program); and (4) social services—helping families help themselves in a variety of ways (from identifying community resources and employment opportunities to offering emergency assistance and crisis intervention). Volunteers, including high school students, are an important part of the program, assisting with indoor and outdoor play, games, storytelling, field trips, parent education and support, and renovation or decoration of Head Start centers. Community organizations and businesses can help by donating classroom space, educational materials, eyeglasses, special equipment for children with disabilities, and medical and dental examinations. For further information on the program or for the location of a program near you, contact the national office. **Volunteer Clearinghouses** (page 6) and **Community Action Agencies** (page 7) often have information on Head Start programs.

Sick Kids (need) Involved People
(see Disabilities, page 192)

Variety Clubs International
1560 Broadway, Suite 1209, New York, NY 10036
(212) 704-9872

Variety Clubs is a nonprofit organization established to aid underprivileged children and children with disabilities. The group sponsors schools, camps, playgrounds, day-care centers, rehabilitation facilities, development centers, hospitals, clinics, and countless other institutions across the country working to ease the pain and better the lot of children of all ages. VCI sponsors several fundraising events, toy campaigns (bringing millions of toys to youngsters worldwide), and the **Sunshine Coach Program**, which transports shut-in children (children confined to their homes or hospital rooms) to picnics, sporting events, and other outings. Volunteers are always appreciated, so if you're interested in getting involved, look up the Variety Club in your community or contact the national headquarters for information on volunteer opportunities near you.

Women in Community Service, Inc.
1900 N. Beauregard St., Suite 14, Alexandria, VA 22311
(703) 671-0500

WICS is an independent, not-for-profit coalition of five major national groups (American GI Forum Women, Church Women United, National Council of Catholic Women, National Council of Jewish Women, and National Council of Negro Women), providing assistance, counseling, and guidance to over a quarter of a million young people during and after their education and training in the Job Corps. Although the coalition's particular focus is helping young women from the Job Corps program, it welcomes both male and female volunteers as mentors, speakers, and trainers. WICS has referred more than 100,000 youth to the Job Corps for education and training. Contact the national headquarters for information on a WICS program near you.

Young Men's Christian Association of the United States of America
(see Doing Good in America, page 21)

Young Women's Christian Association of the United States of America
(see Doing Good in America, page 21)

Youth Development, Inc.
P.O. Box 178408, San Diego, CA 92177-8408
(619) 292-5683
National Youth Crisis Hotline: 1-800-HIT-HOME (448-4663)

A nonprofit organization, **YDI** provides counseling, leadership, and recreational activities for kids in need. Among its activities, YDI offers food, shelter, and transportation to runaways and abandoned children; maintains a crisis hotline (staffed by volunteers); organizes trips taking kids into the wilderness (under the guidance of volunteer outdoorspeople); provides peer support (through volunteer teens); coordinates holiday programs providing kids with food, shelter, small gifts, and compassion; and makes referrals for kids who abuse alcohol or drugs. Volunteers of all ages can help in numerous ways, so write or call and ask for the *YDI Journal*, which lists many of these activities. YDI is an outstanding organization and resource for anyone interested in helping children and young adults.

Youth Law Center
114 Sansome St., Suite 950, San Francisco, CA 94104-3820
(415) 543-3379

YLC is a nonprofit organization established to preserve and protect the rights, health, and lives of children at risk. Programs focus on the problems of low-income children, especially those who are incarcerated or placed outside their families. YLC's hope is to intervene on behalf of children and youth at critical junctures in their lives to improve treatment and conditions to which they are subject, and thereby positively affect their futures. More specifically, YLC works to bring about positive changes in conditions and treatment of poor children in various forms of custody; advocates for legislative and other reforms affecting the legal rights of children and youth; provides specialized information, advice, and other support in youth law matters to parents and children in need, public officials, legal services organizations, private attorneys, social workers, and others working on behalf of children; and writes and widely distributes definitive articles and papers on the legal rights of children (for example, *Making Reasonable Efforts: Steps for Keeping Families Together*, and *Understanding the Foster Care System*). Attorneys and other individuals with legal expertise are welcome to offer their assistance to YLC. Write or call for more information.

National Child Sponsorship Organizations

Children, Inc.
P.O. Box 5381, 1000 Westover Road, Richmond, VA 23220
(804) 359-4562 or 1-800-538-5381

A nonprofit organization, **CI** helps people sponsor children living in poverty-stricken areas. Sponsorships help provide a child with clothing, education, medical care, and other general needs. If you sponsor a child, you'll receive the child's name, address, picture, and history. You can correspond with your child if you wish, and visits can even be arranged. The cost per child ($21 a month) is payable monthly, quarterly, semiannually, or annually. Contact CI for more information and for the newsletter *C.I. NEWS*, which features CI activities and profiles of children who have benefited from the program.

Christian Children's Fund, Inc.
Box 26511, Richmond, VA 23285
1-800-776-6767

CCF is a nonprofit, nonsectarian child-care organization that was established in 1938 to assist orphaned and abandoned children who were victims of the Sino-Japanese war. Today, CCF assists over 510,000 children in twenty-three countries, including the U.S. Assistance is extended to children whose parents have little means of providing even basic needs. These children are given food, clothing, and medical and educational aid, with an emphasis placed on teaching them how to help themselves. Help is extended to their families with the same emphasis, through the teaching of improved agricultural techniques and through the offering of adult literacy classes. This assistance is made possible by sponsors, each of whom sends $21 a month per child. Sponsorship allows a person-to-person relationship, as the sponsor can correspond with his or her child. Besides the sponsorship program, CCF provides assistance to communities by digging wells, establishing sanitary facilities, improving schools, and addressing other community needs.

Feed the Children
P.O. Box 36, Oklahoma City, OK 73101-0036
(405) 942-0228, FAX: (405) 948-8941

An international, nonprofit Christian organization, **Feed the Children** provides food, clothing, medical equipment, and other necessities to people in areas struck by famine, drought, flood, war, or similar calamities. Much of FTC's support comes through food, clothing, and medical supplies donated by corporations and individuals. FTC operates its own fleet of trucks to pick up and transport these emergency supplies. The supplies are sent to countries on five continents, as well as throughout the United States. FTC also coordinates a child-sponsorship program. Through monthly $20 donations, FTC child sponsors help provide for a child's daily physical, spiritual, and educational needs. Sponsors receive a personal history and photo of their child, as well as occasional progress reports from the field.

Futures For Children
805 Tijeras, N.W., Albuquerque, NM 87102
(505) 247-4700 or 1-800-545-6843

FFC is a nonprofit organization that helps American Indian children through sponsorship programs. A monthly donation of $25 provides the financial assistance necessary to help keep an American Indian child in school. Through correspondence with the child, a sponsor can offer emotional support and encouragement that may prove to be more valuable than the monetary donation. FFC also coordinates annual tours, providing each sponsor with the opportunity to meet the child and see the reservation on which he or she lives. Some people also send small gifts on holidays and birthdays. This is an excellent opportunity to learn more about American Indian culture and to make a tremendous difference in the life of a child. Contact FFC and ask for a brochure on this and other programs.

>   **Save the Children**
>   54 Wilton Road, Westport, CT 06880
>   (203) 226-7271 or 1-800-243-5075

A nonprofit organization, **Save the Children** operates in thirty-eight countries, including the U.S., offering training, technical assistance, tools, and humanitarian relief during times of crisis. Save the Children was the first international organization to develop child sponsorship as a method of bringing about lasting improvements in the lives of children and their communities. For $20 a month, sponsors receive a picture, background information, and the opportunity to correspond with their child. Also, the **Save the Children Craft Shop** sells hundreds of beautiful handmade crafts and gifts that support Save the Children and the craftsmakers themselves (see Money Matters, page 28, for a listing of available merchandise). Call *1-800-833-3154* for a free catalog, or write for more information. (If you live in or are visiting Westport, Connecticut, stop by and see the retail store.) Volunteer opportunities are available through Save the Children, so contact the national headquarters for more information.

Adoption
(of Special-Needs Children and Youth)

What You Can Do

☞ **Consider adopting a special-needs child (or children).** Adopting a special-needs child is certainly a great—and rewarding—act of generosity. It is also a serious commitment. If you're interested, contact one of the organizations listed in this section for more information. Some of the national organizations maintain files with photos and descriptions of children and young people who need adoptive families. You can also look under "Adoption" in the phone book, usually under "Community Service Numbers," or in the "Social Services" or "Human Services" section of the government listings.

☞ **If you have friends or relatives who want to adopt, encourage them to consider adopting special-needs children.** Give them a list of the following national organizations. Some people simply don't consider adopting special-needs children until someone reminds them of the need and benefits of doing so.

National Organizations

Adoptive Families of America
3333 Highway 100, Minneapolis, MN 55422
(612) 535-4829

AFA is the largest nonprofit organization in America serving adoptive and prospective adoptive families. AFA can provide you with extensive information on all aspects of adoption and referrals to over 180 adoption and cultural parenting resources. It also maintains a comprehensive support network (including a twenty-four-hour hotline) for families in crisis or for families who simply need information. AFA's *Adoptive Families of America: Adoption Information and Resources* guide, available free of charge, lists hundreds of adoption agencies and adoptive support groups around the country, and tips on finding the right adoption agency. The bimonthly magazine *OURS* features articles on raising adopted children, education, and general adoption issues, parenting resources, and photos of adoptable children. A one-year membership ($24) includes a subscription to *OURS*.

THE CAP BOOK, Inc.
The National Photo Listing of Children Waiting for Adoptive Parents
700 Exchange St., Rochester, NY 14608
(716) 232-5110

THE CAP BOOK is a professionally published, two-volume book (updated every two weeks) containing photographs and biographies of hundreds of hard-to-place children around the U.S. The children, who are of all races and backgrounds, are presently in the foster-care system and are waiting for permanent homes. A one-year subscription to *THE CAP BOOK* (which includes the two volumes and the updates) costs $75. The organization also publishes a free newsletter, *Adoption Link*, which addresses a variety of adoption issues and presents profiles of children waiting to be adopted.

Child Welfare League of America
(see page 129)

National Adoption Center
1218 Chestnut St., 2nd Floor, Philadelphia, PA 19107
(215) 925-0200, (outside PA); 1-800-TO-ADOPT (862-3678)

NAC is a private nonprofit organization that matches children, especially those with special needs, with adoptive families throughout the U.S. Since its formation in 1972, NAC and its affiliate, the **Adoption Center of Delaware Valley**, has found families for 4,000 children. You can also contact, through NAC, **Black Families/Black Children**, a program that works to place some of the 13,000 Black children in this country who are waiting to be adopted. NAC works to increase public awareness of and education about adoption, maintains a comprehensive library of print, video, and audiovisual aids, and provides a database of waiting children and prospective families. It also maintains an electronic mail service and bulletin board to keep members up-to-date on adoption practices, trends, and legislation. NAC is a valuable resource for anyone interested in adopting a child or in adoption issues in the U.S.

National Black Child Development Institute
(see page 134)

National Committee For Adoption
1930 17th St., N.W., Washington, DC 20009
(202) 328-1200

NCFA is a nonprofit support organization that serves as an advocate and resource center for all people touched by or interested in adoption, including adoptees, adoptive parents, and birth parents. The committee creates and supports ethical, nonprofit adoption practices offering quality adoption, maternity, and counseling services; preserves sound adoption practices that protect confidentiality; and works with the media to show that adoption is a loving, natural way to form happy families and to educate the public and professionals about current adoption issues. NCFA is one of the largest sources of materials on adoption issues, with such books as *Successful Adop-*

CHILDREN AND YOUNG ADULTS 145

tion: A Guide to Finding a Child and Raising a Family; A Parent's Guide to Intercountry Adoption; Transracial Adoption: A Point of Reflection?; Why Was I Adopted?; So You're Adopted; and *Adopting the Older Child.* NCFA also has numerous informative brochures, posters, legislative papers and updates, the *Directory of Resources,* (which contains more than 500 listings of maternity and adoption agencies across the country) and the *Adoption Factbook* (which contains comprehensive information on current statistics, regulations, resources, and other important issues).

North American Council on Adoptable Children
1821 University Ave., Suite N498, St. Paul, MN 55104
(612) 644-3036

NACAC is a nonprofit coalition of adoptive-parent support and citizen groups, caring individuals, and agencies. The council is renowned for its commitment to children with special needs who are waiting for adoptive families. The organization maintains a network of adoptive parent support groups. It also publishes *Adoptalk*, a quarterly newsletter that addresses virtually all adoption issues, including legislation, new resources, and interviews and profiles of children in need of parents. The newsletter is an excellent resource for anyone interested in adoption, foster care, parenting, and child advocacy. *Adoptalk* comes with the basic one-year membership fee of $25.

Child Abuse and Neglect

What You Can Do

☞ **Educate your friends, family members, and co-workers about the extent of child abuse in the U.S.** Make them more aware of the problem. Put up hotline numbers, posters, and other informative materials so that abused children and adult abusers in need will know where to go for help. Check the national organizations in this section for materials.

☞ **If you have children, make sure they know how to protect themselves against child abusers.** (See the National Crime Prevention Council's tips on page 162). Unfortunately, child abuse happens every day to boys and girls of all races, religions, and economic backgrounds across America. Many of the national organizations listed in this section can provide you with comprehensive information that will help you talk with your children.

☞ **Since an abused child may be too frightened or confused to talk with someone, know the signs of abuse.** The **National Crime Prevention Council** (page 171) has several informative brochures on child abuse, including *It Shouldn't Hurt to Be a Kid* and *How to Protect Children*. Also check the national organizations in this section for information.

☞ **If a child tells you that he or she has been abused, provide support and encouragement.** Children do make up stories, but according to the **National Crime Prevention Council**, they rarely lie about being victims of abuse. If a child tells you about an assault, take it seriously. How you respond will influence how the child will recover from the abuse. A child often fears that he or she is responsible for the incident. Approach the situation calmly, speaking in a reassuring tone, and find out as much as you can about what happened. (Your greatest challenge may be holding in your own horror about the abuse.) Report the problem *immediately* to the local social-services agency or the police department.

☞ **Volunteer to work on a crisis hotline that helps parents suffering from stress.** This will require a good deal of training, but it is a needed service, and it may keep an adult from lashing out at a child. Check the phone book for "Community Service Numbers," specifically under the headings "Survival" and "Crisis." **Childhelp U.S.A., Inc.** (page 148) also has information on hotlines across the country.

☞ **Support a nonprofit agency working to stop child abuse.** These organizations often need help with administrative work (for example, answering phones, editing newsletters, sending out notices), fundraising, and other services. Check the national organizations listed in this section to see if one is located near you or has an affiliate in your community. (**Childhelp U.S.A., Inc.**, page 148, and the **National Council on Child Abuse & Family Violence**, page 149, are two excellent resources.)

☞ **Volunteer to work at a child-care center that helps abused children.** Volunteers are almost always needed to provide these children with some stability and love. Check the phone book under "Community Service Numbers" for the "Child & Family Services Division" (if it's not listed there, you should find it in the government pages under "Social Services" or "Human Services"). **Childhelp U.S.A., Inc.** (page 148), and the **National Council on Child**

Abuse & Family Violence, (page 149), may also be able to provide you with the necessary referrals. Also, see page 124 for information on children's homes and residential centers that provide treatment and care for children who are emotionally disturbed and/or who have been abused.

☞ **Become a Court-Appointed Special Advocate.** (See **The National Court Appointed Special Advocates Association**, page 150 for more information.) These volunteers often represent the only caring voice for a child in a court of law. You don't need to be a lawyer or even to be entirely knowledgeable about the judicial system; CASA volunteers come from all walks of life, and they represent a variety of professional, educational, and ethnic backgrounds. If your community does not have a CASA program, you can help start one.

National Organizations

American Association for Protecting Children
The American Humane Association
63 Inverness Drive East, Englewood, CO 80112
(303) 792-9900 or 1-800-227-5242

The **AAPC** is the child welfare division of the **AHA**, a nonprofit organization that works to improve the quality of children's and animal's lives. AAPC disseminates books, pamphlets, and educational materials; researches and compiles statistics on child abuse and neglect; monitors legislation; provides expert testimony and advocates for the welfare of children on a national level; and offers training, seminars, and professional assistance in almost every area of child protection. AAPC also publishes *Protecting Children*, a quarterly professional journal which presents a variety of issues related to child protection. An individual membership ($35) includes a one-year subscription to the journal, discounts on publications, and other benefits.

C. Henry Kempe National Center for the Prevention and Treatment of Child Abuse and Neglect
1205 Oneida St., Denver, CO 80220
(303) 321-3963

The **Kempe Center** is a nonprofit organization committed to improving the recognition, treatment, and prevention of all forms of child abuse and neglect. The center develops and operates several programs for the benefit of abused or neglected children, many of which have been successfully replicated throughout the U.S. (including the **Crisis Nursery**, which provides respite care for stressed parents and children at risk, and the **Home Visitor Program**, through which trained laypersons offer support to new parents). It also conducts research and disseminates information on abuse and neglect, in the form of slides and audiovisual materials (for example, *The Breaking Point, A Case of Neglect; Child Abuse: Causes, Consequences, Solutions*) and books (such as *Child Abuse and Neglect: The Family and the Community; Consequences of Child Abuse;* and *Death from Child Abuse . . . And No One Heard*), for community groups, educators, parenting groups, foster parents, and concerned individuals. If you live in the Denver area, the Kempe Center can direct you to several different volunteer opportunities.

Childhelp U.S.A., Inc.
6463 Independence Ave., Woodland Hills, CA 91370
(818) 347-7280
Toll-free National Child Abuse Hotline: 1-800-4-A-CHILD
(1-800-422-4453)

Childhelp is the largest private nonprofit organization in the U.S. dedicated to the research, prevention, and treatment of child abuse and neglect. The group sponsors several programs and services that work to combat child abuse, including a toll-free hotline staffed by professional counselors who handle calls from victims, abusers, and distraught parents; an aggressive public-education campaign, including a national distribution of brochures, posters, and other educational materials through schools, hospitals, and pediatricians' offices, and public service announcements for television, radio, and print; a residential treatment center in California that provides multidisciplinary services for severely emotionally disturbed abused children ages two to twelve; a **Specialized Foster Parent** program; and research to determine the causes of abuse and both the short- and long-term effects. Childhelp is an excellent resource for anyone concerned about child abuse and ready to do something about it.

National Assault Prevention Center
Child Assault Prevention
(see Crime and Victim Assistance, page 169)

National Center for Child Abuse and Neglect
P.O. Box 1182, Washington, DC 20013
(703) 821-2086

NCCAN is responsible for the federal government's activities related to child abuse and neglect. The center coordinates federal efforts to prevent abductions; conducts research; and provides assistance to states, professionals, and local governments developing policies concerning the identification, prevention, and treatment of child abuse. The center also runs the **Clearinghouse on Child Abuse and Neglect and Family Violence Information**, which maintains a database of documents, audiovisual materials, service programs, and ongoing research projects concerning child abuse and neglect. The clearinghouse can provide you with such publications as *Family Violence: Intervention Strategies; Executive Summary: Study of National Incidence and Prevalence of Child Abuse and Neglect;* and *Child Abuse and Neglect: A Shared Community Concern*, which addresses the extent of the problem, discusses how child abuse can be defined, recognized, and reported, and lists state and national organizations concerned with child abuse.

National Committee for Prevention of Child Abuse
332 S. Michigan Ave., Suite 1600, Chicago, IL 60604-4357
(312) 663-3520, FAX: (312) 939-8962

A nonprofit volunteer-based organization, **NCPCA** is dedicated to involving all concerned citizens in the prevention of child-abuse. NCPCA is working to make the public fully aware of the problem of child abuse and how to prevent it; to have important child-abuse-preventive services available to all parents and children; to improve public and private sector policies; and to create a more complete body of child-abuse-prevention knowledge. The organization has chapters in all fifty states and the District of Columbia primarily engaged in public education and awareness, community-based prevention services, advocacy, research, and evaluation. NCPCA offers a free catalog of its publications—informative booklets, pamphlets, and brochures on the subject of child abuse and ways to solve it, parenting tips, and volunteer ideas—and other materials for parents, social workers, educators, and concerned individuals.

National Council on Child Abuse & Family Violence
1155 Connecticut Ave., N.W., Suite 300
Washington, DC 20036
1-800-222-2000

The **National Council on Child Abuse & Family Violence** is a nonprofit private-sector initiative established to end the abuse of children, spouses, and the elderly. The council works to strengthen community prevention and treatment programs through national advocacy, volunteer recruitment and training, professional accreditation and placement, and technical assistance. It publishes *INFORUM*, a free quarterly journal with information on child abuse and family violence and updates on activities and programs across the field. The council also provides referral information to individuals seeking help, professionals seeking information about child abuse and family violence, and volunteers interested in helping agencies working to stop family violence or provide support for those who have been abused (foster-care agencies, shelters for battered women, child-abuse agencies).

The National Court Appointed Special Advocate Association
2722 Eastlake Ave. East, Suite 220, Seattle, WA 98102
(206) 328-8588

The association is a nonprofit membership organization that coordinates **CASA** programs nationwide. Local programs, which are now in most states, recruit and train volunteers to serve as Court-Appointed Special Advocates for abused and neglected children who are in foster care. CASAs are trained to speak for children in court dependency hearings. No special experience is required. Once accepted, volunteers receive approximately fifteen hours of training. Volunteers are taught about courtroom procedure, the social service and juvenile court systems, and the special needs of children who have been abused and neglected. CASAs assist judges and often work with social workers and lawyers. They are responsible for reviewing records and interviewing parents, teachers, neighbors, and the child. Volunteers often appear in court and make recommendations on behalf of the child to whom they are assigned. CASA volunteers are desperately needed because many of the cases are lost in an overburdened child welfare system that cannot pay close attention to each child. Contact the national headquarters if you cannot find a program in your community (or if you would like to start one). Individuals with legal expertise are also needed to train volunteers and provide other services.

Foster Care

What You Can Do

☞ **Volunteer to help your local foster-care agency.** (Check the phone book under "Social Services" or "Human Services.") Among other services, volunteers can assist social workers with basic administrative tasks; work with young people in out-of-home placement; or serve as case aides, visiting a foster child's home and school to gather as much information on the child as possible. In some cases, volunteers can also appear with the child in court. (For more information on this, contact the **National Court Appointed Special Advocate Association**, page 150.) Volunteer opportunities vary significantly from state to state, so contact your local agency to see how you can help.

☞ **Consider becoming a foster parent.** Although this is very different from adopting a special-needs child, it is similar in that foster parents provide one of the most generous and needed services in this country. Look in the phone book under "Community Service Numbers" for "Foster Care." If you don't find a listing there, check the government pages under "Social Services" or "Human Services."

☞ **If you have friends or relatives interested in becoming parents, encourage them to consider foster parenting.** The national organizations listed in this section have excellent publications and materials for interested individuals.

National Organizations

American Foster Care Resources, Inc.
P.O. Box 271, King George, VA 22485
(703) 775-7410

AFCR is a nonprofit organization dedicated to the research, development, and production of informational and educational resources for and about foster care. AFCR provides resource materials for foster parents, foster children, and placement agency staff. AFCR works to increase awareness of available resources; creates and maintains resource networks; and addresses identified knowledge and service gaps. The organization distributes a newsletter, *Foster Care Journal* ($11.50), which is published nine times a year and presents up-to-date information, research, theory, and practical suggestions. It also publishes the quarterly journal *LawNotes*, which offers the layperson news and views regarding the impact of legal issues on foster care and services. If you are interested in becoming a foster parent or if you already are one, AFCR has an outstanding selection of materials and publications (ACFR is *not* a referral or foster-care agency).

Foster Grandparent Program
(see Doing Good in America, page 10)

National Foster Parent Association
Information and Services Office
226 Kilts Drive, Houston, TX 77024
(713) 467-1850

NFPA is a nonprofit organization of foster parents, local and state foster parent associations, agencies, organizations, and other child advocates. The association seeks to improve foster-care services; informs the general public of issues and information related to the well-being of all children, particularly foster children; awards several scholarships, and publishes a variety of materials on foster care. Its bimonthly publication, *The National Advocate*, features notices on NFPA activities and a broad spectrum of information on foster care. Membership ($25) includes a one-year subscription to the newsletter.

Missing Children

What You Can Do

☞ **Keep up on information and legislation pertaining to missing children.** The more people know about how serious the missing-child problem is in America, the more, one hopes, they will be inclined to get involved. Most of the national organizations listed in this section can provide you with up-to-date statistics and information on legislation that works to protect children. (See also Voicing Your Opinion, page 363).

☞ **If you have children, teach them to protect themselves from strangers.** According to **Missing Children . . . Help Center**, every year in America 2 million children are kidnapped or run away; 5,000 of them are murdered and 2,000 are never identified. Make sure that your child isn't one of them. Remember, precautions that may seem obvious to adults are not always obvious to children, who tend to be more trusting and open with strangers. The national organizations listed in this section should have all the information you'll need to educate your children on how to protect themselves. Also, see page 162 for general safety tips children should know.

☞ **Be sure to have current photographs (and videotapes, if**

CHILDREN AND YOUNG ADULTS 153

possible), as well as fingerprints of your children. All of these measures can help authorities working to find missing children. Contact the local police station or sheriff's office for more information (there are some specific things you need to know).

☞ **Help put up posters and distribute pictures of missing children.** Public places such as libraries, supermarkets, synagogues, churches, and schools are good spots. Most of the organizations listed in this section can provide you with missing-child posters. The more people know about missing children, the better the chances are that these children will be found.

☞ **Volunteer at a missing-child organization.** Helping out with administrative work and related services allows the organization to focus better on finding children. Volunteers are always needed to answer phones, mail out pictures of missing children, and help with other administrative tasks. Check with the national organizations listed in this section to see if they have a volunteer opportunity for you. If there isn't an organization near you, call the **National Center for Missing and Exploited Children**'s Toll-free Crisis and Information Hotline (page 156) for a referral.

☞ **Become active in helping to find missing children.** The more people available to look for missing children when searches are conducted, the better the chances are that the children will be found. Most of the national organizations in this section can help you get involved.

☞ **Work to make your community safer for all children.** See the suggestions for making your community safer on page 164.

National Organizations

Adam Walsh Child Resource Center
319 Clematis St., Suite 404, West Palm Beach, FL 33401
(407) 833-9080

A nonprofit organization, the **Adam Walsh Child Resource Center** is dedicated to making America safer for children. Programs are aimed at preventing the abduction and molestation of children and effecting positive changes in systems that serve youth. The center is a powerful legislative force and a primary source of information for people who want to know how to better protect their own children and to bring about positive changes for all children. The organization can send you materials on programs, plus information on the ten model child-protection statutes it believes should be enacted in every state. It also publishes *Adam's Song*, a newsletter with information on relevant legislation, the center's activities, tips for parents and other adults, and pictures of missing children. Contact the center for child-safety tips, legislative information, or volunteer opportunities.

Child Find of America, Inc.
7 Innis Ave., P.O. Box 277, New Paltz, NY 12561-9277
(914) 255-1848, FAX: (914) 255-5706

CFA is a nonprofit organization established to locate missing children and to prevent child abduction. The group conducts investigations and provides mediation for children who have been criminally abducted by parents. Its prevention program consists of a mediation forum for parents in custody conflicts, two videos for children *(Be Smart—Stay Safe* and *The Safety Game)* and safety tips. Hundreds of local groups and individuals from forty-eight states, the District of Columbia, and foreign countries have used the prevention materials. CFA does not charge for its services and has searched for and located children in all fifty states and in six countries. Contact CFA for information on nationwide volunteer opportunities (for example, putting up posters, talking at schools about child safety, and fundraising).

Child Keyppers' International, Inc.
P.O. Box 6456, Lake Worth, FL 33466
(407) 586-6695, FAX: (407) 585-4372

A nonprofit organization staffed and funded by people who care about children, **Child Keyppers'** works to maintain children's safety and to provide assistance and protection for children in need. Its name indicates the goals of the organization: being the "key" to service (s) for children in protection (p), prevention (p), education (e) and recovery, rescue, and records (r). Child Keyppers' believes it is possible to reduce the number of kidnapped, abducted, and missing children through education and good record keeping. Protection of runaways and children who are abandoned, pushed out, or exploited is possible through prevention programs, education, crisis homes (where parents who are under stress and feel that they are on the verge of harming their child can leave the child, temporarily), and speedy recovery systems. Prevention of death from physical abuse is possible through an early-warning tracking system, and conviction of offenders can be increased through record matching. Child Keyppers' also works for the safe care and protection of children with special needs and for the treatment of children who are born addicted to drugs or alcohol. Child Keyppers' is staffed completely by volunteers; no one is paid for the services he or she provides. Contact the national headquarters if you are interested in volunteer opportunities (for example, supporting families who have lost children, putting up posters, educating children), drug prevention and safety programs (for children ages three to seven), information on the **Bite Identification System** (a database of children's bite marks), or a free copy of the *Missing Child Directory*.

Children's Rights of America, Inc.
(see page 130)

Find The Children
11811 W. Olympic Boulevard, Los Angeles, CA 90064
(213) 477-6721

FTC is a nonprofit organization that provides resources for parents, children, and agencies involved in the prevention of child abduction and the recovery of missing children. The organization's objectives are to locate missing children, to educate parents on child safety, to enlighten the media and the public on the problem of missing children, and to support legislation providing position action to ensure the safety of every child in America. FTC provides technical assistance and referrals to attorneys, private investigators, and counselors, and distributes child-safety materials and photos of missing children. The organization also distributes the *FTC Directory*, which lists hundreds of missing children.

Missing Children . . . Help Center
410 Ware Boulevard, Suite 400, Tampa, FL 33619
(813) 623-KIDS (5437)
National hotline: 1-800-USA-KIDS (872-5437)

A nonprofit organization, **MCHC** works to find missing children, to prevent the loss of children, and to help families of missing youngsters. The center helps parents determine proper courses of action and provides individual photo distribution with the assistance of 450 newspapers, magazines, TV stations, and truck trade publications. Its **Multiple Poster Publication** is mailed to truck stops, schools, hospitals, and many other locations around the country. MCHC also has several prevention, education, and litigation programs and can provide safety tips for parents and children.

National Center for Missing and Exploited Children
2101 Wilson Boulevard, Suite 550, Arlington, VA 22201
(703) 235-3900
Toll-free Crisis and Information Hotline: 1-800-843-5678
TDD: 1-800-826-7653

NCMEC is a nonprofit organization established to assist parents searching for missing children and to help law-enforcement and other professionals handle the difficult cases involving missing children or child sexual exploitation. The center offers books and brochures (such as *Child Pornography and Prostitution;* and *Youth at Risk*) and acts as a national center of communication, maintaining a toll-free hotline for people to report cases of sexually exploited or missing children or sightings or to request any of NCMEC's publications. NCMEC also coordinates the necessary persons, in both the public and private sector, to help facilitate the finding of children and the prevention of exploitation.

Vanished Children's Alliance
1407 Parkmoor Ave., Suite 200, San Jose, CA 95126
(408) 971-4VCA (4822), FAX: (408) 971-8516
National Sighting Line: 1-800-VANISHED (826-4743)

VCA is a nonprofit organization dedicated to the prevention and recovery of missing children, including parental abductions, stranger abductions, and runaways. The alliance believes that every missing child is a potentially endangered child and must be found quickly and safely. VCA offers prevention-education materials and presentations, provides support and technical information for searching families and law-enforcement agencies, registers missing children, and assists in locating them. It also maintains a list of reputable and knowledgeable private investigators, attorneys, and therapists. Prevention literature and posters of missing children are available upon request.

CRIME and VICTIM ASSISTANCE

Why Help Is Needed

Anyone who has had a knife flashed in his or her face, been chased by a stranger, or walked into a house that has been ransacked by a burglar knows the impact a crime can have on a person. Too many Americans, unfortunately, know this feeling. According to the Bureau of Justice Statistics' Criminal Victimization Survey, 19.7 million people—approximately one out of every thirteen Americans—were victims of a personal crime in 1989 alone. Almost six million of these offenses were violent crimes (murders, rapes, and simple and aggravated assaults). The Bureau of Justice Statistics also estimates that if crime continues at its current rate, eighty-three percent of children now twelve years old will become victims of actual or attempted violence at some point in their lives.[1] And these statistics are only for personal crimes. The Criminal Victimization Survey reports that 16.1 million property crimes, which include burglaries, household thefts, and motor vehicle thefts, were committed in 1989. All in all, this adds up to 35.8 million criminal acts in one year in this country.

These statistics, however, do not reflect the depth of the problem and its consequences. Statistics cannot express what it feels like to have one's house invaded or to lose a valued possession. They cannot impart the brutality of rape or the lifelong emotional scars it can leave. Nor does a crime have just one victim. If an elderly man is beaten to death, or a young mother is killed by a drunk driver, it is devastating for the victim's family and friends. And, in a much broader sense, crime affects every American. The simple threat of crime keeps children out of certain playgrounds or parks, and even makes adults think twice about traveling in certain areas alone at night. The National Crime Prevention Council estimates that every

---

[1]Ted Gest with Pamela Ellis-Simons, "Victims of Crime," *U.S. News & World Report*, July 31, 1989, 16.

year businesses lose approximately thirty billion dollars to crime from shoplifting, employee thefts, burglaries, and robberies. What is more, according to the Bureau of Justice Statistics, the nation's justice system (federal, state, and local expenditures on civil and criminal justice) costs over sixty-one billion dollars in taxes.[2]

A number like 35.8 million appears to loom invincibly over America. This could not be further from the truth. Individual action has proven to be a swift and effective force against all crime. Concerned citizens, working with their neighbors and local police, have forced drug dealers out of their communities, prevented burglaries by watching one anothers' homes and streets, and provided security and assistance to those more vulnerable to attack, including children, elderly persons, and individuals with disabilities. These community crime fighters demonstrate a courage, power, and determination that would impress any police force. Concerned citizens may not stop all of the crimes in this country, but even one less rape, one less murder, or one less break-in is worth it.

What You Can Do

☞ **Keep up on crime issues in your community and across the nation.** The more you know about crime, the more you will know about what needs to be done. Also, if you are knowledgeable you will be better able to encourage your friends and neighbors to get involved with crime prevention if you can explain how serious the problem is. Many of the national organizations in this chapter have statistics on different crime issues; the **National Institute of Justice** (page 173) is an especially good source of information. To get a better perspective on crime in your community, talk with the local police or sheriff's department. You may also want to consider riding with a police officer or sheriff in his or her precinct. Many law-enforcement offices provide this opportunity.

☞ **If you witness or are aware of a crime or know the whereabouts of a criminal, contact the police department or sheriff's office immediately.** This may sound obvious, but the **National Crime Prevention Council** estimates that only about half of all crimes are ever reported. Even an anonymous tip is better than no call at all. For major crimes (such as arson and drug smuggling)

[2]1988 Statistics.

CRIME AND VICTIM ASSISTANCE 159

you can make an anonymous call to **WeTIP** (page 175) at *1-800-73-CRIME (732-7463)*, and in California *1-800-78-CRIME (782-7463)*. WeTIP informants are eligible for large monetary rewards.

☞ **If you are a witness or are the victim of discrimination on the basis of race, religion, sexual preference, or national origin,** contact the **Justice Department's Community Relations Service (CRS)** hotline at *1-800-347-HATE (4283)*. Hotline operators will pass the information on to the appropriate authorities. The CRS hotline collects statistics regarding discrimination and in some instances, provides conciliation and mediation services for disputes. For more information on discrimination and hate-motivated crimes, see **The National Gay & Lesbian Task Force** (page 172) and the **National Institute Against Prejudice and Violence** (page 172).

☞ **If you know someone who is a recent victim of a crime, offer to help out in any way possible.** If the person needs to go to court, offer to drive, stay with the person for a while if he or she lives alone, or babysit the person's children if he or she needs to go to the doctor, court, police station, etc. Encourage the person to go to a victims' center. These centers not only offer emotional support for people who have experienced traumatic crimes, they help victims understand their rights, victim compensation laws, and how to follow a case's progress. One of the best ways a friend can help is to offer support and assurance. Victims sometimes feel guilty, as if they did not do enough to prevent the crime. Remind them that it's not their fault. The only person responsible for a crime is a criminal.

☞ **Volunteer at a victim's organization or crisis hotline in your community.** Shelters for battered women, centers for abused children, and other victim's organizations need volunteers for a variety of services, ranging from simple administrative work to counseling and support. Check the phone book for "Community Service Numbers," particularly under "Emergency Assistance, Food and Shelter," for shelters for battered women and under "Survival Numbers" for hotline numbers. Call the **National Domestic Violence Hotline** at *1-800-333-7233* for information on shelters for battered women nationwide. You can also contact the **National Coalition Against Sexual Assault** (page 170), the **National Organization for Victim Assistance** (page 174), the **National Victim Center** (page 174), or the **National Woman Abuse and Prevention Project** (page 175) for referrals to community victims' organizations. The national organizations listed in the Children and Young Adults chapter have information on centers and agencies for abused children.

☞ **Offer to help at your local police station or sheriff's office.** Many police stations and sheriff's offices need volunteers to help with administrative and other duties; this frees law-enforcement officers to do other police work. Some departments even have police-trained citizen forces, which have some of the same duties, authority, and responsibilities as the regular force.

☞ **Volunteer to become a Court-Appointed Special Advocate.** (See **The National Court Appointed Special Advocate Association**, page 150.) These volunteers often represent the only caring voice for an abused child in a court of law. You don't need to be a lawyer or even to be entirely knowledgeable about the judicial system; CASA volunteers represent a variety of professional, educational, and ethnic backgrounds. If your community does not have a CASA program, consider starting one. The national headquarters can provide you with the necessary information.

☞ **If you are a law student, lawyer, or paralegal,** give your time to a legal services organization in your community that works to protect the rights of elderly persons, persons with limited incomes, and other individuals who many need legal advice. These organizations are usually listed in the phone book under "Community Service Numbers," specifically under "Legal Services." You can also check the Yellow Pages under "Legal Services" or "Legal Clinics." (See also Children and Young Adults, page 125, for volunteer opportunities for people with legal expertise).

☞ **Volunteer at your local prison to help inmates with their rehabilitation.** Volunteers can help illiterate inmates learn to read, offer counseling, and provide a variety of other services. Many inmates will stand a better chance of contributing to the welfare of society if they are encouraged to succeed and have the resources to do so. The **Salvation Army** (page 18), your local **Volunteer Clearinghouse** (page 6), and **Volunteers of America** (page 20) may have opportunities for interested volunteers.

You can also contact the **Prison Fellowship**, a nonprofit Christian outreach organization that works with prisoners, ex-prisoners, victims, and their families. Prison Fellowship has over 33,000 volunteers who assist with prison evangelism and visitation; prerelease counseling and support (for example, helping inmates set goals and plan their futures); pen-pal correspondences; family assistance (for example, assisting with marriage seminars, providing gifts for children of inmates); and volunteer recruitment and training. Prison Fellowship has fifty-five field offices, managing programs in 632 of the 939 state and federal prisons in the U.S. For more information, write or call *P.O. Box 17500, Washington, DC 20041-0500*; (703) 478-0100.

☞ **If you are a college or university student, help make your campus safer for everyone.** Most colleges have campus escort services that need volunteers to walk with people to their dorms, the library, and other locations. If your school does not have an escort program, consider starting one. Talk with school security for more information. If areas of the campus are poorly lit, talk with the administration about putting in streetlights. Be sure your school doesn't wait until a serious crime has been committed to make safety an issue.

☞ **Work to prevent a crime from happening in your home.** Don't wait until you've been a victim to make your home a safer place. Here are a few suggestions to consider (as adapted, with permission, from information provided by the **National Crime Prevention Council**, page 171):

- **Have the police conduct a free "crime check" of your house** to see if there are any simple changes you can make and to offer some prevention tips.
- **Be sure that important phone numbers (police department, fire department, parents at work, family friend, or trusted neighbor) are clearly written by every telephone in the house,** especially if you have children who may be home alone. A few seconds can make all the difference if there is an emergency.
- **If you've just moved into a house or if you lose your keys, have the locks changed** (and never put an address or name on a key).
- **Don't hide keys near the house, for instance, in mailboxes and planters or under doormats.** Instead, give a duplicate set to a trusted neighbor.
- **Be sure that your windows and doors are sturdy and that they are locked when you are out or asleep.** Almost half of all burglars enter homes through unlocked doors and windows. For more information, see the National Crime Prevention Council's free pamphlet *How to Secure Windows and Doors.*

- **Install a peephole or wide-angle viewer in the front door.**
- **Keep drapes, blinds, and shades drawn at night.**
- **Be sure appliances, televisions, radios, bikes, and other valuable items are marked for identification purposes.** Many local police stations can lend you special pens to engrave a number (your social security number or driver's license number and state are recommended) on valuable items. A burglar will be less inclined to steal identified items (they are harder to sell), and if the items are found, the police can check the numbers against their files and return the items to you. You can also buy an engraving pen at a hardware store for about $20, but be sure to give the ID number you use to the police department and get an "Operation Identification" sticker to put on your window or door to deter burglars.
- **Cut back tree limbs and shrubbery that hide doors, windows, or provide access to second-story windows.**
- **Be sure porches, entrances, and yards are well lit.**
- **Put timers on lights, TVs, and radios when you go on vacation.**
- **Think about installing an alarm system in your house.** Most burglars, not surprisingly, look for houses without them. Choosing the right system is critical to protecting your home and family. Test the alarm regularly.
- **If you suspect that there is a burglar in the house, don't investigate**—call the police.
- **If you wake up and find that someone is in your bedroom looking through your belongings, pretend you are asleep until the intruder has left and then call the police.** It's not worth losing your life over your property.
- **If you see a broken window or an open door when you come home, don't go in.** Go to the nearest available phone and call the police.

☞ **If you have children, teach them about protecting themselves.** What may seem obvious to adults is not always obvious to children, who are often more trusting of strangers. Here are some precautions to teach your children (adapted, with permission, from information provided by the **National Crime Prevention Council**):

- **Never accept rides, candy, money, or anything else from a stranger.** Someone may try to tell you that he or she knows your parents, is an old friend, or is doing your parents a favor

CRIME AND VICTIM ASSISTANCE 163

(such as by picking you up after school), so make sure that you say no to *anyone* you don't know. It's not worth the chance.
- **Never get close to a car if a stranger calls out to you for directions or anything else.** It is easy for a stranger to pull you into the car.
- **Never give your name or address to a stranger.**
- **Never open the door to someone you don't know.**
- **Never tell callers you're home alone.** Say Mom or Dad can't come to the phone, and take a message.
- **Never volunteer family vacation plans, or give other information about your home.**
- **If a stranger in a car bothers you, turn and run in the opposite direction.** It's not easy for a car to change directions suddenly.
- **When frightened, run to the nearest person you can find**—a police officer, a person working in a yard, or a neighborhood house or store. While you should stay away from strangers who approach you, it's okay to ask an adult you don't know for help.
- **If a stranger tries to follow you on foot or tries to grab you, run away, scream, and make lots of noise.**
- **Never play in deserted areas such as woods, parking lots, alleys, deserted buildings, or construction sites.**
- **Always try to play or walk with friends.**
- **Never, ever hitchhike.**
- **Always keep doors and windows locked when you're home alone.**
- **Never display money in public.** Carry money only if necessary and keep it in a pocket until needed.
- **Always tell a family member or other adult in charge where you'll be at all times and what time you'll be home.**
- **If you go out on Halloween, be sure a teenager or adult goes with you.** Don't eat any candy or food that is not wrapped and sealed by the candy company. It's best if you wait until you get home to have your parents look over the candy before you eat it. Also, be sure that you can see out of your costume and that you can move well.
- **If someone older is touching you or talking to you in a way that makes you feel uncomfortable, tell them to stop right away; then run away and tell an adult.** Don't let an adult make you keep a secret about something you don't like doing, and tell your parents if someone tries.
- **Be sure you know how to use a phone.** Dial the operator

("O"), 911, or other emergency numbers if you need help. Memorize your phone number, a parent's work number, and a friend's number, including area codes.

☞ **Never leave children alone or unsupervised in a park, mall, or other public space, no matter how short the time.** Children can be (and have been) abducted in seconds. Don't take the chance. If you go shopping or to a public place, be sure you agree upon a meeting place if you are separated. If you hire a babysitter or put your children in day care, check references carefully. See the sections on Child Abuse and Neglect (page 145) and Missing Children (page 152) in the chapter on Children and Young Adults for additional information on protecting your child.

☞ **Work to make your community safer for all children.** Here are a few suggestions to consider (as adapted, with permission, from information provided by the **National Crime Prevention Council**):

- **Set up "block-parent programs" in the community by designating homes whose residents will assist children who are lost or frightened.** Neighborhood parents, grandparents, or other older adults can be recruited and trained to aid and comfort frightened children. A special sign posted in the window of each such home tells the children that this is a place to go when confronted with a serious problem.
- **Put children in an after-school program instead of leaving them at home alone.** If your community or school has no such program, work to organize one.
- **Encourage crime-prevention curriculum in local schools, after-school programs, or community centers.** Kids should learn basic skills to protect themselves, protect their property, and cope with being at home alone. Talk with the school's administration, the police department, and the PTA.
- **Form block patrols made up of adult volunteers to keep watch and report trouble during the hours that kids are likely to be outside.** Schools are prime locations for child abductors, and children are particularly vulnerable right before and after the school day.
- **Encourage schools to alert parents immediately when their children are not in school.** Many schools don't make these calls until well into the school day. If a child is abducted, this could be too late. If your school is understaffed, suggest that volunteers be used to make such calls.

- **Be sure to have current photographs and videotapes, if possible, as well as fingerprints of your child.** These can all help authorities working to identify missing children. Contact the local police department or sheriff's office for more information (there are some specific things you should know). The National Crime Prevention Council (page 171) can provide you with more information. If your school does not have a fingerprinting program, encourage school officials to start one.

☞ **Help to make your neighborhood a safer place for everyone.** Working with your neighbors is beneficial not only for safety's sake, but for creating a greater sense of community. Citizens working together can also prove to be a powerful force in preventing crime. Here are a few suggestions on increasing community safety (adapted, with permission, from information provided by the **National Crime Prevention Council**):

- **Be an alert and cooperative neighbor.** Watch out for strange activities. Trusted neighbors can also help one another by keeping spare keys, watching each other's children when the children are alone, and picking up newspapers and mail during vacations.
- **Discuss crime with other members of the community** and strive to increase overall crime awareness.
- **Contact the police about training local homebound residents to be "window watchers" or "silent observers,"** who anonymously report crimes, identifying themselves by numbers.
- **Help to remove graffitti and clean up alleys, parks, and other community areas.** Believe it or not, the better a neighborhood is kept up, the less likely it is to attract criminals.
- **If neighborhood parks, playgrounds, lots, and sidewalks are poorly lit, ask officials to install streetlights.** Contact the local Department of Public Works to express your concern.
- **Organize an escort program** for elderly persons, children, or anyone else who may want to be assisted in the evenings or when going into more dangerous areas of a community. Have a telephone network set up so that these individuals can call when they want to go out.

☞ **Start up or participate in a Neighborhood Watch or Apartment Watch program.** You can learn of local programs by contacting the police station or sheriff's office. Community watches are both economical and effective. They are also an excellent way to improve neighborhood unity and spirit. The **National Crime Prevention Council** reports that community watches have reduced overall crime by ten to twenty-five percent, with certain communities reporting even greater improvements.[3] Some cities have even reduced crimes such as rapes and robberies by as much a thirty percent. Here are some suggestions for getting started (adapted, with permission, from materials provided by the **Citizens Committee for New York City**):

- Contact the local police department or sheriff's office. Officers can provide you with information on crime in the community, available resources, prevention techniques, how to make reports, and general suggestions for getting started.
- Get together with neighbors. Try to recruit all members of the community, including teenagers, elderly persons, businesspersons, and civic and religious leaders. See if area businesses will help pay for flyers, newsletters, and other materials to attract attention and publicize the group's activities.
- Establish a trusted core group and block representatives. Don't, however, have one individual be seen as the group leader or driving force. Anonymity is critical to safety.
- Be sure to welcome new neighbors into the group so that they know they are welcome and that they are joining a neighborhood concerned about safety.
- Be sure your goals, plans, and activities are well thought out and articulated so that there is no confusion over direction or responsibilities. It's important that the group works together to achieve its aims, so it is critical that goals are understood by everyone.
- Exchange home and work telephone numbers with group members, and share information about daily routines, vacation plans, etc. A phone "tree," or network, will help you get information out quickly and effectively.
- Work together on home security surveys, "Operation Identification" (engraving ID numbers on valuable possessions), community cleanups, buying dead bolt locks (bulk orders save money), and pushing the local Department of Public Works for better lighting and other improvements.
- Patrol the streets or apartment building at night in small groups. Bring noisemakers (whistles, air horns) to scare away offenders, as well as two-way radios to communicate with patrols

---

[3]National Crime Prevention Council, *Crime and Crime Prevention Statistics*, 1989.

on other blocks. If you or your friends have car phones or CB radios, consider organizing a civilian motor patrol in cooperation with the police. **REMEMBER: Do not put yourself or neighbors in jeopardy by confronting armed or dangerous offenders. Let the law-enforcement officers handle the confrontational work.**

If you do start up a Community Watch, here are some organizations that can provide you with valuable information and ideas:

- **Citizens Committee for New York City.** Although CCNYC focuses on helping New Yorkers, it can provide excellent guidelines and tip sheets on creating safer communities anywhere. Publications include *Tools and Tactics for Building Neighborhood Organizations; Lend a Hand to Improve Your Schools; Strategies for Drug-Free Communities;* and *Improving Intergroup Relations.* If you live in New York, CCNYC is an indispensable resource for information on making the city a better place, providing information on crime, drugs, the environment, education, and a variety of other social issues. Write or call CCNYC at *3 West 29th Street, New York, NY 10001;* (212) 684-6767.
- **National Crime Prevention Council** (page 171) can provide you with or direct you to a variety of informative pamphlets, booklets, and books, and Community Watch posters, signs, and stickers.

See also the Alcohol and Drugs chapter for specific suggestions on fighting alcohol and drugs in your community.

☞ **Work to make your business crime-proof.** The **National Crime Prevention Council** estimates that businesses lose over thirty billion dollars to crime annually from shoplifting, employee theft, and robberies. Increased crime awareness and inexpensive preventive measures can drastically reduce these losses. If you are an employer, here are a few ideas to consider (adapted, with permission, from information provided by the **National Crime Prevention Council**):

- **Contact your local police station or sheriff's office to see if they'll conduct a "crime check" of your business.** Not all stations offer this, but it's becoming increasingly common.
- **Good nighttime lighting can be an effective crime deterrent.** If your business is in a commercial area where lighting is poor, consider joining up with other merchants to petition local officials for improved lighting. If that fails, get together and underwrite the costs yourselves.

- **Maintain strict control over who has keys to your business.** Have DO NOT DUPLICATE engraved on all keys.
- **Consider using an alarm to protect your business.** Alarms should have a battery fail-safe backup, fire-sensing capability, and read-out self-testing ability.
- **Put the safe and cash register up front, where they are easily visible.** Empty cash drawers every night and leave them open so a potential burglar can see that they're empty.
- **Consider marking all property and inventory.** Local police stations can lend you a special engraving pen to mark everything with predetermined numbers.
- **Avoid having only one employee working at any particular time.**
- **Set up a procedure for discreetly signaling other employees that a robbery is taking place.**
- **Teach employees to be alert to potential shoplifting.** Make sure that the merchandise in your store is easily visible and that expensive items are away from exits.
- **Post notices of a policy to prosecute shoplifters.**
- **Require job applicants to give professional and personal references** and check them before you hire.
- **If you suspect a burglary has occurred at your place of business, don't go in**—the criminal(s) may still be inside. Call the police immediately. Don't open for business until the police have been able to search for evidence.
- **If you are robbed, never refuse a robber's demands if he or she is armed.** Try to remember any possible details about the robber that could be used for later identification.
- **After a burglary, keep everyone away from anything the burglar might have touched until the police arrive.**

There is a great deal more that you, as an employer, should be aware of, such as bankruptcy fraud, check and credit card fraud, inventory control, higher-priced crime prevention items—cameras, bulletproof glass, alarms—and computer fraud, so contact the National Crime Prevention Council (page 171) for more information.

National Organizations

Center for the Prevention of Sexual and Domestic Violence
1914 N. 34th St., Suite 105, Seattle, WA 98103
(206) 634-1903 or 1-800-562-6025

CPSDV is a nonprofit organization dedicated to ending sexual violence and the oppression which often accompanies it (racism, sexism, ageism, or anti-Semitism, for example) by working with churches, synagogues, and seminaries throughout the U.S. The center educates clergy and lay leadership and develops programs that strive to bring the secular and religious communities together to end sexual and domestic violence. It also provides publications (such as *Sexual Violence: The Unmentionable Sin;* and *Keeping the Faith: Questions and Answers for the Abused Woman*), videos, sexual-abuse-prevention curricula, and a quarterly newsletter, *Working Together to Prevent Sexual and Domestic Violence* ($15 for a one-year subscription). CPSDV also has specific programs working with schools and the Jewish community. Write or call CPSDV for more information on its publications, resources, and volunteer opportunities (in the Seattle area).

National Assault Prevention Center
P.O. Box 02005, Columbus, OH 43202
(614) 291-2540 (Voice and TTY)

A nonprofit organization, **NAPC** is committed to crime prevention and to making America a safer place. The center works to stop child abuse, assaults against older citizens and people with disabilities, batterings, and violence against teens by educating the public on the causes and consequences of violence. It also seeks to empower vulnerable populations with information, skills, strategies, and researches the causes and consequences of violence, in order to develop methods of effective prevention. NAPC sponsors the **Child Assault Prevention (CAP) Project**, which focuses on children and teens, and the **Assault Prevention Training (APT) Project**, which is for older adults and adults with disabilities. The programs focus on the right to be safe and to feel physically and emotionally strong. NAPC does not focus on fear or avoidance tactics, but on the positive and constructive efforts each person takes. Programs have been used in diverse ethnic and economic communities (more than 230 communities nationwide). The organization strongly supports multi-cultural sensitivity and specificity in its programs. Contact NAPC for more information about its programs for schools, communities, and neighborhoods, and for information on its publications (including *Preventing Assaults Against Older Adults*, and *Parenting to Prevent Abuse*) and the quarterly newsletter *ReCAP*.

National Association of Town Watches
P.O. Box 303, 7 Wynnewood Road, Suite 215
Wynnewood, PA 19096
(215) 649-7055

NATW is a nonprofit organization dedicated to the development and promotion of organized-crime and drug-prevention activities affiliated with law enforcement, especially groups and individuals participating in police-community crime prevention programs. The organization's quarterly newsletter *New Spirit* keeps members updated on the latest crime-and drug-prevention news, programs, products, legislation, and events. NATW also sponsors the annual **National Night Out** crime-prevention event, which involves about twenty-one million people in 8,000 communities nationwide. The event, which is held on the first Tuesday in August, takes place in the evening and encourages people to turn their lights on, talk with their neighbors, sponsor block parties, discuss crime prevention with the local police, and simply increase community spirit (activities vary from community to community). The basic membership fee is $25.

National Coalition Against Domestic Violence
P.O. Box 34103, Washington, DC 20043-4103
(202) 638-6388, TTY: (202) 737-3033

NCADV is a nonprofit, national membership organization dedicated to ending domestic violence. Members include grass-roots shelter and service programs, support organizations, and concerned individuals. NCADV works to educate the public on the severe problem of battering and the need for national action. It serves as an information and referral center, offers technical assistance, sponsors a national conference, develops a variety of publications, sponsors **National Domestic Violence Awareness Month** each October, and produces the quarterly newsletter *THE VOICE*. The organization also distributes brochures, fact sheets, and annotated resource lists, and maintains a film loan library.

National Coalition Against Sexual Assault
2428 Ontario Road, N.W., Washington, DC 20009
(202) 483-7165

A nonprofit organization, **NCASA** is in the forefront of a national movement to end sexual violence and to promote services for the survivors of these crimes. The coalition works to accomplish these goals through a national network of members, and through working relationships with other public and private organizations with similar objectives. Members include rape crisis centers, counseling services, educational programs, women's shelters, and concerned individuals. NCASA monitors public policy and legislation related to sexual violence, and provides testimony to Congress and other decision-making bodies. It also sponsors conferences; acts as a consultant to the media and national groups on sexual violence matters; and works to shape services for survivors, to encourage preventive education, and to keep the public informed. NCASA distributes *The National NCASA News* (quarterly), regional newsletters (two to three times annually), legislative alerts (as needed), and data on services to victims (periodically from the NCASA data bank). Membership costs $25 for individuals, $75 for organizations. Volunteers are needed at NCASA's national office, or if you are interested in volunteering at a crisis or support center, NCASA can provide you with the location of one in your community.

National Council on Child Abuse & Family Violence
(see Child Abuse and Neglect, page 149)

The National Council on Crime and Delinquency
685 Market St., 6th Floor, San Francisco, CA 94105
(415) 896-NCCD (6223), FAX: (415) 896-5109

The nonprofit **NCCD** conducts research, initiates programs to reduce crime and delinquency, and promotes greater safety in the nation's communities. The organization works to influence public policy on the basis of its research. NCCD also encourages citizen involvement in effective, humane, fair, and economically sound solutions to the problems of crime and delinquency. Publications include *What Kind of Future?*, *Violence and Public Safety in the Year 2000; Facts About Juvenile Crime; What's Going On with Gangs;* and *The War on Crack: The Need for Real Solutions*.

National Crime Prevention Council
1700 K St., N.W., 2nd Floor, Washington, DC 20005
(202) 466-NCPC (6272)

A nonprofit organization, **NCPC** is probably one of the most valuable resources listed in this section. The council publishes materials, provides training, and offers information and referral services to help people prevent crime and build safer communities. NCPC works to teach individuals of all ages how to reduce their risk of being victimized and to encourage citizens to look beyond self-protection and involve themselves in community-wide actions that attack the causes of crime. NCPC can send you information on virtually every aspect of crime prevention, including such publications as *Your Inside Look at Crime Prevention* and *Don't Get Scared: Get Organized! A How-To Guide*. NCPC's Information Services has information and materials for college students, elderly persons, teachers, parents, employers, individuals with disabilities, teens, corporations, and anyone else concerned about crime. The organization also publishes a free monthly newsletter, *Catalyst*, which contains information on NCPC activities, national crime statistics and problems, local crime-prevention innovations, and related issues. NCPC's licensees sell T-shirts, bumper stickers, *Neighborhood Crime Watch* signs and notices, posters, videos, comic books, calendars, cups, stickers, caps, desk supplies, and similar items.

The National Gay & Lesbian Task Force
1734 14th St., N.W., Washington, DC 20009
(202) 332-6483

NGLTF is a nonprofit gay-rights organization working to create a society free from violence, bigotry, and discrimination against lesbians and gay men. Its activities include monitoring and influencing public policy and legislation that affects the gay community, organizing grass-roots programs to support programs in communities and on college campuses, working with the media to ensure that gays are represented fairly, and working to end violence and discrimination against lesbians and gay men. Through research, documentation, lobbying, and public education, NGLTF fights for appropriate legislative, political, and community-based responses to violence directed at the gay community. NGLTF also distributes numerous publications, including *Dealing with Violence: A Guide for Gay & Lesbian People; Anti-Gay Violence, Victimization, & Defamation in 1990* (updated yearly); and *Congressional Report Cards*, which rate congressional representatives on their voting records concerning gay and lesbian issues. Membership ($35) includes a subscription to *Task Force Report*, a quarterly newsletter with legislative updates, articles on hate crimes nationwide, notices of NGLTF activities, and other current news and features.

National Institute Against Prejudice and Violence
31 South Greene St., Baltimore, MD 21201
(301) 328-5170

A nonprofit organization, **NIAPV** is the only national resource dedicated to the study and elimination of violence motivated by prejudice against a victim's gender, race, religion, ethnicity, or sexual orientation. NIAPV serves as a clearinghouse by collecting, analyzing, publishing, and distributing materials and information; researches the causes of ethnoviolence and its effect on victims and communities; and emphasizes education, prevention, and effective responses to these crimes by working with communities and legislative advocacy and legal analysis groups. Publications include *Prejudice and Violence: An Annotated Bibliography of Selected Materials on Racial, Religious, and Ethnic Violence and Intimidation; Campus Ethnoviolence and the Policy Options;* and *Ethnoviolence in the Workplace*. NIAPV also has a quarterly newsletter, *FORUM*, which reports on ethnoviolence across the country, legislative information, and related issues.

National Institute of Justice
National Criminal Justice Reference Service
Box 6000, Rockville, MD 20850
(301) 251-5500 or 1-800-851-3420
FAX: (301) 251-5212

The principal criminal-justice research agency of the Department of Justice, **NIJ** gathers information on crime and crime control and shares this information through the **National Criminal Justice Reference Service**. The reference service provides up-to-date research, statistics, and other facts on crime and criminal justice to anyone interested. NCJRS also maintains clearinghouses for other Department of Justice agencies, including the **Juvenile Justice Clearinghouse**, the **Justice Statistics Clearinghouse**, the **National Victims Resource Center**, and the **Bureau of Justice Assistance**. NCJRS has many informative publications, audiovisual materials, and databases. You can call the reference specialists toll-free Monday through Friday, 8:30 A.M. to 7:00 P.M. (EST), for information on such topics as law enforcement, drugs and crime, the courts, juvenile justice, and victims' rights. Specialists can conduct a topical bibliography or search on your specific subject of interest, or a custom search can be tailored to meet your needs. Contact NCJRS for more information.

National Organization for Victim Assistance
1757 Park Road, N.W., Washington, DC 20010
(202) 232-6682

NOVA is a nonprofit organization that works to help victims everywhere, particularly in the following ways: by being a voice for victims' interests in the legislative and executive branches of government, by providing direct services to victims (through a crisis hotline, counseling, etc.), by helping local victim assistance programs expand their skills and services, and by uniting and informing those who are dedicated to establishing victims' rights and services across the U.S. Each year NOVA and its corps of dedicated volunteers help over 10,000 victims of crime. The organization publishes the *Directory of Victim Assistance Programs & Resources*, a state-by-state list of more than 7,000 victim/witness programs, rape crisis centers, police-based victim assistance projects, and domestic violence shelters, and *Victim Rights and Services: A Legislative Directory*, a fifty-state compendium of victim-related statutes and constitutional provisions. Each directory costs $25 ($20 for NOVA members). The basic membership fee is $30, $20 for senior citizens and students. Members receive the monthly *NOVA Newsletter*, which contains timely articles, features, and legislative alerts. If you want the location of centers in your community, or if you need information about the laws in your state, call or write to NOVA.

National Victim Center
307 W. Seventh St., Suite 1001, Fort Worth, TX 76102
(817) 877-3355

A nonprofit organization, **NVC** is dedicated to assisting victims of violent crime and serving the victims' rights movement. Among other things, NVC connects victims to resources and assistance available in their area; builds coalitions of victims' rights groups to help promote legislation; sponsors the **Crime Victims' Litigation Project**, which offers guidance in civil litigation; maintains an extensive resource library containing over 6,000 documents on every aspect of criminal justice and victimology, a national speaker's bureau, and a legislative database which tracks victims' rights legislation in all fifty states and at the federal level; and serves as an information clearinghouse and resource center for grass-roots organizations and concerned individuals. If you are interested in volunteering at a victims' center, send a self-addressed, stamped envelope and NVC will provide you with information on centers in your community. Membership ($18 and up) includes two quarterly newsletters, *NETWORKS* and *Crime, Safety, and You*, legislative updates, and other notifications. (A catalog of NVC publications is available for $3.)

National Woman Abuse and Prevention Project
2000 P St., N.W., Suite 508, Washington, DC 20036
(202) 857-0216

NWAPP is a nonprofit policy resource and information center on violence against women, particularly domestic violence and its effects on victims and the community. The organization publishes up-to-date and authoritative brochures and pamphlets (for example, *Domestic Violence: Understanding a Community Problem; Sad Is How You Feel When Mom Is Being Beat; Physical Abuse: You Don't Have to Take It, You Don't Have to Use It;* and *Helping the Battered Woman: A Guide for Family and Friends*), as well as a quarterly newsletter, *The Exchange*, which covers a variety of issues related to abuse against women. The annual subscription rate is $10. If you're interested in becoming a volunteer at a center for abused women, you can contact NWAPP for information on agencies in your community.

WeTIP, Inc.
P.O. Box 1296, Rancho Cucamonga, CA 91730
(714) 987-5005, FAX: (714) 987-2477
Hotline: 1-800-73-CRIME (732-7463)
In California: 1-800-78-CRIME (782-7463)

A nonprofit organization, **WeTIP** runs a toll-free twenty-four-hour hotline, allowing anonymous callers to provide authorities with leads to catch criminals. Since WeTIP began in 1972, more than 138,000 tips have been received, undoubtedly saving many lives and millions of dollars in property. As a direct result of the hotline, 3,800 criminals have been convicted; in addition, law-enforcement agencies have seized more than $239 million worth of illegal drugs and narcotics and solved 8,800 crimes. WeTIP also offers $1,000 rewards for certain crimes (and up to $10,000 for arson information in particular school districts). If you have information on a major crime or criminal, call WeTIP but do not give your name. The operator will assign you a code name and number, take all the necessary information, then pass the information on to the appropriate law-enforcement officers. If there is an arrest and conviction, you will receive the reward (which comes from money donated by corporations, individuals, and other sources).

DISABILITIES

Why Help Is Needed

According to the National Organization on DisAbility (NOD), approximately 43 million men, women, and children in America—one out of every six people—have disabilities, representing the nation's largest minority. Among these millions of Americans, the National Information Center on Deafness estimates that 21 million are deaf or hard-of-hearing. According to the American Foundation for the Blind, approximately 3 million Americans are severely visually impaired (unable to read a newspaper even with corrective lenses, for example), and an estimated 120,000 are totally blind. NOD also estimates that there are 1.4 million wheelchair users in the U.S. The total number also includes hundreds of thousands of people with multiple sclerosis (or closely related disorders), 14,000 people with spina bifida, 700,000 people with cerebral palsy, and hundreds of thousands of people with neuromuscular diseases.[1] Special Olympics International estimates that nearly seven million people in the U.S. have mental retardation, representing about three percent of the total population.

Volunteers across the nation are providing valuable assistance to many of these individuals, reading to those who are blind, driving those who use wheelchairs to various places and events, offering job counseling, and participating in sports and recreational events with children and adults who have mental retardation. These countless volunteers often begin helping individuals with disabilities as volunteers and quickly find themselves becoming friends.

The need for volunteers to provide assistance for many individuals with disabilities cannot be overemphasized. It also cannot be overemphasized, however, that there are many people with disabilities who are not only functioning quite well on their own, but are excelling in their professions and making valuable contributions to society. They are among the nation's doctors, musicians, artists, teachers,

---

[1] All statistics in this chapter are taken from the related organization (for example, "14,000 people with spina bifida" is from the Spina Bifida Association of America). The Muscular Dystrophy Association provided the information on neuromuscular diseases.

members of Congress, poets, judges, reporters, lawyers, librarians, CEOs, athletes, and volunteers. To name a respected few, there is premier violinist Itzhak Perlman, senators Bob Dole and Daniel Inouye, professor and former congresswoman Barbara Jordan, musicians Stevie Wonder, Ray Charles, Ronnie Milsap, and Jose Feliciano, major league pitcher Jim Abbott, actor Chris Burke, and Academy Award–winning actress Marlee Matlin. Clearly, individuals with disabilities are, first and foremost, individuals who deserve equal treatment and respect like everyone else.

The disability that probably suffers from the most negative stigma is mental illness. Words such as *nuts*, *crazy*, *loony*, and *psycho*, which seem to be common in everyday language, not only hurt people who have mental illnesses, they trivialize the severity and extent of their problems. According to the American Mental Health Fund (AMHF), an estimated 35 million Americans experience mental illnesses every year, which includes, among other things, schizophrenia, severe depression, and anxiety disorders. (Note that these 35 million individuals are not a subset of the 43 million individuals with disabilities, mentioned above.) AMHF also claims that mental illness is the most prevalent disease in America, more so than cancer and heart and lung disease combined. Many people with mental illnesses develop alcohol or drug problems, lose their friends and families, and even commit suicide. Although treating these individuals is the responsibility of professionals, volunteers can offer their skills and time to their local mental health agency or offer their companionship to individuals with mental illnesses on a one-on-one basis.

Medical breakthroughs and modern technology have given many individuals with disabilities a better chance at realizing their potential. No amount of technology, science, and medicine, however, can change people's attitudes concerning disabilities. The word "disability" should not be confused with "unability." Volunteers can work with those individuals with disabilities who need assistance. Everyone can work to stop the inequalities and insensitivities that affect individuals with disabilities everywhere.

What You Can Do

☞ **While people usually have the best intentions when meeting or talking with individuals with disabilities,** they sometimes become uneasy about what to say or how to act. The following suggestions and tips (adapted, with permission, from "Disability Etiquette," © National Easter Seal Society, Chicago, IL) are intended to help people be as considerate and respectful to individuals with disabilities as possible:

- **It's okay to offer your help if it seems needed, but don't overdo it or insist on helping.** Be sure that you wait until your offer is accepted before you help, and listen for any instructions the person may have.
- **Don't feel embarrassed if you happen to use common, accepted expressions** such as "*See* you later" or "Got to be *running* along," that seem related to the person's disability.
- **Don't feel embarrassed if your child asks a person about his or her disability.** Many children are endowed with a natural, uninhibited curiosity and ask questions that many adults consider embarrassing. People with disabilities are well aware of this and recognize that the questions are innocent. Reprimanding a child for asking questions may cause the child to think that there is something "bad" about disabilities. Most people with disabilities will not mind answering a child's question.
- **Treat adults in a manner befitting adults.** Call a person by his or her first name only when extending that familiarity to all others present. Strangely, people sometimes forget such titles as Mr., Ms., Mrs., or Dr. when speaking with or about a person with a disability, even in formal circumstances.
- **When talking with a person who uses a wheelchair,** place yourself at the person's eye level to spare both of you a stiff neck.
- **Don't lean on a person's wheelchair or push any controls if it's electrically operated.** This is an invasion of personal space and can be very discomforting. And remember that when you push someone's wheelchair unexpectedly, it's the same as if someone came up and pushed you.
- **Give your whole, unhurried attention when talking with a person who has difficulty speaking.** Keep your manner encouraging rather than correcting, and be patient rather than speaking for the person or completing sentences for him or her. If necessary, ask questions that require short answers or a nod or shake of the head. Never pretend to understand if you are having difficulty doing so. Repeat what you understand, and work from there.
- **When talking with a person who has a disability, make sure you speak directly to that person** rather than through a companion or interpreter who may be along.
- **When you're giving directions to a person with a phys-

ical disability, consider distance, weather conditions, and physical obstacles such as stairs, curbs, and steep hills.
- **If you are planning to do something with a friend who uses a wheelchair,** check ahead. Be sure that wherever you're going is accessible to your friend.
- **Because a disabling condition may or may not be handicapping, try to use the word "disability" rather than "handicap."**
- **When speaking or writing about a person with disabilities, mention the** *person* before the *disability* out of respect for his or her individual uniqueness and worth. Although "person with a disability" or "individual with a disability" may be longer than "disabled person" or "disabled individual," respecting the individuals involved is more important than speaking quickly. (Some major organizations for individuals with disabilities use the term *handicapped person*, but most of them are changing.) This is especially important for people in the media.

Here are some other word choices to avoid:

Afflicted—This is very negative and should definitely be avoided. Person *who has* is much better.
The Cerebral Palsied, The Disabled, or **The Handicapped**—These sound like inanimate objects. Try to use *person* or *individuals with cerebral palsy* or *disabilities*. This way, you emphasize the person, then the disability.
Crippled or **Deformed**—Don't use these terms under any circumstances. No replacements.
Drain and **Burden**—These are also very negative and should be avoided. If you must, *added responsibility* is much better.
Poor—Physical disabilities have nothing to do with economic status, nor do individuals with disabilities need pity.
Suffers from—It's presumptuous to state what another person "suffers from," for an individual with a disability may not feel that he or she "suffers from" anything. (And he or she would be right.)
Unfortunate—As with *suffers from, unfortunate* is presumptuous and should be avoided.
Victim—Unless you know for certain, don't use this word.
Wheelchair-bound—Leaves the impression that the *wheelchair user* (a better descriptive term) is glued to his or her mode of transportation. And remember, just because people use wheel-

chairs doesn't mean that they're sick. Lots of people who use wheelchairs are healthy and strong.

See also Blindness and Visual Impairments, page 198, and Deafness and Hearing Loss, page 203, for more information.

☞ **Become knowledgeable about physical and cognitive disabilities.** Read about the causes and effects of certain disabilities. This will help you educate others and recognize misconceptions about particular disabilities (for example, that all persons who use wheelchairs are chronically ill or sick). Most of the national organizations listed in this chapter can provide you with extensive information on particular disabilities.

☞ **Keep up on legislation that affects individuals with disabilities.** Many of the national organizations listed in this chapter keep track of legislation. The **Disability Rights Education and Defense Fund** (page 186), in particular, is an excellent source of legislative news and insight. (See also Voicing Your Opinion, page 363).

☞ **Work to eliminate myths and stereotypes about individuals with disabilities in your home, office, school, club, or community.** Write to the editor if you think that a newspaper or magazine article is insensitive to individuals with disabilities or uses misleading descriptions (see above). Put up posters in public places or distribute literature on disabilities. Many of the national organizations listed in this chapter, including the **National Easter Seal Society** (page 189), can provide you with useful educational materials, including posters, videos, and pamphlets. For a great selection of educational posters, videos, and slides, contact the **Human Policy Press** (see **Center on Human Policy**, page 186).

☞ **Don't park in spaces reserved for individuals with disabilities and discourage others from doing the same.** These spaces are specially designed and placed for people who need them. Even parking in such a space for a quick run into a store should be discouraged. These "quick" trips sometimes turn into long ones, and the person who needs the space has no idea how long you'll be gone.

☞ **Work to eliminate architectural and transportation barriers.** This could be as simple as writing letters to state or local government officials about making areas more accessible to individuals with disabilities. Or it could be something more aggressive, such as boycotting restaurants, shops, or other businesses that do not take the needs of individuals with disabilities into consideration. If you do participate in a boycott, be sure, of course, that you inform the management why you will not be a customer.

☞ **Volunteer at an organization that provides services for individuals with disabilities.** Activities may include working directly with individuals with disabilities or assisting with administrative work (for example, sending out notices, editing newsletters, answering phones) and fundraising. Check the national organizations in this chapter for their regional offices or local affiliates. **Volunteer Clearinghouses** (page 6) also have a variety of volunteer opportunities available. If you are a member of a religious congregation, see if there are any activities, services, or programs available for which you can volunteer.

☞ **Volunteer at a center or home for individuals with disabilities if there is one near you.** Volunteers are needed for a variety of services (opportunities may differ from facility to facility), including playing with and taking care of children at the facility, participating in recreational activities, helping with cooking or facility maintenance, and assisting with fundraising and general administrative work. To see if there's a facility near you, send a self-addressed stamped envelope to the **National Association of Private Residential Resources**, *4200 Evergreen Lane, #315, Annandale, VA 22003*; (703) 642-6614.

☞ **Volunteer to work with sports and recreation organizations for individuals with disabilities.** Even if you have no athletic interests or skills, you can always help in some way. Many organizations can use sports equipment and other supplies. Volunteers are also needed as officials, event organizers, fundraisers, even as cheering spectators (schools can help by conducting fundraising programs or opening athletic facilities to sports events). See National Sports and Recreational Organizations for Individuals with Disabilities (page 195) for more information.

☞ **If you are fifty-five or older, consider volunteering for the Family Friends Program** run by the **National Council on the Aging** (see full listing under Elderly Persons, page 241), which matches older volunteers with children who are chronically ill or who have disabilities. Write to or call NCOA at *600 Maryland Ave., S.W., West Wing 100, (After June 1: 409 3rd St., S.W., 2nd floor) Washington, D.C. 20024*; (202) 479-1200.

☞ **Support an organization that provides assistance dogs for individuals with disabilities.** Volunteers are often needed to be "puppy raisers"—that is, to take care of a puppy for a year—walk dogs, and provide a variety of other services. Even if you cannot volunteer your time, many of these organizations need financial support and donations of supplies, such as collars, leashes, and food bowls. If there's an organization near you, call or write to see how you can help out. Here are some of the nation's largest organizations providing assistance dogs to individuals with disabilities:

Assistance Dogs of America, Inc.
P.O. Box 20496
Columbus, OH 43220
(614) 451-2969

Canine Companions for Independence
1215 Sebastopol Road
Santa Rosa, CA 95407-6834
(707) 579-1985
and 6901 Harrisburg Pike
Orient, OH 43146
(614) 871-2554
and P.O. Box 205
Farmingdale, NY 11735-0205
(516) 694-6938
and P.O. Box 547511
Orlando, FL 32854-7511
(407) 682-2535

Eye of the Pacific Guide Dogs and Mobility Services
Room #407, 747 Amana St.
Honolulu, HI 96814
(808) 941-1088

Freedom Service Dogs, Inc.
980 Everett St.
Lakewood, CO 80215
(303) 234-9512

Handi-Dogs, Inc.
P.O. Box 12563
Tucson, AZ 85732
(602) 326-3412

Independence Dogs, Inc.
146 State Line Road
Chadds Ford, PA 19317
(215) 358-2723

The New England Assistance Dog Service, Inc.
P.O. Box 213
West Boylston, MA 01583
(508) 835-3304

Okada, Ltd.
RR 1, Box 640F
Fontana, WI 53125
(414) 275-5226

"Paws with a Cause"
Home of Ears for the Deaf, Inc.
1235 100th St.
Byron, MI 49315
(616) 698-0688

Phydeaux for Freedom
1 Main St.
Laurel, MD 20707
(301) 498-6779

Support Dogs for the Handicapped
301 Sovereign Court, Suite 113
Ballwin, MO 63011
(314) 394-6163

If you cannot find an organization in your area, contact **The Delta Society** (see Animals, page 89) for information on assistance-dog organizations nationwide. All of the organizations listed above train dogs for individuals with physical disabilities that affect their mobility, and some also train dogs for individuals who are deaf and for those who are blind. For information on guide- and hearing-dog organizations, see Blindness and Visual Impairments (page 200) and Deafness and Hearing Loss (page 205), respectively.

☞ **Volunteer to work with an organization that takes individuals with disabilities into the great outdoors.** Here are two that work with volunteers:

- **Environmental Traveling Companions** is a nonprofit organization that coordinates wilderness adventures for disadvantaged youths and individuals with physical and cognitive disabilities of all ages. Trip activities include sea kayaking, skiing, and white-water rafting. Volunteers do not pay for the trips, but do have to pay for the training beforehand (usually over $100). Trips are available year-round and take place primarily in the West. Contact ETC for more information at *Fort Mason Center, Landmark Building C, San Francisco, CA 94123*; (415) 474-7662.
- **Wilderness Inquiry** is a nonprofit organization that organizes wilderness adventures nationwide for individuals with disabilities. WI sponsors kayaking, canoeing, and exploring trips year-round. Each trip includes a focus on the natural history and ecology of the area the groups travel through. For more information on trip activities and volunteer opportunities, contact WI at *1313 5th St., S.E., Box 84, Minneapolis, MN 55414*; (612) 379-3858 (Voice or TTY).

☞ **If you are an employer, make an effort to hire individuals with disabilities.** Millions of individuals with disabilities want to work, have the skills to work, but are still unemployed. Employers should check the phone book (usually in the government pages) under "Vocational Rehabilitation Services" or "Rehabilitation Services," sometimes listed under the "Social Services," or "Human Services" department. You may also want to try the local employment/unemployment office. If you're interested in information on tax credit, contact the IRS Forms and Distribution Center for *General Business Credit* (Publication 572). The toll-free number is *1-800-TAX-FORM* (829-3676). Public libraries should also have these forms. See National Organizations for the Employment of Individuals with Disabilities, page 194, for more information.

☞ **Start up a program for individuals with disabilities in your area, if there is not one already.** Services will vary, depending on the needs of the community, but may include transportation, education, youth, and accessibility programs, along with recreation and culture projects. The **National Organization on DisAbility** (page 191) can help you develop such a project. If you are a member of a religious congregation, service club, or other community group, see how you can use your resources (and facilities, if relevant) to start up a community organization for individuals with disabilities.

☞ **Consider adopting or becoming a foster parent of a child**

with a disability. This is a serious commitment, but if you are interested, see Adoption (page 142) and Foster Care (page 150) for more information. The **Spina Bifida Association of America** (page 193) also has an adoption referral program.

National Organizations

American Cancer Society
1599 Clifton Rd., N.E., Atlanta, GA 30329
(404) 320-3333

ACS is a nonprofit voluntary health organization dedicated to eliminating cancer, saving lives, and diminishing the suffering from cancer to the fullest extent possible. ACS and its more than two million volunteers work to fight cancer and help those with the disease in numerous ways, including researching the causes and effects of cancer; providing services and rehabilitation for people with cancer (for example, driving patients to treatment centers and offering information, counseling, and support to families of patients); and educating the public about recognizing the signs of cancer and about preventive measures that they can take. There are fifty-eight divisions nationwide (including Hawaii and Puerto Rico) and nearly 3,000 units within the states. Whatever your skills or time constraints may be, you can help out your local ACS in a variety of ways, including the services mentioned above, as well as fundraising and administrative work. People who have been treated for cancer are especially needed to help and support new patients. ACS is listed in the white pages of all telephone books. (ACS is not an organization solely for individuals with disabilities, as are the other national organizations listed in this chapter, but it is one of the largest volunteer organizations in the U.S. and it does work with cancer patients with disabilities.)

The Association for Persons with Severe Handicaps
7010 Roosevelt Way, N.E., Seattle, WA 98115
(206) 523-8446

TASH is a nonprofit organization concerned with the human dignity, education, and independence of individuals who have traditionally been labeled ''severely intellectually (or physically) disabled.'' TASH's activities and services include disseminating research findings and practical applications for education and rehabilitation; providing support for parents, educators, and service providers; and advocating comprehensive, high-quality, integrated education and rehabilitation services. In addition, TASH distributes papers, reports, bibliography sheets, books (such as *After the Tears: Parents Talk about Raising a Child with a Disability* and *Home Care for the Chronically Ill or Disabled Child*), and films and videos (including *Regular Lives*, a twenty-eight-minute presentation that documents individuals who have disabilities in typical school, recreational, and work settings and shows the impact integration has had on their lives and the lives of those around them). Membership to TASH costs $49 for students, paraprofessionals, and parents, $72 for others. Anyone, however, can order TASH's publications and audiovisuals or volunteer in one of its many chapters around the country.

Center on Human Policy
Syracuse University
200 Huntington Hall, Syracuse, NY 13244-2340
(315) 443-3851

A nonprofit organization, **CHP** provides training, consultation, and technical assistance to states and communities on integrating individuals with severe disabilities into community life. CHP is also an aggressive advocacy force, working through the press, letter-writing campaigns, public education, and legislation monitoring. Through its **Human Policy Press**, you can purchase posters (for example, *Sticks & Stones Can Break My Bones But Names Will Really Hurt Me* and *Label Jars . . . Not People*), books (such as *Ordinary Moments: The Disabled Experience*), slides, and videotapes. CHP also has numerous informative publications and resource materials.

The Disability Rights Education and Defense Fund
Main Office:
2212 Sixth St., Berkeley, CA 94710
(415) 644-2555, TDD: (415) 644-2627, FAX: (415) 861-8645
Government Affairs Office:
1616 P St., N.W., Washington, DC 20036
Voice or TDD: (202) 328-5185, FAX: (202) 328-5137

The nonprofit **Disability Rights Education and Defense Fund** works to change the policies and attitudes that prevent persons with disabilities from participating in the mainstream of American life. Primarily, the organization lobbies to create laws and policies that challenge the discrimination which has prevented persons with disabilities from being integrated into schools, jobs, and community life. Among many other activities, the group testifies before Congress, advises government policymakers about disability as a civil-rights cause, and provides legal representation for parents of children with disabilities and for adults with disabilities who are discriminated against by employers, landlords, and businesses. Its newsletter, *Disability Rights Education and Defense Fund News*, is an excellent publication for people who want to stay on top of legislation and policy issues concerning individuals with disabilities. The newsletter comes out every three months and is free.

Disabled American Veterans
(see Veterans, page 361)

Epilepsy Foundation of America
4531 Garden City Drive, Landover MD 20785
(301) 459-3700 or 1-800-EFA-1000 (332-1000)
FAX: (301) 577-2684

A nonprofit organization, **EFA** promotes research into the causes and treatments of epilepsy, supports educational and vocational programs for persons with epilepsy, and provides educational information about epilepsy to the general public, including publications and a print and radio campaign on the employability of people with epilepsy. EFA also works with federal government agencies and with Congress to advance the interests of people with epilepsy. Employers can contact EFA for information on hiring individuals who have epilepsy. Volunteers are needed at chapters nationwide (contact the national headquarters if you cannot find one in your area).

Family Friends Program
The National Council on the Aging, Inc.
600 Maryland Ave., S.W., West Wing 100
(after June 1, 1991: 409 3rd St., S.W. 2nd floor)
Washington, DC 20024
(202) 479-1200

The **Family Friends Program**, sponsored by **NCOA** (a nonprofit organization dedicated to improving the quality of life for older Americans), matches volunteers fifty-five and older with children twelve and younger who are chronically ill or who have disabilities. A volunteer visits his or her child at least once a week in the child's home, providing support to the child, parents, and other family members.

If you are interested in becoming involved, contact NCOA (see Elderly Persons, page 241, for full listing) to find out if there's a program near you.

Goodwill Industries of America
9200 Wisconsin Ave., Bethesda, MD 20814
(301) 530-6500, FAX: (301) 530-1516

GIA is North America's leading nonprofit provider of vocational training and services for individuals with disabilities and other special needs. Goodwill is dedicated to discovering the productive capabilities in every person, and to helping people overcome barriers to employment and become full participants in both the work force and the life of the community. Vocational services are provided directly by a network of more than 178 autonomous community-based agencies located throughout the U.S. and Canada. Through its **Goodwill Industries Volunteer Services (GIVS)**, GIA can provide you with a worthwhile volunteer opportunity in your community. More than 14,000 people are part of GIVS, helping achieve the GIA mission by raising funds, promoting donations of household goods, soliciting contracts with businesses, and working directly with individuals with disabilities. Employers nationwide can call GIA for skilled job applicants. Contact the Goodwill chapter in your community or call the national headquarters for more information.

Learning Disabilities Association of America
(see Education and Illiteracy, page 222)

March of Dimes Birth Defects Foundation
1275 Mamaroneck Ave., White Plains, NY 10605
(914) 428-7100

The **March of Dimes** is a nonprofit organization with 300 chapters nationwide and a network of volunteers, scientists, and medical professionals working to fight birth defects. The foundation provides leadership in the treatment and prevention of birth defects through research, health-care programs, and educational services, and monitors public policy at the local, state, and federal levels. Literally millions of volunteers help the March of Dimes each year by promoting and implementing programs in its local chapters and by raising the funds to carry them out. Contact the March of Dimes in your area to receive more information about what the March of Dimes is doing and how you can get involved.

Muscular Dystrophy Association
3561 E. Sunrise Dr., Tucson, AZ 85718
(602) 529-2000

MDA is a nonprofit organization of scientists and concerned citizens dedicated to fighting over forty neuromuscular diseases through an extensive research effort, a nationwide program of medical services, and far-reaching professional and public-education initiatives. The association also sponsors camps, which provide youngsters with neuromuscular diseases the opportunity to develop new friendships, share interests, and build self-confidence. MDA needs volunteers at its camps and local chapters and individuals to help out with the **MDA Labor Day Telethon**. Check the phone book for local chapters or call the national headquarters.

National Easter Seal Society
70 E. Lake St., Chicago, IL 60601
(312) 726-6200

NESS is a nonprofit, nationwide network of 165 affiliates and 400 service programs dedicated to helping persons with disabilities achieve maximum independence. NESS provides direct services to more than a million people each year, serving individuals of all ages with any disability. The society helps communities develop necessary and appropriate services for persons with disabilities; work with and for persons with disabilities to help them attain and protect their legal rights; and create a climate of acceptance in all aspects of society for persons with disabilities. NESS is also a powerful voice with respect to legislative issues and public education. Interested individuals can help the NESS by (among many other activities) serving on volunteer committees, raising funds, providing transportation for individuals with disabilities, assisting in therapy and support groups, and working at Easter Seal camps. Trained volunteers are also needed to check the accessibility of public accommodations in their communities to disabled individuals. Contact the Easter Seal Society in your community for volunteer opportunities, or contact the national headquarters for referrals and information on NESS's publications and public education campaigns (such as *A Safe Home Is No Accident*, a guide to safeguarding one's home against disabling injuries; *Attitudes*, an award-winning campaign that targets myths and facts about disabilities; and *Friends Who Care*, another award-winning disability-awareness campaign for elementary, junior, and senior high school students).

National Head Injury Foundation, Inc.
1140 Connecticut Ave., N.W., Suite 812
Washington, DC 20036
(202) 296-NHIF (6443)

A nonprofit advocacy organization, **NHIF** works to prevent head injuries and to improve the quality of life for head-injury survivors and their families. NHIF's efforts include increasing the public's awareness of head injury and its consequences, developing support systems, encouraging appropriate rehabilitation for head-injury survivors, raising funds to support head-injury research and training, and disseminating information about head injuries. Membership ($35) includes a subscription to the *NHIF Newsletter*, which presents legislative updates, announcements of NHIF activities and events, and head-injury news and related information. Volunteers (members and nonmembers alike) are needed at the local chapters, so contact the national headquarters if you cannot find the affiliate near you.

National Information Center for Children and Youth with Handicaps
P.O. Box 1492, Washington, DC 20013
(703) 893-6061, TDD: (703) 893-8614
1-800-999-5599 (recorded message)

The nonprofit **National Information Center** provides useful publications and other materials to parents, educators, caregivers, advocates, and others helping children and youth with disabilities become participating members of the community. The center can send you a list of important local, state, and national resources and organizations working for the benefit of individuals with disabilities, as well as news digests and publications on virtually all disabilities (including cerebral palsy, Down syndrome, and spina bifida). Single copies of NICHCY materials are free.

National Multiple Sclerosis Society
205 E. 42nd St., New York, NY 10017
(212) 986-3240 or 1-800-624-8236

NMSS is the only nonprofit organization in the U.S. that supports national and international research on the cause, prevention, treatment, and cure of multiple sclerosis. Through its more than 140 chapters across the U.S., NMSS provides referrals, peer counseling, peer support and self-help groups, physical fitness programs, medical equipment assistance, vocational rehabilitation, social and recreational activities, and advocacy for all individuals with multiple sclerosis. Contact the national headquarters if you want to learn more about multiple sclerosis or about what NMSS does, or if you cannot find an NMSS chapter near you.

National Organization on DisAbility
910 16th St., N.W., Suite 600, Washington, DC 20006
(202) 293-5960, TDD: (202) 293-5968, FAX: (202) 293-7999
Toll-free 24-hour hotline: 1-800-248-ABLE (2253)

NOD is a nonprofit organization established to promote full participation of all individuals with disabilities in all aspects of community life. Members are individuals, with and without disabilities, in thousands of communities nationwide who seek to improve attitudes toward individuals with disabilities, expand educational and employment opportunities, address transportation needs, and encourage participation of individuals with disabilities in recreational, social, religious, and cultural activities. Volunteers work to eliminate barriers at shopping centers, hotels, churches, voting centers, theaters, lecture and concert halls, and other public facilities. Whether you're part of a business, religious congregation, social service organization, or simply a concerned individual, your time and abilities are needed at the NOD chapter nearest you. Contact the national headquarters if you cannot find an NOD affiliate near you or if you want to start one up in your community.

National Rehabilitation Information Center
8455 Colesville Road, Suite 935, Silver Spring, MD 20910
(301) 588-9284 (Voice or TDD)
1-800-34-NARIC (346-2742)

NARIC, which is funded by the **National Institute on Disability and Rehabilitation Research (NIDRR)**, provides at little or no cost some of the best information available on disabilities and rehabilitation-related issues. NARIC's professionals are committed to helping anyone who contacts the center, from the most highly skilled researcher to the student writing a paper, find the information and resources that he or she may need. Individuals can call, write, or walk in to NARIC's facility (accessible to all individuals with disabilities) and receive fast, professional help. Its collection includes research reports, policy studies, journal articles, audiovisual materials, periodicals, pamphlets, and monographs. NARIC also publishes a free quarterly newsletter and several directories.

National Spinal Cord Injury Association
600 W. Cummings Park, Suite 2000, Woburn, MA 01801
(617) 935-2722 or 1-800-962-9629

NSCIA is a nonprofit organization with more than sixty chapters and support groups nationwide dedicated to improving the welfare of individuals with spinal cord injuries and related disabilities. The association provides a variety of direct services for people with spinal cord injuries (including therapy and rehabilitation programs), educates the public and professionals about the needs, capabilities, and rights of individuals with disabilities; promotes research; implements a program of public education focusing on prevention; and advocates the elimination of barriers for persons who use wheelchairs. NSCIA also publishes a quarterly news magazine, *Spinal Cord Injury Life*, a full-color publication containing in-depth articles, legislative updates, chapter listings, book reviews, research notes, calendar events, information resources and many other features and departments. A one-year subscription to the magazine costs $20 for nonmembers, but comes free for members. The basic membership fee is $25 for individuals with disabilities or family members and $35 for professionals and interested individuals. Volunteers (members and nonmembers alike) are needed at the local chapters and at the national headquarters for a variety of services.

The Orton Dyslexia Society
(see Education and Illiteracy, page 226)

Project Head Start
(see Children and Young Adults, page 137)

Sick Kids (need) Involved People
c/o SKIP of New York
990 Second Ave., Floor 2, New York, NY 10022
(212) 421-9160

SKIP, a nonprofit organization working with volunteers nationwide, assists the families of children who are chronically ill or who have disabilities. Volunteers provide the families with a variety of services, including offering emotional support, assisting with household chores and errands, helping to find needed services for the children, and caring for the children or siblings. If you are interested in becoming a volunteer, contact the New York office for more information on the program and the location of a family near you.

Spina Bifida Association of America
1700 Rockville Pike, Suite 250, Rockville, MD 20852
(301) 770-SBAA (7222)

The nonprofit **Spina Bifida Association** is dedicated to increasing the emotional and physical well-being of individuals with spina bifida. SBAA sponsors research on the causes, treatment, and prevention of spina bifida; encourages the education, socialization, career development, and rehabilitation of persons with spina bifida; monitors legislation on all levels of government; and promotes public awareness and action. SBAA also provides a support system for parents of infants and children with spina bifida; coordinates **The Adoption Information Referral** program, which helps to match infants and children with spina bifida with loving families; and offers a variety of print and audiovisual materials on spina bifida for professionals and the general public alike. Membership ($25 and up) includes the bimonthly newsletter *INSIGHTS*, which contains news of medical, therapeutic, and rehabilitative advances, legislative updates, and other relevant information. Volunteers (members and nonmembers alike) are needed at SBAA's chapters across the country.

United Cerebral Palsy Associations
7 Penn Plaza, Suite 804, New York, NY 10001
(212) 268-6655 or 1-800-872-1827

UCPA is a nonprofit nationwide network of approximately 180 state and local voluntary agencies that provide services, conduct public and professional education programs, and support extensive research on cerebral palsy. On a national level, UCPA works as an advocate for individuals with disabilities, encouraging legislation for federal, state, and local programs that will benefit those with cerebral palsy and other disabilities. On the local level, UCPA provides direct services to children and adults with cerebral palsy and their families. Services include medical diagnosis, evaluation and treatment, special education, career development, social and recreational programs, counseling for parents, adapted housing, advocacy, and community education. The organization also has informative research updates, pamphlets, and booklets on cerebral palsy and a comprehensive materials mailing list, which contains general information, project materials, and campaign/fundraising materials. UCPA is always in need of volunteers, so check the phone book for the affiliate in your community or contact the national headquarters.

Variety Clubs International
(see Children and Young Adults, page 138)

National Organizations for the Employment of Individuals with Disabilities

Job Accommodation Network
West Virginia University
809 Allen Hall, P.O. Box 6122, Morgantown, WV 26506
(304) 293-7186 or 1-800-526-7234
In West Virginia: 1-800-JAN-INWV (526-4698)

JAN is a nonprofit network established to gather and provide information about practical ways of making accommodations for employees and applicants with disabilities so that these qualified workers may be hired or retained. JAN offers employers comprehensive information on methods and available equipment that have proven effective for a wide range of accommodations, most of which are quite inexpensive. For more information or questions on tax write-offs, etc., call the toll-free number. Callers can speak with JAN's human factors consultants and get immediate suggestions on solutions to accommodation problems. There is no charge for JAN's services. All JAN asks is that you provide information about accommodations you have made so they may be shared with future callers.

Job Opportunities for the Blind
National Federation of the Blind
1800 Johnson St., Baltimore, MD 21230
(301) 659-9314 or 1-800-638-7518

JOB is a project of the **National Federation of the Blind** (see page 202) in partnership with the **U.S. Department of Labor**. If you are an employer who would like to hire a person who is blind, JOB can help you find qualified applicants; assist you and the employee in devising simple, often cost-free alternative techniques to accommodate the individual's needs; provide you with the most current information about computers and other specialized devices used by blind workers; and conduct workshops for your staff to provide them with correct information about blindness. JOB also has many fact sheets, bulletins, and an informative booklet for employers called *Have You Considered . . .* , which discusses all the good reasons employers should hire people who are blind. Contact JOB for more information.

President's Committee on Employment of People with Disabilities
1111 20th St., N.W., Suite 636, Washington, DC 20036
(202) 653-5044

PCEPD is a public-private partnership of national and state organizations and individuals working to improve the lives of individuals with disabilities. Although membership is limited, the general public and employers can call PCEPD with questions on hiring individuals with disabilities or on any other topic, and anyone can obtain PCEPD publications. PCEPD also publishes a free quarterly magazine, *Worklife*, which focuses on information vital to both employers and individuals with disabilities seeking employment.

National Sports and Recreational Organizations for Individuals with Disabilities

National Foundation of Wheelchair Tennis
940 Calle Amanecer, Suite B, San Clemente, CA 92672
(714) 361-6811

A nonprofit organization, **NFWT** works to promote the sport of wheelchair tennis. The group has educational representatives in almost every city in the U.S. and has enlisted the support of such professional tennis organizations as the United States Tennis Association, the United States Tennis Registry, Vic Braden's Tennis Academy, and the U.S. Professional Tennis Association. NFWT sponsors exhibitions, clinics, tournaments, and sports camps, and offers instructional videos and publications. NFWT will gladly help volunteers find existing programs in their communities.

National Handicapped Sports
1145 19th St., N.W., Suite 717, Washington, DC 20036
(301) 652-7505

NHS is a nonprofit organization with sixty chapters nationwide providing year-round sports and recreation activities for persons of all ages with orthopedic, spinal cord, neuromuscular, and visual impairments. NHS publishes a newsletter, *Handicapped Sport Report*, which includes information on national activities and events, profiles of athletes, and other items concerning professional and amateur athletes with disabilities. NHS needs volunteers for an array of activities, so contact the national headquarters for information on a program near you. Contributions of sports equipment are appreciated.

North American Riding for the Handicapped Association, Inc.
P.O. Box 33150, Denver, CO 80233
(303) 452-1212 or 1-800-369-RIDE (7433)

NARHA is a nonprofit organization with more than 450 affiliated therapeutic riding centers across the U.S. and Canada. The association serves nearly 21,000 riders and is supported by a network of more than 13,000 volunteers. Membership ($35) includes a one-year subscription to the bimonthly *NARHA News*, discounts on merchandise (such as posters, videos, mugs, hats, and T-shirts), and the NARHA guide. Volunteers (who need not have any expertise with horses) can contact the national headquarters for information on opportunities in their community.

Special Olympics International
1350 New York Ave., N.W., Suite 500
Washington, DC 20005
(202) 628-3630

Special Olympics is an international nonprofit organization dedicated to sponsoring year-round sports training and athletic competition in a variety of Olympic-type events for children and adults with mental retardation. Currently, more than 750,000 Special Olympics athletes participate in programs in the U.S. and in ninety other nations. The organization gives these individuals the opportunity to develop physical abilities, demonstrate courage, experience joy, and participate in sharing gifts, skills, and friendship with their families, other athletes, and the community. Special Olympics welcomes volunteers (more than 500,000 volunteers are involved already, but more are needed) for coaching, fundraising, officiating, organizing, and countless other services. To find the program near you, check the phone book or call the international headquarters.

U.S. Association for Blind Athletes
33 N. Institute St., West Hall, 3rd Floor
Colorado Springs, CO 80903
(719) 630-0422

The nonprofit **USABA** provides individuals who are blind or visually impaired with opportunities to participate in various sports. USABA is dedicated to emphasizing the abilities of persons who are visually impaired and to encouraging independence and personal confidence through discipline, dedication, and competition. Everyone, sighted or visually impaired, can participate in USABA activities as volunteers, coaches, guides, and fundraisers. Contributions of sports equipment are also appreciated.

United States Cerebral Palsy Athletic Association
34518 Warren Road, Suite 264, Westland, MI 48185
(313) 425-8961, FAX: (313) 425-6510

The nonprofit **USCPAA** offers competitive sports opportunities and support mechanisms to persons with cerebral palsy, as well as to stroke victims and persons with closed-head injuries. Participants range from the beginning athlete to the elite, international-caliber competitor. Because cerebral palsy manifests itself in many ways and in varying degrees, USCPAA offers a broad spectrum of sports so that all athletes will have the opportunity to become truly competitive. Sports offered by USCPAA at local, regional, national, and international levels include archery, bowling, cycling, horseback riding, powerlifting, soccer, slalom, swimming, track/field/cross-country, and wheelchair team handball. Volunteers are needed at local USCPAA programs as coaches, spectators, fundraisers, and coordinators of the sports events (for example, timers and field station operators). Membership ($15 for individuals, $10 for athletes) includes a quarterly newsletter with up-to-date information on the world of CP sports, competition updates, training information, schedule of events, equipment information, and information exchanges from local programs nationwide.

Blindness and Visual Impairments

What You Can Do

☞ **Be sensitive to the needs and dignity of persons who are blind or visually impaired.** Here are some suggestions (adapted, with permission, from the **American Council of the Blind**, page 201), "When You Meet a Blind Person":

- **If you encounter a person who is blind and seems to be in need of help, don't hesitate to ask him or her if you can be of assistance.** This lets the person know you are willing to assist when necessary, but it also indicates your confidence in his or her ability to act independently.
- **If you are going to physically guide a person who is blind, allow him or her to take your arm and follow the movements of your body.** Avoid grabbing the person and pulling or pushing him or her.
- **Never take hold of a guide dog's harness or even pet the dog.** The dog is "on duty" and cannot have any distractions. The dog's owner has received extensive training in handling and working with the dog, and commands given to the dog by a person other than the master can be confusing and dangerous. Talk to the person, not to the dog.
- **Talk with persons who are blind the same way you would with anyone else.** Many people mistakenly seem to think that blind persons are also partially deaf and talk to them too loudly. Speak in a normal tone and directly to the person, not through a third party.
- **Don't feel embarrassed if you use the words *see* or *look*.** This is common language and is perfectly appropriate to use.
- **When approaching a person who is blind, identify yourself by name.** Let the person know that you are talking to him or her by simply tapping the person on the arm. Disguising your voice or playing "guess who" is not amusing and can be quite embarrassing.
- **When traveling alone, persons who are blind often ask directions.** Try to give directions in terms of so many feet to the right, straight ahead, etc. When directing a person who is blind to a seat, place the person's hand on the back or arm of the chair and say, for example, "Your hand is on the left arm of the chair."

- **If you are dining with a person who is blind, you may be of assistance by helping the person locate food on the plate.** If the person has a guide dog, do not feed the dog. All owners depend on their dogs' strict obedience. Plus, most owners watch their dogs' diets very carefully and do not want the mealtime routine and discipline broken.
- **When you leave a person who is blind, remember to tell him or her that you are departing.** It is easy to forget this and leave the person stranded, talking to empty air.
- **Above all, simply use common sense.** Persons who are blind appreciate attention the same way sighted persons do, but they also want their friends and others they encounter to be natural, not unnecessarily solicitous or condescending. Pity should not be a part of your approach to people who are blind. Expect the same level of performance from them as you would from sighted people, even though persons who are blind may use different methods to accomplish the same end.

☞ **Help out at an organization in your area that offers services to individuals who are blind or visually impaired.** Volunteers are needed for a variety of direct services, including providing transportation; reading books or newspapers to persons who are blind; helping with independent living skills, such as cooking, housekeeping, and money management; assisting with summer programs for children who are blind; and visiting the individuals, particularly elderly persons, to make sure everything is in order in the home (checking for broken glass on the floor or for plants in need of water, for instance). Volunteers can also help with administrative duties, fundraising, and recruiting. Also, if you have extra concert tickets, consider donating them to one of these organizations. Check the national organizations listed in this section for referrals to community-based groups (see, in particular, **National Industries for the Blind,** page 203). **Volunteer Clearinghouses** (page 6) should also have available opportunities.

☞ **Volunteer to work for Recording for the Blind** (page 203). If you are an excellent reader and can speak clearly, you can help make tapes for individuals with visual impairments.

☞ **Support organizations that provide guide dogs for individuals who are blind or visually impaired.** Many of these organizations welcome supplies (such as dog bowls, leashes, and food) and volunteers to assist with various activities. The organizations also need "puppy raisers," who take puppies into their homes for about a year. Write to or call a group near you for more information:

Eye Dog Foundation for the Blind
512 N. Larch Mont Boulevard
Los Angeles, CA 90004
(213) 468-8856

Fidelco Guide Dog Foundations
P.O. Box 142
Bloomfield, CT 06002
(203) 243-5200

Guide Dog Foundation for the Blind
371 East Jericho Turnpike
Smithtown, NY 11787
(516) 265-2121

Guide Dogs for the Blind
P.O. Box 151200
San Rafael, CA 94915-1200
(415) 499-4000

Guide Dogs of the Desert
P.O. Box 1692
Palm Springs, CA 92262
(619) 329-6257

Guiding Eyes for the Blind
611 Granite Springs Road
Yorktown Heights, NY 10598
(914) 245-4024

International Guiding Eyes
13445 Glenoaks Boulevard
Sylmar, CA 91342
(818) 362-5834

Leader Dogs for the Blind
1039 South Rochester Road
Rochester, MI 48063
(313) 651-9011

Pilot Dogs, Inc.
625 West Town St.
Columbus, OH 43215
(614) 221-6367

The Seeing Eye
P.O. Box 375
Morristown, NJ 07960
(201) 539-4425

Southeastern Guide Dogs
4210 77th St. E.
Palmetto, FL 34212
(813) 729-5665

If you cannot find a guide-dog organization in your area, see page 182 for more information on dogs for individuals with disabilities.

☞ **If you are an employer, make an effort to hire individuals who are blind or visually impaired.** Check the national organizations listed in the section, National Organizations for the Employment of Individuals with Disabilities, page 194, and the What You Can Do section on page 184.

National Organizations

American Council of the Blind
1155 15th St., N.W., Suite 720, Washington, DC 20005
(202) 467-5081 or 1-800-424-8666

ACB is dedicated to improving the well-being of all people who are blind and visually impaired. The nonprofit council strives to improve educational and rehabilitative facilities and opportunities; to encourage and assist people who are blind to develop their abilities; and to educate the public on the capabilities of people who are blind everywhere. ACB offers numerous books and publications, including a braille newsletter, *The Braille Forum*, and has a toll-free information and referral number. An indispensable resource, ACB can refer volunteers to organizations and programs in their communities that serve individuals who are blind or visually impaired.

American Foundation for the Blind
15 West 16th St., New York, NY 10011
(212) 620-2000 or 1-800-232-5463
TDD: (212) 620-2158, FAX: (212) 727-7418

AFB is a national, nonprofit organization whose primary mission is to ensure the development, maintenance, and constant improvement of services for blind and visually impaired people in the United States. Through its national headquarters, regional centers, and government relations office, AFB provides a continuum of services to help meet the needs of professionals in the blindness and low-vision fields, as well as the needs of those who are blind or visually impaired themselves. These services include (among many others) technological research and development, childhood and school-age education, rehabilitation and employment, and legislative advocacy. (For information specific to legislation, call the Washington, D.C., office at *202-457-1487*.)

Blinded American Veterans Foundation
(see Veterans, page 359)

Blinded Veterans Association
(see Veterans, page 360)

Helen Keller National Center for Deaf-Blind Youths and Adults
(see page 207)

National Federation of the Blind
1800 Johnson St., Baltimore MD 21230
(301) 659-9314

NFB is the largest nonprofit organization of the blind in America (sighted persons are welcome to join, too). NFB is dedicated to integrating individuals who are blind or visually impaired into society by working to remove legal, economic, and social discrimination; educating the public about new issues concerning blindness; and to helping people who are blind exercise their individual talents and capacities to the fullest. NFB also has a catalog of films, videos, and literature in braille and print (including *The Blind in the Medical Profession* and *The Bottom Line Is Respect for People*). The monthly magazine *Braille Monitor* (in braille print, or on record or cassette) covers news of issues important to the blind. Blind individuals and other interested persons can join local chapters for a minimum membership fee.

National Industries for the Blind
524 Hamburg Turnpike, CN969, Wayne, NJ 07474-0969
(201) 595-9200

NIB is a nonprofit corporation representing more than 100 associated industries serving people who are blind in thirty-six states, the District of Columbia, and Puerto Rico. NIB's associated agencies strive to help people who are blind or visually impaired reach their individual potential. Services, which vary nationwide, include providing job and family counseling, instruction in braille and other communication aids, and assistance in independent living skills. Volunteers can help out with all of these services and can also participate in programs aimed specifically at children who are blind. If you are interested in obtaining additional information or need the name of an agency location near you, contact the national headquarters.

Recording for the Blind
20 Roszel Rd., Princeton, NJ 08540
(609) 452-0606

The nonprofit **Recording for the Blind** provides textbooks, library services, and other educational resources to people who cannot read standard print because of visual, physical, or perceptual disabilities. Over the years, RFB has evolved from a small volunteer organization into a major national resource, operating more than thirty recording studios across the country and providing thousands of books to people in all fifty states. All books are recorded by RFB's volunteers (numbering about 4,000). Although RFB provides books that cover a diversity of issues and subjects, volunteers with backgrounds in science and mathematics are especially needed. For more information or the location of an RFB affiliate in your area, call the national headquarters.

Deafness and Hearing Loss

What You Can Do

☞ **Be sensitive to the needs and dignity of individuals who are deaf or hard-of-hearing, especially when you are communicating with them.** Here are some tips to consider (adapted, with permission, from "Communicating with Hard of Hearing People" by the **Alexander Graham Bell Association for the Deaf**, page 206):

- **Be sure that you have the person's attention.** Gently touch his or her arm, wave, or find another way to establish contact.
- **Do not assume that the person can read lips.** If he or she does not, use your imagination to find ways of communicating. Write, draw pictures, or act out what you're trying to say.
- **Move closer to the individual.** Many people raise their voices or shout instead of moving closer. Shouting distorts your features and can be especially discomforting to people with hearing aids. Speak naturally—don't exaggerate mouth movements or talk too slowly (but don't rush, either).
- **If the person has a hearing aid, turn off the radio, television, running water, air conditioner, or anything else that may be making noise.** The noises may not seem loud to you, but they are magnified by a hearing aid and can interfere with communication.
- **Face the individual and speak at his or her own eye level.** Do not chew gum, smoke, or cover your mouth while speaking.
- **If an interpreter is helping you communicate with a person who is deaf, talk to the person, not the interpreter.** For example, don't say, "Does [the person] like this book?" Instead, say, "Do you like this book?" while looking at him or her.
- **If the person does not understand you, try rewording a message instead of repeating it.** Since some words are easier to lipread than others, rephrasing a message may make it easier for the person to understand.
- **Extend extra consideration in a group.** Only one person should be speaking at a time, so try not to talk over others.
- **Use common sense and show special awareness.** Call the person by name to initiate the conversation, and try to give a frame of reference for the discussion by mentioning the topic at the outset. Be patient, and don't talk down to the person.

☞ **Work to eliminate stereotypes, myths, and insensitivity about deafness and hearing loss whenever you are exposed to them.** Educate yourself so that you can educate others. Put up posters or give people information or publications on the abilities and successes of individuals who are deaf or hard-of-hearing.

☞ **Volunteer at an organization in your community that helps** individuals who are deaf or hard-of-hearing. These organizations often need volunteers for various tasks, including direct services, administrative help, and fundraising assistance.

☞ **Support organizations that provide dogs for individuals who are deaf or hard-of-hearing.** Many organizations have on-site volunteer opportunities or need individuals to raise puppies. Write to or call an organization near you to see how you can help out. Here are some of the major U.S. organizations:

Connecticut Canine Education Center
239 Maple Hill Ave.
Newington, CT 06111
(203) 666-4646

Dogs for the Deaf, Inc.
10175 Wheeler Road
Central Point, OR 97502
(503) 826-9220

E.A.R. Foundation
2000 Church St., Box 111
Nashville, TN 37236
(615) 329-7807

Florida Dog Guides for the Deaf, Inc.
P.O. Box 20662
Bradenton, FL 34203
(813) 748-8245

International Hearing Dog
5901 East 89th Avenue
Henderson, CO 80640
(303) 287-EARS (3277)

Red Acre Farm Hearing Dog Program
Box 278
Stow, MA 01775
(508) 897-8343

San Francisco SPCA Hearing Dog Training Center
2500 16th St.
San Francisco, CA 94103
(415) 554-3020

If you cannot find an assistance-dog organization in your area, see page 182 for more information on dogs for individuals with disabilities.

☞ **If you are an employer, make an effort to hire individuals who are deaf or hard-of-hearing.** Check the organizations listed in the section, National Organizations for the Employment of Individuals with Disabilities, page 194 and the What You Can Do section on page 184:

National Organizations

Alexander Graham Bell Association for the Deaf
3417 Volta Place, N.W., Washington, DC 20007
(202) 337-5220, FAX: (202) 337-8314

A nonprofit organization, **AGBAD** promotes public education to encourage early identification of hearing loss, particularly in children; monitors legislation that affects the hard-of-hearing; grants scholarships and financial aid to prelingually deaf students; and provides various other services related to hearing loss, particularly for children. AGBAD has up-to-date information and publications on hearing loss and related issues (for example, *Communicating with Hard-of-Hearing People* and *They Do Belong: Mainstreaming the Hearing Impaired*). You can also order **Hearing Alert!** materials, which are part of a public-information campaign to encourage early detection of hearing loss in children. The materials are appropriate for hospitals, doctors' offices, schools, and service clubs. A $40 membership fee ($20 for students) entitles you to, among other things, *Newsounds*, the AGBAD newsletter; *Our Kids Magazine* (for parents); *The Volta Review*; and discounts on AGBAD publications and materials.

American Deafness and Rehabilitation Association
P.O. Box 251554, Little Rock, AR 72225
(501) 375-6643

ADARA is a nonprofit partnership of national organizations, local affiliates, professionals, and concerned individuals working to ensure that people who are deaf receive the services they deserve. The association, encourages research, runs a forum to help people better understand the needs of deaf individuals, and supports legislative actions in the interest of the deaf community. Regular membership ($21.50) includes one-year subscriptions to the quarterly *Journal of American Deafness and Rehabilitation Association* and the *ADARA Newsletter*, a bimonthly publication with updates on events, legislation, information of national interest, conferences/workshops, and employment opportunities (employers looking for applicants who are deaf can advertise in the newsletter).

Helen Keller National Center for Deaf-Blind Youths and Adults
111 Middle Neck Road, Sands Point, NY 11050
(516) 944-8900 (Voice and TTY)

The **Helen Keller Center** is the only not-for-profit national agency that provides diagnostic evaluation, short-term comprehensive rehabilitation and personal adjustment training, and job preparation and placement for all Americans who are deaf-blind. HKNC's mission is to enable its clients to return to their home communities to live and work as independently as possible and to enjoy a full and productive life. The center operates through its ten regional offices, thirty affiliated agencies, a National Training Team, a Technical Assistance Center (which develops transitional services for youth), National Parent Network, and Services for Older Adults who are deaf-blind. HKNC also serves as a resource center for materials on deaf-blind issues and publishes a magazine in large print and braille, *NAT-CENT NEWS* (a free periodical that comes out three times a year and contains profiles of deaf-blind individuals, new HKNC programs, and related news); a newsletter for parents and families of children who are deaf-blind; and a national directory of agencies serving individuals who are deaf-blind. Contact HKNC if you are looking for applicant referrals and information on hiring individuals who are deaf-blind, or if you want to volunteer at an organization that provides services for individuals who are deaf-blind.

National Association of the Deaf
814 Thayer Ave., Silver Spring, MD 20910
(301) 587-1788 (Voice and TDD)

NAD is one of the oldest and largest national nonprofit consumer organizations of individuals with disabilities. Its primary mission is to ensure that a comprehensive, coordinated system of services is accessible to all persons who are deaf or hard-of-hearing, enabling them to achieve their full potential through increased independence, productivity, and integration into the community. NAD monitors and works to influence legislation affecting individuals who are deaf or hard-of-hearing; sponsors conferences and forums, youth programs, and the Miss Deaf America competition; disseminates information and makes referrals (particularly for individuals who are deaf or for their families); and publishes periodicals and books related to deafness (for example, *Deaf Heritage, A Kaleidoscope of Deaf America*). Membership ($25) includes subscription to the *Deaf American*, a quarterly magazine carrying in-depth articles and features, and the *NAD Broadcaster*, which is published eleven times a year and contains shorter columns and timely articles, including advertisements that are of special interest to the deaf and hard-of-hearing community. Volunteers (members and nonmembers alike) are needed at the local chapters.

National Information Center on Deafness
Gallaudet University
800 Florida Ave., N.E., Washington, DC 20002
(202) 651-5051, TDD: (202) 651-5052

A nonprofit organization, **NICD** serves as a centralized source of accurate, up-to-date information on all aspects of deafness and hearing loss. The center collects, develops, and disseminates information on deafness, hearing loss, organizations, services, and programs. It also offers fact sheets, resource listings, reading lists, and brochures. NICD can provide potential volunteers with information on organizations in their community that work with individuals who are deaf or hard-of-hearing. NICD is a valuable resource for anyone needing information on deafness or hearing loss.

Mental Illness
What You Can Do

☞ **Learn about the causes and effects of mental illness so that you may be better able to recognize if a friend or family member has such an illness.** Mental illnesses are more common than you may think, affecting one out of every four families in America, according to the **American Mental Health Fund**. If you think that you or someone you know may have a mental illness, get help as soon as possible. The AMHF estimates that only one in five people with a mental illness ever seeks professional help. The AMHF claims that with proper treatment, two out of three individuals with mental illnesses can expect to get better. The national organizations listed in this section can give you more information on mental illnesses.

☞ **Help eliminate stereotypes, myths, and insensitive comments concerning mental illnesses.** Not only painful to those individuals who have mental illnesses, these stereotypes discourage people who may need help from finding it. Many of the national organizations in this section offer free posters and materials for use in offices, schools, religious congregations, and other public places.

☞ **Volunteer to work at an organization for individuals with mental illnesses.** Organizations are located across the country and welcome volunteer help for a variety of services, including administrative work and fundraising. **The COMPEER Program** (page 210), in particular, is an excellent person-to-person program in need of volunteers. Check the national organizations listed in this section for other referrals and volunteer opportunities.

☞ **If you are an employer, make an effort to hire persons who have or are being treated for a mental illness.** Check the national organizations listed in the section, National Organizations for the Employment of Individuals with Disabilities, page 194, and the What You Can Do section, page 184.

National Organizations

American Mental Health Fund
P.O. Box 17389, Washington, DC 20041
(703) 573-2200 or 1-800-433-5959 (recorded message)

The nonprofit **American Mental Health Fund** is dedicated to raising public awareness of mental illnesses and to eliminating negative stigmas. The only mental health organization conducting a nationwide educational campaign with the Advertising Council, AMHF provides posters (for example, "Are Your Attitudes about Mental Illness Still in the Dark Ages?", informative booklets (for example, *Understanding Mental Illnesses*), and other educational materials, including an awarding-winning video (many of these materials are free). AMHF offers opportunities for volunteers nationwide in its media network, as well as locally in the Falls Church, Virginia, office.

COMPEER, Inc.
Monroe Square, Suite B-1, 259 Monroe Ave.
Rochester, NY 14607
(716) 546-8280

COMPEER, Inc., a national nonprofit organization, matches trained volunteers with mental-health clients in a one-to-one friendship relationship. The goal of the program is to assist children and adults receiving mental-health treatment to reach their maximum level of functioning by fostering a caring, supportive relationship between each client and volunteer. Volunteers are asked to make a commitment of one hour a week for at least a year (many volunteers, however, extend their commitment past one year and spend more than one hour weekly with their friends). Volunteers are interviewed, receive five hours of formal training from senior resource volunteers and COMPEER staff, and are then matched with a client referral. The criteria used in the matching process include similar interests, age preferences, and geographical proximity. Contact the national headquarters for information on a COMPEER Program near you or for information on starting one in your community.

National Alliance for the Mentally Ill
2101 Wilson Boulevard, Suite 302, Arlington, VA 22201
(703) 524-7600 or 1-800-950-NAMI (6264)

NAMI is a nonprofit organization dedicated to eradicating mental illnesses and improving the quality of life of those affected by these illnesses. NAMI educates the public through radio, television, and press coverage; acts as an advocate for mentally ill people by bringing their problems to the attention of local, state, and federal governments; and informs Congress about the need for more research money. NAMI also has special outreach programs, including **NAMI CAN** (Children and Adolescent Network), which helps children with mental illnesses and their families, and the **Homeless and Missing Mentally Ill Network**, which offers support, education, and assistance to families with missing or homeless loved ones; seeks to reunite families when possible; and works to expand services to assist people with mental illnesses, wherever they are. The organization offers posters and publications about mental illness as well as referrals for volunteers looking for mental-health organizations in their community. An associate membership ($25) includes a subscription to *The Advocate*, NAMI's regular newsletter.

National Mental Health Association
1021 Prince St., Alexandria, VA 22314
(703) 684-7722, For informative materials on mental illnesses:
1-800-969-NMHA (6642)

A nonprofit group, **NMHA** is the only citizen's volunteer advocacy organization concerned with all aspects of mental health and mental illnesses. NMHA has been a leader in research, prevention, and education for decades. At the national level, NMHA advocates for mental-health programs, including research, income support, education, rehabilitation, housing, and rights; the elimination of discrimination against people with mental illnesses; and the refinement of all programs that do not adequately meet the needs of those with mental illnesses. At the local level, NMHA affiliates recruit, train, and place thousands of volunteers in programs and activities to assist persons with mental illnesses and their families. Affiliates serve their communities by organizing self-help and support groups, providing information and referral services, assisting individuals in obtaining desired services and in protecting their rights, educating the public, and lobbying for increased attention to the needs of people with mental illnesses. NMHA has informative publications (such as *Homeless in America: A Photographic Project*), posters, legislative updates, and other materials on suicide, depression, homelessness, stress, and a variety of other topics. Contact NMHA for more information on mental illnesses and volunteer opportunities.

Mental Retardation

What You Can Do

☞ **Educate yourself about mental retardation and work to eliminate myths, stereotypes, and insensitive comments.** All of the national organizations in this section have information on mental retardation, and some have posters, videos, books, and other materials you can use to educate others.

☞ **Volunteer to work at an organization for individuals who are mentally retarded.** These organizations are located across the country and need volunteers for a variety of services, including administrative work, fundraising, working with children, and helping out with summer programs, camps, and dances. Check the organizations listed in this chapter for referrals. You can also check the phone book under "Mental Retardation" or "Association for Retarded Citizens of . . . ".

☞ **Become a volunteer for Special Olympics** (see page 196). Volunteers are needed as coaches, officials, event organizers, and even as cheering spectators. Schools can help out by making their facilities available for Special Olympics events; businesses can donate their services and offer financial assistance.

☞ **If you are an employer, make an effort to hire individuals with mental retardation.** Although many persons with mental retardation cannot perform all of the tasks that other individuals can, there is a great deal they can do. Check the national organizations listed in the section, National Organizations for the Employment of Individuals with Disabilities, page 194, and the What You Can Do section, page 184.

☞ **Consider adopting or becoming a foster parent to a child who is mentally retarded.** Many of the organizations listed in this section have general literature on raising children who are mentally retarded. See Adoption (page 142) and Foster Care (page 150) in the Children and Young Adults chapter for more information.

National Organizations

American Association on Mental Retardation
1719 Kalorama Road, N.W., Washington, DC 20009
(202) 387-1968 or 1-800-424-3688

AAMR is a nonprofit organization of professionals and concerned individuals working to promote the well-being of persons with mental retardation. The association helps review and shape public policies; encourages research and education; fosters communication and excellence among those in the field by advancing the highest standards of service, training, and research; and promotes high-quality services for those with mental retardation and their families. AAMR distributes several publications, including *Parents for Children, Children for Parents: The Adoption Alternative* and *Aging and Mental Retardation: Extending the Continuum.* AAMR has three periodicals: *American Journal on Mental Retardation*, the nation's oldest and most respected journal on mental retardation; *Mental Retardation*, a bimonthly journal of program and research information, featuring lively articles and current trends; and *News & Notes*, a bimonthly newsletter on developments in federal, state, and provincial governments, current projects, job openings, and other news of the field. Student members ($20) and active members ($80) receive all three; associate members ($35) receive just *News & Notes*. Volunteers (members and nonmembers alike) are encouraged to work at any of AAMR's local chapters around the country.

The Association for Persons with Severe Handicaps
(see page 185)

Association for Retarded Citizens
2501 Avenue J, P.O. Box 6109, Arlington, TX 76005
(817) 640-0204

ARC is the largest nonprofit volunteer organization devoted solely to improving the welfare of all children and adults with mental retardation and the welfare of their families. The association works to provide more than seven million Americans who have mental retardation with services that will enable them to reach their highest level of personal achievement. Activities include increasing employment opportunities, training, education, and independent living opportunities; conducting a nationwide television, radio, and print media campaign to educate the public about mental retardation; supporting programs that work to prevent and reduce the effects of mental retardation; and working to ensure that the rights of individuals who are mentally retarded are promoted and protected. ARC has chapters nationwide, so if you are interested in helping out in some way, check the white pages of the phone book under "Association for Retarded Citizens of . . . ," or contact the national headquarters for the chapternearest you. Volunteer opportunities, as well as membership fees, differ from chapter to chapter, but help is always needed.

National Down Syndrome Congress
1800 Dempster St., Park Ridge, IL 60068
(708) 823-7550 or 1-800-232-6372

The nonprofit **NDSC** seeks to promote recognition of the value and dignity of individuals with Down syndrome. Services include advocating for a full range of opportunities and resources that meet individual and family needs; building a sense of community and fellowship for all persons concerned with Down syndrome; encouraging ethically responsible research relating to Down syndrome; educating parents, professionals, and the general public on all aspects of mental retardation and the needs, rights, and capabilities of individuals with Down syndrome (contact NDSC for a full listing of products and publications); encouraging legislation that benefits individuals with Down syndrome and their families; and promoting full participation of persons with Down syndrome in all aspects of community life. Basic membership ($15 and up) includes a subscription to *Down Syndrome News*, a journal published ten times a year, containing up-to-date information on a variety of issues pertaining to Down syndrome.

National Down Syndrome Society
666 Broadway, New York, NY 10012
(212) 460-9330 or 1-800-221-4602

NDSS is a nonprofit organization that works to promote a better understanding of Down syndrome, to encourage scientific research into its causes and effects, and to provide services for families of individuals with Down syndrome. NDSS also has an extensive selection of bibliographies, reading lists, and audio and visual tapes (for example, *The Best of Me*—a cassette with songs and poetry from a parent to her child with Down syndrome; *Gifts of Love*—a 25-minute video that presents the stories of families and children with Down syndrome), and informative fact sheets and brochures addressing facts and myths about Down syndrome. Individuals interested in adopting a child with Down syndrome can call NDSS for referrals and related information.

Education and Illiteracy

Why Help Is Needed

If the specific issues in this book were placed in order of importance, education would have to be put, if not first, then near the beginning. The connection between a lack of education and other societal problems, such as unemployment, homelessness, alcohol and drug abuse, and crime, is often a close one, too close to be overlooked. To address the state of education in America is to begin to address these problems as well. Consequently, education must be a high-priority concern, and the situation could hardly be more urgent.

According to the Business Council for Effective Literacy (BCEL), approximately twenty-seven million Americans over the age of seventeen—one out of every five adults—cannot read or write. That's twenty-seven million adults who cannot read a newspaper headline, a menu, safety instructions on a medicine bottle, or a job application. The Coalition for Literacy[1] reports that another forty-seven million are only minimally literate. The effect of this on the nation's economy is severe. The Coalition estimates that businesses lose approximately 237 billion dollars every year because of illiteracy, and illiterate or minimally literate workers result in lower productivity, wasteful accidents, and poor product quality. Not surprisingly, many people who cannot read often cannot find work; illiterate individuals make up fifty to seventy-five percent of the nation's unemployed, swelling welfare costs and diminishing tax revenues.[2]

There are other costs that cannot be measured. Reading can open the imagination to an infinite universe of places, characters, and perspectives. Reading a novel, poem, play, short story, or editorial can change one's outlook, inspire new ideas, or simply entertain. Anyone who has ever stayed up all night to finish a book, read a bedtime

---

[1]The Coalition for Literacy is a national campaign working to end illiteracy in America. For more information about the campaign, contact the Contact Center, Inc., *P.O. Box 81826, Lincoln, NE 68501*; 1-800-228-8813.
[2]According to the Coalition for Literacy.

story to a child, or written a letter to a friend understands the importance and power of words.

The facts concerning the nation's schools and drop-out rates are also discouraging. The National Dropout Prevention Center (NDPC) estimates that one out of every four American students drops out of school, and in large cities and rural areas, these rates are even higher.[3] The employment rate for dropouts is dismal, with fewer than half finding jobs. What's more, NDPC also reports that more than eighty percent of new jobs require a high school diploma, as does the military, which used to be a primary employer of dropouts. Even students who do graduate may need help: Cities in Schools estimates that 750,000 of them don't have the skills to read their high school diplomas. The Children's Defense Fund reports that American schoolchildren know less about geography than school children in Iran, less about math than school-children in Japan, and less about science than school children in Spain.

Today's students, however, don't have it easy. Many students must juggle schoolwork with a job to help support their families. And there are many students in America who go to schools that more closely resemble war zones than they do educational institutions. Even in many of the nation's private schools violence, crime, and drug and alcohol abuse are serious problems. (This is probably one of the reasons why 135,000 students bring guns to school every day.[4]) And many students must cope with physical and emotional abuse, divorce, and a multitude of other home-related problems.

Many teachers don't have it any easier. Not only must they teach, they often must act as counselors, disciplinarians, coaches, and mentors. A teacher's duties may even include providing the support that an indifferent or working parent does not or cannot offer. Teachers are also finding that they must address issues that were less severe or even unheard of twenty-five years ago, including AIDS, substance abuse, and teenage pregnancy. There may be unqualified teachers in America, but there are also teachers who qualify, quite literally, as saviors.

Clearly, the nation's education and illiteracy problems are too complex and severe to be solved by any one group of persons. To help solve the education crisis, communities must work together, contributing whatever resources and efforts they can. Parents, teachers, students, and concerned individuals must recognize how valu-

---

[3] According to the Children's Defense Fund.
[4] According to Laubach Literacy International.

able they can be in improving our schools, supporting our young people, and fighting illiteracy. Until this nation works together, a vast field of talent, knowledge, and energy will be lost, and this loss will be multiplied into countless other problems.

What You Can Do

☞ **Keep up on issues and legislation related to education and illiteracy.** If you learn of education-related legislation, follow up on it and express your concern or approval to your government representatives. Most of the national organizations listed in this chapter can provide you with a variety of legislative updates and related information on education and illiteracy. (See also Voicing Your Opinion, page 363.)

☞ **Educate your friends, family members, co-workers, and classmates about the need to improve our nation's schools and to encourage people, young and old, to read.** The more people understand the seriousness of the problem, the more, one hopes, they will want to respond. Most of the national organizations listed in this chapter have informative pamphlets and booklets on education and illiteracy. The **American Library Association** (page 228) also distributes a variety of posters encouraging people to read. See if you can put them up in schools, offices, religious organizations, and other public places.

☞ **If you have children or younger siblings, read to them on a consistent basis and encourage them to read and go to the library.** Reading to young children is a constructive way for family members to spend time together. The American Library Association reports that regardless of factors such as the parents' education level or work schedule, or the family's economic status, young people who read a lot perform better in school and on standardized tests than those who do not. **Reading Is Fundamental** (page 231), the **National Parent-Teacher Association** (page 225), and the **Contact Center, Inc**. (page 230) offer a variety of informative brochures and pamphlets for parents aimed at encouraging young people to read.

☞ **At holidays, birthdays, and other celebrations for children, give gifts that foster creativity and thinking.** Books, magazine subscriptions, educational board games, educational video games, and art or science kits are just some of the worthwhile educational gifts available. (See also Animal Town, page 80, for its selection of educational games and toys.)

☞ **Become involved with your children's schooling.** Talk with your children about what they are learning each day, help them with their homework, talk with their teacher(s), and attend school committee meetings and any activities in which your child participates. Parental involvement lets teachers know that they have your support at home and shows your children that their education is important to you.

☞ **Don't throw out books or reading materials you no longer want.** School libraries, public libraries, prisons, hospitals, shelters for the homeless, and other institutions can put these books and materials to good use. Check with friends and neighbors to see if they have anything to donate, too.

☞ **Sponsor a book drive** in your office, school, church, synagogue, or neighborhood. Collect both new and old books for shelters, literacy programs, school libraries, and other institutions.

☞ **Give a child a magazine subscription to encourage him or her to read, or give a subscription to a school library that does not have the funds.** Young children enjoy getting mail in their name, and a magazine subscription gives them something to look forward to on a regular basis. Check your local magazine stand or library for magazines you feel look entertaining and educational.

☞ **Support your local public school.** When searching for volunteer opportunities in their community, people often overlook public schools. If you need information on nearby schools or available volunteer opportunities, contact the local school board. (Note: Bilingual volunteers—especially those who speak Spanish—are often in great demand as tutors or mentors.) Look in the phone book under ''Schools—Public'' for the ''Volunteers'' number (usually in the government pages) or for a ''Public School Information'' listing. Here are a few ways adults (and students) can help out:

- **Tutor students having trouble in particular subjects or help a teacher with general classroom activities.**
- **Become a mentor.** Different from tutors, mentors primarily provide support, encouragement, or simply a listening ear. Mentors can even be students helping out younger students.

EDUCATION AND ILLITERACY

- **Help with administrative or library work.**
- **Help provide supervision** at recess, lunchtime, in the classroom, or after school when kids are being picked up.
- **Offer your expertise in a particular subject,** either in a class discussion (for example, police officers talking about drugs, doctors or scientists talking about AIDS, reporters talking about particular news events) or by inviting a group of kids to your workplace if you feel it would be of interest.
- **Clean up a school playground** or get a group of people together to fix up old rooms, paint over graffiti, or do whatever other odd jobs may be needed.
- **Sponsor a field trip.** This requires a substantial amount of money, but if you can afford it, it is an excellent way to help, especially in inner-city schools.

School Volunteering, a newsletter put out by the **National Association of Partners in Education** (page 223), keeps up on volunteer programs and opportunities in education and provides tips for volunteers working in education. A subscription costs $10—the regular membership fee for NAPE's school volunteer program.

☞ **Find a literacy program in your area and become a volunteer.** Most local libraries have literacy programs, and the Contact Center, Inc. (page 230) maintains a toll-free hotline *(1-800-228-8813)* which can provide you with information on a literacy program near you. You don't need a teaching degree or any special education to become a tutor, only good reading and writing skills and patience. Most centers will give you a short training course, after which only a couple of hours a week are required to prepare lessons and actually tutor someone. Keep in mind that tutoring can be difficult work. A volunteer cannot expect to make up for several years of lost education in a short time. When progress does happen, however, it can be incredibly rewarding for both the tutor and the reader. Even if you don't want to become a tutor, you can help your local center in a variety of ways. Volunteers are often needed to work as librarians, promotional writers, fundraisers, and typists, and to help with transportation and child care.

☞ **If you are part of a business, see how your business and employees can address the educational needs of your community.** Here are just a few ideas:

- **Encourage employees to work as volunteers in local literacy programs or at schools.** Giving them a day or an afternoon off is an excellent start.
- **Set up an employee-training program** to help your employees improve their own reading skills.
- **Donate office supplies and furniture to literacy centers or schools.** Desks, chairs, bookcases, lamps, and even paper and pens may be needed by a local program.
- **If you think that your business would interest schoolchildren, consider inviting them for a field trip** and explain what you do and how the operation works.
- **Help out with publicity.** Whether by encouraging people to volunteer at their local school or by advertising for a literacy program, businesses can help develop, print, and/or distribute materials.
- **Offer literacy programs the use of your facilities.** Programs may need space for teaching, tutoring, or training.
- **Provide grants** for local efforts fighting illiteracy and helping schools in need.

See also the **Business Council for Effective Literacy**, page 229, and the **Contact Center, Inc.**, (page 230) for more information.

☞ **Volunteer to help illiterate prisoners learn to read.** Sixty percent of the nation's prisoners are illiterate, making this volunteer activity a much-needed service. For more information on getting involved, contact your **Salvation Army** (page 18), **Volunteers of America** (page 20), or **Volunteer Clearinghouse** (page 20).

☞ **If you will be graduating from college soon, consider participating in the Teach for America program** (page 228). This program selects graduating seniors from colleges and universities nationwide, prepares them in a highly intensive summer institute, and places them as teachers in areas that have persistent teacher shortages. (For general information on teaching in the U.S., see **Recruiting New Teachers, Inc.**, page 227.)

☞ **If there is no literacy center in your community, consider starting one.** With a dedicated group of friends and volunteers, you could make a tremendous positive impact upon your community. See if you can work through your local library. Write or call the **Contact Center, Inc.** (page 230) for more information.

National Education Organizations

A Better Chance, Inc.
Public School Programs
419 Boylston St., Boston, MA 02116
(617) 421-0950

A nonprofit national talent search and referral organization, **ABC** recruits academically motivated minority high school students and places them in outstanding independent and public high schools. ABC monitors the progress of all enrolled students and provides support services and information on additional educational opportunities. In particular, the **ABC Public School Programs** (PSPs) are community-based efforts in approximately thirty cities nationwide that help college-bound minority youngsters from educationally disadvantaged areas. Students referred to the PSPs live in community-based residential homes and attend the local high school. Individuals who live near a PSP (call for locations) can help by working as tutors, offering counseling, serving as host families for temporary periods of time, raising funds, and assisting with recreational activities.

Cities in Schools
1023 15th St., N.W., Suite 600, Washington, DC 20005
(202) 861-0230

CIS is the most comprehensive nonprofit organization dedicated to dropout prevention in the U.S. Headquartered in Washington, D.C., CIS operates in more than 200 educational sites throughout the U.S., helping more than 26,000 young people. The organization focuses on at-risk students, working to improve their school attendance; enhance their personal, educational, and social development; develop successful employment attitudes and skills; and increase parental involvement in their educational process. Social workers, coaches, educators, health professionals, and volunteers are brought together at each program site to form a support system for at-risk students. These partnerships work to provide needed services such as tutoring, counseling, employment, health services, and recreational and cultural activities. If you are interested in becoming involved with CIS, write or call the national headquarters for more information.

Learning Disabilities Association of America
4156 Library Road, Pittsburgh, PA 15234
(412) 341-1515

A nonprofit organization with fifty state affiliates and more than 775 local chapters, **LDA** is devoted to defining and finding solutions for the broad spectrum of learning problems. The association works to stimulate development of early detection programs; create a climate of public awareness and acceptance; disseminate information; develop and promote legislative assistance; improve regular and special education; establish career opportunities; and promote research on the prevention of learning disabilities. LDA's publications include *Dyslexia, What You Can and Can't Do About It; Learning Disabilities and Juvenile Delinquency;* and *Dispelling the Myths: College Students and Learning Disabilities*. Membership ($20) includes a subscription to *Newsbrief*, which comes out six times a year and covers current developments in the field of learning disabilities. If you're interested in volunteering for LDA, look for the affiliate in your community or contact the national headquarters for the location of the chapter nearest you.

National Alliance of Business
1201 New York Ave., N.W., Washington, DC 20005
(202) 289-2888

NAB is a nonprofit business-led organization working to build business partnerships with government, labor, and education to ensure quality in the American work force. The alliance believes that in order to remain an internationally competitive nation, we must eliminate the growing disparity between the abilities of Americans entering the work force and the skills they need to do their jobs. Specifically, NAB's objectives include helping the business community foster educational change (for example, defining specific roles for businesses in stimulating local and state restructuring initiatives and identifying the skills and resources businesses may have that educators may need to help restructure schools); helping corporations develop internal company-specific plans for long-term corporate involvement with local and state schools; and formulating policies that promote educational reform at the local, state, and national levels. NAB also has numerous publications, including *America's Leaders Speak Out on Business-Education Partnerships; Who Will Do The Work?; A Business Guide for Preparing Tomorrow's Workforce;* and *A Blueprint for Business on Restructuring Education*. If you are interested in involving your business, write or call the national headquarters for more information.

National Association for the Advancement of Colored People
Back to School/Stay in School
(see Children and Young Adults, page 134)

National Association of Partners in Education
National School Volunteer Program
209 Madison St., Suite 401, Alexandria, VA 22314
(703) 836-4880

The **National School Volunteer Program** is a nonprofit coalition of volunteers providing numerous educational services for schools and students throughout the U.S. These services include helping with the schools' administrative functions; supervising playgrounds and cafeterias; and contributing to instructional activities (as classroom aides, tutors, mentors, and guest lecturers). Parents, business employees (often given time off to help), college and high school students, senior citizens, and other interested individuals from all socioeconomic and educational backgrounds constitute the one million volunteers. The **National Association of Partners in Education**, NSVP's umbrella organization, distributes publications (for example, *American Youth: A Statistical Snapshot; Volunteers and Older Students;* and *Tips for Tutoring: A Resource Tool for School Volunteer Tutors*) and audiovisual materials. NAPE publishes *Partners in Education*, a monthly information clearinghouse on school volunteer programs and policy issues of interest to volunteer programs and partnerships, including legislation, research, and sources of funding. The newspaper is included with the regular membership fee of $60. NAPE also publishes *School Volunteering*, a quarterly newsletter for school volunteers containing profiles of outstanding volunteers and tips on good volunteer practices. The newsletter is included with the $10 NAPE membership fee. If you're interested in becoming a school volunteer or using your business's resources to help out, NAPE is one of the most valuable organizations you'll find.

The National Coalition of Advocates for Students
100 Boylston St., Suite 737, Boston, MA 02116
(617) 357-8507

A coalition of twenty-three experienced child advocacy groups in sixteen states, **NCAS** is an excellent resource for individuals looking for information on a broad range of educational issues. The coalition's catalog of publications includes *Barriers to Excellence: Our Children at Risk; Before It's Too Late: Dropout Prevention in the Middle Grades; Analysis of the U.S. Department of Education's Office of Civil Rights Elementary and Secondary School Survey;* and *Adolescent Pregnancy and Parenting: How Schools Can Respond to Children at Risk.* NCAS is dedicated to providing high-quality education for all public-school students, with a special focus on poor and minority students, recent immigrants, and students with disabilities.

National Committee for Citizens in Education
10840 Little Patuxent Parkway, Suite 301
Columbia, MD 21044-3199
(301) 997-9300 or 1-800-NET-WORK (638-9675)

NCCE encourages parent and citizen involvement in improving the quality of education for all children. This nonprofit organization helps train parents and concerned citizens to organize and strengthen their local school(s) in cooperation with teachers, school administrators, and community groups; distributes books (for example, *Dropout Prevention—A Book of Sources; You Can Improve Your Child's School: Practical Answers to Questions Parents Ask Most About Their Public Schools*), fact sheets, (such as *Single Parents and the Schools*), handbooks (for example, *Parents Organizing to Improve Schools*) and other publications; and maintains a toll-free information service (listed above). This bilingual (English and Spanish) help-line is staffed by NCCE professionals and provides callers with information, advice, and assistance on education issues and public-school problems. NCCE also publishes a bimonthly newsletter, *Network for Public Schools*, which contains information on national educational issues, recommended readings, and a listing of NCCE publications. The cost of a one-year subscription is $12.

National Dropout Prevention Center
Clemson University, 205 Martin St., Clemson, SC 29634-5111
(803) 656-2599 or 1-800-443-6392

NDPC is a nonprofit organization committed to keeping youths in school and ensuring that they receive the education that they deserve. The center helps restructure schooling processes; identify at-risk youths and increase their access to education and employment; form public-private partnerships to address the drop-out crisis from a broad perspective, and serves as a national clearinghouse of information (the organization maintains a toll-free number, listed above) to educate the public and policymakers about the nature and impact of the drop-out crisis. NDPC's publications include *Dropout Prevention Research Reports* (which provide in-depth examinations of at-risk issues), *Mentoring Programs for At-Risk Youth* (for people who want to get personally involved with at-risk youths), *Solutions and Strategies* (which covers a variety of issues and statistics in drop-out prevention), *School-Community-Business Prevention Programs*, and a quarterly journal, *National Dropout Prevention Newsletter*, which focuses on current dropout issues and prevention strategies. In addition, a computer database of model drop-out prevention programs, conferences, and references is accessible nationwide.

National Education Association
1201 16th St., N.W., Washington, DC 20036
(202) 833-4000

Although **NEA** is a professional membership organization of teachers, administrators, school support staff, and students who want to become teachers, the organization has some excellent information on a variety of educational issues. The association has a comprehensive catalog of books, films, and videos (available to anyone) on school violence, student suicide, students at risk, homeless students, learning disabilities, nutrition and learning, AIDS, student stress, teacher burnout, student pregnancy, and dozens of other topics.

National Parent-Teacher Association
700 N. Rush St., Chicago, IL 60611-2571
(312) 787-0977

NPTA is the largest nonprofit volunteer association in the U.S. working for the education, health, and safety of all children. Members include parents, teachers, students, school officials, businesspeople, and other individuals who care about children and education. The PTA works on the local, state, and national levels to promote the welfare of children in schools; to involve the community in supporting schools and school activities; to prevent drug and alcohol abuse; to increase appreciation of culture through arts programs; to address the special needs of large city schools; to monitor and influence legislation; and to provide informative books, guides, brochures, and other publications (for example, *Teens, Alcohol, and Drugs: What Parents Can Do; Children and Television: What Parents Can Do; What to Tell Your Child About Prejudice and Discrimination; Help Your Child Get the Most Out of Homework*). NPTA also publishes *PTA Today Magazine*, which focuses on a variety of educational issues as well as children's health and safety ($10 a year for seven issues) and *What's Happening in Washington*, which reports on legislative activities ($4 a year for six issues). Contact the PTA near you or the national headquarters for more information on joining, starting a local affiliate, or purchasing publications.

National Rural and Small Schools Consortium
Western Washington University
Miller Hall 359, Bellingham, WA 98225
(206) 676-3576

The consortium is an action-oriented nonprofit organization of individuals and agencies working to enhance rural and small-school education by increasing recognition of the unique contributions of rural and small schools; enhancing their quality of education; advocating for these schools at the federal, state, regional, and local levels; working to place teachers in rural schools; and providing several other services. NRSSC has a broad range of publications on rural and small schools (such as *Preventing Teenage Pregnancies in Rural America; Serving At-Risk Populations in Rural America;* and *Personnel Recruitment and Retention in Rural America*) and a newsletter, *Classroom Clips*, which comes out every six weeks and contains brief items about rural-school issues, conferences, and successful programs. Three times a year NRSSC also publishes *Journal of Rural and Small Schools*, containing both scholarly and practical field-oriented articles. Contact NRSSC for more information on membership benefits ($45 for individuals, $20 for students and retired professionals), on referrals for working in a rural school, and on recruiting individuals to work in rural schools.

The Orton Dyslexia Society
724 York Road, Baltimore, MD 21204
(301) 296-0232 or 1-800-ABCD-123 (223-3123)

ODS, a nonprofit organization, is the only American association devoted exclusively to studying and distributing information about dyslexia and helping dyslexic individuals nationwide. The society distributes a variety of publications, including *The Many Faces of*

Dyslexia; Intimacy with Language; and *Language and the Developing Child.* Membership ($55 for individuals, $25 for full-time students) includes a subscription to the yearly *Annals of Dyslexia* and the quarterly *Perspectives on Dyslexia.* Contact the national headquarters to see if there's a chapter near you that needs volunteers.

Phi Delta Kappa Educational Foundation
8th & Union, P.O. Box 789, Bloomington, IN 47402-0789
(812) 339-1156

An international professional society of men and women in education working to promote quality education, with particular emphasis on public education, **PDK** is an indispensable resource for anyone looking for up-to-date, authoritative publications and materials on a variety of educational issues. PDK literature includes *The Persistent Problems of Education; What Schools Are For; Responding to Adolescent Suicide; Drug Abuse; Dropouts; Looking into AIDS;* and *The Supreme Court's Impact on Public Education.* The foundation also publishes *Kappan*, a monthly journal (September through June) which is considered education's leading public voice. The journal includes articles and news about significant issues and developments in education. A one-year subscription costs $30.

Recruiting New Teachers, Inc.
6 Standish St., Cambridge, MA 02138
1-800-45-TEACH (458-3224)

RNT is an outstanding nationwide campaign working to encourage people to become teachers and raise the status of the profession. RNT provides interested individuals with a wide variety of materials on teaching, including information on teacher education, financial aid, certification, alternative certification/mid-career opportunities, minority opportunities, and finding a teaching job. The campaign also serves as a clearinghouse, providing recruitment agencies (such as teacher training institutions and school districts) with the names of the thousands of prospective teachers who have called RNT. These recruitment agencies then contact RNT callers with further information about teacher training, financial aid, and jobs, as well as specific information on such topics as geographical preferences (urban, suburban, rural), and teaching preferences (for example, elementary classes, special education, math/sciences, bilingual education). By June of 1990 alone, RNT had received more than 325,000 calls since its **Reach for the Power: Teach** public-service advertisements began in 1988. More than 90,000 callers have provided RNT with information about their educational backgrounds and teaching interests. This information is being shared with hundreds of teacher-recruitment agencies across the country.

Teach for America
Box 5114, New York, NY 10185
(212) 974-2456

This nonprofit organization recruits a national corps of committed individuals to teach in inner cities and rural areas of the United States for two years. The **TFA** program selects graduating seniors from colleges and universities nationwide, prepares them in a highly intensive summer institute, and places them as teachers in areas that have persistent teacher shortages. If you will be graduating from college soon, contact the national headquarters for more information on how to get involved.

National Literacy Organizations

American Library Association
Coalition for Literacy
50 East Huron St., Chicago, IL 60611
(312) 944-6780

ALA is the oldest and largest library association in the world and, through its **Coalition for Literacy** is a leader in fighting illiteracy in the U.S. The association encourages federal funding for literacy efforts; develops and sponsors public-service announcements about the illiteracy problem in the U.S.; and raises funds for literacy organizations and programs nationwide. ALA can provide you with highly informative fact sheets on illiteracy and a listing of literacy contacts in state library agencies. ALA also distributes posters (featuring such celebrities as Bo Jackson, Bette Midler, Goldie Hawn, Bill Cosby, Sting, and Steve Martin), T-shirts, bookmarks, kits, and a variety of other items with messages encouraging people to read. (ALA also has posters of people such as Gandhi, Martin Luther King, Jr., Margaret Sanger, and Eleanor Roosevelt that, while not aimed at illiteracy, are quite stunning.) Contact ALA for more information on its program and its full-color catalog.

Assault on Illiteracy Program
410 Central Park West, New York, NY 10025
(212) 967-4000

A nonprofit coalition of more than ninety national Black-led community uplifting organizations (with many more at the local level), **AOIP** works to remove the "root causes" of illiteracy (for example, lack of self-esteem, pride, hope, or security) among Black Americans and other minorities. The program has two components. One is a special ego-enhancement tutorial process. The other is an overall coordinated community-building activity to build pride and hope in a comprehensive and long-lasting way. If you are interested in becoming a volunteer for an AOIP program, call or write the national headquarters for more information.

The Barbara Bush Foundation for Family Literacy
1002 Wisconsin Ave., N.W., Washington, DC 20007
(202) 338-2006

The mission of the BBFFL is to establish literacy as a value in every family in America and to break the intergenerational cycle of illiteracy through the support of literacy programs that build families and readers. BBFFL is an all-volunteer endeavor, with Mrs. Bush serving as the Foundation's honorary chairperson. Available resources include fact sheets on family literacy, brochures, a videotape highlighting three family literacy programs, and *First Teachers: A Family Literacy Handbook for Parents, Policy Makers, and Literacy Providers*.

Business Council for Effective Literacy
1221 Avenue of the Americas, New York, NY 10020
(212) 512-2412 (or 2415)

BCEL is a national, nonprofit organization dedicated to informing the business community about the adult illiteracy problem and encouraging and assisting business participation in literacy activities at the local, state, and national levels. The council works closely with both the corporate community and adult literacy groups, bringing them together to guide companies toward meaningful involvement. BCEL is active in state and national policy development and provides technical assistance and publications to both the literacy field and businesses that want to start literacy programs. The council distributes books (for example, *Functional Illiteracy Hurts Business; The State*

Directory of Key Literacy Contacts), bulletins (such as *Developing an Employee Volunteer Literacy Program; Make It Your Business: A Corporate Fundraising Guide for Literacy Programs*), monographs, and *The BCEL Newsletter*, a free quarterly journal that focuses on legislation, program developments of national importance, and profiles of model literacy programs.

Christian Literacy Associates
Allegheny County Literacy Council
541 Perry Highway, Pittsburgh, PA 15229
(412) 364-3777

CLA is a nonprofit organization of Christian volunteers who work on a one-on-one basis with thousands of illiterate individuals in dozens of cities throughout the U.S. Volunteers teach adults and children to read through a Bible reading program (in addition to ordinary drill exercises, participants read parables, stories of Jesus, and passages from the Bible). Contact CLA to see if there's an affiliate in your area, if you are interested in receiving materials (textbooks, videos, pamphlets), or if you want information about starting a CLA in your community.

Contact Center, Inc.
P.O. Box 81826, Lincoln, NE 68501
National Contact hotline: 1-800-228-8813
(402) 464-0602, FAX: (402) 464-5931

One of the most effective nonprofit organizations dedicated to ending illiteracy in the U.S., **Contact** maintains the **National Contact Hotline**, which can provide anyone in America with information on volunteer literacy programs in their community. Contact also has several informative brochures and publications, including fact sheets on illiteracy (for example, *How to Tutor Without Being Part of a Formal Program; How to Form a Community Volunteer Literacy Program*) and tips for encouraging children to read. The center also has lists of magazines for children and young adults, and books and journals to help literate adults help their children. For $15 a year, you will receive a subscription to *the written word*, a newsletter that focuses on new approaches to tackling illiteracy, news about a variety of publications, and national, state, and local programs.

Laubach Literacy Action
Box 131, 1320 Jamesville Ave., Syracuse, NY 13210
For volunteer information: 1-800-228-8813
(315) 422-9121

LLA is the nation's largest network of volunteer-based adult literacy programs. There are more than 850 programs in forty-five states which use trained volunteers as tutors for adults or older youths who want to improve their literacy skills. These programs reach more than 120,000 people each year, providing them with basic literacy or English-as-a-second-language instruction. The national office provides print and audiovisual resources, consultation, technical assistance, and on-site training through staff and specialized volunteer consultants. LLA also provides volunteer management resources and, through its training network, will help local leaders plan and implement programs that will meet the needs of the learners in their communities. Information on individual or group membership and available publications may be obtained by contacting the membership office.

Literacy Volunteers of America, Inc.
5795 Widewaters Parkway, Syracuse, NY 13214-1846
For volunteer information: 1-800-228-8813
(315) 445-8000

A nonprofit organization of volunteers working to end illiteracy in America, **LVA** trains volunteers to tutor adults who lack reading, writing, and conversational English skills; matches tutors to students in a way that encourages a comfortable and confidential situation; and provides training in organizational, administrative, and fundraising skills to local literacy programs throughout the country. LVA distributes several informative fact sheets on illiteracy and publishes a quarterly newsletter, *The Reader*, which covers a variety of news items concerning illiteracy, including legislative issues and LVA activities.

Reading Is Fundamental, Inc.
Smithsonian Institution
600 Maryland Ave., S.W., Suite 500, Washington, DC 20560
(202) 287-3371

RIF is a nonprofit organization that works for a literate America by encouraging our nation's young people to read. RIF and its corps of more than 111,000 volunteers work to get youngsters excited about reading by providing them with books of their own—to keep, read, and re-read—at no cost to them or their families. Through a variety of publications and a media campaign, RIF also works to educate the public on the need to encourage the nation's young people to read. RIF's publications list includes informative booklets, brochures for parents (for example, *Family Storytelling; Reading Aloud to Your Children; Choosing Good Books for Children*), and posters. Some of RIF's more recent programs have focused on meeting the literacy needs of teenage mothers, homeless children, and families at risk. RIF has community-based projects in all fifty states, Washington, D.C., Puerto Rico, the Virgin Islands, and Guam, and reaches youngsters at more than 11,000 schools, libraries, community centers, migrant labor camps, shelters, hospitals, and other places where children can often be found. Contact your local RIF program if you'd like to become involved with its programs and activities.

ELDERLY PERSONS

Why Help Is Needed

The American Association of Retired Persons (AARP) estimates that there are more than thirty million people sixty-five or older in America (thirteen million are seventy-five or older). A substantial number of these older Americans are incredibly active and energetic individuals, many of whom, in fact, are organizing and participating in some of the best volunteer organizations in America (Foster Grandparents Program, Senior Gleaners, RSVP). These older volunteers are providing support to veterans in VA medical centers, alerting older voters to legislation that may affect their lives, working to fight illiteracy, helping others fill out their income-tax forms, feeding the hungry, teaching driver-education classes, leading health-education programs, and offering comfort and guidance for children and adults of all ages.

Unfortunately, however, many older Americans are not as active or energetic and need help with daily tasks such as getting out of bed, eating, dressing, and going to the store. What's more, depression is not uncommon among elderly persons. According to the American Association of Suicidology, twenty percent of all suicides in America are committed by elderly persons. Considering that elderly persons represent only about twelve percent of the population, this is clearly indicative of a serious problem. As a group, elderly persons are also one of the poorest in America. The AARP estimates (based on 1988 statistics from the U.S. Bureau of the Census) that three and half million elderly persons live in poverty—the highest rate among adult age groups. Approximately twenty-five percent of America's elderly persons live in homes that have serious problems, including leaking roofs, inadequate plumbing and electrical wiring, and unvented room heaters.[1] For elderly persons who may need money

---

[1] David E. Driver, *The Good Heart Book: A Guide to Volunteering* (Chicago: The Noble Press, Inc., 1989), 180. (This is an excellent resource for anyone interested in volunteering in the U.S. Driver provides numerous stories of individual volunteers in action, and the problems and joys they experience. He also addresses what people should expect when they become volunteers, how to find the right volunteer job, and how to maintain the volunteer spirit.)

for added medical care or hospitalization, poverty can be a constant, terrible threat.

Concerned individuals clearly cannot solve all of these problems. They can, however, provide human warmth and friendship to replace loneliness and depression. They can help with shopping, cooking meals, or household chores. Remembering an elderly person's birthday, bringing a puppy or kitten to visit, or simply sitting and talking can make an immeasurable difference in a person's life. In many ways, visiting and providing care for a homebound or frail elderly person is less of a "volunteer" opportunity than it is a chance to build a friendship with someone who has a great deal to offer.

What You Can Do

☞ **Keep up on legislation that affects the welfare of elderly persons.** Most of the national organizations listed in this chapter have the information you'll need to follow legislation that affects the welfare of elderly persons. Write to your government representatives to express your concern or approval. (See also Voicing Your Opinion, page 363.)

☞ **Encourage friends, family members, and co-workers to volunteer at a home or center for elderly persons.** The American Health Care Association (page 238) can provide you with posters, bumper stickers, and other materials to display at school, at the office, or at a religious organization to encourage people to visit with elderly persons.

☞ **Volunteer to help elderly persons in need of assistance in your community.** If you have an elderly neighbor, see how you can be of assistance. Here are just a few ways you may be able to help out elderly persons who are frail, living in nursing homes, or living at home alone:

- **Drive them to doctor's or dentist's offices, religious services, or other necessary places:** the drugstore, gift shop, barber shop or hair salon, museum, supermarket, or voting center at election time.
- **Help out with shopping or household chores.**

- **Visit on holidays, remembering birthdays, baking a cake, or giving flowers, a houseplant, or a card.**
- **Phone just to see if they're okay** (especially if there's a major storm or blackout).
- **Offer to shovel walks when it snows or mow the lawn in the summer.**
- **Go over to watch a movie, play cards or chess, or listen to music.**
- **Join them for a walk when the weather is nice.**
- **Help them with their taxes and Medicaid forms.**
- **Bring or cook dinner for them.**
- **Bring a new puppy or kitten for a visit** (make sure you check first).
- **Provide emotional support during down times** or when they must enter a hospital or nursing home (even for short periods of time, this can be terrifying).
- **Stop by simply to talk.**

For opportunities in your community, here are a few resources to keep in mind:

- **Look in your phone book under "Community Service Numbers,"** specifically under "Elderly, Services for" or a similar listing or check under "Nursing Homes" or "Senior Citizens Organizations." If you are having trouble finding a nursing home near you, you can also try the **American Health Care Association** (page 238). AHCA can refer you to your state association, which can tell you of a nursing home near you.
- **Look for the local Area Association on Aging**, which may be listed in the government pages under "Aging, Office On" (and see **National Association of Area Agencies on Aging**, page 240 for information on what community AAAs offer).
- **Contact your local Volunteer Clearinghouse** (check your phone book or see Community Resources and Organizations, page 6).
- **See if there's a Meals on Wheels program in your community.** There's no national headquarters, so check your phone book or your local **AAA** (see page 240). These programs take food to elderly persons who are homebound. Volunteers are usually needed as drivers and for other services, depending on the needs of the community.
- **If you belong to a religious congregation, see if it provides any services for elderly persons.** Most churches and synagogues have programs for elderly persons, but if yours does not, consider starting one.

● **Many of the national organizations listed in this chapter can give you referrals to community programs and centers for elderly persons.**

☞ **Join up with Good Bears of the World,** a nonprofit organization that delivers teddy bears nationwide to children and elderly persons in hospitals, institutions, and other places where a little solace and comfort are welcome. You can purchase one of GBW's official teddy bears starting at $8.50 (the price drops depending on the number of bears you buy). Write to GBW for general information or for the GBW chapter near you (or for assistance if you want to start your own) at *2352 Valeway, Toledo, OH 43613.*

☞ **Participate in The Holiday Project,** a nonprofit organization that works with thousands of volunteers (in more than 400 communities nationwide) who visit with people confined to hospitals, nursing homes, and other institutions during the Christmas and Chanuka seasons, as well as other holidays throughout the year. Even if you don't have the opportunity to visit, you can help out The Holiday Project by making or wrapping gifts, donating goods and services, such as providing wrapping paper or driving volunteers, and in various other ways. It's also helpful if you just spread the word; students can encourage their classmates to get involved and religious members can get their congregations involved. Contact The Holiday Project for general information on the location of a Holiday Project chapter near you (or for assistance if you want to start one up) at *P.O. Box 6829, FDR Station, New York, NY 10150*; (212) 532-0353.

☞ **If you are retired, consider becoming part of the Senior Companion Program.** Through SCP, older Americans help frail elderly persons gain the confidence and positive mental attitude needed for successful independent living. (Although most Senior Companion volunteers are low-income persons who receive a modest stipend, individuals who do not meet those income requirements are needed for the program, too.) Most Senior Companions serve the homebound elderly—those needing daily help shopping, visiting the doctor, or managing finances. Companions also help those who have been hospitalized readjust to normal life, assist people facing a terminal illness, and offer support to individuals with mental illnesses. For more information, see **ACTION**, page 9.

☞ **Use your professional skills to help elderly persons in your community.** If you are experienced with filling out income-tax forms, assist elderly persons with their taxes. If you are a musician or singer, entertain at a local nursing home or senior center. If you are a hair stylist or barber, offer your skills at a nursing home or senior center. People who are handy with tools may be needed at a local senior center for small jobs.

☞ **Get your business, religious congregation, or school involved with helping elderly persons.** Businesses can donate supplies to senior centers in the community, religious congregations can sponsor activities for elderly persons (for example, dances, movies, recreational events), and schools can invite elderly persons, particularly those in nursing homes, to school plays, concerts, and other events. A Washington, D.C., school, for example, encourages its students to volunteer at a local nursing home and gives birthday parties for elderly persons from the home, complete with a birthday cake and a full-school round of "Happy Birthday."

☞ **If you are an employer or the administrator of a volunteer organization, recruit older persons whenever possible.** For information on hiring elderly persons, contact your local Area Association on Aging, listed in the government pages of your phone book. For more information on working with older volunteers, contact the **American Association of Retired Persons** (page 238) and request the informative booklet, *Older Volunteers: A Valuable Resource.* Many of the other national organizations listed in this chapter have similar resources.

National Organizations

The Alzheimer's Association
70 East Lake St., Chicago, IL 60601
1-800-621-0379; (in Illinois): 1-800-572-6037

The Alzheimer's Association is the leading, national nonprofit voluntary health organization dedicated to fighting Alzheimer's disease on all fronts. (Alzheimer's disease is the fourth leading cause of death among American adults, claiming more than 100,000 lives annually. Approximately ten percent of those over the age of sixty-five and fifty percent of those over eighty-five are afflicted with the disease.) Working through a network of 210 chapters and 1,600 support groups, and more than 35,000 volunteers nationwide, the organization provides support, guidance, and assistance to America's four million Alzheimer patients, their families, and their caregivers. The organization also funds research into the cause(s), cure, and treatment of Alzheimer's disease; sponsors public-awareness programs; and disseminates literature describing Alzheimer's disease. Whether participating in volunteer/patient day-care programs or serving on local and national committees, volunteers are instrumental in the success and growth of the Alzheimer's Association. Check your phone book for the chapter in your community, or call the national headquarters for one near you.

American Association of Homes for the Aging
901 East St., N.W. Suite 500, Washington, DC 20004-2837
(202) 296-5960, FAX: (202) 223-5920

This is a national, nonprofit organization of nonprofit homes and services for the elderly. **AAHA**'s membership comprises more than 3,500 nursing homes, residential retirement complexes, low-income rental housing, and community service organizations. The association's facilities serve elderly persons of all income levels, creeds, races, and ethnic origins. The facilities care for more than 600,000 older Americans each year and meet the needs of approximately one million older Americans through various outreach programs. If you are interested in helping elderly persons but cannot find a home in your community, AAHA can help you locate a facility near you.

American Association of Retired Persons
1909 K St., N.W., Washington, DC 20049
(202) 872-4700

A nonprofit organization committed to improving the welfare of older Americans, **AARP** helps and encourages people of all ages to become volunteers. If you are interested in becoming a volunteer and helping older persons in need, the organization can provide you with information about getting started. AARP has a booklet *(Older Volunteers: A Valuable Resource)* that addresses the value of older Americans as volunteers and the need for their services in this country. The association can also supply you with a variety of publications concerning the welfare of older Americans, including information on pending and current legislation that may affect the lives of the nation's older citizens. A one-year membership costs $5.

American Health Care Association
1201 L St., N.W., Washington, DC 20005
(202) 842-4444

AHCA, a nonprofit organization, is the country's largest federation of nursing homes and allied long-term health-care facilities. The association is comprised of fifty-one affiliated member associations—one in each state and the District of Columbia. AHCA can provide you with informative brochures and publications that offer general guidelines for becoming a nursing home volunteer and can refer you to your state association, which can then direct you to a local nursing home (send your inquiries to the **Community Relations Manager** at AHCA). The association also sells a variety of materials, such as T-shirts, posters, bumper stickers, key chains, pins, and other items, that encourage people to visit nursing home residents (the items sport such slogans as *Love Is Ageless; Discover Life's Treasures; Old Friends;* and *Memories Were Made to Be Shared*).

Arthritis Foundation
P.O. Box 19000, Atlanta, GA 30326
(404) 872-7100 or *Arthritis Foundation Information Line:*
1-800-283-7800

Formed in 1948, the **Arthritis Foundation** is the only national, nonprofit voluntary health organization working for the estimated thirty-seven million Americans affected by any of the more than 100 forms of arthritis or related diseases. The foundation advocates for people with arthritis and their families; sponsors research; provides community-education programs (for example, self-care skills); disseminates information on arthritis; and offers a variety of other services. Volunteers in chapters nationwide help support research, community-education programs, services for people with arthritis (for example, leading exercise, support, and self-help programs), and government advocacy. They can also help with administrative work, fundraising activities, and other services. Concerned individuals can support the foundation by becoming members. Membership ($20) includes, among other benefits, a one-year subscription to *Arthritis Today*, a bimonthly magazine with news about arthritis research, new treatments, tips on how to cope with arthritis, and stories of others living with arthritis. Check your phone book for a chapter near you (there are seventy chapters nationwide).

Little Brothers—Friends of the Elderly
1658 Belmont Ave., Chicago, IL 60657
(312) 477-7702

This nonprofit organization of male and female volunteers is dedicated to relieving isolation and loneliness among elderly persons in need. **LBFE** provides emotional support to elderly persons through regular and holiday visits, telephone contact, vacation sessions, and holiday and birthday celebrations. Volunteers make deliveries, provide companionship, and transport elderly friends to appointments, shops, movies, and other activities. LBFE's emphasis, however, is on friendship and companionship, not just services such as meals and transportation. LBFE operates in Chicago, Minneapolis, St. Paul, Boston, Philadelphia, San Francisco, and Houghton County, Michigan, and plans to expand. Contact LBFE for information on volunteer opportunities in your area or if you are interested in starting an affiliate in your community.

National Association of Area Agencies on Aging
1112 16th St., Suite 100, Washington, DC 20036
(202) 296-8130

NAAAA is a nonprofit national organization representing the interests of **Area Agencies on Aging** across the country. (AAAs are nonprofit agencies that address the needs and concerns of older Americans at the local level. They provide such services as home-delivered meals, adult day care, legal assistance and counseling, legislative information, chore services, multi-purpose senior centers, recreation, and employment services.) If you are interested in volunteering for an AAA in your community (there are *many* volunteer opportunities), check your phone book first, usually under the government pages. If you cannot find a listing, contact NAAAA for the location of a facility near you (but only as a last resort, simply because the office is not equipped to handle a high volume of calls).

The National Caucus and Center on Black Aged
1424 K St., N.W., Suite 500, Washington, DC 20005
(202) 637-8400

This nonprofit organization is devoted to improving the economic status and quality of life of low-income and minority elderly persons. **NCBA** helps develop rental housing for low-income elderly persons, offering technical services and training to organizations involved in providing housing and living-arrangement services for older persons. NCBA is also a respected organization on Capitol Hill, testifying before congressional committees as a voice for low-income and minority elderly individuals. NCBA's **Senior Employment Program** provides employers with information on employing low-income older persons, the goal being to provide organizations with a talented and productive pool of older individuals while enabling these older Americans to increase their sense of self-worth. NCBA publishes a quarterly newsletter, *Golden Page*, which addresses various issues concerning low-income and minority older persons in America (for example, legislation, national policy). Membership fees are $15 for persons under fifty-five, $7 for persons over fifty-five.

The National Council on the Aging, Inc.
600 Maryland Ave., S.W., West Wing 100
(after June 1, 1991: 409 3rd St., S.W., 2nd Floor)
Washington, DC 20024
(202) 479-1200, FAX: (202) 479-0735

NCOA is a nonprofit organization of more than 6,000 individuals and voluntary organizations dedicated to improving the quality of life for older persons. The council is committed to protecting their rights, improving services directed to them, and expanding their opportunities. Members of NCOA can become affiliated with one or more of the special interest groups which focus on adult day care, community-based long-term care, senior centers, senior housing, older-worker employment, health promotion, and aging in rural areas. The council also distributes numerous publications about older Americans and older-adult programs (for example, *Aging in the Eighties; Facts and Myths About Aging*) and publishes *NCOA Networks*, which reports on legislative activities and significant developments in the field of gerontology; a bimonthly magazine, *Perspective on Aging*, which contains opinion articles, profiles, book reviews, editorials, legislative updates, information on NCOA activities, and other features; and *Abstracts in Social Gerontology: Current Literature on Aging*, a quarterly annotated bibliography. Membership ($60 for individuals; $30 for students and retired persons) includes a subscription to *Perspective on Aging* and other benefits.

National Council of Senior Citizens
1331 F St., N.W., Washington, DC 20005
(202) 347-8800

A nonprofit organization dedicated to increasing the well-being of older Americans, **NCSC** sponsors the **Senior Aides Program**, which provides part-time employment for eligible older persons with limited incomes. (Individuals who are enrolled as Senior Aides must be fifty-five years of age or older, and preference is given to persons age sixty or older. Income limits for eligibility are established by the federal government and are adjusted yearly.) If you are an interested employer (host agencies must be a unit of government or a nonprofit organization classified under Section 501 (c)(3) of the Internal Revenue Code), contact NCSC for its comprehensive booklet on the Senior Aides Program. NCSC can also provide concerned individuals with information on legislation that affects the welfare of older Americans.

National Hispanic Council on Aging
2713 Ontario Road, N.W., Washington, DC 20009
(202) 265-1288

NHCoA is a nonprofit organization of individuals, chapters, professional agencies, and organizations working to eliminate the social, civic, and economic inequalities experienced by elderly persons of Hispanic descent (Mexican-American, Puerto Rican, Cuban-American, and other Latino elderly from Central and South America). The council develops educational materials; sponsors workshops, seminars, and symposia; monitors legislation; and serves as a national focal point for the exchange of information, technical assistance, and consultation to its members and others who work with the Hispanic elderly. Membership ($10 for individuals) includes a subscription to the bimonthly newsletter, *Noticias*, and information on relevant new books (for example, *The Hispanic Elderly: A Cultural Signature*) and videos (for example, *Nosotros Los Viejos; Your Challenge, Your Reward*, which highlights the views of aging Hispanics in America).

National Indian Council on Aging
6400 Uptown Blvd., N.E., City Centre, 510 West
Albuquerque, NM 87110
(505) 242-9505

This nonprofit organization is dedicated to improving services to Indian and Alaskan Native elderly persons. **NICOA** communicates and cooperates with service agencies and advocacy organizations in the field of aging nationwide; provides technical assistance to and training of Indian tribal/organization personnel; provides expert testimony requested by members and staff of Congress; and serves as a clearinghouse for issues affecting the Indian and Alaskan Native elderly. NICOA sponsors conferences and workshops and publishes a newsletter, *Elder Voices*, which provides in-depth articles of concern to the Indian elderly, updates on current events, legislation, and federal-action information, and publications and funding sources relevant to Indian aging programs. The council also distributes books (for example, *American Indian Elderly: A National Profile*), conference reports, monographs, and posters. An associate membership costs $25 (contact NICOA for other membership possibilities).

National Interfaith Coalition on Aging
298 S. Hull St., P.O. Box 1924, Athens, GA 30603
(404) 353-1331

NICA is a nonprofit organization committed to addressing the needs of older Americans and emphasizing the importance of religion and faith in their lives. (NICA is sponsored by national agencies of Jewish, Catholic, and Protestant religious bodies.) The coalition supports the development of religious programs and services for all older persons; develops and distributes resources that help churches and synagogues respond to the needs of older persons; and represents the spiritual concerns of older Americans in public and private forums throughout the U.S. NICA sponsors *The Journal of Religious Gerontology*, a quarterly periodical that includes informative articles, reports of the latest research, and reviews of new books and films on religion and aging. NICA publishes *NICA Inform*, which comes out six times a year and describes new ministries with older adults, keeps members up-to-date on conferences and training events, and reports on legislation and public policy affecting older adults. The yearly membership fee is $20 for retired persons and students, $35 for individuals, and $50 for professionals (contact NICA for information on organizational membership).

National Pacific/Asian Resource Center on Aging
Melbourne Tower, Suite 914
1511 3rd Ave., Seattle, WA 98101
(206) 624-1221

NP/ARCA is a nonprofit organization funded by the Department of Health and Human Services, Administration on Aging and was established to facilitate and improve the delivery of health and social services to Pacific/Asian elderly persons, ensuring that they are afforded a meaningful, secure, and dignified existence. If you are interested in helping the Pacific/Asian elderly, NP/ARCA can provide you with information on homes and centers for the Pacific/Asian elderly near you. NP/ARCA also monitors and works to influence legislation that affects the well-being of all elderly persons.

**North American Association of Jewish Homes
and Housing for the Aging**
2525 Centerville Road, Dallas, TX 75228
(214) 328-0274

This nonprofit organization is dedicated to serving the 105 nonprofit Jewish homes and 110 housing facilities for elderly persons in North America. **NAAJHHA** serves the homes by sponsoring training programs for the administrators; collecting and sharing information with the homes; and assisting with a variety of other services. The homes work to provide assistance to elderly persons (including but not limited to their physical, emotional, social, and religious requirements) through a variety of services and programs, which vary from home to home. NAAJHHA can refer interested individuals to homes for Jewish elderly persons in their community in need of volunteers.

The Environment

Why Help Is Needed

Whether it is the formation of clouds and the falling of rain, the constant changing of the tide, the cycle of birth, growth, and decay, or the activity of the largest whale or the smallest insect, there is an incredible order and balance to the workings of nature. The system, however, is a fragile one. Drastic changes can produce a wave of disastrous effects. While the environment can usually mend itself over time, if pushed too far the consequences can be irreparable. This generation has seen what one oil spill, for example, or one faulty nuclear reactor can do to an "isolated" area. Clearly, the technology and conveniences which most of us depend on bring with them an unprecedented opportunity for destruction.

On land, in the sea, and in the air, pollutants, garbage, and chemicals are wreaking tremendous havoc. According to the Environmental Action Foundation, the United States produces more than a ton of hazardous wastes *per citizen* each year.[1] Inadequate disposal methods allow much of this waste to seep into underground water resources, ultimately poisoning streams, rivers, lakes, and the water people drink.[2] Environmental Action estimates that nearly 117 million Americans rely on groundwater for their source of drinking water.[3] When hazardous wastes leak into these supplies, serious health problems can result. In fact, between 1971 and 1985 alone, more than 100,000 cases of disease in this country were caused by contaminated drinking water.[4] Chemical plants, nuclear power sites, and computer factories all contribute to this contamination, but so do many individuals who pour hazardous wastes (motor oil, antifreeze, paint) down drains or sewers. In fact, one quart of motor oil can contaminate *two*

---

[1] The Earth Works Group, *50 Simple Things You Can Do to Save the Earth* (Berkeley: Earthworks Press, 1989), 12.
[2] Ibid., 15.
[3] Ibid., 15.
[4] Diane MacEachern, *Save Our Planet: 750 Everyday Ways You Can Help Clean Up the Earth* (New York: Dell Publishing, 1990), 2.

million gallons of water.[5] Deicing salts or pesticides and chemicals on lawns, which wash into sewers, also contribute to the problem. In addition, many of the pesticides used on fruits and vegetables have been linked to nervous system, immune system, liver, and kidney disorders, as well as to cancer.[6] Ironically, these pesticides reach only a fraction of the pests they are intended to kill and, instead, create hybrids of pesticide-resistant insects.[7]

Like contamination of the nation's water supplies, air pollution is emerging as a major problem in the United States. An estimated 110 million Americans live in areas with levels of air pollutants that the federal government considers harmful[8] resulting in stinging eyes, burning throats, and more serious health problems such as lung cancer. The Public Interest Research Group reports that lung damage from ozone-polluted air threatens an estimated three out of five Americans.[9] A recent study concluded that up to 100,000 deaths a year may be caused by toxic chemicals in the air.[10]

One of the most devastating side effects of air pollution is acid rain. Acid rain is causing forest damage, polluting streams, lakes, and reservoirs, killing wildlife, damaging crops, and eroding buildings and national monuments. It has even been known to peel the paint off cars.[11] More than 1,700 of our lakes have already been contaminated, and thousands of acres of forest have been destroyed.[12] Even more alarming, a recent congressional study concluded that acid rain caused as many as 50,000 premature deaths in the U.S. and Canada.[13]

Unfortunately, as air pollution continues, we are simultaneously destroying our best defense against it—trees. Trees absorb the carbon dioxide that spews from cars and factories and replenish the oxygen supply. Trees also provide natural beauty, shade, erosion prevention, and support for wildlife. Rapid deforestation, however, is reducing their effectiveness. On a national level, the American Forestry Association reports that in the average American city, for every four trees that die or are removed, only one new tree is planted.[14] On a

---

[5]John Elkington, Julia Hailes, and Joel Makower, *The Green Consumer* (New York: Penguin Books, 1988), 9.
[6]MacEachern, 8.
[7]Ibid., 8.
[8]Elkington, 9.
[9]The Earth Works Group, 10.
[10]MacEachern, 17.
[11]Elkington, 13.
[12]MacEachern, 17.
[13]Elkington, 14.
[14]American Forestry Association, "The Global ReLeaf Action Guide," 3.

global level, between mid-century and 1980, the forested surface of the earth was reduced by an estimated twenty-five percent.[15]

The destruction of rain forests is particularly disturbing. The Rainforest Action Network (RAN) estimates that although rain forests only cover seven percent of the earth's land mass, they are home to about half of the five to ten million plant and animal species in the world. RAN also estimates that a typical four-square-mile patch of rain forest is home to as many as 1,500 species of flowering plants, 750 species of trees, 125 species of mammals, 400 species of birds, 100 species of reptiles, 60 species of amphibians, and 150 species of butterflies.[16] Rain forest plants are vital to medical research; the World Resources Institute (WRI) reports that the drugs used to treat childhood leukemia, Hodgkin's disease, and several cancers are extracted from rain forest plants, as are medicines for heart ailments, hypertension, and arthritis.[17] In fact, WRI claims, one out of four pharmaceuticals used by Western chemists comes from a tropical plant.[18] WRI also estimates that at least twenty-seven million acres of rain forests are lost each year (that's almost 74,000 acres a day—3,000 acres an hour).[19] The burning of rain forests, which is primarily designed to clear the land for agricultural use, also contributes to air pollution by releasing carbon into the atmosphere as carbon dioxide.

There is serious speculation that destroying trees and releasing excess carbon dioxide into the air causes global warming, a problem that could prove to be the greatest environmental threat of all. Global warming, or "the greenhouse effect," is believed to be caused by excess heat trapped in the earth's atmosphere. Each year, billions of tons of carbon dioxide and smaller amounts of CFCs (chlorofluorocarbons) are pumped into the air.[20] These gases "blanket" the atmosphere, preventing heat from escaping into space and, consequently, warming the planet by as much as four to nine degrees Fahrenheit.[21] (This is not, by any means, an insignificant change—in the past 18,000 years, the average global temperature has not varied more than 3.6 degrees Fahrenheit.[22]) This variance could cause the polar caps to melt, consequently raising the level of the oceans by as much as five

---

[15]The Earth Works Group, 78.
[16]Rainforest Action Network, "Facts About Rainforests" (fact sheet).
[17]World Resources Institute, "Keep Tropical Forests Alive," 3.
[18]Ibid., 2.
[19]Ibid., 4.
[20]Elkington, 15.
[21]Jeremy Rifkin (ed.), *The Green Lifestyle Handbook: 1001 Ways You Can Heal the Earth* (New York: Henry Holt and Company, Inc., 1990), xi.
[22]The Earth Works Group. 9.

feet, which in turn would result in massive flooding of coastal areas.[23] An increase in temperature would also create severe drought conditions in noncoastal areas, turning agricultural regions into massive deserts and killing forests.[24] To put this into context, when the U.S. was hit with a three-month drought in the summer of 1988, more than thirty percent of the nation's grain harvest was lost and thousands of livestock animals died. Parched from the heat, forests in the West, including Yellowstone National Park, burned for days, even weeks.[25] It is true that there has been a great deal of controversy concerning global warming in the past few years, but when the consequences are as severe as they are believed to be, making slight changes in our everyday lives does not seem to be a great sacrifice.

CFCs and other chemicals are also depleting the ozone layer, creating the potential for deadly, irreparable damage to the planet. A critical part of the atmosphere, the ozone layer surrounds the planet between twelve and thirty miles above its surface and blocks out most of the sun's radiation. A single CFC molecule, reacting to sunlight, can destroy up to 100,000 ozone molecules.[26] In 1985, a "hole" in the ozone layer, now estimated to be as wide as the United States, was found above Antarctica.[27] Without the ozone layer, the earth and its inhabitants lose their protection against dangerous ultraviolet rays, which can cause skin cancer. In fact, the Environmental Protection Agency estimates that up to 170 million people may develop cancer in the coming decades from exposure to ultraviolet radiation.[28] Ultraviolet radiation can also affect the immune system, making both humans and animals vulnerable to a variety of bacterial and viral diseases.[29]

Many of these environmental problems are interrelated, but, fortunately, so are the solutions. For example, one of the keys to reducing acid rain, global warming, and air pollution is energy conservation. Reducing the amount of coal and oil burned to create electricity reduces the amount of pollutants released into the atmosphere.[30] The American Council for an Energy-Efficient Economy estimates that if every American simply used the most energy-efficient refrigerator, the savings in electricity would eliminate the need for

[23]Rifkin, xi.
[24]Ibid., xi.
[25]Thomas A. Sancton, "What on Earth Are We Doing?" *Time*, January 2, 1989, 27.
[26]Elkington, 18.
[27]MacEachern, 16.
[28]Rifkin, xi.
[29]Ibid., xii.
[30]The Earth Works Group, 17.

twelve power plants.[31] If every American family set its air conditioner six degrees warmer for just one day, 190,000 barrels of oil would be saved.[32] If every commuter car in the U.S. carried just one more passenger, we'd save 600,000 gallons of gasoline a day and keep millions of pounds of carbon dioxide from polluting the atmosphere.[33] Through simple conservation efforts, people can substantially help the environment, not to mention save a good deal of money.

Recycling is another key to preserving the environment. In the past thirty years our waste production has grown more than eighty percent.[34] Today, eighty percent of solid waste is dumped into 6,000 landfills nationwide[35] (the remaining twenty percent is either recycled or incinerated[36]). In the past five years, 3,000 dumps have been closed.[37] By the year 1993, it is estimated that another 2,000 will be filled to capacity.[38] Opening new landfills is difficult (nobody wants one in their community) and is a temporary solution at best. Garbage contains large amounts of hazardous wastes, which can seep into underground water supplies when dumped into landfills. Garbage is also frequently blown or dumped into the ocean (fourteen billion pounds of trash, to be exact[39]). Beachgoers have found medical waste (including syringes and vials of blood), sewage, and a variety of other refuse washing up onto the sand. This trash is also killing marine life. Plastics alone are responsible for killing an estimated one million sea birds, 100,000 marine mammals, and 50,000 fur seals.[40] One balloon in the ocean can be (and has been) enough to suffocate a whale.[41]

Incineration, an alternative to landfills, simply contributes to air pollution and acid rain. Clearly, recycling coupled with intelligent consumption is a real solution to our garbage problems. Other countries demonstrate that it can be done. Japan recycles fifty percent of its garbage, Western Europe thirty percent, while the United States recycles only about ten percent.[42] Several cities, however, have taken an initiative. According to a 1990 report, Seattle, Washington, currently recycles approximately thirty-four percent of its total waste

[31]MacEachern, 46.
[32]The Earth Works Group, 30.
[33]Ibid., 42.
[34]Elkington, 26.
[35]MacEachern, 9.
[36]Elkington, 26.
[37]MacEachern, 9.
[38]John Langone, "A Stinking Mess," *Time*, January 2, 1989, 45.
[39]The Earth Works Group; 13.
[40]Elkington, 9.
[41]The Earth Works Group, 58.
[42]Langone, 46–47.

stream.[43] Much of the city's processed sewage waste is sold as fertilizer, which is then used to preserve Washington state's beautiful forests. Wellesley, Massachusetts, also has an outstanding recycling program. Wellesley's 1989 Department of Public Works report estimates that eighty-two percent of the town's households participate in the program.[44] Almost twenty-five percent of the town's waste is recycled, which keeps thousands of tons of garbage out of landfills and saves the town several hundred thousand dollars a year, primarily from transfer hauling costs.

Water conservation is another key environmental issue. Until recently, water has been an abundant resource, but enormous waste, pollution, and the destruction of our wilderness have made conserving and preserving water serious priorities. Fresh water is one of the world's most precious resources; despite the fact that two-thirds of the planet is covered with water, only three percent is fresh water.[45] This is, without a doubt, still an incredible amount of water, but it is unevenly spread around the world. This problem is evident in the U.S., too. In the spring of 1990, areas of Texas were suffering from massive floods while areas of California were experiencing severe droughts. The average American household consumes over 300 gallons of water a day.[46] With inexpensive water-saving devices and a simple awareness of conservation, water bills can be cut significantly. And if we conserve hot water, the energy needed to heat the water is saved as well. A simple awareness of water preservation can also help keep groundwater supplies, rivers, lakes, and oceans clean and free of toxins and garbage. Proper disposal of wastes, such as antifreeze, motor oil, and paint, is a good start to keeping groundwater pure.

Environmental disasters resulting from accidents like Three Mile Island and the *Exxon Valdez* oil spill may seem to be of too great a magnitude for individual actions to make a difference. This assumption is simply not correct. It is not only these enormous industrial accidents that are causing tremendous damage to nature, but the millions of smaller, less evident actions occurring in households, gardens, and farms nationwide. Consequently, it will take millions of responsible individual actions to preserve and restore the environment for the sake of this generation, and those to come.

---

[43]From a January 17, 1990 Seattle Solid Waste Utility Report before the U.S. House of Representatives Subcommittee on Transportation and Hazardous Materials.
[44]From a December 19, 1989 Wellesley Department of Public Works recycling program report.
[45]The Earth Works Group, 51.
[46]Elkington, 205.

What You Can Do

☞ **Educate yourself on environmental issues, policies, and activities.** The more you are familiar with the problems facing the environment, the more you will know where help is needed most and what you can do. Most of the national organizations listed in this chapter will keep you well informed. Here are a few other important resources:

- **BUZZWORM: *The Environmental Journal*** is a bimonthly magazine full of environmental and public policy news, travel adventures, and information on environmentally friendly products, volunteer opportunities, and environmental organizations. A one-year subscription costs $18. Write to *BUZZWORM* at *P.O. Box 6853, Syracuse, NY 13217-7930.*
- ***E Magazine*** is a bimonthly full-color periodical containing in-depth articles on the most pressing environmental problems of the day (and those to come), interviews, book reviews, classified listings, tips and ideas on saving the environment, and information on dozens of products, publications, and services for people working to create a cleaner, healthier planet. A one-year subscription costs $20. Write or call *E Magazine* at *P.O. Box 6667, Syracuse, NY 13217*; 1-800-825-0061.
- ***ENVIRONMENT*** magazine contains in-depth articles and features on a variety of environmental issues. The magazine comes out ten times a year and costs $24. Write to or call **HELDREF Publications** at *4000 Albemarle St., N.W., Suite 310, Washington, DC 20016*; (202) 362-6445.
- The **Environmental Protection Agency (EPA),** the U.S. government's environmental agency, offers a range of nontechnical publications (for example, fact sheets, posters, pamphlets) on environmental issues, as well as information on its own programs and activities. Write to or call the EPA at *PIC (PM-211B), USEPA, 401 M St., S.W., Washington, D.C. 20460*; (202) 382-2080.
- ***GARBAGE: The Practical Journal for the Environment*** is a bimonthly magazine that focuses on garbage and related issues, such as recycling, toxic chemicals, and water, air, and energy conservation. The magazine also lists important resources, including publications and environmentally friendly products. A

one-year subscription costs $21. Contact *GARBAGE* at P.O. Box 56519, Boulder, CO 80322-6519; 1-800-274-9909.

• **Island Press** is an excellent source for anyone interested in high-quality, informative books on a variety of environmental issues. Here is a partial list of book subjects:

- endangered species
- forestry
- global warming
- hazardous wastes
- pesticides
- pollution
- solid waste and incineration
- sustainable agriculture
- water and wetlands
- wildlife

For a free catalog, contact Island Press at *Box 7, Covelo, CA 95428*; 1-800-828-1302.

☞ **Keep up on environmental legislation and learn how your representatives vote so that you can express your concern or approval.** Although many of the national organizations listed in this chapter have legislative alerts and updates, the **League of Conservation Voters** keeps track of the voting record of all congressional representatives on environmental matters. Write or call LCV for more information on its environmental scorecards and membership fees (starting at $20) at *1707 L St., N.W., Suite 550, Washington, DC 20036*; (202) 785-VOTE (8683). Individual scorecards are available for $5 (which includes postage and handling). The **National Wildlife Federation** (page 107) also maintains a legislative hotline with up-to-date information on current issues. Call anytime (recorded message): *(202) 797-6655*. (See also Voicing Your Opinion, page 363.)

☞ **Be an environmentally conscious consumer.** This means buying products that are not harmful to the environment (nontoxic or free of CFCs and other ozone-depleting chemicals), that are packaged in recycled and/or recyclable materials, and that help conserve the environment. Here are a few mail-order companies that can help you become an environmentally conscious consumer:

• **Earthwise—A Green Store** offers a wide range of environmentally safe products. Here is a partial listing of Earthwise's products:

- air fresheners
- cleaners, detergents, and waxes
- crayons
- food storage bags
- shampoos, conditioners, and soaps
- string and canvas bags

- 100% recycled paper products (for example, napkins, facial tissues, office and printing paper, envelopes, and computer paper)

Write or call for a free catalog and Earthwise's informative pamphlets (for example, *What Is Recycled Paper*; *Why Should You Buy Products Made from Recycled Paper*) at *407 E. Main (Downtown Mall), Charlottesville, VA 22901*; (804) 979-0189.

- **Ecco Bella** is for environmentalists and animal lovers; the products are environmentally safe and their manufacture has not involved the suffering or death of animals. Here is just a partial list of Ecco Bella's eco-safe and cruelty-free items:

  - companion animal products (for example, shampoos and all-natural herbal flea powders)
  - detergents, cleaners, and air fresheners
  - gifts, such as mugs, T-shirts, and handmade jewelry
  - hand lotions
  - makeup
  - medicinal products (for colds, sore throats, headaches, and other ailments)
  - natural gourmet foods (such as pasta, chocolate, fruit spreads, popcorn, and teas)
  - natural soaps and deodorants
  - recycled paper products (including note cards, postcards, copier paper, envelopes, stationery, computer paper, bathroom tissue, and paper towels
  - shampoos and conditioners
  - tanning lotions

Write or call Ecco Bella at *6 Provost Square, Suite 602, Caldwell, NJ 07006*; 1-800-888-5320, (in New Jersey): (201) 226-5799.

- **Jade Mountain** stocks both small and large environmentally friendly products. Here are just a few examples:

  - educational books, games, and toys
  - fluorescent lights
  - nontoxic children's art supplies
  - nontoxic cleaners
  - pedal-operated power generator (creates electricity while you exercise)
  - recycled paper products
  - solar home kits

- solar-powered battery chargers
- solar-powered flashlights
- solar-powered refrigerators
- solar-powered toys and gifts
- water-saving devices
- wind generators

Write or call Jade Mountain at *P.O. Box 4616, Boulder, CO 80306*; (303) 449-6601 or 1-800-442-1972, FAX: (303) 449-8266.

● **Real Goods News** also sells environmentally friendly products. Here are just a few examples:

- books, brochures, and guides on the environment
- energy-efficient clothes washers
- games, T-shirts and other clothing items, posters, maps, and solar educational kits for kids (and adults)
- low-flush toilets
- recycled paper products
- recycling bin
- solar-powered battery chargers
- solar-powered refrigerators
- solar water heaters
- wind generators

Write or call Real Goods News at *966 Mazzoni St., Ukiah, CA 95482*; 1-800-762-7325, in California: 707-468-9214, FAX: (707) 468-0301. A one-year subscription ($20) to *Real Goods News* entitles you to RGN catalogs sent first-class (the number of catalogs varies each year), the *Alternative Energy Sourcebook* (an informative book on alternative energy and energy-saving ideas and appliances), several free gifts, and other benefits.

● **Seventh Generation** offers enough items to stock your home top to bottom with environmentally friendly products. Here is just a partial list:

- baby powders, shampoos, and soaps
- books, toys, and games that encourage environmental consciousness
- faucet aerators
- fluorescent light bulbs
- low-flow shower heads
- nontoxic bathroom supplies (shampoos, toothpastes, soaps, shaving creams)
- nontoxic dishwasher, laundry, glass, oven, floor, and toilet cleaners
- rechargeable batteries

THE ENVIRONMENT 255

- recycled paper products (including note pads, copier paper, wrapping paper, computer paper, stationery, toilet paper, and paper towels)
- recycling bins and can crushers
- soil composters
- solar chargers
- string shopping bags
- toilet dams

SG is an outstanding resource for anyone who wants to help save the earth. Contact Seventh Generation at *Colchester, VT 05446-1672*; Mon.–Fri. 8 A.M. to 8 P.M., Sat. 9 A.M. to 5 P.M., 1-800-456-1177, FAX: (802) 655-2700.

For more information on being an environmentally conscious consumer, consult the following sources:

• **The Consumer's Guide to Planet Earth** is a *very* comprehensive directory of companies and organizations offering environmentally oriented products and services. Here is just a sampling of category listings: Mail-Order Catalogs, Personal Care Products, Household Cleaning Products, Natural Home Products, Recycled Paper Products, Socially Responsible Investing, Solar Energy, Organic Foods, Environmental Publications, and Adventure & Eco-Travel. The guide is updated every six months and costs $6.95, which includes shipping and handling. Contact **Schultz Communications** at *9412 Admiral Nimitz N.E., Albuquerque, NM 87111*; (505) 821-6062, FAX: (505) 822-9122.

• **The Green Consumer** (Penguin Books) by John Elkington, Julia Hailes, and Joel Makower, contains hundreds of tips, resources, products, and publications. It also provides general information on the environment and environmentally safe consumer goods. The book is a valuable resource for environmentally conscious individuals. If you can't find the book at your local bookstore, contact **The Green Consumer** at *1526 Connecticut Ave., N.W., Washington, D.C. 20036*; (202) 332-1700. The price is $10.70 (including shipping and handling). The Green Consumer also publishes a monthly newsletter, *Going Green* ($27 for a one-year subscription), which covers a variety of environmental issues.

See also What You Can Do, pages 279, 302, and 310, for more information on environmentally conscious consumerism.

☞ **Encourage your friends and co-workers to be environmentally conscious.** The best way to do this is to set a good example.

Also, tell them about available products that are environmentally safe and keep them up-to-date on important environmental legislation or issues in the news. Here are some other ideas to consider:

- **Encourage children to participate in environmentally conscious activities**, such as planting trees, recycling, and conserving water and energy around the house. Children can participate in many of the activities listed in this chapter, but if you want more ideas, check out *50 Simple Things Kids Can Do to Save the Earth* (Andrews & McMeel). The book is filled with tips, information, and activities kids can do, including using household items to make art projects, making recycled paper, and learning about acid rain, the greenhouse effect, and water pollution. The book is written by the **The EarthWorks Group** (the same people who wrote the bestseller *50 Simple Things You Can Do to Save the Earth*).
- **Encourage friends, co-workers, family members, classmates, and others to get involved with environmental activities.** This could be simple—asking them to sign a petition on an environmental issue, for example. Or it could be more involved—such as organizing a beach or park cleanup.

☞ **Volunteer to work at an environmental organization near you.** These organizations often need people to help with administrative work, fundraising, reports, newsletters, and similar projects. (This is also an excellent way to learn about environmental issues.) Many of the national organizations listed in this chapter have local chapters or affiliates. Also, check the phone book under "Environmental Organizations."

☞ **Consider a long-term volunteer opportunity with an environmental organization.** This may include working hands-on to preserve the environment or working with an organization for an extended period of time. Here are a few resources and opportunities to consider:

- **American Hiking Society** (page 259) helps people who want to improve and maintain trails all over the country. If you are interested in this type of work, contact AHS and ask for its *Helping Out the Outdoors* directory, which lists internships and individuals positions at state and national parks and forests nationwide. A single current copy is $3, and a two-year (four issues) subscription costs $12.
- Volunteer for the **Earth Conservation Corps.** ECC is a non-

profit program that engages the energies and talents of young Americans (ages 17-21) to solve pressing environmental problems. In particular, ECC volunteers help to improve wetlands; restore urban parks and city blocks; provide emergency services (for example, storm damage clean-up); and plant trees. ECC volunteers receive rigorous training (approximately 1 to 2 weeks) in physical fitness, work safety, and conservation practices. ECC programs run approximately six months, and volunteers can work on the programs for up to two years (ECC pilot programs in 1991 will last only two months). Food, shelter, and a modest stipend for some programs will be provided, and ECC will also coordinate opportunities for volunteers to further their academic skills. Individuals of all socioeconomic backgrounds are welcome to volunteer. For more information, contact ECC at *1090 Vermont Ave., N.W., 3rd Floor, Washington, DC 20005*; (202) 408-7791.

- **EARTHWATCH** is a nonprofit organization providing people with hands-on opportunities to help the environment. EARTHWATCH sponsors expeditions all over the world, enabling individuals of all ages and skills to save endangered species, study rain forests, monitor the activities of whales, help rebuild threatened habitats, and participate in hundreds of other environmental activities. The trips usually last two weeks and cost about $1,000. Membership ($25) includes a one-year subscription to the bimonthly *EARTHWATCH Magazine*, which features science updates, environmental news, and announcements of new expeditions. Members can also attend such events as film and slide shows, and lectures by scientists and others who have worked on expeditions. Call or write for more information: *680 Mt. Auburn, Box 403, Watertown, MA 02272*; (617) 926-8200, FAX: (617) 926-8532.

- ***Environmental Opportunities*** is a twelve-page directory of approximately 100 opportunities for people interested in working with environmental groups or related activities (some positions do require experience and/or special degrees). Topic headings include "Administration," "Ecology/Fisheries/Wildlife," "Nature Center," "Research," "Organizational," "Environmental Education," "Internships," and "Outdoor Education." Although there are numerous volunteer opportunities, most of the opportunities are full-time, paid jobs. The directory comes out monthly. New subscriptions cost $24 for six months, $44 for one year, and $70 for two years. A single copy costs $4.50. Write to or call Environmental Opportunities at *P.O. Box 4957, Arcata, CA, 95521*; (707) 839-4640.

- ***New Careers: A Directory of Jobs and Internships in Technology and Society*** (see **Student Pugwash U.S.A.**, page 273).
- **Smithsonian Associates Research Expedition Program,** part of the **Smithsonian Institution**, is for individuals who want to help scientists and researchers in a variety of areas, including archaeology, volcanology, photographic documentation, folk culture interviewing, wildlife ecology, and archival research. Volunteer opportunities require a good deal of hard work and commitment (contributions are required), but if you are at all interested, write or call for an application from the Smithsonian Associates Research Expedition Program, Smithsonian Institution, *490 L'Enfant Plaza, S.W., Suite 4210, Washington, DC 20560*; (202) 287-3210.
- **Student Conservation Association** is a national nonprofit educational organization providing volunteer opportunities for high school and college students and other interested individuals who want to help protect public lands and natural resources. Since 1957 more than 12,000 SCA volunteers have maintained hiking trails, conducted educational programs, assisted with wildlife monitoring and research, restored fish habitat in streams, and worked in national parks, forests, public lands, and wildlife refuges. In SCA's **High School Program**, individuals ages sixteen to eighteen volunteer during the summer for periods of four to five weeks (food and group camping equipment are provided). In the **Resource Assistant Program**, volunteers eighteen and older work for twelve to sixteen weeks throughout the year (food, travel, and housing are provided). Listings of opportunities and application materials are available from the address given below. SCA also publishes *JOB SCAN*, a national monthly listing of environmental and natural resource management jobs. *JOB SCAN* lists paying positions, internships, volunteer positions, and related information. Single issues cost $4, a six-month subscription costs $22, and a one-year subscription costs $39. Write to or call SCA at *P.O. Box 550, Charlestown, NH 03603*; (603) 826-4301.

☞ **Make environmentally sound monetary investments.** Invest your money with companies that respect the environment. See Money Matters, page 26, for information on investments and investment service organizations that can help you. The **New Alternatives Fund**, for example, invests only in companies involved with solar and alternative energy development.

National Organizations

American Hiking Society
1015 31st St., N.W., 4th Floor, Washington, DC 20007-4490
(703) 385-3252

AHS is the only national nonprofit organization dedicated to protecting the interests of hikers and preserving America's footpaths. The society monitors and influences federal legislation to increase the number of trails and to turn abandoned railroad rights-of-way into trails. AHS members ($25 for individuals, $15 for students and senior citizens) receive information on where to hike, who to contact for detailed directions about specific areas, how to hike safely, and how to protect the environment. Members also receive *American Hiker*, AHS's quarterly magazine on hiking and the outdoors, and AHS's newsletter, published eight times a year, with information on hiking issues and events nationwide. AHS strongly supports and assists volunteers who want to work to improve and maintain trails. The group publishes a directory of internships and volunteer jobs for people who are interested in trail care. The directory, *Helping Out the Outdoors*, costs $3 for a single current copy and $12 for a two-year (four issues) subscription.

American Wildlands
7500 East Arapahoe Road, Suite 295, Englewood, CO 80112
(303) 771-0380

AWL is a nonprofit conservation organization dedicated to protecting and promoting proper management of publicly owned wildland resources, including wilderness, watersheds, wetlands, free-flowing rivers, fisheries, and wildlife. Programs and projects include river conservation, timber management reform, wilderness protection, riparian habitat protection via the reintroduction of beaver, natural resource economic studies, and monitoring of public land and water policy issues. AWL also sponsors **American Wilderness Adventures**, featuring rafting, hiking, backpacking, canoeing, photography, and biological journeys across the U.S. and abroad. Membership starts at $25 and includes *On the Wild Side*, a quarterly journal with articles and editorials about wildland resources, reports on the current status of wilderness/wildlife, and related environmental issues; periodic issue action alerts; and discounts on books, T-shirts, art prints, and other AWL items.

Appalachian Mountain Club
5 Joy St., Boston, MA 02108
(617) 523-0636, FAX: (617) 523-0722

AMC is the nation's oldest nonprofit recreation and conservation organization. It sponsors outdoor activities and educational programs (including cross-country skiing, backpacking, and naturalist guided hikes, map and compass training); works with volunteers to build and maintain more than 1,300 miles of trails in the Northeast; trains teachers and youth workers to take inner-city youths into the mountains and on other outings; and conducts research on such topics as the ozone, solar energy, clean air, and acid rain. AMC also distributes numerous books, guides, maps, and other publications (for example, *AMC White Mountain Guide; AMC River Guide; AMC Field Guide to Trail Building and Maintenance; and North Woods: An Inside Look at the Nature of Forests in the Northeast*). Membership ($40) includes a subscription to the *Appalachia Bulletin*, a monthly magazine with AMC news and activities.

Center for Environmental Information, Inc.
99 Court St., Rochester, NY 14604-1824
(716) 546-3796, FAX: (716) 325-5131

CEI is a nonprofit organization that provides comprehensive materials covering a broad spectrum of environmental and conservation issues. These materials range from the scientific to the nontechnical and can be of use to the professional seeking detailed information, the politician searching for national statistics, or the student looking for general information for a school report. The center also maintains an extensive collection of books, bibliographies, reports, proceedings, and government documents. Requests for information can be answered directly by telephone, letter, or, when possible, by a visit to CEI. If an answer is not directly available, CEI will try to direct you to an appropriate source. Information is free of charge, but there are nominal fees for more comprehensive information. Membership to the center ($25, $10 for students) includes notices of CEI seminars, conferences, and other activities, as well as a one-year subscription to CEI's quarterly newsletter, *Upstate Environment*, which covers a variety of environmental issues (mostly related to New York).

Concern
1794 Columbia Road, N.W., Washington, DC 20009
(202) 328-8160

The nonprofit **Concern** distributes environmental information to community groups, public officials, educational institutions, and interested individuals. Its primary goal is to help communities find solutions to environmental problems that threaten public health and the quality of life. Concern develops and distributes many worthwhile community action guides, which define major issues, explain relevant legislation, describe successful regional, state, and local initiatives, and give resource information. The guides cover such topics as groundwater, drinking water, farmland, and household wastes. Contact Concern for a full listing of its publications.

The Conservation Foundation
(see **World Wildlife Fund and The Conservation Fund**, page 109)

The Cousteau Society
930 W. 21st St., Norfolk, VA 23517
(804) 627-1144

A nonprofit organization, **The Cousteau Society** was founded by the world-renowned environmentalist and underwater explorer Jacques-Yves Cousteau and his son Jean-Michel to protect and improve the environment for present and future generations. The society explores the planet's incredible natural wealth and biological diversity; educates the public about the wonders of the earth; creates new technology for studying and protecting nature (Cousteau helped invent such things as an underwater camera and a regulator for underwater diving); provides data and recommendations about the environment to policymakers all over the world; and works to protect and preserve the resources of the planet. The organization sells Cousteau videotapes (with stunning photography of various subjects), books, calendars, art prints, posters, and T-shirts. Membership ($20) includes a subscription to the bimonthly magazine *Calypso Log*, a full-color publication that features reports on expeditions and environmental issues, interviews, and photography by the Cousteau team. With the family membership ($28), children age seven to fifteen receive *Dolphin Log*, a full-color bimonthly magazine that contains stories, facts, games, and experiments for young readers.

Earth First!
P.O. Box 5871, Tucson, AZ 85703

EF! is a nonprofit group that confronts ecology-related issues more aggressively than most environmental organizations. EF! does not compromise. Its positions are unabashedly hardline, using direct action and even civil disobedience to fight for wild places and wildlife. EF! does not represent any particular religious or political philosophy, but simply believes in wilderness for its own sake. Since EF! is more of a movement than an organization, a good way to learn about its activities (volunteers are needed), regional affiliates, and programs is to subscribe to *The Earth First! Journal*. A free sample copy is available on request. A one-year subscription (eight issues) costs $20. EF! also sells a wide array of books, T-shirts, sweatshirts, slide-show materials, and bumper stickers.

Earth Island Institute
300 Broadway, Suite 28, San Francisco, CA 94133
(415) 788-3666

The nonprofit **Earth Island Institute** develops, promotes, and supports innovative activities to restore and preserve the global environment. Projects include, among many others, the **Climate Protection Institute**, which develops public education and high school curricula materials on climate change problems; **Friends of the Ancient Forest**, which works to inform the public about the value and uniqueness of old growth forests along the Pacific coast; the **International Marine Mammal Project**, which works to stop the slaughter of dolphins, whales, and other marine life; the **Rainforest Health Alliance**, which develops educational materials explaining the medical and scientific needs for preserving plants in rain forest areas; the **Sea Turtle Resoration Project**, which investigates and works to oppose forces that contribute to the destruction of sea turtles; and the **Urban Habitat Program**, which produces information about inner-city conditions and organizes projects to pursue the restoration of urban neighborhoods. Membership costs $25 and includes the quarterly publication *Earth Island Journal*, which contains in-depth articles and features on a variety of environmental and legislative issues, and corporate and government activities. Members also receive special EII campaign updates and a discounts on EII merchandise.

EarthSave
706 Frederick St., Santa Cruz, CA 95062-2205
(408) 423-4069

EarthSave is a nonprofit organization that helps people move toward more healthy and environmentally sound food choices and non-polluting energy sources, and a wiser use of natural resources. Activities include sponsoring seminars, workshops, and media campaigns; creating nutritional and environmental curricula for schools; supporting local environmental projects; researching and developing ecological alternatives to current factory farming practices; advising policymakers; promoting jobs that contribute to ecological balance; and distributing audiotapes, videos, and publications (such as *The Cookbook for People Who Love Animals; Vegan Nutrition: Pure and Simple;* and *Diet for a New America*). EarthSave also sells T-shirts and cloth shopping bags. Membership ($20 for individuals, $15 for students and retired citizens) includes a subscription to *EarthSave News*, a quarterly newsletter that reports on national policies and a variety of environmental and health issues.

Environmental Action Foundation
1525 New Hampshire Ave., N.W., Washington, DC 20036
(202) 745-4870

The nonprofit **Environmental Action Foundation** is dedicated to creating a cleaner, healthier planet through research, public policy, organization, and legal action. EAF focuses on toxics, alternative energy, solid waste, and energy conservation. Among other things, EAF uses a legal and scientific team to hold polluters accountable for toxic waste; promotes safer alternatives to pesticides, recycling, and source reduction; advocates energy-efficiency measures; and distributes a variety of publications (for example, *Building a Brighter Future; Solid Waste Legislative Summaries; Fact Packets on Energy;* and *Wrapped in Plastics*), reports, and newsletters (including *Power Line*, the only publication that covers energy issues from a consumer and environmental perspective). The sister organization, **EA Inc.**, lobbies Congress on environmental issues, endorses political candidates, and publishes *Environmental Action*, a bimonthly magazine that covers health issues, new trends in recycling, renewable energy, and related issues. Membership ($25) entitles you to a one-year subscription to *Environmental Action* and other benefits. If you only want the magazine, a subscription costs $20.

Environmental Defense Fund
257 Park Ave. South, 16th Floor, New York, NY 10010
(212) 505-2100
For recycling information: 1-800-CALL-EDF (225-5333)

EDF is a nonprofit national conservation organization of scientists, economists, lawyers, and concerned individuals working to defend the environment. EDF addresses such issues as water and energy conservation, pesticides, rain forest preservation, wetland conservation, recycling, wildlife and river protection, acid rain, global warming, and the management and disposal of toxic wastes. The organization has numerous publications on all of these topics, particularly on recycling (for example, *Coming Full Circle;* and *If You're Not Recycling, You're Throwing It All Away*). Membership ($20, $10 for students and senior citizens) includes a subscription to EDF's bimonthly newsletter, which covers legislative issues and EDF activities.

Friends of the Earth
218 D St., S.E., Washington, DC 20003
(202) 544-2600

Friends of the Earth is an international nonprofit organization working to influence public policies and attitudes on such issues as tropical rain forest destruction, toxic chemical safety, coal mining, coastal and ocean pollution, global warming, ozone depletion, groundwater contamination, corporate accountability, and nuclear weapons production. Friends of the Earth distributes several in-depth and enlightening publications, posters, and other items. Membership ($25 for individuals, $15 for students/low income) includes a kit highlighting current projects, international affiliates, and the ACTIVIST MEMBERS program (which will give you information on getting involved with environmental issues); discounts on publications (such as *Bottled Water: Sparkling Hype at a Premium Price*) and products (posters, T-shirts, calendars); and a subscription to Friends of the Earth's magazine. The magazine comes out ten times a year and covers environmental issues, legislative developments, and corporate and government activities that affect the environment.

Global Tomorrow Coalition
1325 G St., N.W., Suite 915, Washington, DC 20005-3104
(202) 628-4016

GTC is a nonprofit association of organizations and individuals working to educate community groups, teachers, policymakers, and concerned citizens about critical global issues relevant to the nation's health, security, and long-term sustainability. GTC works to meet these goals by making research and other materials produced by its member groups available to community-based organizations, publishing and distributing such materials as the *Citizen's Guide to Sustainable Development*; producing teacher packets for elementary and secondary levels on such topics as *Tropical Forests*, *Population*, *Marine Resources* and *Biological Diversity;* and briefing U.S. policymakers on global problems. GTC also helps coordinate Global Town Meetings, Global Issues Forums, Cooperative Alliance Forums, and Globescope Assemblies (these forums and assemblies are small groups that discuss environmental issues in communities nationwide—call GTC for more information). GTC sells gift items, including "Earth Cards," postcards, bumper stickers, wipe-off boards, globe paperweights, mugs, and pens. Members ($35 for individuals, $15 for students and retired citizens) receive GTC publications and periodic bulletins on GTC activities and events.

Greenpeace U.S.A.
1432 U St., N.W., Washington, DC 20009
(202) 462-1177

Greenpeace is a nonprofit organization dedicated to protecting and restoring the environment through positive and nonviolent action. Activities include cleaning up the oceans to protect the habitat and lives of marine mammals; stopping toxic pollution at its source and convincing industries to use readily available "cleaner" technologies; establishing the continent of Antarctica as a World Park; stopping the production of fuel for nuclear weapons; and informing the public of the threat of unregulated nuclear navies. Whether the issue is ocean pollution or the clubbing of baby seals, Greenpeace is making a lasting contribution to preserving the world's habitat and environment. A contribution of $15 will get you a subscription to Greenpeace's colorful and highly informative bimonthly magazine of the same name.

INFORM
381 Park Ave., New York, NY 10016
(212) 689-4040

A nonprofit environmental research and education organization, **INFORM** develops practical ways to protect resources and public health, specifically in the areas of hazardous waste reduction, solid-waste management, urban air pollution, and land and water conservation. INFORM's materials and publications are used by federal and state legislators, national and local conservation groups, business leaders, and concerned individuals. INFORM does not lobby or litigate; instead it examines business practices that harm the air, water, and land, and through studies, pinpoints specific ways in which these practices may be amended. Aside from its many publications (such as *A Citizen's Guide to Promoting Toxic Waste Reduction; Drive for Clean Air: Natural Gas and Methanol Vehicles*), INFORM has an informative quarterly newsletter, *INFORM Reports*, which focuses on the organization's research projects and related findings. A subscription costs $35.

The Izaak Walton League of America
1401 Wilson Boulevard, Level B, Arlington, VA 22209
(703) 528-1818

The **IWLA**, one of the oldest and most respected nonprofit conservation organizations in the U.S., works to defend the nation's soil, air, woods, waters, and wildlife. Its 50,800 members promote citizen involvement in local, hands-on environmental protection efforts; educate the public about emerging natural resource threats; represent conservation concerns before Congress, state legislatures, and government agencies, pressing for strong laws, regulations, and funding to protect resources; and enforce these laws when necessary by taking violaters to court. The IWLA operates on local, regional, and national levels. Its projects throughout the country help keep America's lakes, streams, and groundwater clean and safe; protect national forests, parks, and other lands; work to limit harmful air pollutants; and promote farm conservation. Membership ($5 for students, $20 for individuals) includes a subscription to *Outdoor America*, a quarterly full-color magazine of in-depth articles on conservation, outdoor recreation, and IWLA activities.

Kids Against Pollution
P.O. Box 775
Closter, NJ 07624
(201) 784-0668, FAX: (201) 784-0726

KAP was created by a group of elementary school children from the Tenakill School in New Jersey. The students were committed to making others aware of the problems concerning the environment and how young people, in particular, could address these problems. The students focused particularly on their rights and responsibilities as individuals and how they could help the environment by writing letters and influencing legislation. KAP is now a nonprofit organization with approximately 1,000 chapters nationwide (and some worldwide). Membership ($6) includes a certificate of membership; the opportunity to publish 150-word articles in KAP's newsletter, which contains articles on what KAP chapters are doing nationwide, letter-writing campaigns, and related information; and a membership booklet, which is an excellent source of information not only on KAP, but on what people can do in their schools, homes, communities, and businesses to help the environment. KAP has even drawn up a comprehensive amendment to be adopted by U.S. state and national governments and added to their constitutions. KAP is an outstanding example of a grass-roots organization created by concerned young people working to save the environment.

The Land Trust Alliance
900 17th St, N.W., Suite 410, Washington, DC 20006-2596
(202) 785-1410, FAX: (202) 785-1408

LTA is a nonprofit association of America's local and regional land conservation groups. (A land trust is a nonprofit group that protects land by acquiring it through gift or purchase—sometimes for later conveyance to a government agency; establishing conservation easements that place permanent legal restrictions on future development; and negotiating limited development.) LTA works to provide leadership and services that help land trusts protect land. Its expanding array of programs disseminate information, shape public policy, and make the public aware of land trusts and their role in land conservation. If you want to make a donation or volunteer to help a particular land trust or one near you, LTA can help you locate the trust. LTA provides information on land trusts nationwide; sponsors national conferences; sells books and other materials, and publishes a quarterly journal, *Exchange*, which covers such topics as management of protected lands, state and federal policy developments, and legal and organizational matters. An associate membership ($30) includes a one-year subscription to *Exchange* (contact LTA for other membership opportunities).

National Geographic Society
17th and M Sts., N.W., Washington, DC 20036
(202) 857-7000

With almost eleven million members, **NGS** is the world's largest scientific and educational nonprofit organization. NGS's main activities include producing four magazines, books for adults and children, atlases, videos, and other materials; developing television specials; supporting environmental research; and implementing a comprehensive geography education program for schoolchildren. NGS travels around the globe to explore humanity's history, the status of the world's wildlife and wilderness, and other global, environmental, and societal issues. Membership ($21) includes a subscription to *National Geographic* magazine, a stunning and highly informative monthly publication. In addition, NGS has an extensive catalog of maps, books (such as *Images of the World; Nature's Wonderlands: National Parks of the World; The World of the American Indian*), games, children's books and periodicals (for example, *Explore a Tropical Forest* and *WORLD*—a full-color, monthly magazine for children ages eight and older), and videos (including *The Great Whales; The Sharks*).

The National Resources Defense Council
40 West 20th St., New York, NY 10011
(212) 727-2700, FAX: (212) 727-1773

NRDC is a nonprofit organization that has been working for more than twenty years to protect our air, water, and food supplies. It provides effective litigation, persistent advocacy, and hard-hitting research. The council has led the national fight against acid rain and for enforcement of the Clean Air Act. It has sued the country's worst water polluters to force them to stop poisoning rivers, lakes, and streams. NRDC has created programs dedicated to improving the quality of the urban environment, as well as the **Mothers and Others for Pesticide Limits** campaign, which works to keep apple crops free from the pesticide Alar. It also has initiated forest managment reforms and has fought federal coal-leasing and oil-drilling policies that threaten wildlife and delicate ecosystems. NRDC is working to protect unique tropical forests, and is fighting to preserve coastal enviroments around the U.S. The organization has been a leader in promoting environmentally safe energy sources and ideas. Membership ($10) includes subscriptions to NRDC's quarterly publication, *The Amicus Journal*, and to the *NRDC Newsline*, which is published five times a year and keeps members informed of NRDC programs, publications, and activities. The organization also has publications on energy, atmospheric protection, air quality, pesticides, urban environment, species conservation, and many other topics.

The Nature Conservancy
1815 N. Lynn St., Arlington, VA 22209
(703) 841-5300

The nonprofit **Nature Conservancy** works to save rare plants and animals by buying and protecting the places they need to survive. The Conservancy has fifty state offices and a large international operation. The organization maintains the largest private system of nature preserves in the world (about 1,100), ranging in size from less than an acre to an island four times the size of Manhattan. The basic membership fee ($15) includes a subscription to the award-winning *Nature Conservancy Magazine*, filled with photographs, in-depth articles, and ideas for nature trips. If you are interested in becoming a volunteer for TNC, contact the national headquarters for more information and the location of an affiliate near you.

The North American Conference on Christianity and Ecology
P.O. Box 14305, San Francisco, CA 94114
(415) 626-6064

NACCE is the first major, national group working to bring a Christian force to the environmental movement. Its mission is to reach every church in America and to increase environmental consciousness and action among Christians. NACCE sponsors conferences and wilderness retreats. Membership ($25) includes a subscription to the quarterly *FIRMAMENT MAGAZINE*, which provides an overview of NACCE programs and announces new projects and activities. NACCE also distributes literature that focuses on issues and beliefs related to Christian ecology, including *Christian Ecology: Building an Environmental Ethic for the 21st Century*. Contact the national headquarters if you're interested in starting an affiliate in your community.

One Person's Impact
P.O. Box 751, Westborough, MA 01581
(508) 366-0146

OPI is a nonprofit organization dedicated to teaching people how to incorporate social, economic, and environmental responsibility into their daily lives. OPI sponsors workshops and seminars (mostly in

Massachusetts), and issues a variety of publications, including *The Continental Shelf* (a compendium of inspirational and informational resources). Its highly informative bimonthly newsletter, *One Person's Impact: Practical Actions for Conscious Living*, is filled with simple ideas on how to preserve the environment. Individual membership ($24, $100 for corporations) includes a one-year subscription to *One Person's Impact* and all special reports and supplements.

Renew America
1400 16th St., N.W., Suite 710, Washington, DC 20036
(202) 232-2252, FAX: (202) 232-2617

Renew America is a nonprofit environmental education network dedicated to developing a safe and sustainable environment. The organization collects and disseminates information to enable public officials, environmental groups, and individuals to pursue effective solutions to environmental problems. Programs include **Searching for Success**, which identifies successful local and state environmental programs, and **State of the States**, which provides easily understood report cards on environmental protection programs in all fifty states. Membership ($25) includes a subscription to the quarterly newsletter *Renew America Report*, copies of newly released publications and a fifty percent discount on past publications.

Resources for the Future
1616 P St., N.W., Washington, DC 20036
(202) 328-5000

An independent nonprofit organization, **RFF** advances research and public education about the conservation and use of natural resources and the quality of the environment. Research is primarily concerned with the relationship of people to the natural resources of land, water, and air; the products and services derived from these basic resources; and the effects of production and consumption on environmental quality as well as on human health and well-being. Publications include *Public Policies for Environmental Protection; Readings in Risk;* and *Nuclear Imperatives and Public Trust: Dealing with Radioactive Waste.* RFF is not a membership organization, but its publications are available to anyone. Its quarterly newsletter, *Resources*, is free.

Rocky Mountain Institute
1739 Snowmass Creek Road, Snowmass, CO 81654
(303) 927-3851

RMI is a nonprofit research and educational foundation focusing on five areas: agriculture, economic renewal, energy, security, and water. Its agriculture program develops low-cost strategies for water use, energy use, and farming methods that are economically, ecologically, and socially effective and responsible. The economic renewal program develops ideas to make communities economically strong by plugging the unnecessary leaks of money from a community, supporting existing businesses, creating new businesses, and recruiting businesses that have the community's interests in mind. The institute's energy program focuses on energy-efficient lights, motors, appliances, vehicles, and other items that save money and resources and reduce pollution and global warming. The security program explores the more efficient use of resources, such as energy and strategic materials, as a means to reduce international tensions. Finally, the water program explores the many new ways to use water more efficiently. RMI has an incredible catalog of publications (and a few hats, shirts, and videos) on the five issues mentioned above and more. A $10 donation entitles you to RMI's newsletters.

Scenic America
216 Seventh St., S.E., Washington, DC 20003
(202) 546-1100

Scenic America is the only national nonprofit organization dedicated to protecting America's scenic heritage and cleaning up "visual pollution." Among other activities, SA educates the public on the need for billboard and sign control; provides up-to-date information on aesthetic regulation, growth management, and scenic highways controls; regulates the placement of billboards along America's highways; and helps local governments enact effective legislation to protect community appearance, control signs, and preserve trees. SA also sells videos, T-shirts, books, and fact sheets (such as, *Billboard Control: Facts & Myths* and *Billboards and the Environment*). Members ($20) receive *Sign Control News*, a bimonthly newsletter that provides information on relevant legislative issues, SA activities, local and national successes, and information on billboard advertising in general.

The Sierra Club
730 Polk St., San Francisco, CA 94109
(415) 776-2211

Almost 100 years old, the nonprofit **Sierra Club** is dedicated to preserving and restoring the environment by working for clean air, by protecting wildlife, national forests, and national parks, and by conserving oceans, wetlands, and other water resources. Activities include exploring, enjoying, and protecting the wild places of the earth; researching and providing information on toxins and the greenhouse effect; practicing and promoting the responsible use of the earth's ecosystems and resources; and educating and enlisting people to protect and restore the quality of the natural and human environment. The Sierra Club has a broad base of grass-roots volunteers in the U.S. and Canada, who lead the organization's 57 chapters and 375 local groups. Chapter and group volunteers plan outings and programs, sponsor environmental education campaigns, produce newsletters, and are active in local, state, and national political affairs and lobbying. The national and regional offices support the volunteers by providing training, materials, and assistance. The club has a national program that coordinates more than 300 outings a year, and **Inner City Outings** program, which provides wilderness experiences for urban youth, older Americans, and individuals with disabilities. If you're interested in ski touring, hiking, backpacking, bicycling, canoeing, volunteering to help the environment, or just getting out to appreciate America's natural wealth, the Sierra Club can provide you with the assistance and information you'll need. It also has one of the most extensive environmental catalogs available, with over 350 high-quality publications, calendars, videos, and posters. Another available catalog is the *SourceBook*, with many less expensive materials and publications for activists. Membership ($33, $15 for students, senior citizens, and people with limited incomes) includes a subscription to the local chapter newsletter and the bimonthly magazine *Sierra*, an award-winning, full-color publication filled with environmental articles, commentary, and photography. If you cannot find a chapter near you, contact the Volunteer Development office at *(415) 923-5576* at the address given above.

Sierra Club Legal Defense Fund, Inc.
2044 Fillmore St., San Francisco, CA 94115
(415) 567-6100

The **Legal Defense Fund** is a nonprofit public interest environmental law firm that provides legal services to national and local environmental organizations on conservation issues of broad public concern. The firm litigates primarily in federal court, challenging the actions (or lack of actions) of federal agencies responsible for protecting and managing the nation's environmental resources. On a regular basis, the Legal Defense Fund also represents clients before administrative agencies and state courts. Traditionally, the organization selects cases involving not only unique or significant natural resources but issues that have the potential to establish important new precedents for the protection of the environment. Lawyers or paralegals who would like to volunteer their services should contact the national headquarters for more information.

Smithsonian Institution
Office of Environmental Awareness
S. Dillon Ripley Center, Room 3132
Washington, DC 20560
(202) 357-2700

The **Smithsonian Institution's Office of Environmental Awareness** works to increase public awareness and understanding of environmental issues through exhibitions, workshops, publications, and public programs. OEA cooperates with experts within and outside of the Smithsonian to disseminate research results and conservation-related information to the general public and specialized audiences. OEA has done research in areas such as biogeochemical and atmospheric processes, conservation of species, restoration of degraded ecosystems, and the impact of human destruction of rain forests. One of OEA's offerings is *A Better World Starts at Home*, a free poster (designed to fit on a refrigerator) with information on saving energy and water, reducing the use of chemicals, recycling materials, and stopping practices that deplete stratospheric ozone. OEA also has fact sheets on a variety of environmental issues, particularly rain forests. (The phone number above is a general number for the Smithsonian Institution—there's no direct number for OEA; and it's best to contact the organization by mail.)

Student Conservation Association
(see page 258)

Student Pugwash U.S.A.
1638 R St., N.W., Washington, DC 20009
(202) 328-6555

Run by students and young professionals, **Student Pugwash** is a nonprofit educational organization working to provide university and high school students with the resources and information they may need to understand better the social and ethical dimensions of science, technology, and the environment. (SP was named for the town of Pugwash, Nova Scotia, where, in 1957, a group of internationally reknowned scientists met to discuss the social and ethical implications of science and technology.) The group sponsors conferences and local activities at campuses across the country; provides seminars and a referral network to address career issues; and distributes educational materials and publications, including an outstanding guide called *New Careers: A Directory of Jobs and Internships in Technology and Society* for people considering jobs in areas such as the environment, energy, peace, and health. The directory lists about 150 organizations located in more than thirty cities nationwide and costs $20, $12 for students (these prices include $2 for shipping and handling). SP also publishes *Pugwatch*, a monthly newsletter for SP chapters, and *Tough Questions*, a triannual publication addressing a variety of issues related to global security, bioethics, energy, development, and the environment. Contact the national headquarters if you're interested in starting an SP chapter at your school, college, or university.

Trust for Public Land
116 New Montgomery St., 4th Floor, San Francisco, CA 94105
(415) 495-4014

The nonprofit **Trust for Public Land** is dedicated to conserving land across the country by establishing hundreds of land trusts, thus preserving hundreds of thousands of acres (and inhabitants) under public ownership. Programs focus on urban waterfronts, suburban greenways, wetlands, and inner-city open spaces. TPL also works to improve public access to public lands, foster community-owned or -maintained parks and gardens, and establish local community land trusts. TPL is also launching a **National Counselor Program**, which will train land trusts making the transition from volunteer to professional staff in conservation real estate transactions.

20/20 Vision
30 Cottage St., Amherst, MA 01002
(413) 549-4555 or 1-800-347-2767

20/20 is a nonprofit organization working to engage citizens in effective communication with policymakers to redefine American priorities and shift spending from military defense to defense of the environment and human needs. Membership ($20) includes a monthly postcard with background information on a particular policy issue, legislation, or political appointment. The postcard will tell you who to contact (including addresses and phone numbers) to express your views and what to focus on in your correspondence. 20/20 also provides members with a short guide on how to write an effective letter and a brief report every six months on the results of members' actions. (20/20 promises members that they will not receive mountains of mail, be asked to attend meetings, or have their names and addresses given to other organizations.)

The Union of Concerned Scientists
26 Church St., Cambridge, MA 02238
(617) 547-5552, FAX: (617) 864-9405
or
1616 P St., N.W., Suite 310, Washington, DC 20036
(202) 332-0900, FAX: (202) 332-0905

The Union of Concerned Scientists is a nonprofit organization of individuals (scientists and nonscientists alike) concerned about the impact of advanced technology on society. Its programs focus on national energy policy, national security policy, and nuclear-power safety. The organization advocates energy strategies that minimize risks to public health and safety, provide for efficient use of energy resources, and minimize damage to the global environment. UCS also works to support defense policies and negotiated arms agreements that reduce the risk of nuclear war, benefit U.S. security interests, and enhance the nation's economic strength. This is a highly respected organization, often called on by the media, government representatives and officials, and interested individuals. UCS produces books, briefing papers, videos, and other worthwhile and informative materials. The organization also publishes a quarterly newsletter, *Nucleus*, with editorials, in-depth articles, legislative updates, and other features. The suggested membership fee is $20.

U.S. Public Interest Research Group
215 Pennsylvania Ave., S.E., Washington, DC 20003
(202) 546-9707

U.S. PIRG is the national lobbying office for PIRGs across the country. PIRGs are nonprofit, nonpartisan environmental and consumer advocacy organizations working at state and community levels to represent the public interest in areas of environmental protection, energy policy, and government and corporate reform. PIRGs organize grass-roots efforts on campuses across the country. They also run campaigns nationwide on recycling, clean air and water conservation, hazardous waste removal, pollution prevention, and pesticide reform. U.S. PIRG has numerous publications and reports, including *As The World Burns: Documenting America's Failure to Address the Ozone Crisis;* and *Exhausting Our Future: An Eighty-Two City Study of Smog in the 80's.* Membership ($25) includes a subscription to the quarterly newsletter *U.S. PIRG Citizen Agenda*, which contains updates on state and national PIRG campaigns, reports on legislative activities, and other features. Volunteers are needed at some of the local PIRGs. If you are a college student interested in starting a campus program, contact U.S. PIRG for the necessary information.

The Wilderness Society
900 17th St., N.W., Washington, DC 20006-2596
(202) 832-2300

The nonprofit **Wilderness Society** advocates the wise management of America's federal public lands and their wildlife. The society works to educate citizens, public officials, and the media on the need to protect and carefully manage the public lands; testifies at congressional hearings; encourages concerned citizens across the country to participate in programs protecting public lands; sponsors conferences, seminars, and workshops, and cooperates with other conservation organizations to achieve a comprehensive agenda of environmental goals. Members ($15 for first-time members, students, senior citizens, and people with limited incomes, $30 for basic membership) receive *Celebrating the American Earth*, a stunning collection of twenty-six Ansel Adams photographs; *Wilderness* magazine, a quarterly publication filled with high-quality photography and articles; member alerts (periodic warnings of new threats to the environment); and an invitation to apply for the TWS VISA Card (every time you use the card, the society receives a small donation, at no cost to you).

Windstar Foundation
2317 Snowmass Creek Road, Snowmass, CO 81654
(303) 927-4777

The **Windstar Foundation** is a not-for-profit educational organization that conducts research, sponsors educational programs and meetings, and distributes books, videos, and audiotapes on a variety of environmental issues, including chemical pollution, recycling, global warming, responsible diets, and energy. Publications include *Sharing the Joy of Nature; Hug a Tree; Non-Toxic and Natural; Everyday Chemicals; Full Circle: Successful Recycling Today; Diet for a New America;* and *Creating a Healthy World: 101 Practical Tips for Home and Work.* The foundation also sells windsocks, cloth grocery bags, T-shirts, and sweatshirts. All items are available to the general public, but you can become a WF member ($35 and up), which entitles you to discounts on WF products and a subscription to the quarterly newsletter.

World Resources Institute
1709 New York Ave., N.W., Washington, DC 20006
(202) 638-6300

A nonprofit research and policy organization, **WRI** generates information about global resources and environmental conditions, analyzes emerging issues, and develops creative policy responses for governments, the general public, and environmental organizations. WRI's interdisciplinary staff and network of formal advisers carries out policy research projects in such areas as forests and biodiversity, economics, climate, energy, pollution, and natural resources. The institute's catalog includes *Conserving the World's Biological Diversity; Public Policies and the Misuse of Forest Resources; Tropical Forests: A Call for Action;* and *The Greenhouse Trap: What We're Doing to the Atmosphere and How We Can Slow Global Warming.*

World Wildlife Fund and The Conservation Foundation
(see page 109)

Worldwatch Institute
1776 Massachusetts Ave., N.W., Washington, DC 20036
(202) 452-1999

The nonprofit **Worldwatch Institute** informs policymakers and the public about the interdependence of the world economy and the state of the environment. Its research staff analyzes issues from a global, interdisciplinary perspective. Publications produced by WI are highly respected and informative; *World Watch* is probably the most reliable, unbiased, and enlightening magazine you can find on such issues as population growth, global warming, hunger and nutrition, ozone depletion, solar energy, nuclear power, energy efficiency, and national security. A one-year subscription (six issues) costs $15. WI also has an extensive catalog of **Worldwatch Paper Series**, which are detailed reports on particular issues (for example, *Air Pollution; Acid Rain, and the Future of Forests; Conserving Water: The Untapped Alternative*). The organization publishes *State of the World*, an up-to-date guide to the world's resources and how they are being managed. A partial list of the chapters from the most recent edition includes "Slowing Global Warming," "Feeding the World in the Nineties," "Ending Poverty," and "Converting to a Peaceful Economy." It is a valuable source for anyone interested in the state of the world today. A one-year subscription ($25) to the WI library includes *State of the World* and all *Worldwatch Papers* released during the calendar year.

Zero Population Growth
1400 16th St., N.W., Washington, DC 20036
(202) 332-2200

ZPG is a nonprofit organization that promotes a sustainable balance among people, resources, and environment, both in the U.S. and abroad. The group is active in several areas; at the grass-roots level, bringing population education to thousands of young people by training teachers and distributing its innovative and informative materials to educators across the country; on television and radio, providing the facts about population and environmental issues; and on Capitol Hill, providing testimony for committees and lobbying members of Congress. ZPG distributes a variety of informative teaching kits and publications, including *Population & The Greenhouse Effect* and *USA by Numbers*, an up-to-date resource on demographic, social, economic, and environmental trends in the U.S. Membership ($20 or more) includes a subscription to *The ZPG Reporter*, a bimonthly newsletter containing facts, resources, and features on relevant population issues, and *The Activist*, ZPG's quarterly newsletter containing legislative alerts, volunteer opportunities, and other information on ZPG activities and programs.

Air Pollution, Deforestation, and Global Warming

What You Can Do

☞ **Educate yourself on the problems of air pollution, deforestation, and global warming so that you will know what to do to help out. Knowing the issues also makes you able to educate others. Write letters to congressional representatives expressing your opinion regarding environmental legislation. Most of the national organizations listed in this section can provide you with information and legislative updates. (See also Voicing Your Opinion, page 363.)

☞ **Don't use or purchase products containing CFCs** (chlorofluorocarbons) or other ozone-depleting chemicals. Although CFCs were banned from spray cans in 1978, there are still products (such as aerosols used to clean electronic parts for VCRs and TVs) that contain them or other chemicals hazardous to the environment. Most aerosol products are harmful because they directly add pollutants, while most foam products are harmful because their manufacture requires the use of CFCs. Here are some other products to watch out for:

- aerosol dust removers
- carpet pads
- foam cushions
- foam ice chests
- foam mattresses
- Halon fire extinguishers
- home insulation (not all of these contain CFCs; check first)
- Styrofoam
- vinyl car and bicycle seats

☞ **If you eat at fast-food restaurants, patronize those that have switched to paper products.** Express your disapproval to those companies that still use Styrofoam through letters or phone calls.

☞ **Don't burn leaves or other yard debris.** Not only does this contribute to air pollution, it can also be very dangerous. The best thing to do is to compost your yard debris (see page 315) or take debris to a recycler.

☞ **Don't buy wood, wildlife, or plants from tropical forests.** Rain forests are being destroyed at an alarming rate, and buying wood or plants from these forests simply contributes to the problem. (Buying tropical animals isn't good because it removes them from their natural habitats and many die en route to the U.S.) Rosewood and mahogany, parrots and macaws, and orchids and bromeliads are typical rain forest products, so ask before you buy any of these. If you want to buy something that comes from a rain forest but does not contribute to its destruction (and supports rain forest natives), buy **Rainforest Crunch**, a delicious cashew–Brazil nut buttercrunch. A one-pound box costs $9.20 ($14.50 orders come in an attractive, reusable tin), which includes shipping and handling. Twenty percent of the profits go to rain forest preservation organizations. A price list for retailers interested in carrying Rainforest Crunch is available. For all orders or for more information, contact **Community Products, Inc.** at *RD #2, Box 1950, Montpelier, VT 05602*; (802) 229-1840.

☞ **Plant a tree.** Or better yet, plant a whole lot of trees. Trees are truly an environmentalist's best friend: they provide shade, which can help cut down on energy use when planted near homes and buildings; they convert noxious fumes into clean air; they provide homes and shelter for animals; and they make yards, playgrounds, city streets, and countless other areas more attractive. Here are some helpful resources:

- **Go to a local nursery** (check the yellow pages). In addition to providing you with seeds or young trees, nurseries can give you information on planting and maintaining trees and advice on the best trees or plants for your area. Many nurseries also sell gift certificates for people interested in giving a tree to someone for a birthday or holiday.
- The **American Forestry Association** (page 284) runs project **Global ReLeaf**, a program to have 100 million new trees planted in America by 1992. Ask for the free action guide to see how you can get involved.
- The **National Arbor Day Foundation** (page 286) is working to involve the general public in planting trees around homes and in communities. NADF can provide you with free seedlings and informative publications on tree planting and care.
- **TreePeople** (page 289) can provide you with brochures, booklets, and workshop information on tree care and tree planting. Members also receive free seedlings (you must, however, pick them up from the organization's nursery).

If you are interested in planting trees on public property, contact the local Department of Public Works (check the government pages of the phone book). Look for a Tree Maintenance division, which may be listed under "Public Space Maintenance." It may take some searching to find the right office, but you will need to talk with officials to obtain the necessary permission. They may be able to help out with supplies and information, too.

☞ **Limit the amount you drive your car.** There are more than 135 million cars in the U.S.,[47] emitting twenty percent of this country's carbon dioxide—a "greenhouse" gas.[48] Shop by phone instead of driving to stores to see if they have what you want, and plan your errands so that you can make them all in one trip. Remember, when you drive, don't make quick accelerations and fast stops: this can be hard on your car, and it's not good for the environment. Turn off the ignition if the car will be idling for more than a minute.

☞ **Keep your car well-tuned to limit excess fumes and to save gas.** A well-tuned car uses up to nine percent less gasoline than a poorly tuned car.[49] Have your car checked about every five to ten thousand miles or every six months, whichever comes first. Here are some other automotive tips to consider:

- **Be sure brakes are properly adjusted.** Brakes that drag are not only wasting fuel, they are a safety hazard.
- **Use radial tires, check the tire pressure regularly, and be sure that the wheels are properly aligned.** Radial tires can improve fuel economy by several percentage points as compared to non-radials. And properly inflated and aligned tires significantly help fuel economy.
- **Remove unnecessary items from your car** (usually from the trunk area). Heavy items can weigh down your car and waste fuel. Also, remove a ski or bicycle rack when not in use. This is not only added weight, but it causes added wind resistance.
- **Use the car's air conditioner as little as possible.** Air conditioners are a major source of ozone-depleting CFCs, and they also reduce fuel economy by up to two and a half miles per gallon.
- **When you fill up the gas tank, don't "top off" the tank** by pulling the gas nozzle back and filling the tank to the brim. This risks spilling gas on the ground and yourself and sends vapors into the atmosphere.
- **Plan long trips carefully.** Be sure you have a route mapped out.
- **If you're buying a new car, make fuel efficiency a high priority.** Fuel-efficient cars save you money and significantly help the environment. A car that gets 26.5 mpg (the standard for

---

[47] According to the Federal Highway Administration.
[48] The Earth Works Group.
[49] Ibid., 36.

most new cars), will emit twenty tons less carbon dioxide in its lifetime than the average car on the road today.[50]

☞ **Use a bicycle as often as possible and encourage your family, friends, and co-workers to do the same.** Bikes are clean and efficient, and provide excellent exercise. If you are interested in general biking information or vacations, here are some organizations to contact for safety tips, general biking information, and suggestions for biking vacations:

- **Bicycle Federation of America** is a nonprofit organization established to promote the safe use of bicycles for transportation and recreation. BFA organizes conferences; provides information and technical assistance to federal, state, and local agencies, community organizations, and individuals involved in bicycle programs; and publishes *Pro Bike News* ($18), a monthly newsletter with up-to-date information on cycling events. Write to or call BFA at *1818 R St, N.W., Washington, DC 20009*; (202) 332-6986.
- **Bikecentennial** is the largest nonprofit, recreational cycling organization in the U.S. Activities include researching and mapping out a nationwide network of bicycle touring routes, promoting bicycle safety and the benefits of bicycle touring to the American public, and disseminating information on bicycling (for example, the *Cyclosource Catalog*, which contains biking and camping gear and other necessary items, and *Bikecentennial Tours*, which contains information on tours and expeditions nationwide). Membership costs $22 for individuals, $19 for students, and $17 for senior cyclists sixty or older (contact the organization for other membership opportunities). Membership includes a subscription to *BikeReport, The Cyclists' Yellow Pages*, maps, books, and discounts on Bikecentennial maps. If you are interested in touring or biking in general, Bikecentennial is an indispensable resource. Write to or call Bikecentennial at *P.O. Box 8308-PG, Missoula, MT 59807*; (406) 721-1776.
- The **League of American Wheelmen** is a nonprofit organization of bicyclists dedicated to promoting the sport of bicycling and to protecting the needs and interests of bicyclists everywhere. LAW advocates for the rights of bicyclists, promotes bicycling as a pleasurable recreation and fitness alternative, and facilitates communication among bicyclists to encourage cooperation and sharing of useful information. Membership ($25) includes a subscription to *BICYCLE USA*,

---

[50]Ibid., 37.

LAW's full-color magazine that comes out eight times a year; a subscription to the *Almanac* (a special issue of *BICYCLE USA*), which provides state-by-state information on major rides and events; information on books, products, and videos; and riding tips. Members also receive *TourFinder*, which can provide you with information on planning bicycle vacations worldwide. Write to or call LAW at *6707 Whitestone Road, Suite 209, Baltimore, MD 21207*; (301) 944-3399.

☞ **If you cannot bike to work, try to car pool or van pool, or take public transportation.** Start up a car or van pool at work (often, lack of initiative is the only reason a pool doesn't already exist). You can also look up "Car Pooling" or "Van Pooling" in the phone book for referrals and matching services. If you want more information (including fact sheets and information about local agencies that can help you form a car pool or van pool), write to or call the **Association for Commuter Transportation** at *808 17th St., N.W., Suite 200, Washington, DC 20006*; (202) 223-9669.

National Organizations

The Acid Rain Foundation, Inc.
1410 Varsity Drive, Raleigh, NC 27606
(919) 828-9443

ARF is a nonprofit organization working to foster a greater understanding of the acid rain problem and to help bring about its resolution. The foundation seeks to increase the level of public awareness about the severity of acid rain and other air-quality issues (such as global climate change), supplies educational resources and materials to professionals and the general public alike (including videos, films, slides, information packets, lesson plans, and bibliographies), and supports research in the area of acid rain and related issues. Offerings include curriculum materials for students of all ages, puzzles, posters, proceeding reports (for example, *Air Pollutants' Effects on Forests*), resource directories, information packets, and books (such as *Acidification Today and Tomorrow* and *The Air Around Us*). If you are interested in ARF's catalog, please send a self-addressed, stamped envelope to the address given above. Membership ($25) for one year includes the quarterly publication *The Acid Rain Update*.

American Forestry Association
Global ReLeaf Program
P.O. Box 2000, Washington, DC 20013
(202) 667-3300

AFA is one of the most prominent nonprofit organizations working to protect and care for forests worldwide. The association can provide you with numerous publications on planting and caring for trees in your yard and community. One of AFA's biggest projects is **Global ReLeaf**, a massive effort to encourage people to plant trees to help solve many of the world's environmental problems. Anyone can receive a free booklet describing the Global ReLeaf project and providing information on getting involved. Membership ($24) includes discounts on AFA publications and merchandise (books, stickers, action guides, and decals); technical assistance with tree planting; legislative updates on conservation issues; AFA tour opportunities; and *American Forests*, a bimonthly magazine featuring forestry and conservation news, incredible photography, and in-depth articles.

American Lung Association
1740 Broadway, New York, NY 10019
(212) 315-8700

ALA is the oldest nationwide voluntary health agency in the U.S. Originally founded in 1904 to combat tuberculosis, today ALA and its affiliates are dedicated to the prevention, cure, and control of all lung diseases and some of their related causes, including air pollution. The local ALA chapters (there are approximately 130 of them) usually have posters, booklets, legislative information, and other materials to help you, and others, learn about the problems of air pollution and how to get involved. If you cannot find an office in your community, contact the national headquarters for the affiliate near you.

Basic Foundation
P.O. Box 47012, St. Petersburg, FL 33743
(813) 526-9562 or 1-800-752-0668

The nonprofit **Basic Foundation** advocates the balance of conservation of natural resources with the needs of current and future population levels. Over the past few years the organization has committed its resources to promoting public awareness about rain forest conservation. BF sponsors research activities, exhibits, conferences, lectures, and nature tours; publishes and donates educational materials to schools; and manufactures and distributes **Rainforest Crunch** (candy made of cashew and Brazil nuts harvested in the Amazon rain forest), postcards, T-shirts, bumper stickers, sweatshirts, posters, greeting cards, audiocassettes, and books (such as *Nature Hide & Seek Jungles; Journey Through a Tropical Jungle*). BF also has a program that recruits people to donate $5 to plant an endangered tropical tree.

Children of the Green Earth
307 N. 48th, Seattle, WA 98103
(206) 781-0852

CGE is a nonprofit organization dedicated to "regreening" the earth by encouraging young people to plant and care for trees and forests. CGE distributes educational materials, a newsletter, and books. Almost all of its publications provide information on planting and maintaining trees, along with folklore and mythology pertaining to tree planting. Membership ($25) includes a subscription to the newsletter as well as a discount on CGE materials.

Climate Institute
316 Pennsylvania Ave., S.E., Suite 402, Washington, DC 20003
(202) 547-0104, FAX: (202) 547-0111

The nonprofit **Climate Institute** creates an interchange of ideas among climate researchers and analysts, policymakers and planners, opinion makers, and the public, through conferences and symposia, videos, audiotapes, books, and papers. CI is a leading voice working to influence international policy concerning climate change, focusing on developing countries. Publications include *Coping With Climate Change* and the quarterly newsletter *Climate Alert*, which contains information on international policy developments and a calendar of climate-related events. Membership ($35 for individuals, $15 for students) includes a one-year subscription to the newsletter.

Conservation International
1015 18th St., N.W., Suite 1000, Washington, DC 20036
(202) 429-5660 (For information specifically related to North American and Mexican programs and activities):
105 W. Ash St., Portland, OR 97204
(503) 227-6225

CI is a nonprofit organization dedicated to the protection and preservation of natural ecosystems and the species that rely on these habitats for their survival, with a special emphasis on rain forests. It provides resources and expertise in such areas as science, fundraising, conservation planning, and public education. CI works with private organizations, government agencies, native peoples, and universities in Mexico, Indonesia, Brazil, Costa Rica, Bolivia, Peru, Guatemala, Madagascar, and the U.S. (primarily Washington), among other countries, to preserve critical habitats. Membership ($15 or more) includes a subscription to the quarterly newsletter *Tropicus*, which discusses the state of rain forests worldwide and related issues.

The Greenhouse Crisis Foundation
1130 17th St., N.W., Suite 630, Washington, DC 20036
(202) 466-2823

A nonprofit organization, **GCF** is dedicated to creating a global awareness of the greenhouse crisis and related environmental issues. The foundation has sponsored many public information campaigns on such issues as energy conservation, urban reforestation, and mass transit. Jeremy Rifkin, the president of GCF, is the author of several in-depth and highly informative books on the greenhouse effect and the environment, including *ENTROPY: Into the Greenhouse World; Time Wars; Algeny;* and *The Green Lifestyle Handbook: 1,001 Ways You Can Heal the Earth*. GCF also sells *101 Ways to Help Heal the Earth: A Citizen's Guide* ($5), an excellent resource for people who are looking for information on how to improve the environment.

The National Arbor Day Foundation
100 Arbor Avenue, Nebraska City, NE 68410
(402) 474-5655

NADF is a nonprofit organization working to increase the number of trees planted in the U.S., and to educate the public on the need for trees to preserve the environment and enhance communities and homes. Membership ($10) includes free trees, *The Tree Book*, and a subscription to *Arbor Day* magazine, a full-color publication featuring reports on NADF activities and tree care suggestions. NADF can also send you information on Arbor Day activities and on making your community a **Tree City U.S.A.** NADF is a valuable resource for individuals looking for practically any information on trees and what the world would be like without them.

National Parks and Conservation Association
1015 31st St., N.W., Washington, DC 20007
(202) 944-8530

NPCA is the only nonprofit, citizen-funded organization dedicated to protecting, promoting, and enhancing the country's national parks. NPCA educates the public on the need for national parks; fights pressure to open parks to hunting and trapping; works to preserve wildlife in the parks; raises money to buy holdings and create new parks; fights raids on water resources and opposes the building of useless, destructive dams; encourages the creation and preservation of important archaeological sites, historic buildings, and monuments; and encourages park wildlife research and habitat preservation for endangered species. Members ($22, $15 for students and retired citizens) are given opportunities to participate in outdoor events, including tours and white-water–rafting trips. Members also receive guides and maps of the national parks and a subscription to the bimonthly magazine *National Parks*, a stunning, full-color publication containing in-depth articles about the problems and needs of the National Park System and threats to its survival; legislative updates; and other features and departments. NPCA has a catalog of books, regional guides for hikers, bikers, and naturalists, bird and plant guides, children's books, videos, clothing, games, and other items.

Rainforest Action Movement
430 East University, Ann Arbor, MI 48109
(313) 662-0232

The nonprofit **Rainforest Action Movement** is committed to raising awareness about tropical and temperate rain forests, particularly in Alaska, Oregon, Washington, and Hawaii, to prevent their destruction. RAM works to help diverse communities recognize a common interest (and responsibility) in preserving rain forests. It sponsors public-awareness programs and distributes many publications, videos, films, and other materials. RAM also publishes a newsletter, *Tropical Echoes*, which costs $10 and comes out every six weeks.

Rainforest Action Network
301 Broadway, Suite A, San Francisco, CA 94133
(415) 398-4404

RAN is a nonprofit network dedicated to saving rain forests and educating the public about the vital support system rain forests provide for the earth and its people. RAN has worked to convince Burger King to stop purchasing beef from rain forest regions; to force the World Bank and other financial institutions to stop funding (with U.S. tax dollars) rain forest destruction in areas such as Indonesia and the Amazon; and to protect tropical rain forests in the continental U.S., Hawaii, Puerto Rico, the Virgin Islands, and trust territories in the Pacific. RAN has also been working on an extensive national media campaign, researching tropical timber and beef imports, and developing an international directory of organizations involved in preserving rain forests in the Amazon region. RAN can provide you with comprehensive information on rain forests and things you can do to save them, including books (for example, *In the Rainforest; The Primary Source; Lessons of the Rainforest*), slide-show materials, posters, bumper stickers, and calendars. A $25 contribution ($15 for students and people with limited incomes) will entitle you to RAN reports and a subscription to its monthly *Action Alerts* newsletter. RAN welcomes interns and volunteers, so call or write if you're interested.

Rainforest Alliance
270 Lafayette St., Suite 512, New York, NY 10012
(212) 941-1900, FAX: (212) 941-4986

The **Rainforest Alliance** is a nonprofit network of concerned citizens, conservationists, professional organizations, scientists, and members of the business community working together to support education, research, and legislation to conserve and restore tropical forests. RA believes that an informed public will become a concerned, and consequently, active public. Public information offerings include conferences, consumer-awareness brochures, fact sheets, a nationwide directory of speakers on the rain forest, and a quarterly newsletter, *The Canopy*, which includes a variety of highly informative articles and rain forest activity announcements. If you are interested in learning more about rain forests and helping to save them, RA is an essential resource. Membership is $20 ($15 for students and senior citizens).

Save the Redwoods League
114 Sansome St., Room 605, San Francisco, CA 94104
(415) 362-2352

A nonprofit organization **SRL** was established to purchase and protect forests, particularly redwood forests. SRL is working to purchase land for thirty-two California Redwood State Parks, Redwood National Park, Muir Woods National Monument, and Sequoia National Park. Currently, every dollar donated to SRL is allocated to forestland purchase, unless donors specify otherwise. SRL also has postcards and pamphlets, including *Guide to the Redwood Parks; Redwoods of the Past; A Living Link in History;* and *Story Told by a Fallen Redwood.* Membership ($10 and up) includes spring and fall updates on SRL's activities.

TreePeople
12601 Mulholland Drive, Beverly Hills, CA 90210
(818) 753-4600, FAX: (818) 753-4625

TreePeople is a community-based, nonprofit, environmental problem-solving organization dedicated to showing citizens how to plant and maintain trees. TreePeople runs environmental leadership programs for tens of thousands of children a year, gives technical training on tree planting to community groups and interested individuals, and provides its members with six free seedlings. Members also receive *Seedling News*, a bimonthly newsletter addressing global and local environmental issues. TreePeople has an excellent book for people interested in planting and maintaining trees—*The Simple Act of Planting a Tree: A Citizen Forester's Guide to Healing Your Neighborhood, Your City, and Your World* ($12.95). Membership fees start at $25.

Chemicals and Hazardous Wastes

What You Can do

☞ **Educate yourself and others about chemicals and hazardous wastes and the extent to which they contaminate water supplies, cause air pollution, and create a variety of health hazards.** Monitor and work to influence legislation concerning chemicals and hazardous wastes. Many of the national organizations listed in this section can provide you with the necessary information. (See also Voicing Your Opinion, page 363.)

☞ **Use nontoxic cleaners and pesticides.** Here are a few suggestions and resources to consider (see also the environmentally conscious mail-order companies that sell nontoxic items, page 252):

- **Buy low-phosphate or phosphate-free detergents whenever possible.** Phosphates are toxic and are especially harmful to the environment when they get into the water supply. (Check the label on the detergent for *phosphorus*.)[51]

● **Instead of buying expensive, overpackaged cleaning products, use common household items.** Many cleaning, disinfecting, and other household jobs can be taken care of with baking soda, hot water, or vinegar. Here are some nontoxic alternatives to store-bought products:

1. Air fresheners: Instead of using sprays, boil cinammon, spices, or herbal mixtures. Flowers and plants make excellent year-round air fresheners.
2. Appliance surfaces, counters, and faucets: A mixture of vinegar and water or simply baking soda sprinkled on a damp sponge should do the job.
3. Carpets: To freshen your carpets, sprinkle baking soda (a flour sifter works well for this) on the carpet. Let it sit for twenty to thirty minutes, then vacuum.
4. Door hinges: Use mineral oil on sticky hinges.
5. Drain cleaner: To keep your drain clean, pour a quarter of a cup of baking soda and then a half a cup of vinegar down the drain and cover tightly for a minute (remember, the mixture of vinegar and baking soda will foam quickly). Run hot water to rinse.
6. Glass and windows: A vinegar-and-water solution should be enough.
7. Moths: Instead of using mothballs, try using cedar wood or dried lavender.
8. Shower stalls, sinks, toilets, and tubs: Baking soda sprinkled on a wet sponge (or toilet brush, while cleaning the toilet) should clean these.

● **AFM Enterprises, Inc.** offers a large selection of no- or low-chemical supplies for building and household jobs, including:

- all-purpose polish and wax
- carpet adhesive
- carpet shampoo
- jewelry cleaner
- mildew control
- paint
- primer
- rust remover
- shoe polish
- tile grout
- wallpaper adhesive
- wood protective coating

---

[51]Ibid., 51.

Contact AFM Enterprises, Inc. at *1140 Stacy Court, Riverside, CA 92507*; (714) 781-6860 or (714) 781-6861, FAX: (714) 781-6892. (AFM Enterprises does not test its products on animals.)
* **Coherency Co.** sells a variety of natural and nontoxic household and personal products, including:

- adhesives
- all-purpose cleaners
- companion animal products (such as pest controls and shampoos)
- cosmetics
- laundry detergent
- paints
- polishes
- shampoos
- soaps
- suntan lotions
- toothpaste
- waxes
- wood finishes

Write to or call Coherency Co. at *P.O. Box 553, Occidental, CA 95465*; (707) 869-0956. Coherency Co. also takes special orders.
* **Eco Design Co. and Livos Plantchemistry** are mail-order companies that sell a variety of nontoxic products, including:

- all-purpose cleaners
- art supplies (for example, crayons, modeling wax, water colors, finger paints)
- books (for example, *The Healthy Home: An Attic-to-Basement Guide to Toxin-Free Living*; *Rush to Burn: Solving America's Garbage Crisis*; *War on Waste: Can America Win Its Battle with Garbage?*)
- companion animal products (such as flea powder and herbal shampoo)
- floor wax
- furniture polishes
- hand soaps
- paint thinners and paints
- recycled paper products
- skin-and hair-care products
- toothpastes and mouthwashes

Write or call Eco Design Co. and Livos at *1365 Rufina Circle, Santa Fe, NM 87501*; (505) 438-3448.

* **Sinan Co. Natural Building Materials** sells a variety of nontoxic paints, varnishes, waxes, lacquers, polishes, glues, and related household products. For more information, contact Sinan Co. at *P.O. Box 857, Davis, CA 95617-0857*; (916) 753-3104.

☞ **When you go shopping, be sure to read labels carefully.** The fact that the words "Nontoxic," "Natural," or even "Environmentally Safe" appear on a product's label doesn't necessarily mean that the product or packaging is safe for the environment. "Nontoxic," for example, means that the product is not harmful to humans; it may still harm animals or the environment. It's best to use common sense and be wary of labels that seem vague. Also, "Danger" and "Poison" indicate highly toxic products, "Warning" and "Caution" slightly less toxic.

☞ **Don't buy bleached items such as coffee filters, paper towels, and napkins.** See if there's a nonbleached or reusable alternative (for example, small towels or rags instead of paper towels, cloth napkins instead of paper ones).

☞ **Buy organically grown foods and avoid products that contain a lot of preservatives and chemicals.** Foods that are organically grown are good for the environment because they are grown and processed without the use of synthetic pesticides, chemical fertilizers, or growth stimulants. Here are a few resources that can help you maintain a more chemical-free diet:

- The **Center for Science in the Public Interest** is a nonprofit organization that can provide you with informative pamphlets, guides, and books that will help you eat nutritionally and educate yourself about food chemicals and preservatives in food. Write to or call CSPI for more information and a publications catalog: *1875 Connecticut Ave., N.W., #300, Washington, DC 20009*; (202) 332-9110. **Americans for Safe Foods**, a division of CSPI, has a comprehensive list of mail-order suppliers that can provide you with just about every kind of organic food, including fresh and dried vegetables and fruits, pasta, beans, spices, grains, coffee, and breads. For the catalog, send a large self-addressed, stamped (forty-five cents) envelope to **Mail-Order Organic** at the CSPI address given above.
- **The Healthy Harvest Society** works for the preservation and long-term sustainability of the earth and its soils for the production of pesticide-free food. One of HHS's main publications, *Healthy Harvest: A Directory of Sustainable Agriculture and Horticulture Organizations* ($18.95, which includes $2 for shipping and handling), lists hundreds of resources for people looking for organically grown and pesticide-free foods. Membership ($24 for individuals, $50 for organizations) includes discounts on publications and products, and a one-year subscription to *Healthy Harvest News*, a quarterly newsletter that covers a variety of issues concerning pesticide-free food. Write to or call HHS at *1424 16th St., N.W., Suite 105, Washington, D.C. 20036*; (202) 462-8800.

- **The National Organic Wholesalers Directory and Yearbook** is a publication of the **California Action Network**, a grass-roots political organization dedicated to encouraging alternatives in agriculture. The directory costs $28 (which includes $3 for shipping and handling) and lists more than 400 organic food wholesalers and farm suppliers. Write or call CAN at *P.O. Box 464, Davis, CA 95617*; (916) 756-8518.
- The **Public Voice for Food and Health Policy** is a nonprofit organization that, through research, targeted advocacy efforts, and public-education programs, works to advance consumer interests in national food and health policymaking. Public Voice specifically addresses such issues as pesticide and chemical residues in food, food contamination, and agricultural programs. The organization's materials include *A Blueprint for Pesticide Policy: Changing the Way We Safeguard, Grow and Market Food; Back to Basics* (a poster highlighting ten natural steps toward healthier eating); and *Hazardous Fish: The Raw Facts—The Need for a Mandatory Federal Fish Inspection Program*. Membership ($20 and up) includes a subscription to *Action Alert*, a quarterly bulletin that contains legislative news and a variety of articles on food and nutrition. Write or call Public Voice at *1001 Connecticut Ave., N.W., Suite 522, Washington, DC 20036*; (202) 659-5930.

☞ **If you are a gardener, practice chemical-free gardening.** Gardening chemicals can wash into groundwater supplies, ultimately affecting natural water resources. Ask your local nursery about nontoxic pest and weed killers. Here are some publications and organizations that can help you with chemical-free and environmentally conscious gardening:

- **Gardener's Supply Company** is a mail-order company for environmentally conscious gardeners and yardworkers. GSC can supply you with many items, including:

  - compost holders
  - humane, nonkilling, and noninjuring animal traps and deterrents
  - natural bug killers and repellents
  - plant food and fertilizers
  - protective nettings
  - weed controls

  Write to or call GSC at *128 Intervale Road, Burlington, VT 05401*; (802) 863-1700.
- **Necessary Trading Co.** is a mail-order company that sells a

variety of products for environmentally conscious gardening and farming. Here is just a partial list of available items:

- beneficial insects (for example, ladybugs, lacewing larvae, predatory mites)
- books (such as *Color Handbook of Garden Insects; Organic Farming; Alternative Agriculture*)
- companion animal products (such as flea soaps, flea collars, and shampoos)
- compost activators
- composting bins
- cover crop seeds
- fertilizers
- insect killers, traps, and repellents
- plant food

Write to or call NCO at *6177 Salem Ave., New Castle, VA 24127*; 1-800-447-5354, Technical Help Line: (703) 864-5103. Catalogs are $2 (refundable with first purchase).

● **Ringer Lawn and Garden Products** is a mail-order company for people who want keep their yards and gardens healthy without hurting animals or the environment. Ringer distributes a wide array of environmentally friendly products, including:

- bird feeders
- composting bins
- fertilizers
- grass seed
- hand-powered lawn mowers
- insect repellents and killers
- lawn restorers
- quick compost activators
- spray nozzles and sprinkler timers
- tree food

Write to or call Ringer at *9959 Valley View Road, Eden Prairie, MN 55344-3585*; 1-800-654-1047, FAX: (612) 941-5036.

● **Rodale Press** publishes some of the best gardening and environmental books and magazines available. Here are a just few to look for:

The Chemical-Free Lawn
The Encyclopedia of Natural Insect Disease Control
The Encyclopedia of Organic Gardening
How to Grow Vegetables Organically
Organic Gardening magazine ($25 for a one-year subscription—ten issues)

If you cannot find Rodale publications at your local bookstore, contact Rodale Press at *33 E. Minor St., Emmaus, PA 18098*; (215) 967-5171 or 1-800-441-7761.

☞ **Use rechargeable batteries instead of the common alkaline kind.** Although rechargeable batteries are initially more expensive than alkaline varieties, they will save you money in the long run because they can be recharged up to a hundred times. Using rechargeable batteries also reduces the level of toxic materials and packaging waste going into landfills. Stores that carry alkaline batteries should also stock rechargeable ones, but if not, check the mail-order companies in this chapter (page 252).

☞ **Try to limit dry cleaning.** The cleaning solvents used by dry cleaners are harmful to the environment, so hand wash clothes as often as possible and buy clothes that do not require dry cleaning.

☞ **Dispose of hazardous household wastes and oil properly.** Do not pour them down a sewer, toilet, or drain where they can eventually contaminate drinking-water supplies. Hazardous wastes include motor oil, brake fluid, transmission fluids, paints, and antifreeze/coolants (these are not only bad for the environment, but many cats and dogs have died from drinking puddles of contaminated water). Here are some disposal methods to consider:

- **Contact your local sanitation department, Department of Public Works, or the state office of conservation and natural resources to locate a hazardous-waste collection center.** Some communities even have a hazardous-waste collection day. Community officials should know when this takes place.
- **Call your local service station** and see if they accept used motor oil and properly dispose of it. If not, ask if they know where you can take it. Used oil can also be purified, redistilled, and used again. See if your local automotive or hardware store has information on do-it-yourself recycling kits.
- **If you have paint to throw away, consider donating it to a school, shelter for the homeless, or religious congregation that may need it for small jobs.**

☞ **Work with neighbors and local representatives to start up a "Hazardous Waste Day."** On these days, people bring their hazardous household wastes to a specific location or leave them at the curb to be picked up and properly disposed of.

National Organizations

Bio-Integral Resource Center
P.O. Box 7414, Berkeley, CA 94707
(written inquiries are preferred)

BIRC is a nonprofit organization that researches and provides education on the least-toxic methods of managing pests. The center can give you information on managing practically every farm, garden, lawn, and household pest you could imagine, plus materials on safely getting rid of weeds and structural pests (termites, ants, etc.). BIRC also has information on safe bug and worm repellents for companion animals. Associate members ($30) receive a consultation on toxins and least-toxic alternatives, and a subscription to the *Common Sense Pest Control Quarterly*, a nontechnical publication filled with information on least-toxic methods for managing insects, weeds, rodents, and plant diseases. The journal also lists resources for safe pest-control products.

Citizens Clearinghouse for Hazardous Waste
119 Rowell Court, Falls Church, VA 22046
(703) 237-2249

CCHW is a nonprofit organization dedicated to helping people nationwide learn about and prevent environmental catastrophies in their community. CCHW helps people fight for their rights by providing direct, one-on-one assistance and information on what needs to be done and how to do it (CCHW will even send experts to the community in need). The clearinghouse also collects information on chemicals and their effects, various disposal methods, technology for cleanup, activities of generators and disposal companies, and the work of the many other organizations addressing the hazardous waste problem. CCHW has numerous straightforward citizen's guidebooks on a wide variety of topics (for example, *Hazardous Wastes Fact Book*, How to Deal with a Proposed Facility), a bimonthly newsletter, *Everyone's Backyard*, toxic-waste-site lists, and T-shirts and bags. The basic membership fee is $25 for individuals ($15 for students and people on limited incomes) and $35 for citizens' groups.

The Consumer Pesticide Project
425 Mississippi St., San Francisco, CA 94107
(415) 826-6314

CPP, which is affiliated with the **National Toxics Campaign** (see page 298), is a nonprofit organization of concerned individuals and environmental activists working to keep dangerous pesticides out of food and the environment. CPP is particularly interested in getting consumers to encourage supermarkets and family farmers to provide more fresh fruits and vegetables without dangerous pesticides. The organizing kit, *A Practical Strategy to Reduce Dangerous Pesticides in Our Food and the Environment*, is an excellent source of information on forming a community effort to reduce dangerous pesticides. Membership ($10) includes the organizing kit (please make checks out to NTCF—the National Toxics Campaign Fund).

Grass Roots the Organic Way
38 Llangollen Lane, Newtown Square, PA 19073
(215) 353-2838

GROW is a nonprofit organization established to provide information about harmful pesticides and to offer safe and effective alternatives. The group works to heighten public awareness of the dangers of pesticide misuse; to influence legislation pertaining to the spraying of toxic pesticides on lawns, shrubs, and trees in residential communities; and to create an information and resource network on alternatives to toxic pesticides. Members can ask about specific problems and, depending on the problem, an information packet on the specific problem may be available. Membership costs $15. (Please send a stamped, self-addressed envelope for questions, requests, and other information.)

Household Hazardous Waste Project
901 S. National Ave., Box 108, Springfield, MO 65804
(417) 836-5777

HHWP is a nonprofit program of the Missouri State Environmental Improvement and Energy Resources Authority and Southwest Missouri State University. Its community-education program helps the public protect their personal environment by making informed decisions about the purchase, safe use, storage, and disposal of hazardous products and wastes. HHWP addresses such issues as environmental protection, fire safety, recycling, and poison protection. Publications include *Guide to Hazardous Products Around the Home* ($9.95—includes shipping and handling), which helps people understand "signal words" and product labels, select safer products, and locate recycling options in their communities for some types of hazardous waste. The guide also contains more than 150 easy recipes for safe cleaning and pest control at home.

National Coalition Against the Misuse of Pesticides
701 E St., S.E., Suite 200, Washington, DC 20003
(202) 543-5450

The nonprofit **NCAMP** is committed to pesticide safety and to alternative pest-management strategies. NCAMP is working to educate the public on the dangers of pesticides and to push for legislation and policies enforcing pesticide control. Farmers, gardeners, consumers, scientists, physicians, attorneys, and other concerned individuals are all members of NCAMP. NCAMP has numerous materials on pesticides, chemicals, the least-toxic methods of pest control, legislative issues, and issues relating to pesticide use in schools. Membership ($20, $12 for people with limited incomes) includes *Pesticides and You*, a highly informative newsletter keeping readers up-to-date on a range of pesticide issues, including pesticide myths and ideas on how to create a safer environment in the home and community.

National Toxics Campaign
1168 Commonwealth Ave., 3rd Floor, Boston, MA 02134
(617) 232-4014

NTC is a nonprofit network of statewide consumer organizations, environmental groups, family farmers, lawyers, businesspeople, scientists, and concerned individuals working to implement citizen-based preventive solutions to the nation's toxic and environmental problems. NTC can provide organizational, technical, and legal assistance to concerned individuals and communities fighting toxic waste and pollution. It distributes several useful publications, including *A Consumer's Guide to Protecting the Ozone; Once Is Not Enough: A Citizen's Recycling Manual;* and *A Practical Strategy to Reduce Dangerous Pesticides in Our Food and the Environment.* The quarterly magazine *Toxic Times* features national and regional NTC events, articles on grass-roots campaigns, legal tips, and regular columns on solid waste, ozone protection, and related environmental issues. A one-year subscription costs $15 but is free with membership ($25 and up).

Nuclear Information & Resource Service
1424 16th St., N.W., Suite 601, Washington, DC 20036
(202) 328-0002

NIRS is a nonprofit information center and clearinghouse for anyone concerned about nuclear energy and interested in safe, alternative energy sources. NIRS can provide you with organizing assistance, up-to-date information, fact sheets (for example, "Nuclear Basics," "Nuclear Waste," "Energy Efficiency"), and a variety of publications. Membership ($20, $10 for people with limited incomes) includes a subscription to *GROUNDSWELL*, NIRS's quarterly journal containing in-depth analyses of major nuclear issues, as well as information from industry and government and news on citizen actions (and you don't need a Ph.D in nuclear physics to read it).

Pesticide Action Network
North America Regional Center
965 Mission St., #514, San Francisco, CA 94103
(415) 541-9140, FAX: (541) 9253

The **Pesticide Action Network North America Regional Center (PAN NA RC)** is a nonprofit organization working for the adoption of sustainable, nonchemical pest-control methods. PAN NA RC is one of six regional coordinating points throughout the world for **PAN International**, a coalition of more than 300 independent, autonomous citizen organizations working for pesticide reform in more than fifty countries. PAN NA RC links the collective strength and expertise of the North American pesticide reform movement, and individuals within it, with counterpart citizen movements in other countries. The organization also distributes numerous books (for example, *Problem Pesticides, Pesticide Problems; Pesticides: 44 Questions and Answers*) and posters (such as *Pesticides Don't Know When to Stop Killing; Circle of Poison: What Goes Around Comes Around*), and publishes a quarterly newsletter, *Global Pesticide Campaigner* ($25 per year). The newsletter presents information and analysis of international pesticide issues, as well as coverage of PAN's international **Dirty Dozen Campaign** (which focuses on pesticides that activists worldwide have recommended be replaced with safer alternatives). PAN NA RC invites organizations to become affiliates ($50 to $100). Anyone can purchase PAN NA RC publications and posters.

Rachel Carson Council
8940 Jones Mill Road, Chevy Chase, MD 20815
(301) 652-1877

A nonprofit organization, **RCC** works as an information clearinghouse on pesticides and other toxic chemicals. It sponsors conferences and develops and distributes many publications on pesticide and other chemical contamination. Titles include *Losing the War Against Cancer: Who's to Blame and What to Do About It; Pesticides in Contract Lawn Maintenance;* and *How to Control Garden Pests Without Killing Almost Everything Else.*

Radioactive Waste Campaign
7 West St., Warwick, NY 10990
(914) 651-7917

RWC is a nonprofit educational organization working to inform and help citizens confront radioactive waste issues and the environmental and health hazards involved. Serving as a national clearinghouse, RWC conducts research, works with local groups, responds to inquiries, and distributes several publications (including *Living Without Landfills; Radioactive Waste: Buried Forever?; Deadly Defense;* and *Burning Radioactive Waste: What Comes Out of the Stack*). It also publishes a quarterly newsletter, *The RWC Report* ($15 a year, $25 for two years), which covers a broad range of radioactive waste issues. Membership ($25) includes a one-year subscription to *The Report.*

Energy Conservation

What You Can Do

☞ **Educate yourself and others about the need to conserve energy.** Energy conservation is easy and beneficial to the environment, and helps reduce problems such as air pollution and acid rain. Also, the more you know about energy conservation; the easier it is to follow and influence energy-related legislation. Check the national organizations in this section for the necessary legislative information. (See also Voicing Your Opinion, page 363.)

☞ **Be sure that your home is well insulated and weather-**

sealed. Almost half of all the energy used in American homes is wasted, seeping out of windows, through attics, or through cracks.[52] You may have to purchase storm windows, insulation, weather-stripping, and/or caulking, but the savings from these additions will be significant. In some areas, new insulation can pay for itself in a single season; in most areas it takes only one or two years.[53] (Don't forget to insulate electrical outlets and light switches. You can buy a packet of foam insulating plates—ten or a dozen per packet—for just a few dollars. They are easy to install behind the plate; you'll probably need only a screwdriver.) Many of the national organizations listed in this section have information on energy conservation; and here are a few other sources:

- **Contact your local utility company for conservation tips and an energy audit of your house.** Usually, these audits are, if not free, quite inexpensive. Utility companies will often give you a comprehensive analysis of your specific energy problems and the approximate cost of correcting them, and tell you how long it will take for repairs to pay for themselves. Some utilities even supply free materials. Check your utilities bill for a customer-service number.
- *Home Energy* is a bimonthly magazine for conservation professionals as well as for homeowners and tenants who want the most up-to-date information on saving energy. *Home Energy* has information on air conditioning, appliances, insulation, lighting, space heating, ventilation, water conservation, and water heating. A one-year subscription costs $45. Write or call *Home Energy* at *2124 Kittredge St., No. 95, Berkeley, CA 94704*; (415) 524-5405.
- **National Center for Appropriate Technology** has a wide array of materials on energy conservation. The organization's available titles (most of which cost five dollars or less) include:

How to Detect Air Leaks . . . And Decide If You Need to Fix Them
How to Insulate Gas- or Oil-Fired Hot Water Tanks
Natural Cooling for Homes: Low Energy Concepts
Thermostat Timer Control: A Do-It-Yourself Device to Cut Heating Costs and Increase Comforts

Write to or call NCAT at *3040 Continental Drive, P.O. Box 3838, Butte, MT 59702*; (406) 494-4572.

---
[52]Ibid., 76.
[53]Ibid., 76.

- The **U.S. Department of Energy** has an informative booklet, *Tips for Energy Savers*. For this and other publications, see the **Conservation and Renewable Energy Inquiry and Referral Service** (page 307).

☞ **Turn off lights and other appliances when you're not using them.** While lights and appliances take up relatively little energy when compared to larger appliances like refrigerators or air conditioners, it is much easier to flick off a switch when you leave a room than it is to go out and buy a new energy-efficient refrigerator. Also, turning off lights and appliances will, one hopes, encourage others to do the same. It is simply a good habit to get into, and it will make a difference in your energy bill.

☞ **Keep shades and curtains drawn on sunny days.**

☞ **Depend on fans (particularly ceiling fans) on hot days, instead of air conditioners.** Fans use much less energy, don't emit CFCs, and spread cool air efficiently.

☞ **Close the ducts and doors to unused rooms.** Take a quick walk through your home and see if you feel any air coming through the ducts. If these are open or if doors are left open to unused rooms, you are wasting a good deal of energy. To cut down on drafts in rooms, use draft guards. These sand- or pebble-filled "socks" are put at the bottom of a door or windowsill to stop drafts from going out or coming in. Some people even make their own guards with long sports socks or old pantyhose, substituting softer materials for sand or pebbles.

☞ **When it gets cold at night, use extra blankets instead of relying on an electric blanket.**

☞ **Purchase hand-powered appliances whenever possible.** Hand-powered can openers, lawn mowers, juice squeezers, and other such items will save you a substantial amount of money initially and will result in energy-cost savings later. These items also have fewer parts (especially small pieces), which makes them less likely to need repairs. They are also just as (if not more) effective as electrical appliances.

☞ **Be sure you don't waste energy when you cook.** Here are a few things to keep in mind:

- **Toaster ovens, microwaves, and slow cookers generally use less energy than ranges or ovens.** And remember, to-

day's ovens heat quickly, so you don't have to preheat as long as with older models.
- **Plan ahead when you have to defrost frozen foods.** Instead of doing a last-minute defrosting in the oven or microwave, leave the frozen items in the refrigerator or out on the counter (covered) to defrost. It will take longer, but it won't waste energy.
- **Use cool or cold water when cooking** (unless the recipe says otherwise). Waiting for hot water to come out of the faucet wastes water and energy, and cold water works just as well.
- **Use small pots on small burners and large pots on large burners.** Be sure you put lids on the pots so that the contents heat faster.

☞ **Use compact fluorescent bulbs.** Although they are more expensive than standard bulbs, compact fluorescent bulbs are considerably more energy efficient and last longer (some up to nine times longer), saving you money in the long run. They also cut down on waste; since some fluorescent bulbs can last as long as nine standard bulbs, fewer bulbs and less packaging are thrown away. If your local hardware or appliance store does not sell them, check the environmentally conscious mail-order companies starting on page 252. Here are two other companies that can provide you with fluorescent lights:

- **Rising Sun Enterprises** has a large selection of energy-efficient lighting, particularly fluorescent lights, and water-saving products (and comprehensive information on energy efficiency). Write or call RSE at *P.O. Box 586, Old Snowmass, CO 81654*; (303) 927-8051, FAX: (303) 927-3635.
- **White Electric Co. Inc.: The Light Bulb Place** sells fluorescent bulbs, and its ordering brochure has information on suitable and unsuitable fixtures for fluorescent bulbs. Mail orders should be sent to *P.O. Box 11276, Berkeley, CA 94701*; (415) 845-8535, outside California: 1-800-4NU-BULB (468-2852). Send a self-addressed, stamped envelope for information. (If you're in the area, you can visit The Light Bulb Place at *1511 San Pueblo Ave., Berkeley, CA.*)

☞ **If you have a fireplace, be sure that the flue is closed when the fireplace isn't in use.** When you use the fireplace, close all the doors and warm-air ducts in the room (except for one door or window, which should be left open a crack). Keeping the room closed off will prevent heat from being lost throughout the house.

☞ **Plant trees and shrubs around areas of your house that face the sun.** Planting trees around your house can provide enough shade to reduce air-conditioning costs by ten to fifty percent.[54] Trees and shrubs will also usually make a home look more attractive. (Be sure, however, that you don't have large trees or bushes too close to the house that could shield burglars.)

☞ **Lower your thermostat in the winter and fall just a few degrees and wear warmer clothes.** If every household in America lowered its heating temperature about six degrees for only one day, we could save over 570,000 barrels of oil.[55] Also, lower your thermostat several degrees when you're going to bed or leaving your home for more than four hours (most energy companies suggest fifty-five degrees Fahrenheit as the optimum temperature). Thermostat timers will allow you to start warming your home before you get up or before you return home, and consequently, save you energy.

☞ **Save energy by properly maintaining large appliances.** Here are a few of the biggest energy guzzlers to check:

• **Air conditioners:** Set your air conditioner at a reasonable level. When you turn on the air conditioner, don't set it at the highest reading. This does not cool the room any faster, and it only wastes energy. Make sure the filters are clean and replace them about once a month (have the unit professionally cleaned every one or two years). Poorly maintained air conditioners waste a great deal of energy. If you leave the unit in a window during the winter, make sure that the window is properly sealed and insulated so that no drafts come through. Most hardware and appliance stores sell air-conditioner covers that keep the unit in good condition and help prevent drafts.

• **Furnaces:** Check your furnace's air filters and ducts. Have gas furnaces checked every two years, oil furnaces every year; keeping your furnace serviced and in good working condition can increase energy efficiency by five to fifteen percent and will improve the lifespan of the unit. Have a serviceperson lower the furnace temperature to ninety-five degrees (or whatever he or she recommends). During the summer, have gas-furnace pilot lights turned off; this can save ten to fifteen dollars a summer.

• **Radiators:** Be sure that radiators are clean and that nothing is obstructing them and decreasing their effectiveness. Put a re-

[54]MacEachern, 30.
[55]Ibid., 24.

flector behind each radiator in the house so that as much heat as possible comes into the room. You can buy these at appliance or hardware stores or make them by covering a piece of cardboard with aluminum foil.

- **Refrigerators:** Check the temperature levels; the refrigerator should be set around thirty-eight to forty degrees Fahrenheit, and the freezer should be set at about zero degrees. Be sure that the seal on the refrigerator door is tight, so that no cold air leaks out. Clean the coils on the back or bottom of the unit every six months. Sometimes you can just vacuum or carefully wipe these; otherwise, most hardware or appliance stores sell special brushes.
- **Stoves:** If you have a gas stove, be sure the pilot light is blue. If the flame is yellowish in color, the gas is probably not burning cleanly and the stove needs to be adjusted or cleaned. If you are planning to buy a gas stove, look for one with an electric ignition system, which uses about forty percent less gas than a pilot light.
- **Washers and Dryers:** Set the washing machine on "warm" ("cold" is even better) for the wash and "cold" for the rinse. This will get most clothes as clean as a hot wash and save energy. Also, washing machines use almost fifteen percent of the water consumed in a home, so only wash when you have a full load. (The next time you buy a washer, be sure to get a front-loading machine; they use one-third less water than conventional top loaders). Be sure that you clean the lint screen on your dryer so that the air can circulate properly. Air dry your clothes as often as possible. Do your wash in the evening, so that the clothes can dry overnight.
- **Water Heaters:** Turn the water heater down to 130 degrees Fahrenheit (or to the "energy saver" setting if there is one). Many people have their heaters set as high as 170 degrees, which wastes an enormous amount of energy and shortens the lifespan of the unit. Although some environmentalists have recommended turning water heaters down to 120 or 110 degrees, which is certainly hot enough for showering, bathing, etc., this may not be hot enough to kill certain bacteria. A setting of 130 degrees is sufficient to kill bacteria.[56] Insulate the water heater with a special "blanket," available at most hardware or appliance stores. These are easy to put on and can save a significant amount of energy. Also, be sure your accessible water pipes are insulated. Some local utility companies offer free insulation.

---

[56]The Earth Works Group, 25.

☞ **When purchasing large appliances, such as refrigerators, air conditioners, hot water heaters, furnaces, and stoves, look for the ones that have low "Energy Use" ratings.** A large sticker or chart on the appliance should tell you how efficient it is. For a comprehensive listing of efficient appliances, contact the **American Council for an Energy-Efficient Economy** (below) for its publication, *The Most Energy-Efficient Appliances*.

☞ **Consider using solar power,** especially if you are planning to add on to or rebuild part of your house. Solar power is clean, inexpensive, and efficient. You can even take advantage of it with small items such as solar-powered calculators or outdoor lamps. If you cannot find these items at stores near you, see the environmentally conscious mail-order companies starting on page 252.

National Organizations

The Alliance to Save Energy
1725 K St., N.W., Suite 914, Washington, DC 20006-1401
(202) 857-0666

ASE is a nonprofit coalition of government, business, environment, consumer and labor leaders, and concerned individuals dedicated to increasing the efficiency of energy use as an effective means of achieving vital national goals, such as a clean environment, affordable housing for all Americans, greater U.S. competitiveness in international markets, and economic development. To stimulate investment in energy efficiency, ASE conducts research; organizes pilot projects; sponsors educational programs; and formulates policy initiatives. ASE also testifies before legislative and regulatory bodies; publishes policy studies and technical manuals; and provides consumers with information about energy efficiency through booklets (for example, *Make Housing More Affordable Through Energy Efficiency*; *Your Home Energy Portfolio*). Individual memberships are available for $25; contact ASE for further information on obtaining memberships and publications.

American Council for an Energy-Efficient Economy
1001 Connecticut Ave., N.W., Suite 535
Washington, DC 20036
(202) 429-8873

ACEEE is a nonprofit organization dedicated to advancing energy-conserving technologies and policies through research, analysis, advocacy, and information dissemination. Specifically, ACEEE advises governments and utilities on techniques for improving energy efficiency; researches and prepares in-depth studies of energy-efficient technologies, policies, and related issues; and publishes and distributes books, conference proceedings, and reports. ACEEE conducts projects related to energy efficiency and the environment, utilities, transportation, buildings, appliances, lighting, and equipment, conservation research and development, and energy efficiency in developing countries. Publications include *The Most Energy-Efficient Appliances; Saving Energy and Money with Home Appliances;* and *Oil and Gas Heating Systems: Maintenance and Improvement.* ACEEE is not a membership organization, but its publications are available to anyone interested.

American Solar Energy Society, Inc.
2400 Central Ave., B-1, Boulder, CO 80301
(303) 443-3130

ASES is the United States section of the **International Solar Energy Society**. ASES provides a forum for the various disciplines represented by the solar technologies; serves as a source of broad technical and scientific knowledge; and provides a forum to address critical national issues where solar energy technologies offer significant contributions. One of ASES's most noted publications is *Solar Today*, the only national magazine covering all the solar technologies. The magazine is full of in-depth features, national and international news items, advertisements of solar products, and opinions on solar energy. A one-year subscription costs $25 (the magazine comes out seven times a year).

**Conservation and Renewable Energy
Inquiry and Referral Service**
P.O. Box 8900, Silver Spring, MD 20907
1-800-523-2929

CAREIRS is a nonprofit organization, under contract to the U.S. Department of Energy, working to provide the public with both nontechnical and detailed information on renewable energy technologies and energy conservation techniques for both residential and commercial needs. CAREIRS operates a nationwide, toll-free telephone service to answer public inquiries on such issues as passive solar heating, photovoltaics, wind energy, biomass conversion, solar thermal electricity, geothermal energy, small-scale hydroelectricity, alcohol fuels, wood heating, and ocean energy. The service has more than 150 publications, fact sheets, and bibliographies, and 500 computerized letter units available to respond to inquiries. Responses to inquiries are basically automated—usually a computer-generated letter with enclosures. Some inquiries, however, are immediately answered on the phone, individually researched, or referred to other organizations. Ninety percent of CAREIRS' inquiries are answered within two days. Whether you are a homeowner looking for energy conservation tips or a scientist looking for up-to-date research, CAREIRS is an outstanding source.

Critical Mass Energy Project
Public Citizen
215 Pennsylvania Ave., S.E., Washington, DC 20003
(202) 546-4996

A project of Public Citizen (a nonprofit citizen research, lobbying, and litigation organization), **CMEP** is a powerful voice in the movement to end reliance on nuclear power and promote safer energy alternatives. CMEP has three main focuses: rapidly phasing out nuclear power plants presently operating or under construction in the U.S.; promoting new energy-saving technologies, renewable energy resources, and small power systems as alternatives to nuclear power; and publicizing the many economic, safety, social, and environmental problems associated with nuclear power. CMEP can provide you with legislative information, fact sheets, and a variety of publications (for example, *Turning Down the Heat: Solutions to Global Warming; Nuclear Power: Too Costly to Continue;* and *Consequences of a Nuclear Accident*).

Energy Conservation Coalition
(see **Environmental Action Foundation**, page 263)

Rails-to-Trails Conservancy
1400 16th St., N.W., Washington, DC 20036
(202) 797-5400

Established by trails enthusiasts, **RTC** is a nonprofit organization dedicated to converting abandoned railroad corridors into trails for public use. RTC publicizes rails-to-trails issues throughout the country; provides legal and technical assistance for public and private agencies advocating trail conservancy; notifies trail advocates and local officials of upcoming abandonments of train rails; and pushes for funding programs and simplified regulations to promote rail-trail conversions. RTC sells several publications for trail enthusiasts, including *Converting Rails to Trails: A Citizen's Manual; A Guide to America's Rail-Trails;* and *Great Rail Trails of the Great Lakes.* Membership ($18) includes discounts on publications and products, as well as a subscription to the quarterly newsletter *Trailblazer,* which keeps members up-to-date on rail-trail regulations, newly or soon-to-be converted trails, and other relevant issues.

Safe Energy Communication Council
1717 Massachusetts Ave., N.W., Suite LL215
Washington, DC 20036
(202) 483-8491

SECC is a nonprofit coalition of ten national energy, environmental, and public-interest media organizations. The council works to demonstrate the serious economic liabilities of nuclear power and show that efficient use of energy as well as renewable energy (for example, wind and solar power) can meet an increasing share of our nation's energy needs. SECC produces public service announcements and advertisements; and provides 1,000 newspapers, 300 newsletters and magazines nationwide with an op-ed service, *VIEWPOINT*, and with *ENfacts*, a graphics service on energy and environmental issues. SECC also publishes an ongoing series of reports, *MYTHBusters*, which challenges claims of the nuclear industry. The organization cooperates with activists from every state, providing information, assisting with media, and organizing strategies. Contact SECC for more information on its programs and price listings for its publications.

Recycling
What You Can Do

☞ **Educate others on the need to recycle.** Encourage family members, friends, and neighbors to recycle. You may even want to alternate trips to the local recycling center with a neighbor to save you both time.

☞ **Write letters to government representatives** on recycling issues, especially on the need for more recycling facilities. If your city or town does not have an established recycling program, work with officials to help start one. (See also Voicing Your Opinion, page 363.)

☞ **Recycle and cut down on waste as much as possible in your home.** According to the **Pennsylvania Resources Council,** almost one-half of what Americans throw away is recyclable. Begin by finding out what your local recycling center actually accepts, then set up a system for sorting waste into the basic groups: newspapers, other paper products, aluminum, glass, organic wastes, and plastics. Assign a specific bin or place in the kitchen or garage for each material (some of the environmentally conscious mail-order companies listed on page 252 sell recycling bins). Many communites sponsor roadside pickups of recycled waste, but if yours does not, you may need to take waste to the local recycling center. Look up "Recycling" in the phone book for a center near you. The **Environmental Defense Fund** (page 264) has a toll-free recycling hotline—leave your name and address and EDF will send you a comprehensive packet of information on recycling and the location of a center near you. The number is *1-800-CALL-EDF (225-5333)*. Here are some other recycling ideas to keep in mind:

- **Mend and repair household items instead of tossing them away.** Shoes, bicycle tires, clothing, furniture, and other goods can often be fixed with little effort. If you no longer want an item, see if a church, shelter for the homeless, school, or local **Goodwill** or **Salvation Army** can use it.
- **See if you can reuse materials around the house.** With some imagination, many items in the home can be used for another purpose. Here are a few suggestions to get you started:

- Use newspaper for packing paper or for wrapping gifts (the comics are especially good for children's gifts).
- Use margarine tubs and similar containers to hold leftover food.
- Use the back of discardable paper for scrap paper.
- Reuse foil and other food wraps.
- Save paper towels from drying clean hands, wiping glasses, and other light cleanup jobs for really heavy messes.
- Tear newspapers into handy-size sheets, then store them in the kitchen to be used when you are slicing or peeling vegetables, cutting nuts, or making other messes that require easy wrap-up and disposal.
- Use rinsed mayonnaise or peant butter jars to hold homemade salad dressing, rice, raisins, sugar, and other items.
- Save jars and containers that hold specific amounts (cups, pints, quarts) to be used as measuring cups.
- Package lunches in reusable containers.

- Use old clothes that are too beat up to be donated as cleaning rags.
- Cut off the tops of plastic soda bottles to use as funnels (these are especially useful with thick, messy liquids, such as paint or oil).
- Save dishwasher-safe plastic plates and trays that come from frozen dinners.
- Give egg cartons, scrap cardboard, and other containers to young children to use in art projects—with a little glue, crayons, and paint, kids can be very creative.

☞ **If you do take items to be recycled,** be sure they are ready; throw away bottle caps and check that the bottles are unbroken and relatively clean (a quick rinsing should do it). Be sure you take the "glossy" inserts out of newspapers to be recycled.

☞ **When you go shopping, keep recycling and "pre-cycling" in mind.** Careful buying habits are important because packaging alone, according to the **Pennsylvania Resources Council**, represents almost thirty percent of America's municipal waste. It may take you a few trips before you get into the habit of environmentally conscious shopping, but once you do, it's easy. Here are some ideas to consider:

- **Shop carefully.** This may seem obvious, but the **San Francisco Recycling Program** estimates that Americans throw away one-third of the food they buy.
- **Take your own bags when you go to the grocery store.** Both plastic and paper bags create waste problems (plastic isn't biodegradable; paper takes up much more space and may not degrade well in landfills anyway), so your best bet is to reuse the bags you get or to buy cloth or string sacks (see the environmentally conscious mail-order companies listed on page 252 for more information). If you have leftover grocery or shopping bags, use them as garbage bags or lunch bags, or for other jobs.
- **Don't use a bag if you're buying only a single item or if you're going to use the item as soon as you leave the store.**
- **Buy products that are easily recyclable**, such as aluminum, glass, or paper. Try to find alternatives to Styrofoam, plastic, and other items that are difficult to recycle or cannot be recycled at all. Remember, paperboard packages like cereal boxes with gray interiors are made from recycled paper.
- **Buy in bulk whenever possible**, especially items such as

tissue and toilet paper, cereals, juices, and other supplies. Buying in bulk saves you trips to the supermarket, saves you money, and helps cut down on waste. Also, try to buy items that come in concentrates, such as juices and liquid detergents. These are usually less expensive, too.

- **Buy items that come unwrapped or find replacements for overpackaged products**. For example, instead of buying liquid soap that comes in a plastic container, buy soap bars. If you're buying fruits or vegetables, buy loose ones instead of those wrapped in cellophane.
- **Look for items in containers that can be reused**, such as jars, resealable containers, and dishwasher-safe plates and trays from frozen foods.
- **Use reusable, durable products in place of cheap, throwaway items**. Use rechargeable batteries instead of the alkaline varieties; washable cups, dishes, and utensils instead of Styrofoam, plastic, or paper disposable items; rags or sponges instead of paper towels; cloth napkins instead of paper ones; and refillable supplies such as pens, lighters, tape dispensers, and razors instead of disposables (this may be more of a problem than you think—every year, Americans throw away 1.6 billion pens, two billion razors and blades,[57] and 500 million lighters[58]). When you throw away disposable items, you're not just throwing away the product, you're throwing away all of the packaging that goes with it, and that adds up.

The **Pennsylvania Resources Council** publishes an excellent shopping guide, *Environmental Shopping*, a twenty-page product list of 400 items in recycled or recyclable packaging ($5, which includes postage and handling). The organization also publishes two newsletters, the triannual *PRC News*, which covers primarily Pennsylvania recycling news, and the quarterly *All About Recycling* which covers national and international recycling issues. Membership ($30 for individuals, $35 for nonprofits, $50 and up for businesses) includes one-year subscriptions to the newsletters. Write to or call PRC at *P.O. Box 88, Media, PA 19063*; (215) 565-9131. Volunteers and interns are needed at the PRC office—call for more information.

☞ **Use recycled paper products.** The production of a ton of paper from discarded waste paper, as opposed to virgin wood pulp, requires sixty-four percent less energy, results in seventy-four percent less air

---

[57]Langone, 45.
[58]The Earth Works Group, 10.

pollution and thirty-five percent less water pollution, saves seventeen pulp trees, and reduces solid waste.[59] Check the Yellow Pages for "Recycled Paper Products," or you can order high-quality, recycled paper products from the following companies:

- **Acorn Designs** is a mail-order company that sells a variety of recycled paper and environmental-awareness products, including:

  - beeswax candles
  - bookmarks
  - bumper stickers
  - envelopes
  - holiday greeting cards
  - note cards
  - notepads
  - stationery
  - T-shirts

  Write to or call Acorn Designs at *5066 Mott Evans Road, Trumansburg, NY 14886*; (607) 387-3424.

- **Atlantic Recycled Paper Co.** has a large selection of recycled paper products for the home and office, including:

  - computer paper
  - copy paper
  - envelopes
  - facial tissues
  - fax paper
  - file folders
  - legal pads
  - looseleaf paper
  - mailing labels
  - napkins
  - paper towels
  - toilet paper

  Contact Atlantic Recycled Paper Co. at *P.O. Box 11021, Baltimore, MD 21212*; (301) 323-2676 or 1-800-323-2811.

- **Conservatree Paper Company** is a valuable resource for offices and businesses looking for high-quality office products made from recycled paper. Products include:

  - computer paper
  - envelopes
  - high-speed Xerox paper
  - letterheads

  Contact Conservatree at *10 Lombard St., Suite 250, San Francisco, CA 94111*; (415) 433-1000, outside California: 1-800-522-9200, FAX: (415) 391-7890. Minimum orders are $100.

- **Earth Care Paper's** *Recycled Paper Catalog* is a valuable resource for consumers looking for a variety of high-quality recycled paper products. Here is a partial list of its products:

  - books and games
  - calendars
  - fold-up notes
  - gift wrap

---

[59] Elkington, 48.

- greeting cards
- holiday note cards and postcards
- lined paper, pads, and envelopes
- office and printing paper
- posters
- stationery

Write to or call Earth Care Paper, Inc. at *P.O. Box 7070, Madison, WI 53707-7070*; (608) 227-2900.

● **Save Our ecoSystems, inc.**, is a mail-order company that sells attractive, high-quality recycled paper products, including:

- copier paper
- envelopes
- greeting cards
- mailing labels
- note cards
- stationery

Write to or call SOS at *407 Blair Boulevard, Eugene, OR 97402*; (503) 484-COPY (2679).

See also the environmentally conscious mail-order companies (page 252), that sell recycled products.

☞ **Stop companies and organizations from sending you junk mail.** According to the U.S. Postal Service, every American receives an average of 248 pieces of third-class "junk mail" each year.[60] Much of this is immediately discarded, wasting paper and adding to the garbage filling up America's landfills. So, call or write to the business(es) that send you junk mail and tell them to stop. To keep your name from being added to other large mailing lists, contact **Mail Preference Service, Direct Marketing Association** at *11 W. 42nd St., P.O. Box 3861, New York, NY 10036*; (212) 768-7277.

☞ **If you have a baby, use cloth diapers.** Disposable diapers are quite literally burying our country, and anyone who has handled a baby's diaper knows that that's not a pleasant thought. *Eighteen billion* disposable diapers are thrown out each year, burdening landfills with millions of pounds of plastic and "baby-waste."[61] In the U.S. alone, disposable diapers use 100,000 tons of plastic and 800,000 tons of tree pulp per year.[62] And because landfill waste is highly composted, biodegradable diapers may not decompose in the suggested amount of time. Buy cloth diapers instead and wash them at home

---

[60] According to the San Francisco Recycling Program. For more information about the program, contact SFRP at *Room 271, City Hall, San Francisco, CA 94102 (415) 554-6193.*
[61] MacEachern, 58.
[62] Ibid., 59.

or use a local diaper service (and ask that they use a nonchlorine bleach). Cloth diapers can also save you a significant amount of money. Look under "Diaper Services" in the phone book for a service near you.

☞ **If you buy a Christmas tree, dispose of it properly or buy a living treet and plant it outside after Christmas.** Each year, most of the thirty-five million Christmas tree owners simply throw their Christmas trees away.[63] Discarded trees take up an incredible amount of landfill space. Check with your local nursery; some accept Christmas trees to turn into mulch or wood chips.

☞ **Save leftovers and make a meal out of them once a week.** This will save you money and also cut down on the amount of waste.

☞ **Compost yard and food wastes instead of throwing them away.** Approximately twenty-five percent of what Americans throw away is composed of organic kitchen and yard wastes.[64] Composting will take care of a substantial amount of waste, and you'll have an excellent mulch or fertilizer for yardwork. Here are a few suggestions about making and using a compost pile:

- **Pick a level part of your yard that gets a lot of sun and set up a compost bin**. You can make a "hoop" composter by circling some chicken wire (or similar wire sheet) and securing it with hooks or wire (suggested size is three feet by three feet). For fancier bins, your best bet is often to buy one (see pages 293 and 294).
- **Add grass clippings, leaves, sawdust, flowers, wood ash, and foods** (fruits, vegetables, grains, for example). But *do not* add meat, bones, dairy products, fish, greasy foods, dog or cat waste, or diseased plants. If you compost food wastes, be sure that the composting bin is animal-proof. Otherwise, a hungry dog, cat, or rodent will make a mess of your pile.
- **Be sure that your bin has enough openings to let air into all parts of the pile**. Don't let it get higher than three feet. As you build the pile, sprinkle it occasionally with water and mix up the contents as much as possible. Depending on the climate, the organic materials in the pile, and other variables, it will take a few months for the pile to decompose. Check the mail-order com-

---

[63]Elkington, 159.
[64]Ibid., 27.

panies on pages 293 and 294 for bioactivators, which make the pile decompose faster.

☞ **Your local nursery should have the supplies you'll need for a compost pile.** Otherwise, here are several resources and organizations that can provide you with the necessary information and/or supplies:

- See **Gardener's Supply** (page 293) and **Ringer** (page 294) for composting bins and composting activators. Also, some of the environmentally conscious mail-order companies (page 254) sell composting bins.
- *Let It Rot! The Home Gardener's Guide to Composting*, by Stu Campbell (Storey Communications). This book is filled with illustrations, facts, suggestions, and basically all the information you need to compost successfully. If your local bookstore or library doesn't have *Let It Rot!*, contact Gardener's Supply.

☞ **Encourage recycling in your local schools.** Recycling is habit-forming—if kids learn to recycle early on, they will take the awareness home with them and recycling will become a normal part of their lives. Encourage students to form a school environmental group and initiate recycling efforts, as well as other environmental projects. Also, talk with the school's administration about setting up recycling bins for paper, soda cans, and other discarded materials.

☞ **Recycle at the office and encourage co-workers to do the same.** According to the **San Francisco Recycling Program**, the average businessperson throws away a half pound of high-grade recyclable paper every day at work. Most office waste, including mail, stationery, corrugated cardboard, newspapers, and some plastics, can be recycled. Here are some ideas for recyling paper and other items:

- Make two-sided copies.
- Use scrap paper for drafts of memos and reports.
- Use coffee mugs instead of Styrofoam cups.
- Donate old office furniture or supplies to charitable organizations instead of throwing it away.
- Set up a recycling bin; co-workers can take turns taking the materials to be recycled.
- Encourage your company to buy recycled paper (see the recycled paper companies listed on page 313).
- Put a recycling bin for cans near the soft-drink machine.

☞ **Encourage your local supermarket to be recycling-conscious.** Ask the store to:

- Offer incentives or discounts for people who bring their own shopping bags or reuse store bags.
- Offer dry foods (candies, nuts, etc.) in large, open bins, so people can buy in bulk (this cuts down on packaging).
- Cut down on prepackaged produce.
- Display posters and notices encouraging people to buy recycled and recyclable products, and to recycle as much as possible at home.

☞ **Encourage businesses to be environmentally conscious, and advocate recycling.** Encourage restaurants and airlines to stop using disposable utensils, cups, and plates. Urge your local newspaper to use recycled paper. Encourage companies to use recycled materials in products and packaging. A letter, editorial, or petition can make a difference.

National Organizations

Environmental Action Coalition
625 Broadway, New York, NY 10012
(212) 677-1601

The nonprofit **Environmental Action Coalition** works to protect and enhance the quality of the environment, particularly by promoting the benefits of recycling. Although it is active primarily in New York, EAC is a valuable resource for anyone in the country interested in recycling. The coalition has numerous publications, including *Don't Waste Waste*, *Woods and Water*, and *City Trees, Country Trees*. EAC also has videos and films and information on numerous other publications. Membership ($20) includes a subscription to *CYCLE*, a quarterly newsletter that covers a variety of environmental issues.

Keep America Beautiful, Inc.
Mill River Plaza, 9 West Broad St., Stamford, CT 06902
(203) 323-8987

KAB is a nonprofit public education organization dedicated to improving waste-handling practices in America's communities. When

KAB was founded in 1953 by members of private industry, it focused its efforts on litter prevention. While the organization continues to address littering in America, it now informs and educates citizens on all the alternatives for handling solid waste, including source reduction, recycling, waste-to-energy, sanitary landfills, and composting. Through its principal program, the **KAB SYSTEM**, the organization is influencing more responsible attitudes and behavior toward the environment for seventy-four million Americans living in more than 450 SYSTEM communities, ranging in size from 350 to several million people. The KAB SYSTEM operates under the philosophy that solutions to reduce litter and promote recycling work best when they are organized at the grass-roots level, and not imposed from above. If you are interested in involving your community in a KAB SYSTEM, contact the national headquarters for more information.

National Recycling Coalition, Inc.
1101 30th St., N.W., Suite 305, Washington, DC 20007
(202) 625-6406, FAX: (202) 625-6409

NRC is a nonprofit educational and technical organization dedicated to developing solutions to the nation's solid waste problems. NRC's activities include providing technical education, increasing public understanding of and support for effective recycling and conservation programs, and promoting the implementation of sound laws and regulations. Ongoing NRC initiatives include the **Peer Match** program, which provides technical assistance to local communities, universities, and other groups interested in implementing recycling programs. Individual membership ($30, $15 for students and elderly persons) includes a one-year subscription to the bimonthly newsletter *NRC Connection*, which covers NRC activities, legislative updates, and national recycling news. Membership also includes discounts on a variety of environmental literature addressing the benefits of recycling. (Membership is available for government agencies, businesses, recycling associations, and other organizations—contact NRC for more information.)

Pennsylvania Resources Council
(see page 312)

Water Conservation and Preservation of Natural Resources
(Particularly Lakes, Oceans, and Rivers)

What You Can Do

☞ **Educate yourself and others about the need to conserve water and protect water resources.** Most of the national organizations listed in this section have general information and legislative news to help you educate others and express your concern or approval to government representatives. (See also Voicing Your Opinion, page 363.)

The **Water Pollution Control Federation**, in particular, has some informative materials. WPCF is a nonprofit educational organization made up of water-quality specialists. Among its free brochures are *Clean Water: A Bargain at Any Cost; Wetlands: More Important Than You Think; Household Hazardous Waste: What You Should and Shouldn't Do;* and *Groundwater: Why You Should Care.* Write or call WPCF at *601 Wythe St., Alexandria, VA 22314-1994*; (703) 684-2438.

☞ **Be sure there are no leaks in your house.** Even the smallest drip from a leaky faucet can waste more than fifty gallons a day.[65] To check for leaks, be sure no water is running in the house, then check the water meter. About thirty to forty minutes later, check the meter again. If the dial has moved, you have a leak. To check for leaks in your toilet, put a couple of drops of food coloring in the toilet tank. If you see any coloration in the toilet bowl after about an hour, you have a leak. (Checking toilets is important—a leaky toilet can waste 200 gallons of water a day.[66]) If you're not certain how to fix a leak, call a plumber, talk with someone at a hardware store, or call the local utility company (the number should be on your water bill). Water utilities also usually have general water-conservation tips.

☞ **Use water-conserving devices on shower heads and in faucets.** A low-flow faucet aerator can reduce water consumption by fifty percent. The aerator works by mixing air with the water so the flow will seem basically the same. Check your local hardware store or the environmentally conscious mail-order companies listed on page

---
[65]The Earth Works Group, 66.
[66]Elkington, 206.

252 for these items. Depending on use, these devices can pay for themselves in saved water and energy (with hot water) in a few months. Be sure not to confuse low-flow aerators with screen aerators. Screen aerators help more air get into the water but do not reduce the flow rate.

☞ **Install a water-saving device (or "displacement") device in your toilet tank.** Displacement devices are easy to install and save a significant amount of water. Forty percent of the pure water used in the average home is flushed down the toilet, and fifteen to forty percent of that can be saved with a simple water-saving device.[67] Your local hardware or plumbing store should sell these, but if not, check the environmentally conscious mail-order companies listed on page 252 or your local utility company. (*Don't* put a brick or stone in your tank—sediment can wear off and clog the drain.)

☞ **Don't use your toilet as a trash receptacle.** Flushing an extinguished cigarette, piece of tissue paper, or any other such item down the toilet is simply a waste of water.

☞ **Don't let the tap run while you are brushing your teeth or shaving.** Running water is an incredible waste—at three to four gallons per minutes, you can easily waste ten to fifteen gallons of water if you leave the tap running while simply shaving.

☞ **Keep a bottle of drinking water in the refrigerator.** This way, you won't need to run the tap until the water gets cold. If you buy fruit juice or any other liquid that comes in a large jar, save the jar and use it for water. (You can remove the residual taste from a jar by washing it with baking soda.)

☞ **Take showers (and try to keep them short—five minutes or less) instead of baths.** With low-flow shower heads, you'll really save water.

☞ **Wait until you have a full load before washing clothes.** And use low-sudsing detergents when doing the laundry, because such detergents require less water during the washing. Low-sudsing detergents are usually identified as such on their labels. (Remember to buy phosphate-free detergents—see page 289 for more information.) The next time you buy a washer, be sure to get a front-loading machine; most consume one-third less water than conventional top loaders.

[67]The Earth Works Group, 48.

☞ **Rake or sweep sidewalks, driveways, and patios instead of hosing them down.** The job can be done just as thoroughly with a rake or broom.

☞ **Don't waste water in your garden.** Here are a few suggestions to consider:

- **Water the lawn when it really needs it**. Overwatering wastes water and is not good for the lawn. A lawn should be watered if the grass does not spring back when you step on it.
- **Water in the early morning or evening when the sun won't evaporate the water as quickly**. If you water in the heat of the day, as much as one-third of the water will evaporate before it even gets to the plants. Also, be sure that you have a spray nozzle to control the flow of the water.
- **Use a sprinkler that produces large drops and not a fine mist, which evaporates more quickly**. You won't have to water as long with the larger spray. Be sure you use a timer or alarm so that you don't forget the sprinkler is on.
- **Leave an empty, clean trash can outside to collect rainwater**. The water then can be used for gardening purposes.
- **Keep your grass about two to three inches long.**

This length holds water better and the grass won't dry out as quickly. It is also the best length for a healthy lawn.

☞ **If you live near a beach, work to keep it clean.** Get a group of friends or neighbors together, scout out the beach to determine how much equipment (trash bags, gloves, etc.) you'll need, and get to work. Even one person armed with a trash bag can make a significant difference—and encourage others to get involved, too. Here are two resources to consider for information on getting involved in a beach cleanup:

- For information on organizing a beach cleanup, contact the **Oregon Department of Fish and Wildlife** for its free *Get the Drift and Bag It: A Nuts and Bolts Guide to Organizing a Beach Cleanup Campaign the Easy Way*. The publication has helpful information on organizing and working with volunteers and sponsors, finding the necessary equipment, and other tips. Write or call ODFW at *P.O. Box 59, Portland, OR 97207*; (503) 229-5400 (ext. 432—Public Affairs).
- Join **COASTWEEKS**, which sponsors both three-week beach cleanups conducted around the country and public-education campaigns aimed at increasing awareness of our nation's saltwater and freshwater shores. COASTWEEKS also sponsors boat

cruises, coastal walks, seminars, conferences, art shows, photography contests, and library and museum exhibits. For information on becoming involved with the next COASTWEEKS and a calendar of events, contact the **Coastal States Organization** at *Hall of the States, 444 N. Capitol St., N.W., Suite 312, Washington, D.C. 20001;* (202) 628-9636.

See also What You Can Do, page 289, for suggestions on keeping chemicals out of water supplies.

National Organizations

American Littoral Society
Sandy Hook, Highlands, NJ 07732
(201) 291-0055

ALS is a nonprofit conservation organization that works to preserve the littoral zone, the area where the sea meets the shore. Activities include monitoring and improving coastal beaches, wetlands, rivers, and estuaries, and promoting increased protection of critical habitat. ALS also offers public education, media coverage, and testimony in state capitals and Congress, and sponsors river and sound keeper projects. ALS chapters sponsor field trips, beach cleanups, nest patrols, and turtle nest watches. Membership ($20, $15 for students) includes the quarterly newsletter *Underwater Naturalist*; the bimonthly newsletter *Coastal Reporter*; chapter newsletters; periodical bulletins, which cover coastal topics such as coral reef ecology, barrier islands and dunes, marine mammals, coastal birds, Florida's everglades, and the rise in sea levels; and environmental action reports. Members also receive free copies of selected ALS books. Publications include *Marine Gamefish of the Middle Atlantic* and *And Two If By Sea: Fighting the Attack on America's Coasts.*

American Oceans Campaign
725 Arizona Ave., Suite 102, Santa Monica, CA 90401
(213) 576-6162, FAX: (213) 576-6170

AOC is a nonprofit organization dedicated to the restoration and preservation of America's oceans. AOC works to make the public, Congress, and state legislators aware of the plight of the oceans, the harm of sewage dumping, and the need for a National Oceans Policy. It is also working to create protected marine areas on both coasts, including the Florida Keys, George's Bank (Massachusetts), Bristol Bay

(Alaska), the Mendocino Coast and Santa Monica Bay (California), the Olympic Peninsula (Washington), and parts of the Oregon coast. Membership ($25 or more) includes a subscription to *Making Waves*, AOC's quarterly newsletter featuring articles on ocean pollution, offshore oil developments, and pertinent legislation.

American Rivers
801 Pennsylvania Ave., S.E., Suite 400, Washington, DC 20003
(202) 547-6900

American Rivers is the only nationwide nonprofit organization working to preserve and maintain the nation's rivers and their landscapes. Since its founding in 1973, AR has helped preserve more than 9,300 miles of prime natural rivers, protected millions of acres of adjacent lands, and stopped scores of ecologically destructive dams. AR monitors and influences river-protection legislation; distributes publications on rivers and related resources; educates the public on the need for saving our nation's rivers; and brings together local organizations, federal and state agencies, and private citizens to inventory a state's rivers so that the proper maintenance, legislation, and other protective programs will be implemented. Membership begins at $20 and includes action alerts to keep you up on river-conservation issues; an application for an American Rivers MasterCard (for every purchase you make, AR receives a small contribution at no cost to you); listings of river outfitters and other important retailers that support river conservation; discounts on publications; AR's annual, full-color poster; and a subscription to *American Rivers*, AR's quarterly newsletter.

Clean Water Action
1320 18th St., N.W., Washington, DC 20036
(202) 457-1286

CWA is the only national, nonprofit grass-roots organization working to promote clean and safe water, control toxic chemicals, and protect the nation's natural resources. CWA focuses on pesticide safety and groundwater protection, protection of the nation's coastal and inland resources, and safe alternatives to incineration. CWA has sponsored a national campaign against toxic chemicals and pollution, lobbied for strict environmental regulations, and formed the largest, most effective grass-roots organization working to protect and preserve the Atlantic shore, the Great Lakes, the Gulf shore, and the New England coast. CWA has twenty-four field offices nationwide. Membership ($24) includes monthly regional newsletters and a subscription to the quarterly *Clean Water Action News*, which offers legislative updates, environmental news (on a variety of topics—not just water), interviews, and activities reports. Volunteers are often needed to help out with fundraising, lobbying, community organizing, and a variety of related activities. Contact the national headquarters for more information.

The Cousteau Society
(see page 261)

The Freshwater Foundation
2500 Shadywood Road, P.O. Box 90
Navarre, MN 55392-0090
(612) 471-8407

The nonprofit **Freshwater Foundation** works to keep water usable for human consumption, industry, and recreation. The foundation offers water education programs for children and adults, including school curriculum and teacher training, public-education classes and field trips (primarily in the Minnesota area), television and video publications, and brochures (such as *Pesticides and Groundwater: A Health Concern for the Midwest; Understanding Your Shoreline: Protecting Lakes, Rivers, and Streams; Hazardous Waste in Our Homes—and in Our Water*). The organization also conducts research and information analyses to assist public and private policymakers in the development of environmentally sound and realistic water policy alternatives. Write or call the foundation for more information on its programs, publications, and volunteer opportunities and internships (in the Minnesota area).

Friends of the River
Fort Mason Center, Building C, San Francisco, CA 94123
(415) 771-0400

FOR is a nonprofit organization dedicated to preserving and protecting rivers, stopping dam projects that threaten rivers, and educating the public about their beauty and importance. FOR is active in river-conservation efforts and has successfully fought for preservation of the Tuoumme, Kings, Kern, and Merced rivers in California (although most of FOR's work is done in California, the group sponsors canoe, kayak, and raft trips in several states). Membership ($25) includes action alerts and a subscription to the bimonthly newsletter *Headwaters*, as well as discounts on river trips.

THE ENVIRONMENT

Greenpeace U.S.A.
(see page 265)

International Oceanographic Foundation
4600 Rickenbacker Causeway, Virginia Key, Miami, FL 33149
(305) 361-4888

A nonprofit organization, **IOF** works to provide the public with authoritative, unbiased information about the world's oceans and their importance to the human race and to encourage scientific investigation of the oceans. IOF also serves as an information clearinghouse for its members; distributes a variety of publications; and conducts land and sea explorations, including whale-watching and bird-watching tours, trips through the Everglades, and coral-reef tours. Membership ($18) includes a subscription to *Sea Frontiers*, a bimonthly, full-color publication (the photography is stunning) containing up-to-date articles written for the layperson and scientist alike and reports on current oceanographic developments and research.

National Water Center
P.O. Box 264, Eureka Springs, AR 72632
(501) 253-9755

NWC is a nonprofit organization that collects and disseminates information on water conservation and related issues, emphasizing personal responsibility for human and hazardous waste. NWC distributes T-shirts, calendars, posters, postcards, and books (for example, *Drinking Water: A Community Action Guide; We All Live Downstream;* and *Groundwater: A Community Action Guide;* NWC publications are enlightening and useful for anyone interested in working for cleaner water. *We All Live Downstream*, for example, contains information on how serious the water pollution problem is and tips and resources on things that can be done to solve it. Membership ($10) includes a subscription to the newsletter *Water Center News*.

North American Lake Management Society
1000 Connecticut Ave., Suite 300, N.W.
Washington, DC 20036
(202) 466-8550

NALMS is a nonprofit organization dedicated to promoting a better understanding of lakes, ponds, reservoirs, impoundments, and their

North American Lake Management Society
1000 Connecticut Ave., Suite 300, N.W.
Washington, DC 20036
(202) 466-8550

NALMS is a nonprofit organization dedicated to promoting a better understanding of lakes, ponds, reservoirs, impoundments, and their watersheds. NALMS works to protect, restore, and maintain these natural resources by promoting exchange of information about lake management; and encouraging research on lake ecology and watershed management. NALMS has numerous publications, videos, slide-show materials, and a bimonthly, full-color newsmagazine, *Lake Line*, which reports on national lake association activities and lists current journal articles, jobs, and meetings for researchers. Membership costs $55 ($25 for students) including a subscription to the magazine. Without the magazine subscription, membership is $25.

Ocean Alliance
Fort Mason Center, Building E, San Francisco, CA 94123
(415) 441-5970

A nonprofit organization, **OA** is dedicated to protecting the world's oceans, coastal waters, and wetlands. OA fights pollution and other abuses (including oil spills, toxic and nuclear wastes, sewage, industrial charges, and resources exploitation), and promotes conservation, education, and research to improve understanding of the world's oceans. Local, national, and international activities include creating marine sanctuaries; working on international whaling bans; reducing gill and drift net use; educating boaters on the dangers of pollution from recreational boating; developing a national model for curriculum reform (using ocean studies as a vehicle for improving other disciplines) for kindergarten through eighth grade; and sponsoring a sea camp for children. OA also sponsors the **Adopt-A-Beach** program, which recruits students and concerned individuals to keep beaches clean and litter-free, and the **Adopt-A-Whale** project, which works to protect gray whales. Membership ($30 for individuals, $20 for students and senior citizens) includes *Ocean Ally*, a quarterly newsletter with information on legislation, OA activities; and international news related to oceans and their inhabitants, and discounts on programs and special events. Contact OA for more specific information on its programs and volunteer opportunities.

Oceanic Society
(see **Friends of the Earth**, page 264)

Homelessness and Housing

Why Help Is Needed

Homelessness in the United States is at its highest level since the Depression of the 1930s and is rapidly getting worse.[1] The National Coalition for the Homeless estimates that upwards of three million Americans are homeless (more conservative reports put this number somewhere between 250,000 and 600,000). This number is believed to be growing at an annual rate of as much as twenty-five percent. And homelessness is not only increasing in numbers, it is broadening in reach. After surveying twenty-seven major U.S. cities, the U.S. Conference of Mayors[2] estimated that approximately twenty-five percent of the homeless population are individuals with severe mental illnesses, four percent are unaccompanied youth, fourteen percent are single women, twenty-four percent are employed, and twenty-six percent are veterans. The traditional image of homeless individuals as unemployed, middle-aged, male "skid-row" alcoholics is inaccurate. Today's homeless are surprisingly young; the National Alliance to End Homelessness (NAEH) estimates that sixty percent of homeless individuals are under thirty years of age. NAEH also reports that there are an estimated four to fourteen million people on the brink of homelessness. One lost paycheck, one medical problem, a fire or other emergency will put them out of their homes and onto the street.

One of the most troubling aspects of the problem is the enormous number of homeless families with young children. These families represent up to thirty-three percent of the homeless population, according to NAEH. NEAH also reports that the fastest-growing segment of the homeless population is children, who represent one in four home-

---

[1]According to a special report, *The Homeless: Myths vs. Reality* (February 18, 1987) put out by the Democratic Study Group, *U.S. House of Representatives, 1422 House Office Building, Washington, DC 20515*.
[2]The United States Conference of Mayors is located at *1620 Eye St., N.W., Washington, DC 20006*, (202) 293-7300.

less people. It is estimated that as many as 100,000[3] to 500,000[4] children are homeless in America. Probably no other group of homeless individuals is harder hit than the children. They suffer more from the lack of proper nutrition, they do not receive an adequate education, and they are often forced to witness the breakup of their families and horrifying aspects of street life, including drug abuse, prostitution, and violence. In almost every respect, homeless children are deprived of the stability and comfort of a normal childhood.

The problems of many homeless people have become so extensive that they can't simply "pick themselves up by their bootstraps" and make a life for themselves. Employers seldom hire people who are illiterate (fifty to seventy-five percent of all unemployed individuals in America, according to the Coalition for Literacy, are illiterate), have no permanent address, no recommendations, and no change of clothes. Many of the shelters, particularly those in large cities, are terribly overcrowded, and some are unsafe. Unquestionably, legislation and public policy are important to assist homeless individuals, but the participation of concerned individuals is important, too. Volunteers can help provide counseling, resources, and support for those people who are looking for work and a place to live. They can also simply work to remind others that being homeless means more than living on the street; it means losing contact with friends and family members, not knowing where the next meal is coming from, raising your children in an unstable environment, and having no secure home base to depend on in good times and bad. Contrary to what many people believe, few people choose to live such a life. No one should have to.

What You Can Do

☞ **Educate yourself and your friends and family members about homelessness and related issues.** Homelessness is a complex problem, but the more you know about it, the more you will know where help is needed most and how you can become involved. Most of the national organizations listed in this chapter have informative materials and ideas. For a more in-depth look at homelessness, read Jonathan Kozol's *Rachel and Her Children: Homeless Families in America* (Fawcett, $8.95), a powerful study of the day-

---

[3] According to The Better Homes™ Foundation, an independent nonprofit organization dedicated to funding programs and facilities to help America's homeless; *189 Wells Ave., Newton Centre, MA 02159.*
[4] According to the Children's Defense Fund.

to-day problems and experiences of homeless individuals. If you're interested in photography, *Homeless in America: A Photographic Project* (Acropolis Books) is a striking collection of black-and-white photographs documenting homelessness in the U.S. Check your local bookstore. The softcover version is $19.95, the hardcover $29.95, and the video version (VHS format) $29.95. The **National Mental Health Association** (see page 211) distributes both the book and the video.

☞ **Keep up on legislation that affects homeless and low-income individuals,** and express your concern or approval to your government representatives. Many of the national organizations listed in this chapter have legislative updates; the **National Low Income Housing Coalition** (page 337) and the **Coalition on Human Needs** (page 333) are especially good resources. (See also Voicing Your Opinion, page 363.)

☞ **Donate household items or other necessities, new or old, to a shelter for the homeless in your community.** Before you decide to throw something away, consider if it can be used at a shelter or soup kitchen. Go through your home to see if there are any items you no longer use that can be donated. Here are some items that are needed at most shelters:

- bathroom supplies
- bedding
- Bibles and other books
- building equipment and tools
- cleaning products
- clothing
- crutches
- eyeglasses
- food
- furniture
- hats and gloves
- kitchen utensils
- lamps
- rugs
- towels

Shelters with children often need toys, games, stuffed animals, and diapers.

☞ **Volunteer to help out at a nonprofit organization working to end homelessness.** These organizations often need volunteers to answer phones, write letters, edit newsletters, or help with fundraising. See if there's a national organization based near you or a regional office in your community (see the national organizations listed in this chapter).

☞ **If you belong to a religious congregation, see if there are** any programs that work to help individuals who are homeless. Even if the congregation does not maintain a shelter or soup kitchen, most religious congregations sponsor clothing drives, toy drives for children, and canned food drives, especially around holidays. If there are no such programs, consider starting one.

☞ **Volunteer to work at a shelter in your area for individuals and families who are homeless.** No matter what skills or interests you may have, volunteers are needed at homeless shelters for a variety of services. People are usually needed to cook or serve food, read stories to homeless children, provide transportation to school for homeless children, care for homeless children while their parents look for jobs, teach illiterate adults to read, help decorate or renovate the facility, provide job counseling, or help out with simple administrative work. Shelters for battered women may need people to inform women of their legal rights or to drive individuals to court, social services agencies, or hospitals (see Crime and Victim Assistance, page 159, for more information on helping victims of abuse). Check out a shelter near you to see what help it may need. Here are some resources and organizations for finding a shelter or similar facility in your area:

- Check the phone book under "Community Service Numbers" for shelter listings, usually under "Emergency Assistance, Food, Clothing, and Shelter." The local social services or human services department should also be able to help you locate shelters.
- **The Hope Foundation** (page 335) has a national listing of thousands of shelters in need of volunteers.
- Contact the **International Union of Gospel Missions** (page 335) for a referral to one of its shelters nationwide.
- The **National Volunteer Clearinghouse for the Homeless** (page 338) can send interested individuals a listing of shelters in their area in need of volunteers.
- See if there's a **Travelers Aid** in your community (see **National Organization of Travelers Aid Societies**, page 338).
- Review Doing Good in America for national organizations and resources that can refer people to shelters, particularly the **Salvation Army** (page 18), **United Way** (page 7), **United Black Fund** (page 7), and **Volunteer Clearinghouses** (page 6).

☞ **Use your professional skills or business resources to help a shelter in your community.** Doctors and dentists can provide medical care (check with your insurance company and the shelter first), lawyers can provide legal services, financial experts can help with finances, teachers can tutor in specific subject areas, psychiatrists can help with counseling, caterers can provide food, carpenters or hardware stores can provide building materials or services, etc. Here are two of the many professional associations with established programs:

- The **American Bar Association** sponsors the **Representation of the Homeless Project** for attorneys, law students, paralegals, and anyone else who has knowledge of the law, specifically with expertise in real estate, tax, civil rights, and business law. For more information, contact the ABA at *1800 M St., N.W., Washington, DC 20036*; (202) 331-2291, FAX: (202) 331-2220.
- The **American Institute of Architects**, along with **The American Institute of Architecture Students** and **the Neighborhood Reinvestment Corporation**, page (339), sponsors **The Search for Shelter Program**, which works to expand architects' involvement in meeting the housing needs of the nation's poor. The architects, in conjunction with other members of the community, assist in the design and construction management of facilities for the homeless. Although established to address national needs, the program works with state and local affiliates who are responsible for initiating, soliciting, and facilitating community participation. For more information, contact AIA at *1735 New York Ave., Washington, DC 20006*; (202) 626-7468.

☞ **Help build or fix up houses or shelters for individuals who are homeless or whose incomes are limited.** This is probably one of the most rewarding hands-on volunteer opportunities around. See **Project Head Start** (page 137), **Christmas in April** (page 333), **Habitat for Humanity International** (page 334), and the **NeighborWorks** program (see **Neighborhood Reinvestment Corporation**, page 339). Most shelters and day-care centers for low-income children appreciate all the assistance they can get, whether or not it comes through an organization. Encourage your friends, co-workers, and family members to participate. Schools, businesses, and religious congregations are especially good places to round up a group of people to help out.

☞ **Make socially responsible investments that work to enhance low-income neighborhoods and communities. See Money Matters (page 26) for socially responsible investment suggestions and organizations, including the **Cooperative Development Foundation** (page 34) and **The Institute for Community Economics** (page 35).

☞ **Assess the specific needs and problems of homeless individuals in your community and work to address those needs.** Use the resources around you and encourage your friends, family members, co-workers, and classmates to work with you. Concerned individuals have begun some of the most creative and highly effective programs around for individuals who are homeless. Here are just three such programs that are doing a great deal to help homeless individuals help themselves:

- In 1987, Guy Polhemus began a program called **We Can**, which is cleaning up the streets of New York and employing thousands of homeless persons. We Can is a nonprofit operation that accepts refundable bottles and cans and gives the proceeds to the homeless. Numerous schools, businesses, offices, and other institutions in the New York area have set up bins where cans can be deposited and are then picked up by workers. The We Can operation employs homeless individuals to pick up and process the cans and do administrative work at the central office. For more information, contact We Can at *630 Ninth Ave., Room 900, New York, NY 10036*; (212) 262-2222.
- *Street News*, also originating in New York, is a semi-monthly newspaper sold by homeless persons. The publication is filled with poems, stories, news articles, and comments by famous music and TV personalities, comedians, authors, and homeless persons. Homeless distributors buy the paper at a low price, then sell it for one dollar a copy. If you would like a one-year subscription ($18) to *Street News*, or for more information, write to or call **Street Aid** at *1457 Broadway, Suite 305, New York, NY 10036*; (212) 768-7290. *Street News* is expanding to other cities, so keep an eye out for it where you live.
- In 1989, Carolyn Pringle, a former schoolteacher and mother of three, worked for months to get the funds and services to start up a nonprofit school program for homeless children in Seattle called **First Place**. The children at First Place are not only given an excellent education, they are given the encouragement and confidence to develop their abilities. These children do not have to confront the stress of being teased about being homeless, as

they often are at regular schools. For more information on First Place, send a business-sized, stamped, self-addressed envelope to First Place, *P.O. Box 15112, Seattle, WA 98115-0112.*

See also **Seeds**, page 341, for *The Hunger Action Handbook*, a comprehensive guide to fighting hunger and poverty. The book gives detailed information on starting and maintaining facilities for individuals who are homeless.

☞ **If you are an employer, hire individuals who are homeless.** Here, probably more than anywhere else, is where myths about the homeless keep concerned individuals from helping. There are homeless individuals who desperately want to work but need an employer to give them a chance. Check the phone book under "Community Service Numbers" for the local employment/unemployment services office for more information on finding qualified applicants.

National Organizations

Christmas in April U.S.A.
1225 Eye St., N.W., Suite 600, Washington, DC 20005
(202) 326-8268

Christmas in April is a nonprofit organization of dedicated volunteers from all faiths and walks of life who help renovate—at no cost—the homes of low-income individuals, especially elderly persons and individuals with disabilities. One day each year (usually, but not always, in April), the organization gathers volunteers and donated materials to paint, repair, and renovate homes and shelters and, in the process, bring some cheer and goodwill. Homeowners participate in the work as much as they are able. Since 1983, dozens of Christmas in April programs across America have repaired almost 6,000 homes. Contact the national headquarters for information on a program near you or if you would like to start one (you can also ask for a poster to put up to encourage interest).

Coalition on Human Needs
1000 Wisconsin Ave., N.W., Washington, DC 20007
(202) 342-0726

The nonprofit **Coalition on Human Needs** works to ensure that the basic needs of poor minorities, children, women, elderly persons, and individuals with disabilities are met by compassionate, cost-effective government programs. The coalition monitors and reports on government actions that affect the nation's disadvantaged citizens, works to influence public policy (especially budget and tax issues), and helps local groups organize to protect human-service programs in their communities. The coalition also publishes in-depth and authoritative books, case studies, fact sheets, brochures, and directories on poverty in the U.S. (including *How the Poor Would Remedy Poverty*) and a bimonthly newsletter *Insight/Action*, which provides up-to-date information on public policy issues that affect low-income people. There is no set subscription fee for the newsletter, but a contribution would be appreciated.

Community for Creative Non-Violence
425 2nd St., N.W., Washington, DC 20001
(202) 393-4409 or (202) 393-1909

CCNV is a nonprofit organization dedicated to assisting homeless individuals. CCNV works to educate the public about the plight of the homeless in the U.S.; to express the needs of the homeless on the local, state, and national levels; and to provide thousands of homeless individuals with daily food, shelter, medical care, and other services. The organization runs **The National Volunteer Clearinghouse for the Homeless** (page 338), which can supply individuals anywhere in the country with possible volunteer opportunities in shelters and other facilities for the homeless. CCNV publishes *Homelessness in America: A Forced March to Nowhere* ($5), which looks at the causes and dimensions of the problem of homelessness. The group welcomes inquiries from anyone who is interested in becoming part of CCNV's work.

Feed The Children
(see Children and Young Adults, page 141)

Habitat for Humanity International
121 Habitat St., Americus, GA 31709-3498
(912) 924-6935, FAX: (912) 924-6541

HHI is a nonprofit organization dedicated to eliminating poverty, inadequate housing, and homelessness in America and abroad. HHI is, quite literally, working to build a better America by building and repairing homes at no charge (potential homeowners work alongside volunteers and then pay small, no-interest mortgages on their homes and help with other HHI projects). HHI needs volunteers, but even if you can't hammer a nail, you can help in a variety of ways, including assisting with fundraising and other administrative activities. HHI also has long-term volunteer opportunities for those interested. Although HHI is a Christian organization, everyone interested is encouraged to join. Contact the national headquarters for information on activities near you.

Homelessness Information Exchange
1830 Connecticut Ave., N.W., 4th Floor
Washington, DC 20009
(202) 462-7551

HIE is the nonprofit organization to contact if you want information on the homeless or information on how to create or improve programs and policies for the homeless. HIE disseminates various informative resources, including an annotated bibliography of more than 750 references, and numerous comprehensive publications (such as *Helping the Homeless in Your Community; Transitional Housing; Coalition Building to Address Homelessness: Guidelines/Models/Accomplishments;* and *Family and Child Homelessness*). HIE's quarterly newsletter, *Homewords*, contains updates on effective national and local programs and resources that address homelessness. A one-year subscription costs $10.

The Hope Foundation
1555 Regal Row, Dallas, TX 75247
(214) 630-5765
National toll-free pledge and volunteer hotline: 1-800-843-4073

A nonprofit organization, **THF** is dedicated to helping the homeless in three ways: by providing funding for emergency shelters nationwide; by serving as a volunteer resource information center offering volunteers information on where they can go to donate time, food, clothing, household goods, professional expertise, and other services; and by raising public awareness about the problem of homelessness and the role of well-managed shelters. You can call the toll-free number to find out more about shelters in your community (THF has a computer database with more than 6,000 shelters listed).

International Union of Gospel Missions
1045 Swift Street N., Kansas City, MO 64116
(816) 471-8020

IUGM is a nonprofit Christian association of inner-city missions that serve hundreds of thousands of homeless persons every year. IUGM missions and volunteers offer emergency food and shelter, youth and family services, jail ministry, rehabilitation, and specialized programs for individuals with mental illnesses, elderly persons, and street youths. Its purpose is to provide education and training to enable local missions to better serve the homeless and poor in their communities; to help start new shelters and programs for the needy; and to provide networking and sharing of vital information. Volunteers can help with Bible study programs, feeding the hungry, office assistance, and professional expertise (for example, medical, including dental, or legal assistance). Missions provide approximately 15,000 beds for the homeless on any given night and 17.5 million meals each year. Contact the national headquarters for the location of an IUGM mission near you (or for information on starting one up).

The National Alliance to End Homelessness, Inc.
1518 K St., N.W., Suite 206, Washington, DC 20005
(202) 638-1526: FAX: (202) 638-4664

A nonprofit organization, **NAEH** works to bring together all sectors of society in a program of research, advocacy, project operation, and education to address the long-term problems of homelessness. NAEH has several informative publications, including *Housing and Homelessness: A Report of The National Alliance to End Homelessness* and a monthly newsletter, *ALLIANCE*, which contains legislative updates, general articles, and information on important resources related to homelessness ($25 for a one-year subscription).

The National Coalition for the Homeless
1621 Connecticut Ave., 4th Floor, Washington, DC 20009
(202) 265-2371, FAX: (202) 265-2615

NCH is a nonprofit federation of individuals, agencies, and organizations committed to the principle that decent shelter, affordable housing, and basic sustenance are fundamental rights in a civilized society. NCH seeks adequate and safe emergency shelter as a first step to prevent more Americans from literally dying on the streets of U.S. cities. The coalition approaches homelessness and related issues from a long-term perspective and therefore works to ensure that more rational housing, employment, and mental health policies are implemented on a local and national level. NCH also works to educate the public on the needs of the homeless and serves as a clearinghouse for nationwide resources on homelessness. It publishes a free monthly newsletter, *Safety Network*, which addresses legislative and public policy issues.

National Housing Institute
439 Main St., Orange, NJ 07050
(201) 678-3110

The nonprofit **National Housing Institute** provides a powerful voice for the housing interests of moderate and low-income families. NHI serves as a resource center, offering information, materials, and support for housing advocates and concerned individuals nationwide; NHI has also created its own innovative community-development programs. NHI distributes videos, status reports, and other informative materials. NHI's bimonthly magazine, *Shelterforce*, contains information on affordable housing strategies, legislation, industry issues, and forecasts. A one-year subscription to *Shelterforce* costs $15 for individuals, $25 for organizations.

National Low Income Housing Coalition
1012 14th St., N.W., Suite 1500, Washington, DC 20005
(202) 662-1530

NLIHC is a nonprofit organization dedicated to advocating, organizing, and informing the public, the media, and the government about the need for decent housing for all low-income people. Members receive two publications: *Call to Action*, which alerts them to pending votes in Congress, and *Memos to Members*, which provides detailed analyses of new developments in federal housing policy, such as the Low Income Housing Tax Credit and the Bush housing proposals. NLIHC is affiliated with the **Low Income Housing Information Service** (located in the same office), a nonprofit educational group that can provide you with numerous informative publications, including *Low Income Housing in America: An Introduction; Out of Reach: Why Everyday People Can't Find Affordable Housing;* and *Low Income Housing Needs*. LIHIS also has bumper stickers (*Housing Is a Human Right*), buttons, and a full-color poster. Contact the organizations for information on membership fees ($10 to $300, depending on type of membership).

National Mental Health Association
(see Disabilities, page 211)

National Organization of Travelers Aid Societies
1001 Connecticut Ave., N.W., Suite 504
Washington, DC 20036
(202) 659-9468

Travelers Aid is a nonprofit, nationwide service providing emergency relief for homeless and poor individuals, runaways, victims of abuse, and other persons on the move who need a safe, supportive rest place. The agency provides information and referrals, counseling, food and shelter, resettlement support, financial assistance, and more, depending on the needs of the individual or family. Travelers Aid programs are always in need of volunteers. Check the phone book for the program near you or call the national headquarters.

The National Resource Center on Homelessness and Mental Illness
Policy Research Associates, Inc.
262 Delaware Ave., Delmar, NY 12054
1-800-444-7415

Funded by the **National Institute of Mental Health, NRCHMI** is the only national source of information specifically focusing on the mental health aspects of homelessness. The center maintains and updates a database of both published and unpublished materials and disseminates information through annotated bibliographies, specialized searches, information packets, and a quarterly newsletter, *Access*, which features in-depth articles, legislative information, and a calendar of events. NRCHMI also has a comprehensive referral list *(Organizations Concerned with Homelessness and Mental Illness)* of national and state organizations that work to help homeless and mentally ill persons. The referral list and newsletter are free.

National Student Campaign Against Hunger and Homelessness
(see Hunger, page 347)

The National Volunteer Clearinghouse for the Homeless
425 2nd St., N.W., Washington, DC 20001
1-800-HELP-664 (435-7664)

NVCH is a nonprofit program run by the **Community for Creative Non-Violence** (page 334) that provides volunteers anywhere in the country with information on local agencies helping the homeless.

NVCH can tell you what the service offers the homeless, its hours of operation, and what they need the volunteers to do. When you call the toll-free number, you will get a recording asking you to leave your name and address. Since NVCH is run completely by volunteers who must perform a variety of other services, it may take a few weeks before you get the information (although it may take only a few days).

Neighborhood Reinvestment Corporation
1325 G St., N.W., Washington, DC 20005
(202) 376-2400

Neighborhood Reinvestment is a congressionally chartered, nonprofit corporation that works to improve and offer hope to disadvantaged neighborhoods nationwide. Neighborhood Reinvestment has helped initiate hundreds of neighborhood partnerships, and provided ongoing technical services and training (for example, information on processing loans, fundraising, media coverage) for the volunteers and paid staff who run the partnerships. Its revitalization program, the **NeighborWorks** network, is active in more than 300 neighborhoods in 139 cities nationwide and is responsible for rehabilitating more than 100,000 homes in the past twenty years. The people working with the NeighborWorks network include residents who want decent, affordable housing and members of the business community and concerned individuals willing to help out. Volunteers can help a local NeighborWorks program in several ways (actions vary in different neighborhoods, however): rehabilitating houses, cleaning up or painting community areas and houses, and providing financial expertise, fundraising, and organizing assistance. Write to Neighborhood Investment to see if there's a NeighborWorks project in operation near you.

Hunger

Why Help Is Needed

At one time or another, everyone has experienced the feeling of hunger, whether from missing a meal, dieting, or simply not having time to grab a bite to eat. According to Second Harvest National Food Banks Network (see page 349), however, twenty million people in America suffer from hunger for at least a few days every month, representing the largest number of hungry people in America in the last twenty-five years. There is a substantial difference between feeling hungry and suffering from hunger. Suffering from hunger is not only missing meals on a constant basis, it is not knowing where the next meal is coming from, or if it will come at all. Even more discouraging is the fact that many of these hungry people are children who depend on others for their food. Second Harvest estimates that one out of every five children in this country lives in poverty and is unable to maintain a minimally adequate diet. The U.S. Department of Agriculture estimates that more than half of the people who participate in the nation's food stamp program are children.[1]

The effects of hunger, especially on a developing child, can be devastating. According to Second Harvest, the chances of permanent tissue damage and susceptibility to illness all increase as a result of malnutrition. The Food Research and Action Center (FRAC) reports that improper nourishment can also affect a child's ability to succeed in school, reinforcing the cycle of poverty. An empty stomach, after all, can be a powerful distraction.

During the past ten years, the hunger problem, according to FRAC, has significantly increased in America. The coming years are not expected to be any different. Based on a survey of twenty-seven major cities, the U.S. Conference of Mayors reports that almost ninety percent of these cities expect the demand for emergency food assistance to increase. Already, in nearly three-fourths of the cities surveyed,

---

[1] According to the U.S. Department of Agriculture Food and Nutrition Service's April 1, 1990 "Food Stamp Program" report.

emergency food-assistance facilities have had to turn away people in need because of lack of resources.

One of the most frustrating aspects of America's hunger problem, as *Seeds* magazine reports, is that the food is there.[2] The U.S. government stores enough surplus wheat to provide every person in the world with seven loaves of bread.[3] And according to the San Francisco Recycling Project, Americans throw out one-third of the food they buy at the grocery store. This is where concerned individuals are so important. Volunteers can help locate, collect, and distribute much of the food in America that would otherwise go to waste. "Gleaning" programs, which harvest food that would otherwise go to waste from orchards, community gardens, and other areas—such as those initiated by Senior Gleaners and the Contra Costa Food Bank—effectively demonstrate how excess food can be collected to feed hungry individuals. Extra hands at a soup kitchen or food bank are also essential in getting available food to those who need it. It is a real tragedy that while perfectly edible food slowly spoils in warehouses, fields, orchards, and kitchens across America, so many millions of people, young and old, do not have enough to eat.

What You Can Do

☞ **Stay informed on hunger and related issues.** The more you know about the hunger problem, the better you can educate your friends and family members and the better you will know where help is needed most. Although most of the national organizations listed in this chapter have newsletters and updates, here are three that are particularly informative:

- *Hunger Notes* (see **World Hunger Education Service**, page 350).
- ***Seeds*** is a nonprofit, bimonthly magazine whose focus is ending U.S. and world hunger. Each issue of the magazine contains feature stories and analytical articles on domestic and international hunger issues, profiles, news updates, cartoons, book reviews, resources, and information on national hunger-related events and activities. A *Guide to Volunteer Opportunities* is published each year (usually the Sept./Oct. issue) with information

---

[2] *Seeds* magazine, *Hunger Action Handbook: What You Can Do and How to Do It* (edited by Leslie Withers and Tom Peterson), 1985.
[3] Frances Moore Lappé, and Joseph Collins, *World Hunger: 12 Myths* (New York: Grove Hill, Inc., 1986), 14.

on short- and long-term volunteer projects in the U.S. and abroad. A one-year subscription costs $16 ($2.50 for the *Guide* alone). Also available is the *Hunger Action Handbook: What You Can Do and How to Do It* ($9.15, including shipping and handling), an outstanding resource for fighting hunger and poverty. Among many other things, it tells how to start or become involved with short- and long-term activities, from soup kitchens and shelters for the homeless to legislative action and wise investment. Write or call *Seeds* for more information at *222 East Lake Drive, Decatur, GA 30030*; (404) 371-1000.

- **WHY, Challenging Hunger and Poverty** (see **World Hunger Year** page 351).

☞ **Contact your government representatives to express your opinion regarding existing policies and legislation relating to hunger and poverty.** Many of the national organizations listed in this chapter have legislative updates and information. (See also Voicing Your Opinion, page 363.)

☞ **Set up a "Hunger Bank" in your home for spare change.** After several months you could have a substantial amount of money to donate to a hunger-related charity. And if you don't clip coupons for your own sake, use them and contribute the savings to your "Hunger Bank."

☞ **Give to food drives and other projects working to collect food.** Volunteers are also often needed to help pick up, organize, and distribute the food.

☞ **Sponsor a child living in a poor part of the United States through a child sponsorship organization** (see Children and Young Adults, page 140). A primary goal of these organizations is to provide proper nourishment for hungry children. Sponsors can directly help a poor child receive the food and other necessities he or she would otherwise do without. Sponsors can also correspond with (and sometimes even meet) their children to see how they are progressing.

☞ **If you belong to a religious congregation, see if there are any hunger programs that need volunteers.** If your congregation does not already have programs to help the hungry, try to start one with other members. For information on starting such an operation, see *Seeds* (page 341) for its *Hunger Action Handbook*.

☞ **Encourage restaurants, dining services, and other food service organizations to donate leftover food to food banks.** **Share Our Strength** (page 350), a nonprofit organization of creative professionals, including chefs and restaurateurs, who have joined together to end hunger, can help you help them put excess food to good use. If you have a lot of excess food or think that you may have some left over from a party, wedding, or other occasion, SOS can provide you with the necessary information on getting it to a food bank. If you are interested in supporting restaurants affiliated with SOS, the organization can send you a free list of the more than 1,000 SOS member restaurants.

☞ **Find a food bank near you and volunteer your time, energy, and/or supplies.** Food banks collect food for distribution to soup kitchens, drug-rehabilitation centers, shelters for the homeless, and other programs for the hungry. In addition to food, food banks need kitchen supplies (pots, pans, bowls, cooking utensils, etc.) and people to make deliveries or pick up donated food. **Second Harvest** (page 349) can provide you with the location of a food bank near you.

☞ **Volunteer at a soup kitchen or shelter near you.** Each facility has different needs, so call to see how you can help out. Encourage friends and family members to come with you. The more help, the better. Here are a few suggestions to help you find a facility in your area:

- Check the phone book under "Community Service Numbers" for "Emergency Assistance, Food, Clothing and Shelter" or for "Food and Nutrition."
- Check with your local government's human services or social services department, especially an Office of Emergency Shelters.
- **The National Volunteer Clearinghouse for the Homeless** (page 338) and **The Hope Foundation** (page 335) can give you the location of shelters in your community.

Considering the close connection between hunger and homelessness, check out the chapter on Homelessness and Housing (page 327) for more information on helping people living in poverty.

☞ **Volunteer to help out at a nonprofit organization working to end hunger.** These organizations often need volunteers to answer phones, write letters, edit newsletters, or help with fundraising. See if there's a national organization based near you or a regional office in your community (see the national organizations listed in this chapter).

☞ **Encourage classmates, co-workers, members of your religious congregation, and friends to make and donate sandwiches and other foods for shelters or soup kitchens in the community.** Whether it's once a month or once a week, extra help and food is almost always needed. Students could also check to see if the school cafeteria throws out any food that could be put to good use. Before you start such an operation, contact the organization to be sure there won't be any health-code problems regarding the food.

☞ **Organize a canned food (or other nonperishable goods) drive at your office, school, religious congregation, or club.** A food drive may not be set up already simply because of a lack of initiative. With help from others, it's not that difficult. Make up announcements, set up a drop-off spot for the food, and deliver it to a food bank, shelter, or soup kitchen in your area.

☞ **Start a food bank or distribution center for the hungry in your community if there isn't one already.** This task requires a great deal of work. If you are interested, however, check with a food bank or distribution center in a community near you, and contact *Seeds* (page 341) for its *Hunger Action Handbook*. The book can provide you with practically all the information you'll need.

☞ **Organize a "gleaning" program in your area.** Gleaning is collecting perfectly edible food (from orchards, farms, and other places) that would go to waste if it weren't picked up. Here are two organizations, in particular, that run outstanding gleaning programs:

- The nonprofit **Contra Costa Food Bank** is a nonprofit organization that runs **Project Glean**, a gleaning program that harvests tons of food a year from backyards, farms, orchards, and other areas. In 1989 alone, Project Glean harvested 288,000 pounds of food, which eventually went to help low-income elderly persons and children, soup kitchens, and shelters. For more information on Project Glean or for suggestions on starting a similar program in your community, write to or call CCFB at *5121 Port Chicago Highway, Concord, CA 94520*; (415) 798-8666 or (415) 676-7543. CCFB welcomes volunteers in the Contra Costa and San Joaquin regions.
- **Senior Gleaners** is a nonprofit organization of volunteers age

fifty and older that operates one of the largest food bank operations in America. The gleaners contribute more than 400,000 hours annually collecting fruit and vegetables from farms and orchards and salvaging damaged or outdated canned or packaged food from stores. These individuals supply, per year, more than thirteen million pounds of food that goes to nearly 100 charitable organizations. They also handle all of the necessary trucking, warehousing, and administrative work. Although Senior Gleaners is a local California organization, it has informative packets that can help you begin a similar program in your area. Gleaning is one of the most productive ways of fighting hunger in America, and the success of Senior Gleaners is an excellent example of its effectiveness. Write to or call SG at *3185 Longview Drive, North Highlands, CA 95660*; (916) 971-1530.

☞ **Consider a long-term volunteer commitment**, such as an internship, summer program, or position on a Native American reservation. Here are two helpful resources:

- *Going Places*, compiled and published by the **National Student Campaign Against Hunger and Homelessness** (page 347), is a listing of internships and other long-term volunteer opportunities with organizations fighting hunger and poverty. The directory costs $5.
- *Seeds* magazine (page 341) highlights long-term volunteer opportunities for students and adults (usually in its Sept./Oct. issue).

See also Doing Good Full-Time and for the Long Term (page 22).

National Organizations

Bread for the World
802 Rhode Island Ave., N.E., Washington, DC 20018
(202) 269-0200
24-hour update on legislative issues
(recorded message): (202) 269-0494

A nonprofit organization rooted in the Christian faith, **BFW** lobbies policymakers, engages in research, and works to educate the public about hunger-related issues. Members are taught to become effective hunger activists and media coordinators. Although BFW is a lobbying group, it does have volunteer opportunities (call the number listed above and ask for the volunteer coordinator). BFW also publishes a variety of legislative updates, books, and educational materials that focus on hunger, including *The Face of Hunger in a Land of Plenty; The Causes of World Hunger; Cry Justice: The Bible Speaks on Hunger and Poverty; Gentle, Angry People* (a thirty-minute video that examines the problems of poor women and children in the U.S.); and *U.S. Hunger: The Problem Grows*. BFW is a valuable source for authoritative information on hunger and legislative issues. A one-year membership costs $25; to become a member, call *1-800-82-BREAD (822-7323)*.

Feed The Children
(see Children and Young Adults, page 141)

FOOD FIRST
Institute for Food and Development Policy
145 9th St., San Francisco, CA 94013
(415) 864-8555
(for book orders and membership): 1-800-888-3314

FOOD FIRST is a nonprofit research and education organization dedicated to increasing public education and participation in solving critical social problems on local, national, and global levels. Its three primary objectives are to dispel myths that deny hope and block action against hunger, poverty, and other social problems; to inform people about positive democratic developments in the U.S. and in other societies; and to help define and develop the core public values necessary to guide democratic social change. The organization sells T-shirts and distributes numerous publications, including *Rediscovering America's Values; World Hunger: Twelve Myths; Food First: Beyond the Myth of Scarcity; Diet for a Small Planet;* and *A Fate Worse Than Death*. Membership ($25 and up) includes a free book and a subscription to the quarterly newsletter *FOOD FIRST NEWS*, containing legislative updates and national and international hunger news.

Food Research and Action Center
1875 Connecticut Ave., N.W., 5th Floor
Washington, DC 20009
(202) 393-5060

A nonprofit organization, **FRAC** is the leading national organization working to end hunger and malnutrition in America. FRAC documents the extent and impact of hunger within the U.S. monitors federal legislative and regulatory developments; serves as a clearinghouse for organizations and individuals seeking information on hunger; conducts media and public information campaigns on hunger; and provides legal assistance (primarily to state welfare and food stamp offices). It also maintains a national listing of food resource centers. Publications include *The Relationship Between Nutrition and Learning* and *A National Survey of Nutritional Risk Among the Elderly*. FRAC's bimonthly newsletter, *Foodlines: A Chronicle of Hunger and Poverty in America*, monitors political, legislative, and administrative developments affecting hunger and poverty in the U.S.

Freedom from Hunger Foundation
1644 DaVinci Court, P.O. Box 2000, Davis, CA 95617
(916) 758-6200, FAX: (916) 758-6241

The nonprofit **Freedom from Hunger Foundation** sponsors self-help programs for poor families in the U.S. and abroad so that they may eliminate hunger and malnutrition in their homes and communities. For example, FFHF shows villagers ways to increase crop yields, teaches families how to improve nutrition, health, and hygiene, instructs volunteer health workers on methods to improve sanitation and prevent illness, and provides small community-level loans for income-producing activities. The free quarterly newsletter *Newsbrief* covers development issues and program progress. Other publications include *A Geography of American Poverty: U.S. Strategy Assessment for the Meals for Millions/Freedom from Hunger Foundation* and *Combating Chronic Hunger: Women, Credit, and Education*.

National Student Campaign Against Hunger and Homelessness
29 Temple Place, 5th Floor, Boston, MA 02111-9907
(617) 292-4823

NSCAHH is a nonprofit organization made up of students from more than 500 schools and campuses nationwide united to fight hunger and homelessness in the U.S. and abroad. The group promotes letter-writing campaigns for federal housing and hunger legislation, provides immediate relief to the hungry, transports unused food from school dining halls and neighborhood restaurants to local meals programs, serves as a clearinghouse for new project ideas and activities of local groups, and provides many other services, activities, and conferences. Publications include *Going Places* ($5), a comprehensive listing of internships and volunteer travel and career opportunities with organizations working to fight poverty; *Students Making a Difference* ($15), a monthly newsletter that reports on hunger- and homelessness-related news, resources, and activities nationwide; and the *Hunger Cleanup Manual*, which addresses fundraising, media connections, recruitment, and other information on sponsoring volunteer events (such as fixing up homeless shelters or cleaning a local park). One copy of the manual is free, but each additional copy costs $4. For any student (college or high school) interested in fighting hunger and homelessness, this is an outstanding resource.

PLENTY USA
P.O. Box 2306, Davis, CA 95617
(916) 753-0731

PLENTY is a nonprofit development, relief, hunger, environment, and education organization dedicated to enhancing the self-sufficiency, self-determination, health, and well-being of disadvantaged people everywhere, with a special focus on indigenous people. PLENTY provides information on and assistance in agriculture, nutrition, primary health care, potable water, sanitation, alternative energy, and microeconomic development projects. Volunteers are employed primarily on a short-term basis in projects which offer substantial opportunities for intercultural learning and exchange. PLENTY also publishes a quarterly newsletter, *PLENTY Bulletin*, which contains updates on PLENTY activities and projects. A one-year subscription costs $10.

Public Voice for Food and Health Policy
1001 Connecticut Ave., N.W., Suite 522
Washington, DC 20036
(202) 659-5930

Through research, targeted advocacy efforts, and public education programs, the nonprofit **Public Voice** works to advance consumer interests in national food and health policymaking, including issues related to hunger. The organization distributes such publications as *Off to a Poor Start: Infant Health in Rural America; Full Fields, Empty Cupboards: The Nutritional Status of Migrant Farm Workers; Patterns of Risk: The Nutritional Status of the Rural Poor;* and *Making the Grade: A Healthier Course for School Lunches*. Membership ($20 and up) includes a subscription to *Action Alert*, a quarterly bulletin that contains legislative news and a variety of articles on food and nutrition.

RESULTS
236 Massachusetts Ave., N.E., Suite 300
Washington, DC 20002
(202) 543-9340

RESULTS is a nonprofit, grass-roots lobbying organization dedicated to creating the political will to end hunger. Local RESULTS groups, active in more than 100 communities nationwide, educate themselves about government programs and legislation that address hunger and hunger-related issues in the U.S. and abroad. The groups then share that information with their elected representatives, the general public, and the press, urging support of programs and proposals that are effective in combating hunger. RESULTS also publishes a quarterly action report, *Entry Point*, which presents issues, interviews, and legislation dealing with hunger ($25 for a one-year subscription). If you would like to join a RESULTS group, contact the national headquarters for the location of one near you.

The Salvation Army
(see Doing Good in America, page 18)

Second Harvest National Food Bank Network
116 S. Michigan Ave., Suite 4, Chicago, IL 60603
(312) 263-2303

Second Harvest is America's only charitable national network of food banks and the nation's largest nongovernmental food program. The organization solicits donated, surplus food products from the nation's food industry and other sources, and channels them through some 200 Second Harvest food banks to nearly 40,000 soup kitchens, church pantries, senior and day-care centers, and other food programs that serve America's needy. Each year, Second Harvest distributes more than 400 million pounds of food, valued at more than $845 million. Contact Second Harvest for a list of food banks in your area or for information on volunteer opportunities.

Share Our Strength
1511 K St., N.W., Suite 623, Washington, DC 20005
(202) 393-2925 or 1-800-222-1SOS (1767)

SOS is a nonprofit organization established to bring creative professionals from a variety of fields together to help fight hunger. SOS organizes benefits, such as **Taste of the Nation**, a nationwide food- and wine-tasting event held each spring in sixty-five cities to raise money for hunger relief. It also publishes *Louder Than Words*, an anthology of short stories by twenty-two of America's top writers, and the *Great Chefs of America* calendar. More than 1,000 restaurants across America are members of SOS (SOS can provide you with a free list of member restaurants, as well as with information on becoming a member). Many of the member restaurants are involved in the **Fight Food Waste** campaign, in which SOS encourages restaurants to salvage their leftover food and donate it on a consistent basis to food banks and homeless shelters in the area. If you know of a restaurant, food service, or grocery store that would like to become involved in SOS activities, or if you are aware of someone who has a lot of leftover food from a party or other function, have them contact SOS. Further information is available by writing to SOS.

USA Harvest
P. O. Box 628, Louisville, KY 40201-1628
1-800-USA-4-FOOD (1-800-872-4366)
(502) 583-7756

USA Harvest is a nonprofit organization that provides food donated by hospitals, restaurants, hotels, bakeries, caterers, wholesalers, and retailers to hungry men, women, and children at centers nationwide. It is a unique nonprofit organization in that it does not accept monetary donations—only offerings of food, time, and materials. Volunteers, using vans or their own vehicles, transport food from donors to centers maintained by USA Harvest. Contact the national headquarters for the location of an affiliate in your area (or if you want to start one).

World Hunger Education Service
P.O. Box 29056, Washington, DC 20017
(202) 298-9503

A nonprofit organization, **WHES** disseminates information on the extent, causes, and consequences of the hunger problem. Its quarterly newsletter, *Hunger Notes*, provides current facts and insights on hunger and related topics ($18 for a one-year, individual subscription). WHES also operates a large library out of Washington, D.C., offering books, periodicals, audiovisual materials, teaching kits, and files on hunger-related issues and organizations. (If you live in the Washington, D.C., area, WHES could use your help with editing, researching, and writing for *Hunger Notes*, maintaining the library, and various other tasks.) WHES also distributes educational curricula and books (for example, *Have You Ever Been Hungry*, *Monsoon*, and *Who's Involved with Hunger*—a guide to 400 organizations in the U.S. providing information and publications on hunger, poverty, food, and related issues).

World Hunger Year
261 W. 35th St., Room 1402, New York, NY 10001-1906
(212) 629-8850

WHY is a nonprofit organization that works to inform the general public, the media, and policymakers on the extent and causes of hunger in the U.S. and abroad. It also initiates, organizes, and participates in programs promoting more effective government and private sector policies to eliminate hunger, homelessness, and poverty. WHY publishes a quarterly resource newsletter, *Hungerline Reports*, as well as *WHY, Challenging Hunger and Poverty*, a *very* informative magazine filled with in-depth articles, interviews, and book reviews. A one-year subscription costs $18. WHY can also provide you with information on joining or forming a WHY chapter, participating in its *Hungerthon*, and other volunteer activities.

SUICIDE

Why Help Is Needed

Without a doubt, the death of a friend, family member, or loved one can be an absolutely devastating experience. This grief can be terribly compounded, however, when the death is by suicide. According to the American Association of Suicidology (AAS), approximately 30,000 Americans kill themselves every year, leaving behind countless friends and family members to endure this grief—and often tremendous feelings of helplessness and guilt as well.

Suicide among young people is especially hard to accept. It is the third leading cause of death among young people ages fifteen to twenty-four years old (suicide is the eighth leading cause of death among all persons). The Youth Suicide National Center reports that 5,000 young people kill themselves every year, and even more staggering, for every suicide, an estimated 100 others have been attempted. This means that every day in America, approximately 130 young people will try to kill themselves. And every day, thirteen will succeed.

Suicide is not, however, just an issue among young people; it cuts across all age groups, and economic, social, and ethnic boundaries. The youngest known suicide victim, according to AAS, was five years old. Elderly persons represent twenty percent of all suicides in America, according to AAS (some estimates go much higher[1]). What many of these people share is the desire to live. They are just unable to see alternatives to their problems. AAS also believes that most suicidal persons give definite warnings of their intentions. Unfortunately, others are either unaware of the significance of these warnings or do not know how to respond to them.

The situation is certainly not hopeless; many people benefit from counseling and treatment and are able to work through their problems. And although treatment should be left to the professionals, suicide prevention can be everybody's business. Knowing the signs of

---

[1]David E. Driver, *The Good Heart Book: A Guide to Volunteering* (Chicago: The Noble Press, 1989), 182.

SUICIDE 353

suicide, volunteering at crisis centers, educating others about the need to help, or simply helping depressed family members or friends to find the treatment they need will work to solve the problem. Not every suicide can be prevented, but by encouraging a general awareness of suicide and providing necessary support and encouragement for those in need, there is no telling how many tragedies can be avoided.

What You Can Do

☞ **Learn the signs that suicidal people usually exhibit as warnings of their intentions**, because these signs are often calls for help. All of the national organizations listed in this chapter can give you information on warning signs and dos and don'ts to keep in mind if you think a friend (or family member) may be suicidal.

☞ **Put up posters and other informative materials on suicide in your school, office, or place of worship.** This will help others to recognize that suicide is a problem and that they can help prevent it. All of the national organizations listed in this chapter have useful materials.

☞ **Volunteer to work for a suicide prevention organization in your community.** These centers often need volunteers to staff the crisis hotlines, and although the work is quite challenging and requires a lot of training, you may quite literally help save lives. Colleges also usually have suicide or "rap" lines that often need volunteers. Centers may need volunteers to help with other services, including administrative work (for example, editing newsletters, word processing, sending out notices) and fundraising. Look in the phone book under "Community Service Numbers" or in the Yellow Pages under "Suicide Prevention," or check the **American Association of Suicidology** for information about the services in your area.

National Organizations

American Association of Suicidology
2459 S. Ash, Denver, CO 80222
(303) 692-0985

AAS is a nonprofit organization that works to understand and prevent suicide in the U.S. The association develops public-service announcements, sponsors conferences and seminars, organizes school suicide prevention programs, and serves as a national clearinghouse on suicide information and resources. AAS also publishes the quarterly newsletter *Newslink*, which informs readers of current activities in the suicide-prevention field; *Suicide and Life-Threatening Behavior*, a quarterly journal that contains research, articles, and reviews; and the *Directory of Suicide Prevention and Crisis Intervention Agencies in the U.S.* If you want to volunteer at a suicide crisis center in your community but are having trouble finding one, AAS can help you locate a center near you. Membership rates start at $20 (for volunteers and students) and go up to $150 (for organizations).

The Samaritans
(there is no headquarters—check the phone book for the center in your community)

The Samaritans is a volunteer suicide prevention organization with branches in the U.S. and throughout the world. Each chapter runs a suicide hotline and works to help anyone who feels suicidal, lonely, depressed, or who just needs someone to talk to. The local chapters have a variety of informative fact sheets and booklets available for parents, friends, teachers, coaches, and concerned individuals, including *Teen Suicide: Information and Guidelines for Parents; Elderly Suicide: Information and Guidelines;* and *Depression, Suicide, and the College Student* (publications may vary from chapter to chapter). The Samaritans are always in need of volunteers, so check the phone book for a chapter near you. Chapters are presently in Washington, D.C.; Boston, Cape Cod (Falmouth), Merrimack Valley, Framingham and Fall River/New Bedford, Massachusetts; Providence, Rhode Island; Albany, New York; New York City; and Manchester and Keene, New Hampshire.

Task Force on Youth Suicide Prevention
Union of American Hebrew Congregations
1330 Beacon St., Suite 355, Brookline, MA 02146
(617) 277-1655, FAX: (617) 277-3491

The **Task Force**, a program administered by the nonprofit UAHC, is dedicated to informing the public about youth suicide and about ways suicide can be prevented. The organization can provide you with informative pamphlets (such as *About Suicide; Suicide and How to Prevent It;* and *Youth Suicide Prevention*—with a comprehensive reading list on adolescent suicide), books (for example, *When Living*

Hurts), posters, films, and videos (Billy Joel's *You're Only Human, Second Wind, Inside I Ache*). It also offers a kit, *Youth Suicide Prevention: Programs and Resources for Congregations*, which includes a reading list, program suggestions and model formats, a discussion guide, high school–related materials, a guide to the Reform Jewish view of suicide, film and media resources, a poster, and informative booklets and pamphlets.

Youth Suicide National Center
204 E. 2nd Ave., Suite 203, San Mateo, CA 94401
(415) 347-3961

A nonprofit organization, **YSNC** was established as a reaction to increasing numbers of young people in the U.S. who are committing suicide. Its purpose is to facilitate effective action on both the local and national levels by serving as a national clearinghouse, developing and distributing educational materials, coordinating a national awareness campaign, reviewing current youth suicide prevention and support programs, and encouraging research. Publications include, *Suicide in Youth and What You Can Do About It; Helping Your Child Choose Life: A Parent's Guide to Youth Suicide; Film and Media Resources on Youth Suicide;* and a *Youth Suicide Information Packet*, which contains several informative booklets and pamphlets, information on current legislation, statistics, and relevant articles.

Veterans

Why Help Is Needed

According to the Department of Veterans Affairs (VA), there are approximately 27.1 million American veterans. The VA also reports that more than ninety percent of them are leading productive lives, and they represent one of America's most productive corps of volunteers. Not all veterans, however, are as fortunate. The U.S. Conference of Mayors estimates that approximately twenty-six percent of homeless men are veterans, and the VA estimates that over four percent of all veterans—almost 1.1 million—are unemployed. VA hospitals annually treat more than one million veterans a year, many of whom appreciate assistance with daily activities, as do many of the three million veterans who have disabilities.

Traditionally, veterans have held an honored and respected place in this country. Unfortunately, however, there have been times when people who have disagreed with the nation's wars, particularly the Vietnam War, have transferred their disapproval to the individuals involved. Thousands of men and women who served in Vietnam returned to the U.S. to face indifference and even hostility. Fortunately, the past few years have marked a period of openness toward and reconciliation with the events of the Vietnam War. The national monument in Washington, D.C., and the various popular films about Vietnam (and the public's response to these films) indicate that Americans recognize the nation's veterans have suffered and that many continue to do so. Blame directed toward Vietnam veterans is passing, and the present provides an opportunity to revitalize a national concern for all veterans.

Almost all of the organizations and volunteer ideas in this chapter could have been placed in other chapters, such as those on disabilities, homelessness, or elderly persons (the VA estimates that twenty-four percent of all veterans are over sixty-five). It seems only fitting, however, to devote a chapter to veterans. Veterans have offered their lives to preserve America, qualifying them, one may argue, as the nation's ultimate public servants. The U.S. government can provide the financial compensation and essential services that veterans need, but volunteers are needed to provide the companionship, respect, and assistance that only a caring individual can offer another individual.

What You Can Do

☞ **Keep up on veterans' issues, such as legislation and the creation of local and national monuments.** The more people recognize how many veterans are in need of help, the more they will know where help is needed most and how they can help. Most of the national organizations listed in this chapter can provide concerned citizens with legislative information and news on a variety of veterans issues. (See also Voicing Your Opinion, page 363.)

☞ **Become part of Operation Appreciation,** which works to bring holiday cheer to hospitalized veterans (it is sponsored by the **Non-Commissioned Officers Association of the United States**, a nonprofit organization dedicated to promoting, protecting, and increasing the well-being of noncommissioned officers and petty officers as well as their families). Prior to several holidays each year, including Easter, the 4th of July, Memorial Day, Veteran's Day, and Christmas, NCOA sends a greeting card or message to participants asking that the card be personalized with a short note for a hospitalized veteran. The cards are returned to NCOA to be packaged and sorted, and then delivered to hospitalized veterans on the holiday. There is no fee for participating. Write or call NCOA for more information at *225 N. Washington St., Alexandria, VA 22314*; (703) 549-0311.

☞ **Become part of Help Hospitalized Veterans.** This nonprofit organization was established to distribute arts-and-crafts kits, free of charge, to patients in VA and military hospitals. Since the project's inception, in 1971, HHV has delivered more than sixty-five million dollars worth of kits to more than 260 hospitals in all fifty states. The kits do a great deal to help overcome boredom, boost morale, and restore self-confidence and faith. They include models, paint-by-numbers sets, and poster art. For more information, write or call HHV at *2065 Kurtz St., San Diego, CA 92110-2014*; (619) 291-5846, FAX: (619) 291-3842.

☞ **Join the Department of Veterans Affairs' Voluntary Service Program** (see the **Department of Veterans Affairs,** page

361). Men and women of all ages are welcome in this comprehensive program. You will receive complete training on working with veterans and can get involved in chaplaincy, community activities, counseling, extended care for elderly persons, library work, escorting patients, recreational activities, and social work. Here are some other examples of what you can do as part of the Voluntary Service Program (as adapted from the Department of Veterans Affairs' *Community Service Volunteers*):

In nursing homes:

- **Friendly visiting.** Help the patients get acquainted with other nursing home residents and activities within the nursing home environment.
- **Assist patients with games, crafts, and social activities**, and help them to develop special interests of their own.
- **Escort patients to social outings**, church, synagogue, shopping trips, or out to handle personal business affairs.
- **Write letters and help with other personal services.**
- **Remember the person on birthdays and other special occasions.** Bring them an American flag on Flag Day or Veteran's Day.
- **Observe the patient's morale and progress in adjusting to a new situation and report to the social worker.** Volunteers can also help evaluate and refer special needs.

In community residential homes and group living facilities:

- **Work with individual patients who need special, friendly support.**
- **Work with a group of other volunteers in expanding patient participation in recreational, social, and educational opportunities in the community.**
- **Assist the VA staff member in locating suitable new community residential homes.**
- **When appropriate, assist the veteran in finding employment or volunteer tasks in the community.**

☞ **Volunteer to assist veterans with disabilities. Disabled American Veterans** (page 361), in particular, has a wide array of volunteer opportunities. Through its **Older Veterans Assistance Program**, volunteers can help retirement-age veterans with everyday duties, including getting adequate food, shelter, and clothing; maintaining a balanced diet; getting to the store and to doctors appointments; and doing minor repairs on their homes. Through the **DAV Transportation Network**, volunteers provide transportation to and from VA hospitals and clinics for veterans with disabilities. (See also **Blinded American Veterans Foundation**, below, and **Blinded Veterans Association**, page 360, for more volunteer opportunities.)

☞ **Work at a veterans' organization** (usually the local post or chapter of a national organization). Volunteers are often needed to help with a variety of administrative duties, fundraising activities, and services to veterans in the community. Organizations should be listed in your phone book under "Veterans." You can also get a listing of veterans organizations in your community by sending a stamped, self-addressed envelope to the **Department of Veterans Affairs**, Attn: Deputy Assistant Secretary for Veterans Liaison at *810 Vermont Ave., Washington, DC 20420.*

☞ **If you are an employer, make an effort to hire veterans.** Look in the phone book under "Veterans Employment Representative" or "Employment Services, Department of" (usually under the government pages). These offices have a veterans' coordinator who can help you find qualified applicants. If there is no such listing, or if you are having trouble finding the office, check with the local government's veterans office.

National Organizations

Blinded American Veterans Foundation
P.O. Box 65900, Washington, DC 20035-5900
(202) 462-4430, FAX: (202) 265-0833

BAVF is a nonprofit organization established to increase the well-being of blinded and other sensory-disabled veterans across the U.S. The foundation assisted in the research and development of the Americane, a telescoping aid for the blind. It distributes these canes (which cost BAVF $20) free to needy veterans, provides audiotapes (including an audio version of the U.S. Constitution and veterans benefits), conducts studies on blinded veterans, and contributes thousands of dollars for the purchase of computers to train blinded veterans. BAVF can also provide employers with lists of blinded veterans who would like to be employed. Donations of audiotapes (old or new) are appreciated.

Blinded Veterans Association
477 H St., N.W., Washington, DC 20001-2694
(202) 371-8880 or 1-800-669-7079

This congressionally chartered nonprofit veterans' service organization was established to promote the welfare of blinded veterans nationwide. **BVA** helps in numerous ways, including searching out and targeting blinded veterans and their families who need services; providing compassion and support; serving as an advocate for blinded veterans in the private and public sectors; lobbying for legislation and monitoring Congress on issues that affect the well-being of blinded veterans; providing scholarships for dependents of blinded veterans; and increasing public awareness on both the needs and capabilities of blinded veterans. BVA has a field service program with eight field representatives throughout the U.S. and a network of volunteer national service officers to assist blinded veterans. There are chapters nationwide and volunteers are welcome (and needed). There is also an auxiliary made up of spouses, family, and friends of members.

BRAVO
Brotherhood Rally of Veterans Organizations
23919 Craftsman Road, Calabasas, CA 91302
(818) 999-4174, FAX: (818) 888-VETS (8387)

A nonprofit corporation that serves as a multimedia clearinghouse for veterans' activities worldwide, **BRAVO** focuses on bringing news and information on veteran problems and solutions to the public and veterans; VA benefits and abuses; legislation affecting veterans; Agent Orange treatment and compensation; and a variety of related issues. BRAVO supports local and national veterans' activities through its national media (including a weekly public-access TV show, a weekly radio program, and a newspaper, *Veteran's Outlook*) and via state and international chapters; encourages local programs that aid veterans by establishing neighborhood veteran community-service centers and veterans' advisory committees to local, county, and state government offices; and advocates veteran training and employment. BRAVO encourages participation in veterans' organizations, clubs, and activities through *Veterans Outlook*, a newspaper that comes out ten times a year and features stories on issues of interest to veterans of all wars and their families (call for rates). The newspaper also provides veterans with opportunities to find their buddies. There is a one-time, life-time registration fee of $10 for veterans, organizations, and interested individuals. Write or call BRAVO for information on its volunteer opportunities nationwide (such as gathering information for news stories, disseminating information, serving on committees, and supporting events sponsored by veterans and civic organizations).

Department of Veterans Affairs
Voluntary Service
810 Vermont Ave. (161A), Washington, DC 20420
(202) 233-4110

The **Department of Veterans Affairs**, a federal cabinet branch, operates the **Voluntary Service** program, which encourages volunteers (of practically all ages) nationwide to work in nursing homes and VA Medical Centers. (You can also look these up in your phone book, usually under the government pages.) Volunteers help veterans through various services, including simply coming to visit; bringing books or small gifts; remembering birthdays and other special occasions; escorting veterans to social outings, church, synagogue, shopping trips, and the like; and playing games. Volunteers, if needed, will receive free orientation, training, and staff guidance. The Voluntary Service program has been running for almost forty-five years and is an outstanding program for volunteers and veterans alike.

Disabled American Veterans
3725 Alexandria Pike, Cold Spring, KY 41076
(606) 441-7300
or
807 Main Ave., S.W., Washington, DC 20024
(202) 554-3501

This nonprofit organization provides numerous services for disabled veterans. **DAV** activities include claims representation to all veterans, their dependents, and survivors regarding government benefits and rights concerning veterans benefits; a transportation network that takes disabled veterans to VA hospitals; an emergency relief fund for veterans; a scholarship fund; and an employment program that encourages public- and private-sector employers to provide job opportunities to veterans with disabilities. Volunteers are needed nationwide for many activities, especially to help out at veterans' hospitals, clinics, nursing homes, and DAV chapters.

USO
(see Doing Good in America, page 19)

Veterans of the Vietnam War, Inc.
Pocono Park Office, Jumper Rd., Wilkes-Barre, PA 18702
(717) 825-7215

Despite its name, **VVnW** is a nonprofit organization dedicated to helping veterans *of all wars*. VVnW provides numerous services to veterans, such as assistance in filing claims for disability and compensation, and referrals to rehabilitation or training programs. Membership costs $10 and includes a subscription to *The Veteran Leader*, a bimonthly newsletter that contains up-to-date news and information on Agent Orange legislation, POW-MIA issues, and news updates, and offers various mail-order items (including patches, bumper stickers, pins, hats, flags, and T-shirts).

Vietnam Veterans of America, Inc.
1224 M. St., N.W., Washington, DC 20005
(202) 628-2700, FAX: (202) 628-5880

A nonprofit organization, **VVA** is the only congressionally chartered, national Vietnam veterans' service organization devoted exclusively to the issues of Vietnam-era veterans and their families. VVA has more than 36,000 active members nationwide and abroad, many of whom are located in one of its 491 chapters or thirty-six state councils. VVA has been a leader when it comes to virtually every issue that affects Vietnam-era veterans. VVA fights for veterans' legislation; works with state employment agencies to help veterans find jobs; works with volunteers at local VA hospitals; and provides leadership in the construction of state and local Vietnam veterans' memorials. VVA has an extensive catalog of books, flag, stickers, patches, pins, and other products. There is also a monthly publication, the *Veteran*, full of in-depth articles, book reviews, and information on upcoming VVA events and chapter news. Membership costs $20. Veterans' information and services are available through the national office and local VVA Chapters.

VOICING YOUR OPINION

How to Contact Government Representatives

Although often overlooked, expressing your views to your government representatives can be one of the most effective ways to create change. The belief that just one letter, phone call, or visit cannot make a difference is simply false; every opinion is noted and addressed. One letter, in fact, can represent the views of several hundred people, so if there's an issue that you're steamed about or an issue you want endorsed, let your representatives know about it. If you are not certain whom your representatives are, contact your local town hall or library.

If you want more information on expressing your views, following political candidates, and learning about other political matters, contact **The League of Women Voters**. LWV is a nonprofit, nonpartisan organization that encourages the informed and active participation of citizens in government and influences public policy through education and advocacy. LWV's informative publications include *Tell It to Washington; Vote! The First Steps; How to Judge a Candidate; How to Watch a Debate;* and *Unmet Needs: The Growing Crisis in America*. Write to or call LWV for more information at *1730 M St., N.W., Washington, DC 20036*; (202) 429-1965.

When you're writing a letter to your representative, here are a few suggestions to keep in mind:*

- **The best time to contact your representative is right after a bill has been introduced**. When mentioning the bill, try to cite it by number or title. (If the bill is getting a lot of publicity, the popular title is usually enough.) However, if it is a more obscure bill, call the representative's office and ask for the specific legislation identification number. The congressional operator's telephone number is *(202) 224-3121*. You can also get

*With special thanks to congressional aide Peter Shakow.

copies of bills by sending a self-addressed mailing label (they'll supply the envelopes) to the **House Document Room**, *Annex 2, Room B-18, Washington, DC 20515*; (202) 225-3456, or the **Senate Document Room**, *SH-B 04, Washington, DC 20510*; (202) 224-7860. When writing, you can indicate how you wish your representative to vote, ask him or her to co-sponsor the bill, or offer any amendments.

- **If you are criticizing your representative or offering a differing opinion, try to be as constructive as possible.** Angry, insulting letters are certainly noticed, but they are not as influential as letters that make the same point in a levelheaded manner.
- **Try to avoid form letters.** Form letters are not dismissed, but they are not as influential as letters that show effort and thought. It is also best to type or neatly handwrite your letter.
- **If you have any experience with the issue or have a report or statistics to back your point, don't hesitate to use them.** Make sure you staple together all the material you send in, and don't send in anything you want mailed back to you.
- **If you are not satisfied with the response you receive,** don't hesitate to write another letter indicating that your concerns were not adequately addressed. If you are satisfied with the response, don't hesitate to send a quick thank-you note.

For Senators

The Honorable *(full name)*
United States Senate
Washington, DC 20510

For Congresspersons

The Honorable *(full name)*
United States House of Representatives
Washington, DC 20515

Here is a sample letter to give you an idea of how you may want to express your views:

Date

Dear Senator (*last name*),
or
Dear Congressman or Congresswoman (*last name*),

It has come to my attention that the Volunteer Recognition Bill (H.R. 927) will soon be on the floor of the House of Representatives. I am strongly in favor of this bill, and I hope that you will support it.

It is clear that volunteerism is essential to the welfare of this country, and this bill will insure that the efforts of volunteers nationwide will be better recognized. This will, I believe, encourage others to volunteer their time and effort. I understand that the bill may create added costs to the budget, but I believe that the benefits of additional volunteers will offset these costs.

I know that you have supported and encouraged volunteerism in the past, and I hope that you will continue to do so, particularly by supporting this bill. Please let me know your position on it. Thank you.

Sincerely,
Your Name
Address
Telephone Number

For the President

Surprisingly, it is not uncommon for representatives of the president to respond to comments, opinions, or general greetings. Some people are even fortunate enough to receive a handwritten response from the president, though this is quite rare. If you're interested, here's where to write:

The President
The White House
Washington, DC 20500

It is most proper to begin the letter with *Dear President (last name)*.

You can also express your views to the White House by calling the **White House Comment Line** is *(202) 456-7639*. The line is open from 9 A.M. to 5 P.M., Monday through Friday. Each day, the opinions and comments that are called in (usually relating to current events or legislation) are tabulated and condensed into a concise report, which is relayed to the president.

WISE GIVING

Tips on Making Charitable Donations

If you make a charitable donation, be sure your money is going to a reputable organization and will not be wasted. Here are a few suggestions to keep in mind when making a donation.*

General Rules

- **Do not give cash;** always make contributions by check and make the check out to the charity, not the individual collecting the donation.
- **Keep records of your donations** (receipts, canceled checks, and bank statements) if you wish to document your charitable giving at tax time. Although the value of your time is not tax deductible, out-of-pocket expenses (including transportation costs) directly related to your volunteer service are.
- **Don't confuse *tax deductible* with *tax exempt*.** Contributions to tax-exempt organizations are not always tax deductible. Tax exempt simply means that the organization does not pay federal income tax. Tax deductible means that the donor can deduct contributions to the organization from his or her federal income tax.
- **If you are suspicious of an organization's soliciting methods, check out the organization with the local charity registration office** (usually a division of the state attorney general's office) and with the **Better Business Bureau** (if it's a local charity, contact the area office of the bureau; if it's a national charity, contact the bureau's headquarters at the address given on page 368).

*The material in this chapter has been excerpted and adapted, with permission, from *Tips on Charitable Giving*, copyright 1986, **Council of Better Business Bureaus, Inc.**, *4200 Wilson Boulevard, Arlington, VA 22203*, (703) 276-0100.

- **Ask if the charity is licensed by state and local authorities.** Registration or licensing is required by most states and many communities. Bear in mind, however, that registration in and of itself *does not* imply that the state or local government endorses the charity.

Telephone, Door-to-Door, and Street Solicitations

- **Ask for the charity's full name and address and identification from the solicitor.** Don't be fooled by a name that looks impressive or that closely resembles the name of a well-known organization.
- **Don't succumb to pressure to give money on the spot or to allow a "runner" to pick up a contribution.** The charity that needs your money today will welcome it just as eagerly tomorrow.
- **When you're asked to buy candy, magazines, cards, or tickets to a dinner or show to benefit a charity, be sure to ask what the charity's share will be.** You cannot deduct the full amount paid for any item, as the IRS considers only the part above the fair market value of the item to be a charitable contribution. For example, if you pay $10 for a box of candy that normally sells for $8, only $2 can be claimed as a charitable donation.
- **Call the local office of the Better Business Bureau if a fundraiser uses pressure tactics**, such as intimidation, threats, or repeated or harassing calls or visits. Such tactics violate the bureau's recommended "Standards for Charitable Solicitations."

Mail Appeals

- **Mail appeals should clearly identify the charity and describe its programs in clear and specific language.** Beware of appeals that bring tears to your eyes but tell you nothing about the charity or what it's doing about the problems it describes.
- **Appeals should not be disguised as bills or invoices.** It is illegal to mail a bill, invoice, or statement of account due that is in fact an appeal for funds unless it bears a clear and noticeable

disclaimer stating that it is an appeal and that you are under no obligation to pay unless you accept the offer.
- **It is also against the law to demand payment for unordered merchandise.** If unordered items such as key rings, stamps, greeting cards, or pens are enclosed with an appeal letter, remember that you are under no obligation to pay for or return the merchandise. If payment is requested, inform the local office of the Better Business Bureau.
- **Appeals that include sweepstakes promotions should disclose that you do not have to contribute to be eligible for the prizes offered.** To require a contribution would make the sweepstakes a lottery, and it is illegal to operate a lottery through the mail.
- **Matching check appeals are not subject to any particular legal requirements.** Donors should keep in mind, however, that they do not have to return the checks if they don't contribute. The checks do not have any real value in and of themselves.

Additional Resources from PAS/CBBB

To order one of the following publications, write to the **Philanthropic Advisory Service, Council of Better Business Bureaus**, *Dept. 024, Washington, DC 20042-0024*. Please enclose a self-addressed, business-sized envelope, with fifty cents postage for all nonsubscription orders. Make checks payable to the **CBBB Foundation**. The prices noted are for 1990 and are subject to change.

- ***Give But Give Wisely*™**—A bimonthly list of those national charities generating the most inquiries to PAS. This will give you a concise summary of who meets and does not meet CBBB standards. Single issues cost $2. One-year subscriptions cost $12.
- ***Annual Charity Index***—A companion to *Give But Give Wisely*™, this compact paperback contains the addresses, establishment dates, purposes, and major programs of about 200 charities that were among those that generated the greatest number of inquiries to PAS in the past year. $9.95 a copy.
- ***Insight***—A quarterly newsletter featuring timely articles about fundraising and trends in philanthropy. One-year subscriptions cost $15.
- ***PAS Subscription Package***—One-year subscriptions cost $30 and include six issues of *Give But Give Wisely*™, the *Annual Charity Index*, and four issues of *Insight*.
- ***PAS Reports on Specific Nonprofit Organizations***—One-

to four-page summaries of individual soliciting organizations whose programs or fundraising efforts are national or international in scope. Reports include information about the group's background, current programs, governing body, fundraising practices, tax-exempt status, and finances, as well as an explanation of whether the group complies with CBBB standards. Reports are free. PAS asks that you limit requests to three specific national nonprofit organizations at a time.

- ***Tips on Charitable Giving***—A pamphlet containing practical advice to donors about making informed giving decisions. Free.
- ***Tips on Tax Deductions for Charitable Contributions***—A brochure explaining tax exemption and the tax deductibility of charitable gifts. $1 per copy.
- ***Tips on Solicitations by Police and Firefighter Organizations***—A booklet outlining points for individuals and businesses to keep in mind when asked to contribute to police and firefighter organizations. $1 per copy.
- ***Tips on Handling Unwanted Direct Mail from Charitable Organizations***—A brochure addressing steps individuals can take to remove their names from soliciting organizations' mailing lists. $1 per copy.
- ***The Responsibilities of a Charity's Volunteer Board***—A brochure outlining the duties and responsibilities involved in serving on a nonprofit organization's board of directors. $2 per copy.

General Index

The Acid Rain Foundation (ARF), Inc., 283
Acorn Designs, 313
ACTION, The National Volunteer Agency, 9–13
  Foster Grandparent Program (FGP), 10
  Retired Senior Volunteer Program (RSVP), 10
  Senior Companion Program (SCP), 10, 236
  Student Community Service Program (SCSP), 11
  Volunteers In Service To America (VISTA), 11
Adam Walsh Child Resource Center, 153
Adoption Center of Delaware Valley, 144
Adoptive Families of America (AFA), 143
Adult Children of Alcoholics (ACA) Interim World Service Organization, 74
Affirmative Investments (AI), 32
AFM Enterprises, 290–91
AIDS Action Council (AAC), 41, 47
AIDS Coalition To Unleash Power (ACT UP), 47
AIDS Project Los Angeles (APLA), 48
  Buddies Program, 48
  Case Management Program, 48
  Hospital Visitation Volunteers Program, 48
  Necessities of Life Program, 48
Al-Anon/Alateen Family Group Headquarters, 75
Alcoholics Anonymous (AA) World Services, 75
Alexander Graham Bell Association for the Deaf (AGBAD), 204, 206
  Hearing Alert!, 207
The Alliance to Save Energy (ASE), 306
The Alzheimer's Association, 237–38
American Anti-Vivisection Society (AAVS), 86
American Association for Protecting Children (AAPC), 147
American Association of Children's Residential Centers (AACRC), 124
American Association of Homes for the Aging (AAHA), 238

American Association of Retired Persons (AARP), 233, 237, 238
American Association of Suicidology (AAS), 119n, 352, 253–54
American Association on Mental Retardation (AAMR), 212–13
American Bar Association (ABA), Representation of the Homeless Project, 331
American Cancer Society (ACS), 185
American Cetacean Society (ACS), 101
American Council for an Energy-Efficient Economy (ACEEE), 248, 306
The American Council for Drug Education (ACDE), 62
American Council of the Blind (ACB), 198, 201
American Deafness and Rehabilitation Association (ADARA), 206
American Forestry Association (AFA), 246n, 284
  Global ReLeaf, 280, 284
American Foster Care Resources (AFCR), Inc., 151
American Foundation for AIDS Research (AmFAR), 48
  ART AGAINST AIDS, 49
  Community-Based Clinical Trial Network, 49
American Foundation for the Blind (AFB), 176, 202
American Health Care Association (AHCA), 234, 235, 238–39
American Hiking Society (AHS), 256, 259
American Humane Association (AHA), 98–99
  Adopt-a-Cat, 99
  Adopt a Pet from Your Local Animal Shelter, 99
American Association for Protecting Children (AAPC), 147
  Be Kind to Animals Week, 99
American Institute of Architects (AIA), The Search for Shelter Program, 331
American Library Association (ALA), 217, 228
  Coalition for Literacy, 228

American Littoral Society (ALS), 322
American Lung Association (ALA), 284
American Mental Health Fund (AMHF), 177, 208, 209
American Oceans Campaign (AOC), 322-23
American Red Cross, 13, 111, 113
National Tissue Services, 116
American Rivers (AR), 323
American Social Health Association (ASHA), 49
National AIDS Hotline, 42, 44, 49
The American Society for the Prevention of Cruelty to Animals (ASPCA), 87
Pet Adoption Vans, 87
American Solar Energy Society (ASES), Inc., 307
American Vegan Society (AVS), 85
American Wildlands (AWL), 259
American Wilderness Adventures, 259
The Animal Legal Defense Fund (ALDF), 87
Animal Protection Institute (API) of America, 81, 88-89
Animal Rights Mobilization! (ARM!), 88
Animals, 79
The Animals' Agenda, 79-80
The Animals' Voice Magazine, 80
Animal Town, 80, 218
Animal Welfare Institute (AWI), 88
Appalachian Mountain Club (AMC), 260
Arthritis Foundation, 239
The ASPIRA Association, Inc., 126
Assault on Illiteracy Program (AOIP), 229
Assistance Dogs of America Inc., 182
Associated Humane Societies (AHS), 97, 99
Share-a-Pet, 99
Association for Commuter Transportation, 283
The Association for Persons with Severe Handicaps (TASH), 185

Association for Retarded Citizens (ARC), 213
Association of Jewish Family & Children's Agencies, 13
Athletes and Entertainers for Kids (AEFK), 126
Back to School and Stay in School, 127
Kareem's Kids, 126
The Ryan White National Program, 126
Atlantic Recycled Paper Co., 313

BACCHUS (Boost Alcohol Consciousness Concerning the Health of University Students) of the U.S., Inc., 63
The Barbara Bush Foundation for Family Literacy (BBFFL), 229
Basic Foundation (BF), 284-85
Beauty Without Cruelty (BWC) U.S.A., 81, 89
A Better Chance (ABC), Inc., 221
Public School Programs (PSPs), 221
The Better Homes Foundation, 328n
Bicycle Federation of America (BFA), 282
Big Brothers/Big Sisters of America (BB/BSA), 123, 127
Bikecentennial, 282
Bio-Integral Resource Center (BIRC), 296
Blinded American Veterans Foundation (BAVF), 359
Blinded Veterans Association (BVA), 359, 360
The Body Shop, 81
The Box Project (TBP), 14
Boys & Girls Clubs of America (BGCA), 123, 128
Boy Scouts of America (BSA), 125, 127-28
BRAVO (Brotherhood Rally of Veterans Organizations), 360-61
Bread for the World (BFW), 345-46
Business Against Drunk Drivers (BADD), Inc., 72
Business Council for Effective Literacy (BCEL), 215, 220, 229-30
Business Ethics, 5, 26

GENERAL INDEX 373

Buzzworm: The Environmental Journal, 257

California Action Network (CAN), 293
Calvert Group, 32
  Calvert-Ariel Appreciation Funds, 33
  Calvert Social Investment Fund (CSIF), 32
Camp Fire Boys and Girls, 125, 128–29
CAMPUSES WITHOUT DRUGS, Inc., 63
Campus Outreach Opportunity League (COOL), 14
Canine Companions for Independence, 182
THE CAP BOOK, Inc., 143
Catalyst, 29
Catholic Charities U.S.A., 15
Center for Environmental Information (CEI), Inc., 260
Center for Marine Conservation (CMC), 102
Center for Science in the Public Interest (CSPI), 292
  Americans for Safe Foods, 292
Center for the Prevention of Sexual and Domestic Violence (CPSDV), 168
Center on Human Policy (CHP), 186
Centers for Disease Control (CDC), 40
The Chemical People Institute (CPI), 64
C. Henry Kempe National Center for the Prevention and Treatment of Child Abuse and Neglect, 147
  Crisis Nursery, 148
  Home Visitor Program, 148
Child Find of America (CFA), Inc., 154
Childhelp U.S.A., Inc. 146, 148
  Specialized Foster Parent program, 148
Child Keyppers' International, Inc., 154
  Bite Identification System, 155
Children, Inc. (CI), 140
Children of the Green Earth (CGE), 285
Children's Defense Fund (CDF), 119n, 120, 129–30, 216, 328n
Children's Rights of America (CRA), 130
  National Youth Crisis Hotline, 130
Child Welfare League of America (CWLA), 120, 129
  Center for Program Excellence, 129
  Children's Campaign, 129
Christian Children's Fund (CCF), Inc., 141
Christian Literacy Associates (CLA), 230
Christmas in April U.S.A., 331, 333
Cities in Schools (CIS), 221
Citizens Clearinghouse for Hazardous Waste (CCHW), 296
Citizens Committee for New York City (CCNYC), 60, 61, 62, 166, 167
Clean Water Action (CWA), 323–24
The Clean Yield, 27
Climate Institute (CI), 285
Coalition on Human Needs, 329, 333–34
Coalition for Literacy, 215n
Coastal States Organization, COASTWEEKS, 101, 321–22
Cocaine Anonymous (CA) World Services, 76
Cocaine Helpline, 58
Coherency Co., 290
Commission on Voluntary Service and Action (CVSA), 24
Committees of Correspondence (COC), Inc., 64
Community Action Agency (*see* National Association of Community Action Agencies)
Community Careers Resource Center, 23
Community for Creative Non-Violence (CCNV), 334
  The National Volunteer Clearinghouse for the Homeless (NVCH), 330, 334, 338–39, 343
Community Jobs, 23
Community Products, Inc., 280
Community Servings, 43
The Compassionate Consumer, Inc., 81–82
CompCare Publishers, 64

374 GENERAL INDEX

COMPEER, Inc., 209–10
Concern, 260
Connecticut Canine Education Center, 205
Connections, 23
Conservation and Renewable Energy Inquiry and Referral Service (CAREIRS), 307–8
Conservation International (CI), 285–86
Conservatree Paper Company, 313
The Consumer Pesticide Project (CPP), 296–97
The Consumer's Guide to Planet Earth, 255
Contact Center, Inc., 217, 219, 220, 230
    Coalition for Literacy, 215n
    National Contact Hotline, 230
Contra Costa Food Bank (CCFB), 341, 344
    Project Glean, 344
Co-op America, 28, 33
Cooperative Development Foundation (CDF), 34, 332
The Corporate Examiner, 26
COSSMHO (The National Coalition of Hispanic Health and Human Services Organizations), 50
Council of Better Business Bureaus (CBBB), Inc., 366n
    Philanthropic Advisory Service (PAS), 368
Council on Economic Priorities (CEP), 27, 30
The Cousteau Society, 261
Covenant House, 124, 130–31
    Faith Community, 131
    Nineline, 131
    Rights of Passage, 131
Critical Mass Energy Project (CMEP), 308
Cure AIDS Now, 43

Deafness Research Foundation, National Temporal Bone Banks Program, 114, 118
Defenders of Wildlife, 4, 105
The Delta Society, 89, 183
Dembner Books, 23
Department of Veterans Affairs (VA), 356, 357, 358, 359, 361
    Voluntary Service, 357, 361
Direct Marketing Association, Mail Reference Service, 314
The Disability Rights Education and Defense Fund, 180, 186
Disabled American Veterans (DAV), 361
    Older Veterans Assistance Program, 358
    Transportation Network, 359
Dogs for the Deaf, Inc., 205

E.A.R. Foundation, 205
Earth Care Paper Company, Inc., 313–14
Earth Conservation Corps (ECC), 257
Earth First! (EF!), 262
Earth Island Institute, 262
    Climate Protection Institute, 262
    Friends of the Ancient Forest, 262
    International Marine Mammal Project, 262
    Rainforest Health Alliance, 262
    Sea Turtle Restoration Project, 262
    Urban Habitat Program, 262
EarthSave, 263
EARTHWATCH, 256
Earthwise—A Green Store, 252–53
The Earthworks Group, 245n, 246n, 247n, 249n, 250n, 256
Ecco Bella, 253
Eco-Choice, 82
Eco Design Co., and Livos Plant Chemistry, 291
Elsa Wild Animal Appeal (EWAA), 104–5
E. Magazine, 251
Environment, 251
Environmental Action Coalition (EAC), 317
Environmental Action Foundation (EAF), 245, 263
Environmental Defense Fund (EDF), 264, 310
Environmental Opportunities, 257
Environmental Protection Agency (EPA), 251
Environmental Traveling Companions (ETC), 184
Epilepsy Foundation of America (EFA), 187

Ethical Investments (EI), 34
EveryBody Ltd., 82–83
Eye Bank Association of America (EBAA), 116
Eye Dog Foundation for the Blind, 200
Eye of the Pacific Guide Dogs and Mobility Services, 182

Families Anonymous (FA), 76
Family Friends Program, 125, 181, 187
Family Service America (FSA), 15, 124
Farm Animal Reform Movement (FARM), 86, 90
   The Great American Meatout, 90
   Veal Ban Campaign, 90
   World Farm Animals Day, 90
Feed the Children (FTC), 141
Fidelco Guide Dog Foundations, 200
Find The Children (FTC), 155
First Place, 332
Florida Dog Guides for the Deaf, Inc., 205
Food & Friends, 43
FOOD FIRST: Institute for Food Development Policy, 346
Food Research and Action Center (FRAC), 346
Four-One-One, 16
   Super Volunteers, 16
Fourth World Movement (FWM), 25
Franklin Research and Development Corporation (FRDC), 34
Freedom from Hunger Foundation (FFHF), 347
Freedom Service Dogs, Inc., 182
The Fresh Air Fund, 131
The Freshwater Foundation, 324
Friends of Animals (FoA), 90–91
Friends of the Earth, 264
   ACTIVIST MEMBERS program, 264
Friends of the River (FOR), 324
The Fund for Animals (TFA), Inc., 91
Futures For Children (FFC), 141–42

GARBAGE: The Practical Journal for the Environment, 251–52
Gardener's Supply (GSC), 293, 316
Gay Men's Health Crisis (GMHC), 50
The Giraffe Project (TGP), 5

Girl Scouts of the United States of America (GSUSA), 125, 132
Global Tomorrow Coalition (GTC), 264–65
God's Love We Deliver, 43
Good Bears of the World (GBW), 122, 236
GOOD MONEY (GM) Publications, 30
Goodwill Industries of America (GIA), 188, 310
Goodwill Industries Volunteer Services (GIVS), 188
Good Works: A Guide to Careers in Social Change, 23
Grass Roots the Organic Way (GROW), 297
The Green Consumer, 255
The Green Consumer, 255
The Greenhouse Crisis Foundation (GCF), 286
Greenpeace U.S.A., 265
Guide Dog Foundation for the Blind, 200
Guide Dogs for the Blind, 200
Guide Dogs of the Desert, 200
Guide to Volunteer Opportunities, 341
Guiding Eyes for the Blind, 200

Habitat for Humanity International (HHI), 331, 334–35
Handi-Dogs, Inc., 182
Hazeldon Educational Materials, 65
Head Start (*see*: Project Head Start)
Health Education Resource Organization (HERO), 41, 51
The Healthy Harvest Society (HHS), 292
Heartland Products, Ltd., 83
HELDREF Publications, 251
Helen Keller National Center (HKNC) for Deaf-Blind Youths and Adults, 207
Help Hospitalized Veterans (HHV), 357
The Holiday Project, 122, 236
Home Energy, 301
Homelessness Information Exchange (HIE), 335
Home of Ears for the Deaf, Inc., "Paws with a Cause," 183
Home Service Products Co., 83
The Hope Foundation (THF), 330, 335, 343

House Document Room, 364
Household Hazardous Waste Project (HHWP), 297-98
The Humane Farming Association (HFA), 86, 91
Humane Society of the United States (HSUS), 91-92, 97
Human Policy Press, 180, 186

In Defense of Animals (IDA), 92
  World Laboratory Animal Liberation Week, 92
Independence Dogs, Inc., 183
INDEPENDENT SECTOR (IS), 16
  Give Five, 17
INFORM, 265-66
The Institute for Community Economics (ICE), 35, 332
  Revolving Loan Fund, 35
Institute for Food and Development Policy (See: FOOD FIRST)
Institute on Black Chemical Abuse (IBCA), 65
Interfaith Center on Corporate Responsibility (ICCR), 26-27, 31
International Child Health Foundation (ICHF), 125, 132
International Council for Bird Preservation (ICBP), 106
International Guiding Eyes, 200
International Hearing Dog, 205
International Liaison of Lay Volunteers in Mission, 24
International Oceanographic Foundation (IOF), 325
International Society for Animal Rights (ISAR), Inc., 78, 92, 98
International Union of Gospel Missions (IUGM), 330, 335-36
International Wildlife Coalition (IWC), 100, 102
  Whale Adoption Project, 102
Investor Responsibility Research Center (IRRC) 31
Island Press, 252
The Izaak Walton League of America (IWLA), 266

Jade Mountain, 253
Jewish Community Centers Association of North America, 7-8

Job Accommodation Network (JAN), 194
Job Opportunities for the Blind (JOB), 194-95
Joint Action in Community Services (JACS), Inc., 132
Junior League of Washington, 4
"Just Say No" International, 66

Keep America Beautiful (KAB), Inc., 317-18
  KAB SYSTEM, 318
Kids Against Pollution (KAP), 266-67

The Land Trust Alliance (LTA), 267
The Latham Foundation (TLF), 93
Laubach Literacy Action (LLA), 220, 231
Leader Dogs for the Blind, 200
League of American Wheelmen (LAW), 282-83
League of Conservation Voters (LCV) 252
The League of Women Voters (LWV), 363
Learning Disabilities Association (LDA) of America, 222
LifeBanc, 116
lion & lamb, inc., 83
Literacy Volunteers of America (LVA), Inc., 231
Little Brothers—Friends of the Elderly (LBFE), 239-40
The Living Bank (TLB), 117
Lutheran Volunteer Corps (LVC), 25

Mail for Tots, 122
Making the Grade, 133
March of Dimes Birth Defects Foundation, 188
Massachusetts Society for the Prevention of Cruelty to Animals (MSPCA), 79
Mennonite Board of Missions, 24
Message! Check (M!C) Corporation, 27
Missing Children . . . Help Center (MCHC), 152, 155
  Multiple Poster Publication, 155
Mothers Against Drunk Driving (MADD), 72

Drive for Life, 72
Keep It a Safe Summer (KISS), 72
National Red Ribbon Campaign, 72
Project Prom/Graduation, 72
Moveable Feast, 44
Muscular Dystrophy Association (MDA), 176n, 189
MDA Labor Day Telethon, 189

The Names Project Foundation, 51
AIDS Memorial Quilt, 51
Nar-Anon Family Group Headquarters, Inc., 76
Narcotics Anonymous (NA), 77
Narcotics Education, Inc. (NEI), 66
National Adoption Center (NAC), 144
Black Families/Black Children, 144
National AIDS Hotline (see: American Social Health Association)
National Alliance for Animal Legislation (ALLIANCE), 80, 93
National Alliance for the Mentally Ill (NAMI), 210
Homeless and Missing Mentally Ill Network, 210
NAMI CAN (Children and Adolescent Network, 210
National Alliance of Business (NAB), 222–23
The National Alliance to End Homelessness (NAEH), Inc., 327, 328, 336
National Anti-Vivisection Society (NAVS), 81, 94
The National Arbor Day Foundation (NADF), 280, 286
National Asian Pacific American Families Against Substance Abuse (NAPAFASA), 66
National Assault Prevention Center (NAPC), 169
Assault Prevention Training (APT) Project, 169
Child Assault Prevention (CAP) Project, 169
National Assembly of National Voluntary Health and Social Welfare Associations, Making the Grade, 133
National Association for Children of Alcoholics (NACoA), 67

National Association for the Advancement of Colored People (NAACP) Youth and College Division, 134
Academic, Cultural, Technological and Scientific Olympics (ACT-SO), 134
Back to School/Stay in School, 134
Resumé Retrieval Project, 134
National Association of Area Agencies on Aging (NAAAA), 235, 240
Area Agencies on Aging (AAAs), 240
National Association of Community Action Agencies (CAAs), 7, 138
National Association of Partners in Education (NAPE), National School Volunteer Program (NSVP), 219, 223
National Association of Private Industry Councils (PICs), 125–26
National Association of Private Residential Resources, 181
National Association of Service & Conservation Corps (NASCC), 17
National Association of the Deaf (NAD), 207
National Association of Town Watches (NATW), 170
National Night Out, 170
National Association on Drug Abuse Problems (NADAP), 67
National Audubon Society (NAS), 78, 106–7
National Black Alcoholism Council (NBAC), 68
BADD (Blacks Against Drunk Driving), 68
Black Alcoholism Institute, 68
National Black Child Development Institute (NBCDI), 123, 134
The National Caucus and Center on Black Aged (NCBA), 240–41
Senior Employment Program, 240
National Center for Appropriate Technology (NCAT), 301
National Center for Child Abuse and Neglect (NCCAN), 148
Clearinghouse on Child Abuse and Neglect and Family Violence Information, 149

National Center for Missing and Exploited Children (NCMEC), 153, 156
The National Center for Youth Law (NCYL), 125, 135
National Clearinghouse for Alcohol and Drug Information (NCADI), 68
National Coalition Against Domestic Violence (NCADV), 170
National Domestic Violence Awareness Month, 170
National Coalition Against Sexual Assault (NCASA), 159, 170
National Coalition Against the Misuse of Pesticides (NCAMP), 298
National Coalition for Marine Conservation (NCMC), 103
The National Coalition for the Homeless (NCH), 327, 336–37
The National Coalition of Advocates for Students (NCAS), 223–24
The National Coalition of Hispanic Health and Human Services Organizations (COSSMHO), 50
National Collegiate Athletic Association (NCAA) Committee on Competitive Safeguards and Medical Aspects of Sports, 68
National Youth Sports Program (NYSP), 69
Youth Education through Sports (YES), 69
National Commission Against Drunk Driving (NCADD), 73
Network of Employers for Traffic Safety (NETS), 73
National Committee for Adoption (NCFA), 144
National Committee for Citizens in Education (NCCE), 224
National Committee for Prevention of Child Abuse (NCPCA), 149
National Council of Senior Citizens (NCSC), 241–42
Senior Aides Program, 241
National Council on Alcoholism and Drug Dependence (NCADD), 55, 59, 69
Hotline, 58
National Alcohol Awareness Month, 69

National Alcohol-Related Birth Defects Awareness Week, 69
National Council on Child Abuse & Family Violence, 146, 149
The National Council on Crime and Delinquency (NCCD), 171
The National Council on the Aging (NCOA), Inc., 241
Family Friends Program, 125, 181, 187
The National Court Appointed Special Advocate (CASA) Association, 125, 147, 150, 151, 160
National Crime Prevention Council (NCPC), 56, 62, 145, 146, 157–58, 161, 162, 164, 165, 166, 167, 171–72
National Criminal Justice Reference Service (NCJRS), 173
National Criminal Justice Assistance, 173
Bureau of Justice Assistance, 173
Justice Statistics Clearinghouse, 173
Juvenile Justice Clearinghouse, 173
National Institute of Justice (NIJ), 158, 173
National Victims Resource Center, 173
National Dog Registry (NDR), 98, 99
Rescue Fund, Inc., 100
National Domestic Violence Hotline, 159
National Down Syndrome Congress (NDSC), 213
National Down Syndrome Society (NDSS), 214
National Dropout Prevention Center (NDPC), 216, 224–25
National Easter Seal Society (NESS), 177, 180, 189
National Education Association (NEA), 225
National Families in Action (NFIA), 69
National Federation of Parents (NFP) for Drug-Free Youth, 70
Lifers, 70
National Red Ribbon Campaign, 70
REACH (Responsible Educated Adolescents Can Help), 70

National Federation of State High
  School Associations (NFSHA),
  TARGET, 70
National Federation of the Blind
  (NFB), 202
  Job Opportunities for the Blind
    (JOB), 194
National Foster Parent Association
  (NFPA), 152
National Foundation of Wheelchair
  Tennis (NFWT), 195
National 4-H Council, 125, 135–36
The National Gay & Lesbian Task
  Force (NGLTF), 159, 172
National Geographic Society (NGS),
  80, 267–68
National Handicapped Sports (NHS),
  196
National Head Injury Foundation
  (NHIF), Inc., 190
National Hispanic Council on Aging
  (NHCoA), 242
National Housing Institute (NHI), 337
National Indian Council on Aging
  (NICOA), 242–43
National Industries for the Blind (NIB),
  199, 203
National Information Center for
  Children and Youth with Handicaps
  (NICHCY), 190
National Information Center on
  Deafness (NICD), 176, 208
National Institute Against Prejudice
  and Violence (NIAPV), 159, 172–73
National Institute for Urban Wildlife
  (NIUW), 107
National Institute of Justice (NIJ), 158,
  173
National Institute on Disability and
  Rehabilitation Research (NIDRR),
  191
National Institute on Drug Abuse
  Drug-Free Workplace Helpline, 58
National Institute on Drug Abuse
  Information and Referral Line, 58
National Interfaith Coalition on Aging
  (NICA), 243
The National Kidney Foundation
  (NKF), Inc., 115n, 117
National Low Income Housing
  Coalition (NLIHC), 329, 337

Low Income Housing Information
  Service (LIHIS), 337
National Marrow Donor Program
  (NMDP), 114, 117
National Mental Health Association
  (NMHA), 211, 329
National Minority AIDS Council
  (NMAC), 52
  Project HEAL (Health Education and
    AIDS Leadership), 52
National Multiple Sclerosis Society
  (NMSS), 190
The National Network of Runaway and
  Youth Services, 124, 136
  Safe Choices, 136
  Youth-to-Youth, 136
*The National Organic Wholesalers
  Directory and Yearbook*, 293
National Organization for Victim
  Assistance (NOVA), 159, 174
National Organization of Travelers Aid
  Societies, 330, 338
National Organization on Disability
  (NOD), 176, 184, 191
National Pacific/Asian Resource Center
  on Aging (NP/ARCA), 243
National Parent-Teacher Association
  (NPTA), 217, 225–26
National Parks and Conservation
  Association (NPCA), 287
National Recycling Coalition (NRC),
  Inc., 318
  Peer Match, 318
National Rehabilitation Information
  Center (NARIC), 191–92
The National Resource Center on
  Homelessness and Mental Illness
  (NRCHMI), 338
The National Resources Defense
  Council (NRDC), 268
  Mothers and Others for Pesticide
    Limits, 268
National Runaway Switchboard (NRS),
  124, 136–37
National Rural and Small Schools
  Consortium (NRSSC), 226
National Spinal Cord Injury
  Association (NSCIA), 192
National Student Campaign Against
  Hunger and Homelessness
  (NSCAHH), 345, 347–48

National Temporal Bone Banks
   Program (see: Deafness Research
   Foundation)
National Toxics Campaign (NTC), 297,
   298
National Urban League (NUL), Inc., 18
   AIDS Initiative, 18
   Comprehensive Youth Development
   Program, 18
   Stop The Violence Campaign, 18
National Victim Center (NVC), 159,
   174
   Crime Victims' Litigation Project,
   174
The National Volunteer Clearinghouse
   for the Homeless (NVCH), 330, 334,
   338-39, 343
National Water Center (NWC), 325
National Wildlife Federation (NWF),
   80, 107, 252
National Woman Abuse and
   Prevention Project (NWAPP), 159,
   175
The Nature Conservancy (TNC), 269
Necessary Trading Co. (NCO), 293-94
Neighborhood Reinvestment
   Corporation, 339
   NeighborWorks, 339
   The Search for Shelter Program, 331
New Alternatives Fund (NAF), 36, 258
*New Careers: A Directory of Jobs and
   Internships in Technology and
   Society*, 23
The New England Assistance Dog
   Service Inc., 183
Non-Commissioned Officers
   Association (NCOA) of the United
   States, Operation Appreciation, 357
North American Association of Jewish
   Homes and Housing for the Aging
   (NAAJHHA), 244
The North American Conference on
   Christianity and Ecology (NACCE),
   269
North American Council on Adoptable
   Children (NACAC), 145
North American Lake Management
   Society (NALMS), 325
North American Riding for the
   Handicapped Association (NARHA),
   Inc., 196

North American Vegetarian Society
   (NAVS), 85
North American Wildlife Foundation
   (NAWF), 108
Nuclear Information & Resource
   Service (NIRS), 298-99

Ocean Alliance (OA), 100, 326
   Adopt-A-Beach, 326
   Adopt-A-Whale, 326
Okada, Ltd., 183
One Person's Impact (OPI), 269-70
Opportunity to Serve!, 24
Oregon Department of Fish and
   Wildlife, 101, 321
The Orton Dyslexia Society (ODS),
   226-27

Parents' Resource Institute for Drug
   Education (PRIDE), 71
   America's PRIDE Program, 71
The Parnassus Fund, 36
"Paws with a Cause" (see Home of
   Ears for the Deaf, Inc.)
Pax World Fund (PWF), 36
Pediatric AIDS Foundation (PAF), 42,
   52
Pennsylvania Resources Council, 311,
   312
People for the Ethical Treatment of
   Animals (PETA), 78, 81, 94, 97
People with AIDS (PWA) Coalition, 53
Pesticide Action Network North
   America Regional Center (PAN NA
   RC), 299
   Dirty Dozen Campaign, 299
Phi Delta Kappa (PDK) Educational
   Foundation, 227
Philanthropic Advisory Service (PAS),
   368
Phoenix House Foundation, 55n
Phydeaux for Freedom, 183
Physicians Committee for Responsible
   Medicine (PCRM), 95
Pilot Dogs, Inc., 201
PLENTY USA, 348
President's Committee on
   Employment of People with
   Disabilities (PCEPD), 195
PRIDE (see Parents' Resource Institute
   for Drug Education)

GENERAL INDEX 381

Prison Fellowship, 160
Private Industry Council (*see* National Association of Private Industry Councils)
Progressive Asset Management (PAM), 37
Progressive Securities Financial Services, 37
Project Angel Food, 44
Project Concern International (PCI), 125, 137
    CHAP, 137
    OPTIONS/SERVICE, 137
    WALK FOR MANKIND, 137
Project Head Start, 124, 137–38, 331
Project Open Hand, 44, 53
Project Open Hand Atlanta, Inc., 44
Public Voice for Food and Health Policy, 293, 348

Rachel Carson Council (RCC), 300
Radioactive Waste Campaign (RWC), 300
Rails-to-Trails Conservancy (RTC), 308–9
Rainbow Concepts, 83
Rainforest Action Movement (RAM), 287
Rainforest Action Network (RAN), 247, 287–88
Rainforest Alliance (RA), 288
Rainforest Crunch, 280, 285
Reading Is Fundamental (RIF), Inc., 217, 231–32
Real Goods News, 254
Recording for the Blind (RFB), 199, 203
Recruiting New Teachers (RNT), Inc., 220, 227–28
Red Acre Farm Hearing Dog Program, 205
Remove Intoxicated Drivers (RID), 73
    Sane National Alcohol Policy, 74
Renew America, 270
    Searching for Success, 270
    State of the States, 270
Representation of the Homeless Project, 331
Resources for the Future (RFF), 270
RESULTS, 349

Ringer Lawn and Garden Products, 294, 316
Rising Sun Enterprises (RSE), 303
The Response, 24
Rocky Mountain Institute (RMI), 271
Rodale Press, 294–95

Safe Energy Communication Council (SECC), 309
St. Vincent Pallotti Center for Apostolic Development, 23
The Salvation Army (TSA), 18, 160, 220, 310, 330
The Samaritans, 354
San Francisco AIDS Foundation (SFAF), 41, 53
    AIDS Food Bank Program, 53
    Emergency Housing Program, 53
San Francisco Recycling Program (SFRP), 311, 314*n*, 316, 341
San Francisco SPCA Hearing Dog Training Center, 206
Save Our ecoSystems (SOS), inc., 314
Save the Children, 28, 142
Save the Children Craft Shop, 4, 28, 142
Save the Redwoods League (SRL), 288–89
Scenic America (SA), 271
Schultz Communications, 255
Scientists Center for Animal Welfare (SCAW), 95
Sea Shepherd Conservation Society (SSCS), 103
Second Harvest National Food Bank Network, 340, 343, 349
Seeds, 331, 333, 341–42
The Seeing Eye, 201
SELFHELP Crafts, 29
Senate Document Room, 364
Senior Gleaners (SG), 341, 344
Service Civil International/USA (SCI/USA), 24
Seventh Generation (SG), 254–55
Sex Information and Education Council of the U.S., 41
Share Our Strength (SOS), 343, 350
    Fight Food Waste, 350
    Taste of the Nation, 350
SHIRTS BY ZACK, 52
Shopping for a Better World, 27

GENERAL INDEX

Sick Kids (need) Involved People (SKIP), 192
The Sierra Club, 272
　Inner City Outings, 272
Sierra Club Legal Defense Fund, Inc., 272–73
Sinan Co. Natural Building Materials, 291
　Smithsonian Associates Research Expedition Program, 258
Smithsonian Institution
　Office of Environmental Awareness (OEA), 273
Social Investment Forum (SIF), 38
Southeastern Guide Dogs, 201
Spare the Animals, Inc., 84
Special Olympics International, 176, 196–97, 212
Spina Bifida Association of America (SBAA), 176n, 185, 193
　The Adoption Information Referral, 193
Street Aid, 332
Street News, 332
Student Action Corps for Animals (SACA), 84, 95–96
Student Conservation Association (SCA), 258
　High School Program, 258
　Resource Assistant Program, 258
Student Pugwash (SP) U.S.A., 24, 273–74
Students Against Driving Drunk (SADD), 74
　Student Athletes Detest Drugs, 74
Sunrise Lane, 84
Support Dogs for the Handicapped, 183

TARGET, 70
Task Force on Youth Suicide Prevention, 354–55
Teach for America (TFA), 220, 228
TOYS FOR TOTS, 122–23
Trade Wind, 28–29
TreePeople, 280, 289
Trust for Public Land (TPL), 274
　National Counselor Program, 274
20/20 Vision, 274–75

Union of American Hebrew Congregations (UAHC), Task Force on Youth Suicide Prevention, 354
The Union of Concerned Scientists (UCS), 275
United Action for Animals (UAA), Inc., 96
United Black Fund (UBF), 7
United Cerebral Palsy Associations (UCPA), 193–94
United Neighborhood Centers of America (UNCA), Inc., 8
United Network for Organ Sharing (UNOS), 113
U.S. Association for Blind Athletes (USABA), 197
United States Cerebral Palsy Athletic Association (USCPAA), 197
U.S. Conference of Mayors, 327, 340, 356
U.S. Department of Agriculture, 340
U.S. Department of Education, 58
U.S. Department of Energy, 302
U.S. Department of Justice, Community Relations Service (CRS), 159
U.S. Department of Labor, Job Opportunities for the Blind (JOB), 194
U.S. Fish and Wildlife Service, 78
　Division of Endangered Species, 104
U.S. House Select Committee on Children, Youth, and Families, 120
United States Marine Corps Reserve, TOYS FOR TOTS, 122–23
U.S. Public Interest Research Group (PIRG), 246, 275–76
United Way of America, 7, 132, 330
USA Harvest, 350
USO (United Services Organization), 19
　Airport Centers, 19
　Celebrity Entertainment, 20
　Family and Community Centers, 20
　Fleet Centers, 19–20
　Orientation and Intercultural Programs, 20

Vanished Children's Alliance (VCA), 156
Variety Clubs International, 123, 138
　Sunshine Coach Program, 138

Vegetarian Awareness Network
  (Vegenet), 85–86
Vegetarian Times, 86
Veterans of the Vietnam War (VVnW),
  Inc., 362
Vietnam Veterans of America (VVA),
  Inc., 362
Volunteers for Peace (VFP), 26
  International Workcamps, 26
Volunteers of America (VOA), 20, 160,
  220, 235
Volunteer Program Guide, 24
*Volunteer! The Comprehensive Guide
  to Voluntary Service on the U.S.
  and Abroad*, 24
VOLUNTEER—The National Center, 6,
  20, 132, 138, 160, 181, 199, 220,
  330

Water Pollution Control Federation
  (WPCF), 319
We Can, 332
WeTIP, Inc., 159, 175
White Electric Co., Inc.: The Light
  Bulb Place, 303
White House Comment Line, 365
Wilderness Inquiry (WI), 184
The Wilderness Society (TWS), 276
Wildlife Information Center (WIC),
  Inc., 108
Wildlife Preservation Trust
  International (WPTI), 109
Will Rogers Institute, 56
Windstar Foundation (WF), 276–77
Women in Community Service,
  (WICS), Inc. 138

Working Assets Funding Service, 38
Working Assets Long Distance, 38
Working Assets Mastercard, 38
Working Assets Travel Service, 38
Working Assets VISA, 38
Working Assets Money Fund, 38
World Hunger Education Service
  (WHES), 341, 350–51
World Hunger Year (WHY), 342, 351
World Resources Institute (WRI), 247,
  277
Worldwatch Institute (WI), 277–78
World Wildlife Fund and The
  Conservation Foundation (WWF and
  TCF), 109–10
The Write Cause (TWC), 80, 96

Xerxes Society, 110

Young Men's Christian Association
  (YMCA) of the United States of
  America, 21
Young Women's Christian Association
  (YWCA) of the United States of
  America, 21
  ENCORE, 22
  Mothers' Center, 22
Youth Development, Inc. (YDI), 124,
  139
Youth Law Center (YLC), 125, 140
Youth Service America (YSA), 22
Youth Suicide National Center (YSNC),
  352, 355
Youth to Youth (YtY), 71

Zero Population Growth (ZPG), 278

Geographical Index

The following is a state-by-state index of all the organizations listed in this book. Many organizations—Goodwill, YMCA, Volunteer Clearinghouses, United Way, etc.—have affiliates or offices nationwide, and there may be an affiliate in your state even if it's not listed below. If there's an organization you're interested in and the national office is not listed in your state, read the full description of the organization (check the general index for the page number) to see if it has local offices.

ALABAMA
ACTION, The National Volunteer Agency, 12

ALASKA
ACTION, The National Volunteer Agency, 13

AMERICA SOMOA
ACTION, The National Volunteer Agency, 12

ARIZONA
ACTION, The National Volunteer Agency, 12
Earth First! (EF!), 262
Handi-Dogs, Inc., 182
Muscular Dystrophy Association (MDA), 176*n*, 189

ARKANSAS
ACTION, The National Volunteer Agency, 12
American Deafness and Rehabilitation Association (ADARA), 206
National Water Center (NWC), 325

CALIFORNIA
ACTION, The National Volunteer Agency, 12
Adult Children of Alcoholics (ACA) Interim World Service Organization, 74
AIDS Project Los Angeles (APLA), 48
American Cetacean Society (ACS), 101
American Foundation for AIDS Research (AmFAR), 48
American Oceans Campaign (AOC), 322-23
The Animal Legal Defense Fund (ALDF), 87

Animal Protection Institute (API) of America, 81, 88
Athletes and Entertainers for Kids (AEFK), 126
The Ryan White National Program, 126
Bio-Integral Resource Center (BIRC), 296
BRAVO (Brotherhood Rally of Veterans Organizations), 360-61
California Action Network (CAN), 293
Canine Companions for Independence, 182
Childhelp U.S.A., Inc., 146, 148
Cocaine Anonymous (CA) World Services, 76
The Consumer Pesticide Project (CPP), 296-97
Contra Costa Food Bank (CCFB), 341, 344
Project Glean, 344
The Disability Rights Education and Defense Fund, 180, 186
Earth Island Institute, 262
EarthSave, 263
Elsa Wild Animal Appeal (EWAA), 104-5
Environmental Traveling Companions (ETC), 184
Eye Dog Foundation for the Blind, 200
Families Anonymous (FA), 76
Find The Children (FTC), 155
FOOD FIRST, The Institute for Food Development Policy, 346
Freedom from Hunger Foundation (FFHF), 347
Friends of the River (FOR), 324
Guide Dogs for the Blind, 200
Guide Dogs of the Desert, 200
Help Hospitalized Veterans (HHV), 357
The Humane Farming Association (HFA), 86, 91

In Defense of Animals (IDA), 92
   World Laboratory Animal Liberation Week, 92
Institute for Food and Development Policy (see: FOOD FIRST)
International Guiding Eyes, 200
"Just Say No" International, 66
The Latham Foundation (TLF), 93
The Names Project Foundation, 51
   AIDS Memorial Quilt, 51
Nar-Anon Family Group Headquarters, Inc., 76
Narcotics Anonymous (NA), 77
National Association for Children of Alcoholics (NACoA), 67
The National Center for Youth Law (NCYL), 125, 135
The National Council on Crime and Delinquency (NCCD), 171
National Foundation of Wheelchair Tennis (NFWT), 195
The North American Conference on Christianity and Ecology (NACCE), 269
Ocean Alliance (OA), 100, 326
The Parnassus Fund, 36
Pediatric AIDS Foundation (PAF), 42, 52
Pesticide Action Network North America Regional Center (PAN NA RC), 299
PLENTY USA, 348
Progressive Asset Management (PAM), 37
Project Angel Food, 44
Project Concern International (PCI), 125, 137
Project Open Hand, 44, 53
Rainforest Action Network (RAN), 247, 287–88
San Francisco AIDS Foundation (SFAF), 41, 53
   AIDS Food Bank Program, 53
   Emergency Housing Program, 53
San Francisco Recycling Program (SFRP), 311, 314n, 316, 341
San Francisco SPCA Hearing Dog Training Center, 206
Save the Redwoods League (SRL), 288–89

Sea Shepherd Conservation Society (SSCS), 103
Senior Gleaners (SG), 341, 344–45
The Sierra Club, 272
Sierra Club Legal Defense Fund, Inc., 272
TreePeople, 280, 289
Trust for Public Land (TPL), 274
Vanished Children's Alliance (VCA), 156
WeTIP, Inc., 159, 175
Working Assets Funding Service, 38
Working Assets Money Fund, 38
The Write Cause (TWC), 80, 96
Youth Development, Inc., (YDI), 124, 139
Youth Law Center (YLC), 125, 140
Youth Suicide National Center (YSNC), 352, 355

COLORADO
ACTION, The National Volunteer Agency, 12
American Association for Protecting Children (AAPC), 147
American Association of Suicidology (AAS), 119n, 352, 353–54
American Humane Association (AHA), 98, 147
American Solar Energy Society (ASES), Inc., 307
American Wildlands (AWL), 259
BACCHUS (Boost Alcohol Consciousness Concerning the Health of University Students) of the U.S., Inc., 63
C. Henry Kempe National Center for the Prevention and Treatment of Child Abuse and Neglect, 147
Freedom Service Dogs, Inc., 182
International Hearing Dog, 205
North American Riding for the Handicapped Association (NARHA), Inc., 196
Rocky Mountain Institute (RMI), 271
U.S. Association for Blind Athletes (USABA), 197
Windstar Foundation (WF), 276–77

GEOGRAPHICAL INDEX

CONNECTICUT
ACTION, The National Volunteer Agency, 11
The Box Project (TBP), 14
Connecticut Canine Education Center, 205
Fidelco Guide Dog Foundations, 200
Friends of Animals (FoA), 90
Keep America Beautiful (KAB), Inc., 317
Save the Children, 28, 142
Save the Children Craft Shop, 28–29

DELAWARE
ACTION, The National Volunteer Agency, 12

DISTRICT OF COLUMBIA
ACTION, The National Volunteer Agency, 9, 12
  Foster Grandparent Program (FGP), 10
  Retired Senior Volunteer Program (RSVP), 10
  Senior Companion Program (SCP), 10, 236
  Student Community Service Program (SCSP), 11
  Volunteers In Service To America (VISTA), 11
AIDS Action Council (AAC), 41, 47
Alexander Graham Bell Association for the Deaf (AGBAD), 204, 206
The Alliance to Save Energey (ASE), 306
American Association of Children's Residential Centers (AACRC), 124
American Association of Homes for the Aging (AAHA), 238
American Association of Retired Persons (AARP), 233, 237, 238
American Association on Mental Retardation (AAMR), 212–13
American Bar Association (ABA), Representation of the Homeless Project, 331
American Council for an Energy-Efficient Economy (ACEEE), 248, 306–7
American Council of the Blind (ACB), 198, 201
American Forestry Association (AFA), 246n, 284
American Health Care Association (AHCA), 234, 235, 238–39
American Hiking Society (AHS), 256, 259
American Institute of Architects (AIA), The Search for Shelter Program, 331
American Mental Health Fund (AMHF), 177, 208, 209
American Red Cross, 13, 111, 113
American Rivers (AR), 323
Animal Welfare Institute (AWI), 88–89
The ASPIRA Association, Inc., 126
Association for Commuter Transportation, 283
The Barbara Bush Foundation for Family Literacy (BBFFL), 229
Bicycle Federation of America (BFA), 282
Blinded American Veterans Foundation (BAVF), 359
Blinded Veterans Association (BVA), 359, 360
Bread for the World (BFW), 345–46
Catholic Charities U.S.A., 15
Center for Marine Conservation (CMC), 102
Center for Science in the Public Interest (CSPI), 292
  Americans for Safe Foods, 292
Children's Defense Fund (CDF), 119n, 120, 129–30, 216, 328n
Child Welfare League of America (CWLA), 120, 129
Christmas in April U.S.A., 331, 333
Cities in Schools (CIS), 221
Clean Water Action (CWA), 323–24
Climate Institute (CI), 285
Coalition on Human Needs, 329, 333–34
Coastal States Organization, COASTWEEKS, 101, 321–22
Community Careers Resource Center, 23
Community for Creative Non-Violence (CCNV), 334
  The National Volunteer Clearinghouse for the Homeless (NVCH), 330, 334, 338–39, 343

388 GEOGRAPHICAL INDEX

Concern, 260–61
Conservation International (CI), 285–86
Co-op America, 28, 33
Cooperative Development Foundation (CDF), 34, 332
COSSMHO (The National Coalition of Hispanic Health and Human Services Organization), 50
Council of Better Business Bureaus (CBBB), Inc., Philanthropic Advisory Service (PAS), 368
Critical Mass Energy Project (CMEP), 308
Defenders of Wildlife, 4, 105
Department of Veteran's Affairs (VA), 356, 357, 358, 359, 361
Voluntary Service, 357, 361
The Disability Rights Education and Defense Fund, 180, 186
Disabled American Veterans(DAV), 361
Earth Conservation Corps (ECC), 257
Environmental Action Foundation (EAF), 245, 263
Environmental Protection Agency (EPA), 251
Eye Bank Association of America (EBAA), 116
Food & Friends, 43
Food Research and Action Center (FRAC), 346–47
Friends of the Earth, 264
Global Tommorrow Coalition (GTC), 264–65
The Greenhouse Crisis Foundation (GCF), 286
Greenpeace U.S.A., 265
The Healthy Harvest Society (HHS), 292
Homelessness Information Exchange (HIE), 335
Humane Society of the United States (HSUS), 91–92, 97
INDEPENDENT SECTOR (IS), 16
International Council for Bird Preservation (ICBP), 106
International Liaison of Lay Volunteers in Mission, 24
Investor Responsibility Research Center (IRRC), 31

Joint Action in Community Services (JACS), Inc., 132
Junior League of Washington, 4
The Land Trust Allaince (LTA), 267
League of Conservation Voters (LVC), 252
The League of Women Voters (LWV), 363
Lutheran Volunteer Corps (LVC), 25
National Allaince for Animal Legislation (ALLIANCE), 80, 93
National Alliance for Business (NAB), 222–23
The National Alliance to End Homelessness (NAEH), Inc., 327, 328, 336
National Assembly of National Voluntary Health and Social Welfare Associations, Making the Grade, 133
National Association of Area Agencies on Aging (NAAAA), 235, 240
National Association of Community Action Agencies (CAAs), 7, 138
National Association of Private Industry Councils (PICs), 125-26
National Association of Service & Conservation Corps (NASCC), 17
National Black Alcoholism Council (NBAC), 68
National Black Child Development Institute (NBCDI), 123, 124
The National Caucus and Center on Black Aged (NCBA), 240
National Center for Child Abuse and Neglect (NCBA), 148
Clearinghouse on Child Abuse and Neglect and Family Violence Information, 149
National Coalition Against Domestic Violence (NCADV), 170
National Coalition Against Sexual Assault (NCASA), 159, 170
National Coalition Against the Misuse of Pesticides (NCAMP), 298
The National Coaltion for the Homeless (NCH), 327, 336–37
National Commission Against Drunk Driving (NCADD), 73
National Committee For Adoption (NCFA), 144

National Council of Senior Citizens
(NCSC), 241
National Council on Child Abuse &
Family Violence, 146, 149
The National Council on the Aging
(NCOA), Inc., 241
Family Friends Program, 125, 181,
187
National Crime Prevention Council
(NCPC), 56, 62, 145, 146, 157-58,
161-62, 164, 165, 166, 167, 171-72
National Education Association (NEA),
225
The National Gay & Lesbian Task
Force (NGLTF), 159, 172
National Geographic Society (NGS),
80, 267-68
National Handicapped Sports (NHS),
196
National Head Injury Foundation
(NHIF), Inc., 190
National Hispanic Council on Aging
(NHCoA), 242
National Information Center for
Children and Youth with Handicaps
(NICHCY), 190
National Information Center on
Deafness (NICD), 176, 208
National Low Income Housing
Coalition (NLIHC), 329, 337
Low Income Housing Information
Service (LIHIS), 337
National Minority AIDS Council
(NMAC), 52
The National Network Of Runaway
and Youth Services, 124, 136
National Organization for Victim
Assistance (NOVA), 159, 174
National Organization of Travelers Aid
Societies, 330, 338
National Organization on Disability
(NOD), 176, 184, 191
National Parks and Conservation
Association (NCPA), 287
National Recycling Coalition (NRC),
Inc., 318
The National Volunteer Clearinghouse
for the Homeless (NVCH), 330, 334,
338, 343
National Wildlife Federation (NWF),
80, 107, 252

National Woman Abuse and
Prevention Project (NCWAPP), 159,
175
Neighborhood Reinvestment
Corporation, 339
NeighborWorks, 339
The Search for Shelter Program,
331
North American Lake Management
Society (NALMS), 325
Nuclear Information & Resource
Service (NIRS), 298-99
People for the Ethical Treatment of
Animals (PETA), 78, 81, 94, 97
Physicians Committee for Responsible
Medicine (PCRM), 95
President's Committee on
Employment of People with
Disabilities (PCEPD), 195
Prison Fellowship, 160
Project Head Start, 124, 137-38, 331
Public Voice for Food and Health
Policy, 293, 348-49
Rails-to-Trails Concervancy (RTC),
308-9
Reading Is Fundamental (RIF), Inc.,
217, 231-32
Renew America, 270
Resources for the Future (RFF), 270
RESULTS, 349
Safe Energy Communication Council
(SECC), 309
St. Vincent Pallotti Center for
Apostolic Development, 23
The Samaritans, 354
Scenic America (SA), 271
Share Our Strength (SOS), 343, 350
Smithsonian Associates Research
Expedition Program, 258
Smithsonian Institution Office of
Environmental Awareness (OEA),
273
Special Olympics International, 176,
196-97, 212
Student Action Corps for Animals
(SACA), 84, 95-96
Student Pugwash (SP) U.S.A., 24,
273-74
The Union of Concerned Scientists
(UCS), 275
United Black Fund (UBF), 7

United Neighborhood Centers of America (UNCA), Inc., 8
U.S. Conference of Mayors, 327, 340, 356
U.S. Department of Agriculture, 340
U.S. Department of Education, 58
U.S. Department of Energy, 302
U.S. Department of Justice, Community Relations Service (CRS), 159
U.S. Department of Labor, Job Opportunities for the Blind (JOB), 194
U.S. Fish and Wildlife Service, 78
Division of Endangered Species, 104
U.S. House Select Committee on Children, Youth, and Families, 120
U.S. Public Interest Research Group (PIRG), 246, 275
USO (United Services Organization), 19
Vegetarian Awareness Network (Vegnet), 85–86
Vietnam Veterans of America (VVA), Inc., 362
The Wilderness Society (TWS), 276
World Hunger Education Service (WHES), 341, 350–51
World Resources Institute (WRI), 247, 277
Worldwatch Institute (WI), 277–78
World Wildlife Fund and The Conservation Foundation (WWF and TCF), 109–10
Youth Service America (YSA), 22
Zero Population Growth (ZPG), 278

FLORIDA
ACTION, The National Volunteer Agency, 12
Adam Walsh Child Resource Center, 153
Basic Foundation (BF), 284–85
Canine Companions for Independence, 182
Child Keyppers' International, Inc., 154
Children's Rights of America (CRA), 130
National Youth Crisis Hotline, 130
Cure AIDS Now, 43
Florida Dog Guides for the Deaf, Inc., 205
International Oceanographic Foundation (IOF), 325
Missing Children . . . Help Center (MCHC), 152, 155
Southeastern Guide Dogs, 201

GEORGIA
ACTION, The National Volunteer Agency, 12
American Cancer Society (ACS), 185
Arthritis Foundation, 239
Centers For Disease Control (CDC), 40
Habitat for Humanity International (HHI), 331, 334–35
National Coalition for Marine Conservation (NCMC), 103
National Families in Action (NFIA), 69
National Interfaith Coalition on Aging (NICA), 243
Parents' Resource Institute for Drug Education (PRIDE), 71
Project Open Hand Atlanta, Inc., 44

GUAM
ACTION, The National Volunteer Agency, 12

HAWAII
ACTION, The National Volunteer Agency, 12
Eye of the Pacific Guide Dogs and Mobility Services, 182

IDAHO
ACTION, The National Volunteer Agency, 13

ILLINOIS
ACTION, The National Volunteer Agency, 12
The Alzheimer's Association, 237–38
American Library Association (ALA), 217, 228
Coalition for Literacy, 228
Little Brothers—Friends of the Elderly (LBFE), 239–40

GEOGRAPHICAL INDEX 391

National Anti-Vivisection Society
(NAVS), 81, 94
National Committee for the Prevention
of Child Abuse (NCPCA), 149
National Down Syndrome Congress
(NDSC), 213
National Easter Seal Society (NESS),
177, 180, 189
National Parent-Teacher Association
(NPTA), 217, 225-26
National Runaway Switchboard (NRS),
124, 136-37
North American Wildlife Foundation
(NAWF), 108
Second Harvest National Food Bank
Network, 340, 343, 349
Young Men's Christian Association
(YMCA) of the United States of
America, 21

INDIANA
ACTION, The National Volunteer
Agency, 12
Mennonite Board of Missions, 24

IOWA
ACTION, The National Volunteer
Agency, 12

KANSAS
ACTION, The National Volunteer
Agency, 12
Commission on Volunteer Service and
Action (CVSA), 24
National Collegiate Athletic
Association (NCAA) Committee on
Competitive Safeguards and Medical
Aspects of Sports, 68

KENTUCKY
ACTION, The National Volunteer
Agency, 12
Disabled American Veterans (DAV),
361
USA Harvest, 350

LOUISIANA
ACTION, The National Volunteer
Agency, 12
Volunteers of america (VOA), 20, 160,
220, 235

MAINE
ACTION, The National Volunteer
Agency, 11

MARYLAND
ACTION, The National Volunteer
Agency, 12
The American Council for Drug
Education (ACDE), 62
Calvert Group, 32
Conservation and Renewable Energy
Inquiry and Referral Service
(CAREIRS), 307-8
Epilepsy Foundation of America
(EFA), 187
Farm Animal Reform Movement
(FARM), 86, 90
Fourth World Movement (FWM), 25
Goodwill Industries of America (GIA),
188, 310
Health Education Resource
Organization (HERO), 41, 51
International Child Health Foundation
(ICHF), 125, 132
League of American Wheelmen (LAW),
282-83
Moveable Feast, 44
National Asian Pacific American
Families Against Substance Abuse
(NAPAFASA), 66
National Association for the
Advancement of Colored People
(NAACP) Youth and College
Division, 134
Back to School/Stay in School,
134
National Association of the Deaf
(NAD), 207-8
National Clearinghouse for Alcohol
and Drug Information (NCADI), 68
National Committee for Citizens in
Education (NCCE), 224
National Criminal Justice Reference
Service (NCJRS), 173
Bureau of Justice Assistance, 173
Justice Statistics Clearinghouse, 173
Juvenile Justice Clearinghouse, 173
National Institute of Justice (NIJ),
158, 173
National Victims Resource Center,
173

National Federation of the Blind
  (NFB), 202
  Job Opportunities for the Blind
    (JOB), 194
National 4-H Council, 125, 135-36
National Institute Against Prejudice
  and Violence (NIAPV), 159, 172-73
National Institute for Urban Wildlife
  (NIUW), 107
National Institute of Justice (NIJ), 158,
  173
National Institute on Disability and
  Rehabilitation Research (NIDRR),
  191
National Rehabilitation Information
  Center (NARIC), 191-92
The Orton Dyslexia Society (ODS),
  226-27
Phydeaux for Freedom, 183
Rachel Carson Council (RCC), 300
Scientists Center for Animal Welfare
  (SCAW), 95
Spina Bifida Association of America
  (SBAA), 716n, 185, 193
  The Adoption Information Referral,
    193

MASSACHUSETTS
ACTION, The National Volunteer
  Agency, 11
Affirmative Investments (AI), 32
Appalachian Mountain Club (AMC), 260
A Better Chance (ABC), Inc., 221
The Better Homes Foundation, 328n,
Committees of Correspondence (COC),
  Inc., 64
Community Servings, 43
Deafness Research Foundation,
  National Temporal Bone Banks
  Program, 114, 118
EARTHWATCH, 256
Franklin Research and Development
  Corporation (FRDC), 34
The Institute for Community
  Economics (ICE), 35, 332
International Wildlife Coalition (IWC),
  100, 102
Mail for Tots, 122
Massachusetts Society for the
  Prevention of Cruelty to Animals
  (MSPSA), 79

The National Coalition of Advocates
  for Students (NCAS), 223-24
National Spinal Cord Injury
  Association (NSCIA), 192
National Student Campaign Against
  Hunger and Homelessness
  (NSCAHH), 345, 347-48
National Toxics Campaign (NTC), 297,
  298
The New England Assistance Dog
  Service Inc., 183
One Person's Impact (OPI), 269-70
Recruiting New Teachers (RNT), Inc.,
  220, 227
Red Acre Farm Hearing Dog Program,
  205
The Samaritans, 354
Students Against Drunk Driving
  (SADD), 74
Task Force on Youth Suicide
  Prevention, 354-55
20/20 Vision, 274-75
The Union of Concerned Scientists
  (UCS), 275

MICHIGAN
ACTION, The National Volunteer
  Agency, 12
"Paws with a Cause,"
Leader Dogs for the Blind, 200
Home of Ears for the Deaf, Inc. 183
Rainforest Action Movement (RAM),
  287
United States Cerebral Palsy Athletic
  Association(USCPAA), 197

MINNESOTA
ACTION, The National Volunteer
  Agency, 12
Adoptive Families of America (AFA),
  143
Campus Outreach Opportunity League
  (COOL), 14
Ethical Investments (EI), 34
The Freshwater Foundation, 324
Institute on Black Chemical Abuse
  (IBCA), 65
National Marrow Donor Program
  (NMDP), 114, 117
North American Council on Adoptive
  Children (NACAC), 145

Social Investment Forum (SIF), 38
Wilderness Inquiry (WI), 184

MISSISSIPPI
ACTION, The National Volunteer
 Agency, 12

MISSOURI
ACTION, The National Volunteer
 Agency, 12
American Red Cross National Tissue
 Services, 116
Camp Fire Boys and Girls, 125, 128–29
Household Hazardous Waste Project
 (HHWP), 297–98
International Union of Gospel Missions
 (IUGM), 330, 335–36
National Federation of Parents
 (NFP)for Drug-Free Youth, 70
National Federation of State High
 School Associations (NFSHA),
 TARGET, 70
Support Dogs for the Handicapped,
 183

MONTANA
ACTION, The National Volunteer
 Agency, 12
Bikecentennial, 282
National Center for Appropriate
 Technology (NCAT), 301

NEBRASKSA
ACTION, The National Volunteer
 Agency, 12
Contact Center, Inc., 217, 219, 220,
 230
 Coalition for Literacy, 215n
 National Contact Hotline, 230
The Natioanl Arbor Day Foundation
 (NADF), 280, 286

NEVADA
ACTION, The National Volunteer
 Agency, 12

NEW HAMPSHIRE
ACTION, The National Volunteer
 Agency, 11
Pax World Fund, 36

The Samaritans, 354
Student Conservation Associates
 (SCA), 258

NEW JERSEY
ACTION, The National Volunteer
 Agency, 11
American Littoral Society (ALS), 322
American Vegan Society (AVS), 85
Associated Humane Societies (AHS),
 97, 99
Association of Jewish Family &
 Children's Agencies, 13
God's Love We Deliver, 43
Kids Against Pollution (KAP), 266–67
National Housing Institute (NHI), 337
National Industries for the Blind (NIB),
 199, 203
Recording for the Blind (RFB), 199,
 203
The Salvation Army (TSA), 18, 160,
 220, 310, 330
The Seeing Eye, 201

NEW MEXICO
ACTION, The National Volunteer
 Agency, 12
Futures for Children (FFC), 141–42
National Indian Council on Aging
 (NICOA), 242–43

NEW YORK
ACTION, The National Volunteer
 Agency, 11
AIDS Coalition to Unleash Power (ACT
 UP), 47
Al-Anon/Alateen Family Group
 Headquarters, 75
Alcoholics Anonymous (AA) World
 Services, 75
American Foundation for the Blind
 (AFB), 176, 202
American Lung Association (ALA),
 284
The American Society for the
 Prevention of Cruelty to Animals
 (ASPCA), 87
Assault on Illiteracy Program (AOIP),
 229
Beauty Without Cruelty (BWC) U.S.A.,
 81, 89

GEOGRAPHICAL INDEX

Boys & Girls Clubs of America (BGCA), 123, 128
Business Council for Effective Literacy (BCEL), 215, 220, 229-30
Canine Companions for Independence, 182
THE CAP BOOK, Inc., 143
Center for Environment Information (CEI), Inc., 260
Center on Human Policy (CHP), 180, 186
Child Find of America (CFA), Inc., 154
Citizens Committee for New York City (CCNYC), 60, 61, 62, 166, 167
COMPEER, Inc., 209, 210
Council on Economic Priorities (CEP), 27, 30
Covenant House, 124, 130-31
Environmental Action Coalition (EAC), 317
Environmental Defense Fund (EDF), 264, 310
The Fresh Air Fund, 131
The Fund for Animals (TFA), Inc., 91
Gay Men's Health Crisis (GMHC), 50
Girl Scouts of the United States of America (GSUSA), 125, 132
God's Love We Deliver, 43
Guide Dog Foundation for the Blind, 200
Guiding Eyes for the Blind, 200
Helen Keller National Center (HKNC) for Deaf-Blind Youths and Adults, 207
The Holiday Project, 122, 236
INFORM, 265-66
Interfaith Center on Corporate Responsibility (ICCR), 26-27, 31
Jewish Community Centers Association of North America, 7-8
Laubach Literacy Action (LLA), 220, 231
Literacy Volunteers of America LYA), Inc., 231
March of Dimes Birth Defects Foundation, 188
National Association on Drug Abuse Problems (NADAP), 67
National Audubon Society (NAS), 78, 106-7

National Council on Alcoholism and Drug Dependence (NCADD), 56, 59, 69
National Dog Registry (NDR), 98, 99-100
Rescue Fund, Inc., 100
National Down Syndrome Society (NDSS), 214
The National Kidney Foundation (NKF), Inc., 115n, 117
National Multiple Sclerosis Society (NMSS), 190
The National Resource Center on Homelessness and Mental Illness (NRCHMI), 338
The National Resources Defense Council (NRDC), 268
National Urban League (NUL), Inc., 18
New Alternatives Fund (NAF), 36, 258
North American Vegetarian Society (NAVS), 85
People with AIDS (PWA) Coalition, 53
Phoenix House Foundation, 55n
Radioactive Waste Campaign (RWC), 300
Rainforest Alliance (RA), 288
Remove Intoxicated Drivers (RID), 73
The Samaritans, 354
Sex Information and Education Council of the U.S., 41
Sick Kids (need) Involved People (SKIP), 192-93
Street Aid, 332
Teach for America (TFA), 220, 228
United Action for Animals (UAA), Inc., 96
United Cerebral Palsy Association (UCPA), 193
Variety Clubs International, 123, 138
We Can, 332
Will Rogers Institute, 56
World Hunger Year (WHY), 342, 351
Young Women's Christian Association (YWCA) of the United States of America, 21

NORTH CAROLINA
The Acid Rain Foundation (ARF), Inc., 283

GEOGRAPHICAL INDEX 395

ACTION, The National Volunteer Agency, 12
American Social Health Association (ASHA), 49
National AIDS Hotline, 42, 44, 49

NORTH DAKOTA
ACTION, The National Volunteer Agency, 12

OHIO
ACTION, The National Volunteer Agency, 12
Assistance Dogs of America Inc., 182
Canine Companions for Independence, 182
Good Bears of the World (GBW), 122, 236
LifeBanc, 116
National Assault Prevention Center (NAPC), 169
Pilot Dogs, Inc., 201
Youth to Youth (YtY), 71

OKLAHOMA
ACTION, The National Volunteer Agency, 12
Feed the Children (FTC), 141

OREGON
ACTION, The National Volunteer Agency, 13
Dogs for the Deaf, Inc., 205
Oregon Department of Fish and Wildlife, 101, 321
Progressive Securities Financial Services, 37
Xerxes Society, 110

PENNSYLVANIA
ACTION, The National Volunteer Agency, 12
Adoption Center of Delaware Valley, 144
American Anti-Vivisection Society (AAVS), 86
Animal Rights Mobilization! (ARM!), 88
Big Brothers/Big Sisters of America (BB/BSA), 123, 127

CAMPUSES WITHOUT DRUGS, Inc., 63
The Chemical People Institute (CPI), 64
Christian Literacy Associates (CLA), 230
Grass Roots the Organic Way (GROW), 297
Independence Dogs, Inc., 183
International Society for Animal Rights (ISAR), Inc., 78, 92, 98
Learning Disabilities Association (LDA) of America, 222
National Adoption Center (NAC), 144
National Association of Town Watches (NATW), 170
Pennsylvania Resources Council, 311, 312
Veterans of the Vietnam War (VVnW), Inc., 362
Wildlife Information Center (WIC), Inc., 108
Wildlife Preservation Trust International (WPTI), 109

PUERTO RICO
ACTION, The National Volunteer Agency, 11

RHODE ISLAND
ACTION, The National Volunteer Agency, 11
The Samaritans, 354

SOUTH CAROLINA
ACTION, The National Volunteer Agency, 12
National Dropout Prevention Center (NDPC), 216, 224-25

SOUTH DAKOTA
ACTION, The National Volunteer Agency, 12

TENNESSEE
ACTION, The National Volunteer Agency, 12
E.A.R. Foundation, 205

TEXAS
ACTION, The National Volunteer Agency, 12

Association for Retarded Citizens (ARC), 213
Boy Scouts of America (BSA), 125, 127–28
The Hope Foundation (THF), 330, 335, 343
The Living Bank (TLB), 117
Mothers Against Drunk Driving (MADD), 72
National Foster Parent Association (NFPA), 152
National Victim Center (NVC), 159, 174
North American Association of Jewish Homes and Housing for the Aging (NAAJHHA), 244

UTAH
ACTION, The National Volunteer Agency, 12

VERMONT
ACTION, The National Volunteer Agency, 11
Catalyst, 29
GOOD MONEY (GM) Publications, 30
Volunteers for Peace (VFP), 26

VIRGINIA
ACTION, The National Volunteer Agency, 12
American Foster Care Resources (AFCR), Inc., 151
Children, Inc. (CI), 140
Christian Children's Fund (CCF), Inc., 141
Citizens Clearinghouse for Hazardous Waste (CCHW), 296
Council of Better Business Bureaus (CBBB), Inc., 366n
The Cousteau Society, 261
Four-One-One, 16
The Izaak Walton League of America (IWLA), 266
National Alliance for the Mentally Ill (NAMI), 210
National Association of Partners in Education (NAPE), National School Volunteer Program (NSVP), 219, 223
National Association of Private Residential Resources, 181

National Center for Missing and Exploited Children (NCMEC), 153, 156
National Mental Health Association (NMHA), 211, 329
The Nature Conservancy (TNC), 269
Non-Commissioned Officers Association (NCOA) of the United States, Operation Appreciation, 357
Service Civil International/USA (SCI/USA), 24
United Network for Organ Sharing (UNOS), 113
United Way of America, 7, 132, 330
VOLUNTEER—The National Center, 6, 20, 132, 138, 160, 181, 199, 220, 330
Water Pollution Control Federation (WPCF), 319
Women in Community Service (WICS), Inc., 138

VIRGIN ISLANDS
ACTION, The National Volunteer Agency, 11

WASHINGTON
ACTION, The National Volunteer Agency, 13
The Association for Persons with Severe Handicaps (TASH), 185
Center for the Prevention of Sexual and Domestic Violence (CPSDV), 168–69
Children of the Green Earth (CGE), 285
The Delta Society, 89, 183
First Place, 332–33
The Giraffe Project (TGP), 5
Message!Check (M!C) Corporation, 27
The National Court Appointed Special Advocate (CASA) Association, 125, 147, 150, 151, 160
National Pacific/Asian Resource Center on Aging (NP/ARCA), 243
National Rural and Small Schools Consortium (NRSSC), 226

WASHINGTON, D.C., see **DISTRICT OF COLUMBIA**

GEOGRAPHICAL INDEX

WEST VIRGINIA
ACTION, The National Volunteer Agency, 12
Job Accommodation Network (JAN), 194

WISCONSIN
ACTION, The National Volunteer Agency, 12

Business Against Drunk Drivers (BADD), Inc., 72
Family Service America (FSA), 15, 124
Okada, Ltd., 183

WYOMING
ACTION, The National Volunteer Agency, 12